D1712949

STEFAN ZWEIG

UNIVERSITY OF NORTH CAROLINA
STUDIES IN THE GERMANIC LANGUAGES
AND LITERATURES

For other volumes in this series see page 191.

NUMBER FIFTY

UNIVERSITY
OF NORTH CAROLINA
STUDIES IN
THE GERMANIC LANGUAGES
AND LITERATURES

STEFAN ZWEIG

A BIBLIOGRAPHY

BY

Randolph J. Klawiter

CHAPEL HILL
THE UNIVERSITY OF NORTH CAROLINA PRESS

Printed in The Netherlands by Royal VanGorcum Ltd., Assen

PREFACE

To compile a completely comprehensive bibliography is a task as futile as it is seemingly vain. No matter how hard one tries to gather in all the pertinent information, let him but look at one more book and without fail there he will find another indispensable entry for his already "completed" list. More than once the bibliographer is sorely tempted to doubt the efficacy of his protracted labors and to end them all with a slight touch of sulfur. But here as elsewhere "conscience doth make cowards of us all," and we carry on towards our goal, as arbitrary as it may seem to be.

From such scholarly pangs of conscience I too have suffered more than once, knowing that I couldn't possibly do justice to my undertaking and yet fearing that were I not at least to try, the project might never be attempted. Which would be worse – to make an effort and fall short of the desired goal or make no effort at all, waiting for the day when someone more competent should have the time and desire to do that which I could but hope to accomplish in part? It is to be hoped that my choice of the former alternative may nevertheless prove beneficial to those interested in the works of Stefan Zweig for their own sake or those engaged in future Zweig scholarship.

Admitting without reserve the incompleteness of the following bibliography and taking upon myself the onus of any factual as well as all typographical errors, I nevertheless take great pleasure in acknowledging my sincere debt of gratitude to the many people without whose efforts I would most assuredly have been able to accomplish little: in sequence of time I must first mention Dr. F. X. Braun of the University of Michigan under whose guidance I wrote my doctoral dissertation on Stefan Zweig and to whom I owe the idea of assembling the present bibliography; to Mrs. Friderike M. Zweig my thanks must surely prove inadequate to the amount of encouragement and friendship that she has shown me; for much material that I would never have otherwise seen and for his ever ready assistance in so many instances I wish to thank Dr. Harry Zohn of Brandeis University; for permission to compare my efforts with his unpublished American Zweig Bibliography I likewise thank Dr. Thomas L. Broadbent of the University of Utah; for information on recent articles about Zweig appearing in foreign periodicals as well as for copies of her own lectures my appreciation is extended to Mrs. Mimi Grossberg of New York City; to the many friends of Stefan Zweig in Germany, Austria, France, Italy, Holland, Japan and India who so willingly gave of their time to correspond with me concerning problems that arose with respect to articles and translations of Zweig's works in these respective languages my gratitude is without limit; for many enjoyable hours spent together searching library stacks I tip my hat to my friends Michael C. Downs and Ralph Kent, students at the University of Notre Dame, who likewise shared the joys and sorrows of the several proofreadings of the typescript, a dubious honor shared by many other friends and most of my family; for the financial support at every step of the way as well as the unflagging moral and morale support I take special pleasure in paying herewith in some small manner the enormous debt I owe to my parents; for the many long hours spent behind her relentless typewriter with an equally relentless script of undecipherable languages before her I thank Mrs. M. Webber, the most perfect secretary any language department could ever hope to acquire; and to my wife I also owe more than I can here express, not only for her willingness to shoulder all the domestic responsibilities while I wiled away the fruitful hours among the weeds and flowers of literary scholarship but perhaps even more am I indebted to her sense of practicality and self-discipline, both of which effectively made me realize that the business at hand was a task to be accomplished and not a life-long dedication. It would also indeed be remiss on my part were I to fail to mention the many services rendered to me by the library staffs of the Universities of Notre Dame, Michigan, and Chicago without whose ready assistance the information needed from far and near would never have been made available. Lastly I might erect a type of prefatory altar to the forgotten god upon which is to be placed anyone whom I have inadvertently forgotten to mention or whom perhaps I have never met, but to whom nevertheless my debt of gratitude is rendered with the utmost sincerity.

University of Notre Dame   Randolph J. Klawiter
Notre Dame, Indiana   June, 1964.

TABLE OF CONTENTS

ABBREVIATIONS

1. GENERAL

a.	year (Cf. also J. = year)
cf.	compare, see
col.	column
diss.	dissertation
ed(s).	editor(s), edition(s), edited by
enl.	enlarged
esp.	especially
f.m.	frequently mentioned
fr.	foreword, foreword by
intro.	introduction, introduction by
Lit. Beil.	literary supplement (Literarische Beilage)
m.	mentioned, scattered references
n.d.	no date given
N.F.	new series (Neue Folge)
n.l.	no place given
n.p.	no publisher given
opp.	opposite
p.	page
pp.	pages
pref.	preface, preface by
rev.	review, reviewed by, revised
sel.	selected by
ser.	series
tr.	translator, translation, translated by
Tsd.	thousand
vol.	volume

2. GERMAN ABBREVIATIONS IN THE APPENDIX

Bl.	sheet
d.	the
e.	a
f.	for
Frhrn v.	Baroness of (Freiherrin von)
Gr.	format, size
Ms(s).	manuscript(s)
S.	page(s)
Slg.	collection
Tl.	part
u.	and
u.a.	and others
usw.	and so forth, etc.

3. ZWEIG'S WORKS

Balzac	*Balzac. Der Roman seines Lebens.* Stockholm: Bermann-Fischer, 1946 (Or later eds. as indicated).
Begegnungen	*Begegnungen mit Menschen, Büchern, Städten.* Wien-Leipzig-Zürich: Herbert Reichner, 1937 (Pagination quoted from the 1955 ed., Berlin-Frankfurt am Main: S. Fischer).
Brasilien	*Brasilien, Land der Zukunft.* Stockholm: Bermann-Fischer, 1941.
Calvin	*Castellio gegen Calvin oder ein Gewissen gegen die Gewalt.* Wien: Herbert Reichner, 1936.
Drei Dichter	*Drei Dichter ihres Lebens: Casanova - Stendhal – Tolstoi.* Leipzig: Insel, 1928.
Drei Meister	*Drei Meister: Balzac – Dickens – Dostojewski.* Leipzig: Insel, 1920 (Or later eds. as indicated).
Durch	*Durch Zeiten und Welten.* Graz-Wien: Stiasny, 1961.
Erasmus	*Triumph und Tragik des Erasmus von Rotterdam.* Wien – Leipzig – Zürich: Herbert Reichner, 1934 (Or later eds. as indicated).
Europäisches Erbe	*Europäisches Erbe.* Frankfurt am Main: Fischer, 1960.
Fahrten	*Fahrten, Landschaften und Städte.* Leipzig – Wien – Zürich: E. P. Tal, 1919.
Fouché	*Joseph Fouché. Bildnis eines politischen Menschen.* Leipzig: Insel, 1929 (Or later eds. as indicated).
Heilung durch den Geist	*Die Heilung durch den Geist: Franz Anton Mesmer – Mary Baker Eddy – Sigmund Freud.* Leipzig: Insel, 1931 (Or later eds. as indicated).
Kampf mit dem Dämon	*Der Kampf mit dem Dämon: Hölderlin – Kleist – Nietzsche.* Leipzig: Insel, 1925.
Magellan	*Magellan. Der Mann und seine Tat.* Wien – Leipzig – Zürich: Herbert Reichner, 1938 (Or later eds. as indicated).
Marceline Desbordes-Valmore	*Marceline Desbordes-Valmore. Das Lebensbild einer Dichterin.* Leipzig: Insel, 1920 (Or later eds. as indicated).
Marie Antoinette	*Marie Antoinette. Bildnis eines mittleren Charakters.* Leipzig: Insel, 1932 (Or later eds. as indicated).
Rolland	*Romain Rolland. Der Mann und das Werk.* Frankfurt am Main: Ruetten and Loening, 1921.
Sternstunden	*Sternstunden der Menschheit. Fünf historische Miniaturen.* Leipzig: Insel, 1927 (Or the later expanded *Zwölf historische Miniaturen.* Stockholm: Bermann-Fischer, 1945 (Or later eds. as indicated)).
Verhaeren	*Erinnerungen an Emile Verhaeren.* Wien: Christoph Reissers Söhne, 1917 (Or later eds. as indicated).
Verlaine	*Paul Verlaine. Eine Monographie.* Berlin – Leipzig: Schuster and Loeffler, 1904.
WvG	*Die Welt von Gestern. Erinnerungen eines Europäers.* Stockholm: Bermann-Fischer, 1944 (Or later eds. as indicated).
Zeit und Welt	*Zeit und Welt. Gesammelte Aufsätze und Vorträge 1904-1940.* Stockholm: Bermann-Fischer, 1943 (Pagination quoted from the 1946 ed.).

4. MONOGRAPHS

ALA	*Anthologie des Lyriques allemands contemporains depuis Nietzsche.* Ed. Henri Guilbeaux. Paris: E. Figuière and Cie, 1913.
Antlitz	Gustav Settler. *Vom Antlitz junger Menschen. Acht Radierungen.* Grenchen (die Schweiz): Verlag Gute Graphik, 1956.
Blätter	*Blätter der Internationalen Stefan Zweig Gesellschaft.* Wien.
Brod	*Max Brod. Festschrift zum fünfzigsten Geburtstag.* Ed. Felix Weltsch. Mährisch-Ostrau, 1934.

Carossa	*Buch des Dankes für Hans Carossa*. Ed. Albrecht Schaeffer.
Ceterum	Emanuel Bin Gorion. *Ceterum Recenso. Kritische Aufsätze und Reden*. Tübingen: Alexander Fischer, 1929.
CGP	*Contemporary German Poetry*. Tr. and ed. Jethro Bithell. London-New York: Walter Scott, 1909.
Crumbs	M. Burrell. *Crumbs are also Bread*. Toronto: Macmillan, 1934.
CurBio	*Current Biography. Who's News and Why*. 1942. New York: H. W. Wilson, 1942.
DdG	*Dichter der Gegenwart*. Vol. IV. Ed. Toni Meder. Bamberg-Wiesbaden: Bayerische Verlagsanstalt, 1955.
DeB	*Der ewige Brunnen. Ein Volksbuch deutscher Dichtung*. 2. ed. München: Beck, 1959.
Diktate	*Diktate aus dem deutschen Schrifttum*. Ed.Willi Hopff, Hans Thiel and Wilhelm Reininghaus. 8. ed. Frankfurt am Main – Berlin – Bonn: Mantz Diesterweg, n.d.
DuZ	*Dichter unserer Zeit*. Vol. II. Ed. Hans Göttling. Bamberg: Buchners, 1954.
EdD	*Erzählungen deutscher Dichter*. Vol. III. Ed. Wilhelm Helmich and Paul Nentwig. n.l.: Georg Westermann, 1958.
Europäer	*Der grosse Europäer Stefan Zweig*. Ed. Hanns Arens. München: Kindler, 1956.
Francé	*R. H. Francé. Festschrift zu seinem fünfzigsten Geburtstag*. Heilbronn: Seifert, 1924.
Franz Dichter	*Französische Dichter des XIX. und XX. Jahrhunderts in deutscher Übertragung*. Sel. and Intro. Otto Heuschele. Bühl in Baden: Roland, 1948.
Franz Lyrik	*Französische Lyrik aus acht Jahrhunderten*. Ed. Franz von Rexroth. Saarbrücken: Saar Verlag, 1946.
Frau	*Die Frau von Morgen, wie wir sie wünschen* (Von Max Brod, Arnolt Bronnen, Axel Eggebrecht, Stefan Zweig *et al.*). Ed. Friedrich M. Huebner. Leipzig: Seemann, 1929.
Geistesleben	*Deutsches Geistesleben der Gegenwart*. Ed. Otto Koischwitz. New York: Knopf, 1928 (School ed.).
Gewalt	*Gewalt und Gewaltlosigkeit. Handbuch des aktiven Pazifismus*. Ed. Franz Kobler. Zürich: n.p., 1928.
Herz	*Das Herz Europas. Österreichisches Vortragsbuch*. Wien: n.p., 1935.
Herzl	*Theodor Herzl. A Memorial*. Ed. Meyer W. Weisgal. New York: The New Palestine, 1929.
HLAS: 1941	*Handbook of Latin American Studies: 1941*. Ed. Miron Burgin. Cambridge (Mass.): n.p., 1941.
Hofmannsthal	*Hugo von Hofmannsthal. Der Dichter im Spiegel der Freunde*. Ed. Helmut A. Fiechtner. 2. ed. Bern – München: Francke, 1963.
Hommage	*Hommage à Romain Rolland*. Ed. Charles Baudoin. Genève: Les Editions du Mont Blanc, 1945.
Journeys	*Journeys in Time*. Ed. B. R. Niles. New York: Coward-McCann, 1946.
Juden	*Von Juden in München. Ein Gedenkbuch*. Ed. Hans Lamm. München: Ner-Tamid Verlag, 1958.
Karussell	*Das Karussell. Geschichten aus dieser Zeit*. Vol. III. 2. ed. Ed. Walter Urbanek. Bamberg: Buchners, 1962.
Kippenberg	*Navigare necesse est. Festschrift für Anton Kippenberg*. Ed. P. Jessen. Leipzig: Insel, 1924.
Kraus	*Rundfrage über Karl Kraus*. Ed. L. von Ficker. Innsbruck: n.p., 1917.
Leben-Werk	*Stefan Zweig. Sein Leben – sein Werk*. Ed. Hanns Arens. Esslingen: Bechtle, 1949.

Librarians	*Of, By and For Librarians. Further Contributions to Library Literature* Ed. J. D. Marshall. New York: Shoe String Press, 1960.
Life-Work	*Stefan Zweig. A Tribute to His Life and Work.* Ed. Hanns Arens. Tr. from the German. London: n.p., 1951.
Liliencron	*Österreichischer Dichter. Zum sechzigsten Geburtstag von Detlev von Liliencron.* Ed. Adolf Donath. Wien: Carl Konegen, 1904.
Lyrik	*Lyrik des Abendlands.* Ed. Georg Britting. München: Hanser, 1948.
Mann-Werk	Erwin Rieger. *Stefan Zweig. Der Mann und das Werk.* Berlin: Spaeth, 1928.
Masereel	*Frans Masereel* (Mit Beiträgen von Stefan Zweig, Pierre Vorms, Gerhard Pommeranz-Liedtke und einer Bibliographie von Hanns Conon von der Gabelentz). Dresden: Verlag der Kunst, 1959.
Moissi	*Moissi. Der Mensch und Künstler in Worten und Bildern.* Ed. Hans Böhm. Berlin: Eigenbrödler, 1927.
Negen Vuurmakers	*Negen Vuurmakers voor het Kampvuur.* Utrecht: Vrijzinnig Christelijke Jeugd Centrale, 1946.
PeR	M. Robertazzi. *Poesia e Realtà.* Modena: Guandi, 1934.
Ramuz	*Hommage à Ramuz, zum sechzigsten Geburtstag.* Lausanne: Porchet and Cie, 1938.
Schmidtbonn	*Chor um Wilhelm S. Schmidtbonn. Zum 50sten Geburtstag, 6. Feb. 1927.* Ed. Herbert Saekel. Stuttgart – Berlin – Leipzig: Deutsche Verlagsanstalt, 1926.
Schmitz	*Oskar A. H. Schmitz zum fünfzigsten Geburtstage.* München: Georg Müller, 1923.
Schorer	Henri Delarue and Paul F. Geisendorf. *Calvin, Stefan Zweig et M. Jean Schorer.* Genève: Librairie de l'Université – Georg and Cie, 1949.
Schweitzer	*Albert Schweitzer, Genie der Menschlichkeit.* Frankfurt am Main-Hamburg: Fischer, 1955 (Fischer Bücherei, No. 83).
Spectrum	*Spectrum. Modern German Thought in Science, Literature, Philosophy and Art.* Ed. W. P. Lehmann, Helmut Rehder and Hans Beyer. New York: Holt, Rinehart and Winston, 1964.
Spiegelungen	*Stefan Zweig. Spiegelungen einer schöpferischen Persönlichkeit.* Ed. Erich Fitzbauer. Wien: Bergland, 1959 (Erste Sonderpublikation der Stefan Zweig Gesellschaft).
SZ	Friderike Maria Zweig. *Stefan Zweig, wie ich ihn erlebte.* Stockholm – New York: Neuer Verlag, 1947.
SZG	Paul Zech. *Stefan Zweig. Eine Gedenkschrift.* Buenos Aires: Quadriga, 1943.
Tag	*Der Tag bricht an* (Neue Gedichte von Waldemar Bonsels, Felix Braun, Hermann Hesse, Stefan Zweig *et. al.*). Ed. Carl Seelig. Dortmund: Der Garten Eden, 1921.
Wedekind	*Das Wedekindbuch.* Ed. Joachim Friedenthal. München – Leipzig: n.p., 1914.
Weltdichtung	*Lyrische Weltdichtung in deutscher Übertragung aus sieben Jahrhunderten.* Ed. Julius Petersen and Erich Trunz. Berlin: Juncker and Dünnhaupt, 1933.
Zdz	*Zeichen der Zeit. Ein deutsches Lesebuch in vier Bänden.* Vol. IV. Ed. Walther Killy. Frankfurt am Main – Hamburg: Fischer, 1961 (This work also appeared as one volume in Fischer, 1962).

5. NEWSPAPERS AND PERIODICALS

A	America (New York)
AAP	Atti della Accademia Pontaniana (Napoli)

AB	Atlantic Bookshelf (Boston)
Abl	Abendland (Köln)
Äbl	Ärzteblatt (Bremen)
Abz	Arbeiterzeitung (Wien)
AdP	Almanach der Psychoanalyse (Wien)
ADV	Almanach des deutschen Volkstheaters (Leipzig – Wien – Zürich)
AfdW	Alles für die Welt (Baden-Baden)
AH	The American Hebrew (New York)
AHR	American Historical Review (New York)
AIR	Adam. International Review (London)
AJPH	American Journal of Public Health (Boston)
AL	Art Libre (Bruxelles)
AM	Atlantic Monthly (Boston)
AMoz	Acta Mozartiana. Mitteilungen der deutschen Mozart Gesellschaft (Kassel-Wilhelmshöhe)
An	Athenaeum (London)
APL	Les Annales Politiques et Littéraires (Paris)
APzt	Augsburger Postzeitung (Augsburg)
AR	American Review (New York)
ARsch	Autographen Rundschau
As	Asia (Concord, N.H.)
Ate	Atenea (Concepción de Chile)
Au	Aufbau (Berlin)
AUC	Anales de la Universidad de Chile (Santiago de Chile)
Auf	Aufstieg (Wiesbaden)
Au(NY)	Aufbau (New York)
AWJD	Allgemeine Wochenzeitung der Juden in Deutschland (Düsseldorf)
AZ	Allgemeine Zeitung (München)
AZJ	Allgemeine Zeitung des Judentums (Leipzig – Berlin; Superseded in 1922 by the Central Verein Zeitung)
BA	Books Abroad (Norman, Oklahoma)
Bb	Blaubuch (Berlin)
BBB	Baden-Badener Bühnenblatt (Baden-Baden)
BBC	Berliner Börsen Courrier (Berlin)
BBM	Blätter der Bücherstube am Museum (Wiesbaden)
BBSF	Blätter der bayerischen Staatsoper. Festspiele 1962. Tagesprogramm. Ed. Rudolf Hartmann.
BBZ	Berliner Börsen Zeitung (Berlin)
Bd	Bund (Bern)
BdBh	Börsenblatt für den deutschen Buchhandel (Leipzig)
BdTG	Blätter des deutschen Theaters in Göttingen (Göttingen)
BET	Boston Evening Transcript (Boston)
BF	Bibliografia Fascista (Roma)
Bg	Bergstadt (Breslau)
Bib	Der Bibliothekar (Leipzig)
BibS	Biblioteca Selecta (Panama)
BIG	Bayrisch-israelitische Gemeindezeitung (München)
Bkg	Boekengids (Antwerpen)
Bks	Boekenschouw (Amsterdam)
Bl	Booklist (Chicago)
BM	Biochemische Monatsblätter (Leipzig)
Bm	Bookman (New York)
BMB	Bulletin Bibliographique et Pédagogique du Musée Belge (Louvain)
BMCN	Book of the Month Club News (New York)
BN	Baseler Nachrichten (Basel)
Bng	Die Besinnung (Nürnberg)

Br	Brunsviga
Bre	Brecha (San José, Costa Rica)
BrsZ	Breslauer Zeitung (Breslau)
Brü	Brücke. Blatt für Heimatvertriebene (München)
BS	Best Sellers (Scranton, Pa.)
BT	Berliner Tageblatt (Berlin)
Btr	Boston Transcript (Boston)
BU	Bibliothèque Universelle et Revue de Genève (Genève)
BüB	Bücherei und Bildungspflege (Leipzig-Stettin)
Büg	Büchergilde (Frankfurt am Main)
Büh	Die Bücherhalle (Leipzig)
BuI	Berichte und Informationen (Salzburg)
BüK	Bücher-Kommentare (Stuttgart-Berlin)
BuL	Buch und Leben (Stuttgart)
BV	Bogens Verden (København)
BW	Bühne und Welt (Berlin-Leipzig-Wien)
BWk	Book Week (Chicago)
BZ	Berliner Zeitung (Berlin)
C	Colliers (New York)
Car	Carrefour (Paris)
CC	Christian Century (Chicago)
CdS	Cahiers du Sud (Marseille)
CDT	Chicago Daily Tribune (Chicago)
CF	Canadian Forum (Toronto)
CH	Current History (Chicago)
CHF	Current History and Forum (New York)
Chm	Churchman (London)
Chr	Christendom (Chicago)
Cht	Chantecler
ChW	Die christliche Welt (Marburg)
CJR	Contemporary Jewish Record (New York)
ClW	The Classical Weekly (New York)
CM	Civilta Moderna (Firenze)
Cmy	Commentary (Chicago)
Coe	Coenabium (Lugano)
Colq	Colloquium (Berlin)
Com	Commune (Paris)
ConR	Contemporary Review (London)
ConW	Congress Weekly (New York)
CorS	Corriere della Sera (Milano)
COS	Cleveland Open Shelf (Cleveland, Ohio)
CR	Chicago Review (Chicago)
CV	Caritas. Zeitschrift des schweizerischen Caritasverbandes (Luzern)
CVZ	Central Verein Zeitung (Berlin; Cf. AZJ above)
CW	Catholic World (New York)
Cwl	Commonweal (New York)
D	Demain (Genève-Paris)
DA	Dresdener Anzeiger (Dresden)
DAnq	Das Antiquariat (Wien)
DAZ	Deutsche Allgemeine Zeitung (Berlin)
DB	Die Bühnenkritik (Augsburg)
DBa	Die Barke (Frankfurt am Main)
DBei	Deutsche Beiträge (München)
DBib	Deutsche Bibliographie (Frankfurt am Main)
DBK	Deutscher Bibliophilen Kalender (Wien; Later became Jahrbuch deutscher Bibliophilen)

DBP	Deutsche Blätter in Polen (Posen)
DBu	Das deutsche Buch (Leipzig)
DD	Deutsche Dichtung (Berlin)
DDi	Die Dichtung (Berlin-München)
DDr	Das deutsche Drama (Berlin)
DeG	De Gids (Amsterdam)
DeuE	Deutschlands Erneuerung (München)
DeuR	Deutsche Rundschau (Berlin)
DeuV	Deutsches Volkstum (Hamburg)
DF	Die Fackel (Wien)
DFa	Der Fackelreiter (Hamburg-Bergedorf)
DFR	Deutsch-französische Rundschau (Paris)
DFu	Der Funke (Leipzig)
DG	Die Getreuen (Hamburg)
DgD	Das ganze Deutschland (Detmold)
DGT	Das goldene Tor (Lahr)
DH	Die Horen (Berlin)
Di	Dial (New York)
DIZ	Deutsche Internierten Zeitung (Bern)
DJZ	Das junge Zentrum
DK	Die Kultur (Stuttgart)
DKw	Der Kunstwanderer (Berlin)
DL	Die Literatur (Berlin; Before 1923 called Das literarische Echo)
DlDÖ	Das literarische Deutsch-Österreich (Wien)
DLE	Das literarische Echo (Berlin; After Vol. XXV (1923) renamed Die Literatur, see above)
DLe	Die Lebenden (Görlitz)
DLW	Die literarische Welt (Berlin)
DLZ	Düsseldörfer Lokal-Zeitung (Düsseldorf)
DLz	Der Lesezirkel (Zürich)
DLZg	Deutsche literarische Zeitung (Berlin)
DM	Die Masken (Düsseldorf)
DMfC	Deutsche Monatshefte für Chile
DMo	Der Monat (München)
DMW	Deutsche medizinische Wochenschrift (Leipzig)
DN	Die Nation (Berlin)
DNE	Das neue Europa (Zürich)
DNG	De nieuwe Gids (Den Haag)
DNN	Dresdener Neueste Nachrichten (Dresden)
DNS	Die neueren Sprachen (Marburg)
DNSch	Die neue Schau (Kassel)
DNZ	Die neue Zeit (New York-Leipzig)
DNZg	Die neue Zeitung (München)
Do	Donauland (Wien)
DoA	Dorem Afrike (Johannesburg)
DoiB	Doitsu Bungaku (Tokyo)
DPbl	Deutsches Pfarrerblatt (Stuttgart)
DPr	Die Presse (Wien)
DR	Deutsche Republik (Berlin-Frankfurt am Main)
DRa	Die Rampe (Hamburg)
DRg	Der Ring (Berlin)
DRZ	Deutsche Reichs-Zeitung (Bonn)
DS	Die Schrift (Brünn)
DSa	Die Sammlung (Göttingen)
DSch	Die Schaubühne (Berlin)
DSL	Die schöne Literatur (Leipzig; After 1930 called Neue Literatur)

DSlb	Das Silberboot (Salzburg)
DSt	Der Strom (Köln)
DSta	Der Start. Illustriertes Blatt der jungen Generation (Berlin)
DT	Die Tat (Leipzig-Jena)
DTb	Das Tagebuch (Berlin)
DTg	Der Tag (Berlin)
DTp	Deutsche Tagespost
DV	Der Vormarsch (Berlin)
DW	Die Wage (Wien)
DWB	Dietsche Warande en Belfort (Amsterdam)
DWe	Der Weg. Zeitschrift für Fragen des Judentums (Berlin)
DWk	Das Werk (Düsseldorf)
DWo	Die Wochenpost (Stuttgart)
DWr	Der Werker (Berlin)
DZ	Deutsche Zeitung (München)
DZe	Die Zeit. Wochenzeitung für Politik, Wirtschaft, Handel und Kultur (Hamburg-Frankfurt am Main)
DZfS	Deutsche Zeitung für Spanien
E	Europa (Paris)
Ea	Europa XX Wieku. Zycie Literackie (Krakow)
EAP	Erkenntnis. Annalen der Philosophie (Leipzig)
EC	Etudes Classiques (Namur)
Eck	Eckart. Blätter für evangelische Geistesarbeit (Berlin)
Ed	Edda (Oslo)
EeL	Evangile et Liberté (Paris)
EN	L'Europe Nouvelle (Paris)
Èn	Ère Nouvelle (Paris)
EPCJ	Etudes des Pères de la Compagnie de Jesus (Paris)
Er	Erasmus (Basel)
Erz	Erzählung (Konstanz)
ES	Englische Studien (Leipzig)
EuG	Europäische Gespräche (Hamburg)
F	Freistatt (München)
FdT	Fortschritte der Therapie (Berlin)
Fi	Finanstidende (København)
Fk	Finsk Tidskrift for Vitterhet, Vetenskap Konst och Politik (Helsingfors)
Fm	Freeman (New York)
Fo	Forum (New York)
Fr	Die Frau (Berlin-Leipzig)
FrA	Frauenzimmer-Almanach (Wien)
Frw	Forward (New York)
FT	Fränkische Tagespost
FTb	Freiburger Theaterblätter (Freiburg i.B.)
Fu	Die Furche (Berlin)
FuS	Form und Sinn (Augsburg)
FuT	Forum und Tribüne (New York)
FVb	Freie Volksbildung (Frankfurt am Main)
FW	Free World (New York)
FZ	Frankfurter Zeitung (Frankfurt am Main)
G	Goetheanum (Dornach)
GB	Golden Book (New York)
GdG	Der Geisteskampf der Gegenwart (Gütersloh)
Gdl	Gesundheitslehrer (Berlin)
Ge	Die Gesellschaft (München)
Germ	Germania (Berlin-Leipzig)

GermR	The Germanic Review (New York)
Gespr	Gespräche. Freundesbund für Hermann Hesse (Frankfurt am Main)
GJ	The Geographical Journal (London)
GLL	German Life and Letters (London)
GN	Groot-Nederland (Amsterdam)
GoeJb	Goethe Jahrbuch (Frankfurt am Main)
GOM	Glocke. Okkultische Monatsschrift
GQ	The German Quarterly (Appleton, Wis.)
GR	La Grande Revue (Paris)
Gr	Der Gral (München-Essen)
Grf	Der Greif. Cotta'sche Monatsschrift (Stuttgart-Berlin)
GRM	Germanisch-Romanische Monatsschrift
GS	Generalanzeiger (Stettin)
Gwt	Gegenwart (Berlin)
HaN	Hallische Nachrichten (Halle)
HAR	Hamburger Akademische Rundschau (Hamburg)
HFbl	Hamburger Fremdenblatt (Hamburg)
Hg	Hellweg (Essen)
HK	Hannoverscher Kurier (Hannover)
Hl	Hochland (Dresden-München)
HM	Harper's Magazine (New York)
HN	Hamburger Nachrichten (Hamburg)
HO	Historical Outlook (Philadelphia)
HSFS	Die höhere Schule des Freistaates Sachsens
HT	Historisk Tidskrift (Stockholm)
Hw	Hochschulwissen (Warnsdorf)
Hy	Hygeia (Athens-Chicago-London)
I	L'Illustration (Paris)
IAR	Internationale Antiquitäten Rundschau (Zürich)
IBra	Illustraçao Brasiliera (Rio de Janeiro)
IC	Il Convegno (Milano)
ICS	Italia che Scrive (Roma)
ID	Il Dramma. Revista Mensile di Commedie di Grande Successo (Turin)
IF	Israel Forum (Rothenburg ob der Tauber)
ILN	Illustrated London News (London)
IM	Irish Monthly (Dublin)
Im	Imago (Wien)
Imp	Imprimatur (Hamburg)
IN	Inter-Nationes (Bonn)
In	Das Inselschiff (Leipzig)
InA	Insel Almanach (Leipzig)
IP	Il Ponte (Firenze)
Isb	Istanbul (Istanbul)
J	Jeschurun (Berlin)
JA	Jewish Affairs (Johannesburg, South Africa)
Ja	Janus (München)
JD	Journal des Débats (Paris)
JDB	Jahrbuch deutscher Bibliophilen (Wien; Formerly Deutscher Bibliophilen Kalender)
JdG	Journal de Genève (Genève)
JDSG	Jahrbuch der deutschen Shakespeare Gesellschaft
JeA	The Jewish Advocate (Boston)
JLG	Jewish Literary Gazette (London)
JMH	Journal of Modern History (Chicago)

JNMD	Journal of Nervous and Mental Diseases (Richmond, Va.)
JR	Jüdische Rundschau (Berlin)
JSp	Jewish Spectator (New York)
JüAl	Jüdischer Almanach (Berlin)
JüGbl	Das jüdische Gemeindeblatt für die britische Zone (Düsseldorf)
JulR	The Julliard Review (New York)
K	Kirkus (New York)
KAZ	Königsberger Allgemeine Zeitung (Königsberg)
KD	Katholischer Digest (Aschaffenburg)
KdöL	Die Kritik des öffentlichen Lebens (Berlin)
KHZ	Königsberger Hartung'sche Zeitung (Königsberg)
KNN	Kasseler Neueste Nachrichten (Kassel)
KöT	Kölner Tageblatt (Köln)
KP	Kasseler Post (Kassel)
Kr	Der Kreis (Berlin)
Krl	Kristall (Hamburg)
KrZ	Karlsruher Zeitung (Karlsruhe)
KS	Kirjath Sepher (Jerusalem)
KT	Kasseler Tageblatt (Kassel)
Kt	Der Kunstwart (München)
KVZ	Kölnische Volks-Zeitung (Köln)
KZ	Kölner Zeitung (Köln)
L	Leonardo (Firenze)
LA	Living Age (Boston)
LAM	L'Approdo Musicale (Roma)
LB	Literarische Blätter (Genf)
LC	Le Carmel (Zürich)
LCfD	Literarisches Centralblatt für Deutschland (Leipzig)
LCP	Les Cahiers Protestants
LCQ	The Lutheran Church Quarterly (Gettysburg, Pa.)
LD	Literary Digest (New York)
LF	La Flamberge (Mons, Belgium)
LGRP	Literaturblatt für germanische und romanische Philologie (Heilbronn-Leipzig)
LH	Literarischer Handweiser (Regensburg-Münster)
LI	Il Libro Italiano (Roma)
Lib	Librarians (Northwestern University Library, Evanston, Ill.)
LJ	Library Journal (New York)
LJZ	Leipziger jüdische Zeitung (Leipzig; Later Leipziger jüdisches Familienblatt)
LLM	Les Langues Modernes (Paris)
LM	The London Mercury (London)
LMF	Le Monde Français (Paris-Montreal)
LNE	La Nouvelle Equipe (Bruxelles)
LNL	Les Nouvelles Littéraires (Paris)
LNN	Leipziger Neueste Nachrichten (Leipzig)
LNR	La Nouvelle Relève (Montreal, Canada)
LP	La Libre Pensée (Lausanne-Paris)
LT	London Times (London)
LTbl	Leipziger Tageblatt (Leipzig)
LW	Literarische Wochenschrift (Weimar)
M	Der Merker. Österreichische Zeitschrift für Musik und Theater (Wien)
MA	Musical America (New York)
MaL	Music and Letters (London)
März	März (Leipzig)

MAZ	Münchener Allgemeine Zeitung (München)
MB	More Books (Boston Public Library)
MC	Musical Courier (New York)
Mer	Merian. Das Monatsheft der Städte und Landschaften (Hamburg-Salzburg)
MF	Mercure de France (Paris)
MfDU	Monatshefte für deutschen Unterricht (Madison, Wis.)
MfFL	Morgenblatt für Freunde der Literatur (Berlin)
MfL	Magazin für Literatur (Leipzig)
MG	Manchester Guardian (Manchester, New York)
MH	Mental Hygiene (Concord, N.Y.)
MJ	Menorah Journal (Harrisburg, Pa.)
Mkg	Musikerziehung (Wien)
MLJ	Modern Language Journal (Buffalo, New York)
MLN	Modern Language Notes (Baltimore, Md.)
MMN	Mitteilungen zur Geschichte der Medizin und Naturwissenschaft (Hamburg)
MMW	Münchner medizinische Wochenschrift (München)
MNN	Münchener Neueste Nachrichten (München)
Mo	Der Morgen (Berlin)
Mon	Monatsschrift (Paderborn; Later Wochenschrift für katholische Lehrerinnen)
MP	Münchner Post (München)
MS	Le Messager Social
Ms	Manuscripts (New York)
Mu	Musica (Kassel)
MZ	Magdeburger Zeitung (Magdeburg)
N	Nation (New York)
NA	Nuova Antologia (Roma)
NaQ	Notes and Queries (London)
NAR	North American Review (New York)
NASG	Neue Auslese aus dem Schrifttum der Gegenwart (München)
NB	Neue Bücher (Bonn)
NBKL	Neue Blätter für Kunst und Literatur
NBL	Neue Badener Landeszeitung
NBRMMLA	News Bulletin of the Rocky Mountain Modern Language Association
NC	Nineteenth Century (London)
NDH	Neue deutsche Hefte (Gütersloh)
NDL	Neue deutsche Literatur. Monatsschrift für Schöne Literatur und Kritik (Berlin)
Ne	Newsweek (New York)
Nef	La Nef. Revue Mensuelle (Paris)
NFP	Neue Freie Presse (Wien)
NFP-Jb	Jahrbuch der Neuen Freien Presse (Wien)
NG	Die neue Generation (Berlin)
NK	Nowa Kultura (Warszawa)
NL	Neue Literatur (Berlin; Formerly Die schöne Literatur)
NLAS	Nouvelles Littéraires Artistiques et Scientifiques (Paris)
NLW	Nowiny Literackie i Wydawnicze (Warszawa)
NlW	Neue literarische Welt (Heidelberg)
NLZ	Neue Leipziger Zeitung (Leipzig)
NM	New Masses (New York)
NMz	Neue Musikzeitschrift (München)
NphZ	Neuphilologische Zeitschrift (Hannover)
NR	Neue Rundschau (Berlin-Leipzig)

Rad	Radio (Wien)
RaE	Review and Exposition (Louisville, Ky.)
RB	Revue Bleue (Paris; Also called Revue politique et littéraire)
RC	Revue Catholique des Idées et des Faits (Bruxelles)
RCC	Revue des Cours et Conférences (Paris)
RD	Reader's Digest (Pleasantville, N.Y.)
RdA	Revista de América (Bogotá, Colombia)
RdC	Rivista delle Colonie (Roma)
RdF	La Revue de France (Paris)
RdlI	Revista de las Indias (Bogotá, Colombia)
RdO	Revista de Occidente (Madrid)
RdP	Rivista di Psicologia (Bologna)
RdV	Revue des Vivants (Paris)
RE	La Revue Européenne (Paris)
Ré	Réforme (Paris)
REH	Revue des Études Historiques (Paris)
REI	Revue Économique Internationale (Paris)
RELV	Revue de l'Enseignement des Langues Vivantes (Paris)
RG	Revue Germanique (Paris)
RH	Revue Historique (Paris)
RHb	Revue Hebdomadaire (Paris)
RHEF	Revue d'Histoire de l'Église de France (Paris)
RHPR	Revue d'Histoire et de Philosophie Religieuse (Paris)
RM	Rivista Marittima (Roma)
RMd	Revue Mondiale (Paris)
RN	Rassegna Nazionale (Roma)
RoR	Die Roman-Rundschau (Wien)
RP	Revue de Paris (Paris)
RQH	Revues des Questions Historiques (Paris)
RR	Review of Reviews (New York)
RRev	The Romanic Review (New York)
RRh	La Revue Rhénane (Rheinische Blätter)
RT	Rheinische Thalia. Blätter für badische und pfälzische Kultur (Mannheim)
RvB	Roland von Berlin (Berlin)
Rx	Reflex (Chicago)
S	Sonntag (Berlin)
SAQ	South Atlantic Quarterly (Durham, N.C.)
SC	Suisse Contemporaine (Lausanne)
SchM	Schwäbische Merkur (Stuttgart)
SchMz	Schweizerische Musikzeitung (Zürich)
SchR	Schweizerische Rundschau (Stanz-Einsiedeln)
SE	Social Education (New York)
SeR	Sewanee Review (Sewanee, Tenn.)
SFC	San Francisco Chronicle (San Francisco)
SG	Survey Graphic (New York)
SGM	Scottish Geographical Magazine (Edinburgh)
Si	Sign (Union City, N.J.)
SLR	Saint Louis Review (Saint Louis)
SLzt	Saarbrücker Landeszeitung (Saarbrücken)
SM	Soziale Medizin (Berlin)
SNT	Stuttgarter Neues Tageblatt (Stuttgart)
SoM	Sovjetskaja Muzyka (Moskva)
SoS	Social Studies (Philadelphia)
Soz	Der Sozialist (Berlin)
SP	Strassburger Post (Strassburg)

WU	World Unity (New York)
WuW	Welt und Wort (Tübingen)
WW	Wirkendes Wort (Düsseldorf)
W-Z	Weser – Zeitung (Bremen)
WZV	Weg zur Vollendung (Darmstadt)
Ybk	Yearbook of the Leo Baeck Institute of Jews from Germany (London)
YCD	Yearbook of the Cemetery Department. Jewish Workmen's Circle (New York)
YR	Yale Review (New Haven, Conn.)
Z	Die Zukunft (Berlin)
ZB	Zeitschrift für Bücherfreunde (Bielefeld-Leipzig)
ZD	Zeitschrift für Deutschkunde (Leipzig)
Ze	Die Zeit (Wien)
ZFEU	Zeitschrift für französischen und englischen Unterricht (Berlin)
ZfG	Zeitschrift für Geopolitik (Darmstadt)
ZP	Zeitschrift für Politik (Berlin)

INTRODUCTION

STEFAN ZWEIG - BIOGRAPHICAL SKETCH

"Paix adviendra et malheur cessera.
Mais entre deux que mal l'on souffrera!"[1]

On February 22, 1942, Stefan Zweig and his second wife, Lotte Altmann Zweig, committed suicide. To those who loved him the news was a terrible blow; to those who considered him to be a stalwart ally against the madness of the times, his death came almost as a willful desertion of a common cause. But in the minds of all the same question was evident: why? Indeed, his was not a solitary fate - one need but mention Tucholsky, Toller, Hasenclever, E. Weiss, Friedell – many had preceded him, others were to follow him and yet for some reason his fate does seem unique. Kurt Böttcher would see in Zweig a singular, representative figure who realized in his person:

> ... jenes Charakteristische also für eine Gruppe von humanistischen bürgerlichen Schriftstellern mit gleicher oder ähnlicher gesellschaftlicher und geistiger Position sowie menschlicher Beschaffenheit.[2]

Undoubtedly there is some partial justification for this view but it would seem to fall far short of explaining the individual magnetism and creative spirit which was Zweig's. If he must be a symbol, in justice to him, the symbol should be that of a life dedicated to international understanding and not merely that of a certain social-intellectual reserve.

Zweig was born on the 28th of November, 1881, into a wealthy Jewish family, which, having made a fortune in the textile industry in Czechoslovakia, removed to Vienna about the middle of the nineteenth century. Stefan's father, Moritz Zweig, married an Italian-German girl whose father was an international banker of great repute, having done business even for the Vatican.[3] In keeping with customs of the time, Stefan and his older brother were cared for almost entirely by nurses and governesses. This obvious lack of motherly affection and the many restrictions placed on children, in keeping with social decorum, often arrested the growing spirits of the younger generation.

His mother was a very vivacious woman, but one of very fixed, often obstinate ideas, a trait which Stefan seems to have inherited, along with an unbending resentment of his systematized life as a child.[4]

The family vacations were usually spent dashing from one spa to another amid baggage far in excess, noise, and a regular domestic cortege. As a result, when older, Zweig never took anything with him when he traveled, leaving for anywhere on the spur of the moment.[5]

At the age of six Zweig started his school career – a long, dull struggle in dark rooms with bored teachers, whose lives did not correspond with their contemporary society. Sports and dating were still unheard of, their stead being filled with cultural pursuits: literary-philosophical debates in cafés, extensive reading, regular attendance at opera premières or theatrical performances in Vienna's Burgtheater.[6]

The turn of the century saw an almost revolutionary change in attitude and mode of expression in European Letters. As the onesided, aggressive, tendentious Naturalism had thirty years previously supplanted the historic Epigonentum of the 1860s and 1870s, so in its turn was Naturalism supplanted by a vogue of Impressionism – Expressionism. French, Belgian, Norwegian painting and literature were everywhere considered to be of leading significance; Debussy and Strauss dominated the field of music as did Nietzsche the realm of philosophy. Rimbaud, Verlaine, Zola, Hauptmann, Rilke, Dostoyevsky – such were the dominant figures of the age, names which today seem enwrapped in the sobering effects of distance, but which at that time were names of a younger generation struggling to attain new forms of expression to correspond to their new forms of thought. This new literary movement was amply represented in the "Jung Wien" school which boasted such members as Schnitzler, Hermann Bahr and the young Hofmannsthal, who at nineteen had become the hero of his generation through an essay on art and his exquisitely mature poems.[7]

Having graduated from the Gymnasium in 1900, Zweig enrolled immediately at the University of Vienna. He attended very few classes but read everything of modern literature that he could find. Fearing little success, he nevertheless sent an article to the editor of the leading Viennese newspaper, *Die Neue Freie Presse*, Theodor Herzl,[8] requesting its publication in Herzl's Feuilleton section which normally contained articles on art, music, the theater and literature, contributed only by well known writers. When his article was accepted and appeared on the first page it seemed to Zweig that a dream had been realized. By nature modest, Zweig was embarrassed by the prestige and popularity that he had attained, in his own eyes prematurely. To escape unwelcome celebrity as well as to gain more personal freedom, Zweig transferred to the University of Berlin

(1902), where in a milieu of international intellectualism he formed friendships and ties with artists of other nations which lasted throughout his life (e.g. Ellen Key, Giobanni Cena, Georg Brandes, Peter Hille, Rudolf Steiner).[9]

Through his contacts with local journals in Berlin Zweig was soon introduced into a club known as "Die Kommenden" which consisted of individuals from all social strata, nationality and profession, all united through a common bond: their Bohemian life. The club resembled the literary-café groups which Zweig had frequented in Vienna but how far intellectually superior were the debates, how far more perfected the artistry in Berlin! Zweig actually felt embarrassed in their midst, his self-confidence diminished considerably. He soon realized how childish, how deprived of knowledge of real life his works were. A novel begun in Vienna was soon filed in the stove, its successor appearing only 37 years later. The greater part of the time Zweig spent observing and studying all types of people, from the best to the worst. This psychological curiosity lasted throughout his entire life and by many is considered to be his outstanding characteristic.[10]

By 1910 Zweig could boast of two volumes of verse (*Silberne Saiten* (1902) and *Die frühen Kränze* (1906)), a volume of four Novellen (*Die Liebe der Erika Ewald* (1904)), and a drama, *Tersites* (1907) - all of which were begun under the influence of the new psychological literature predominating in Austria, wherein aestheticism joined forces with irrationalism and cosmic mysticism to produce a neo-romanticism characterized by melodiousness of sound and hues.[11] Realizing his own inadequacies and short-comings, however, Zweig all but completely abandoned his own writings and dedicated himself almost exclusively to translating foreign works into German: some poems of Baudelaire and Verlaine, a drama by Charles van Lerberghe, a novel by Camille Lemmonier and by 1910 the complete works of Emile Verhaeren. Though translation is difficult, demanding a precise knowledge of the nuances of one's own as well as the foreign language, the effort expended is commensurately rewarding in its formative effects.

> Und wenn ich heute einen jungen Schriftsteller beraten sollte, der noch seines Weges ungewiss ist, würde ich ihn zu bestimmen suchen, zuerst einem grösseren Werke als Darsteller oder Übertragender zu dienen. In allem aufopfernden Dienen ist für einen Beginnenden mehr Sicherheit als im eigenen Schaffen, und nichts, was jemals hingebungsvoll geleistet, ist vergebens getan.[12]

The summer of 1902 Zweig spent in Belgium, where through the mediation of the sculptor van der Stappen, he met Emile Verhaeren for the first time. The two became extremely close friends, a friendship which meant much more to Zweig than companionship, for from Verhaeren Zweig acquired that very quality which was so painfully missing in his own works – a love of and direct contact with daily life and an awareness that work and responsibility are moral values of the international credo. It is at this period that his former Viennese bourgeois concepts began to dissolve, but to be sure literature still remained for him "eine Steigerungsform der Existenz." Until the outbreak of the First World War in 1914 (and Verhaeren's death in 1916) Zweig spent a few weeks each summer with his beloved friend at the latter's summer residence, Caillou-qui-bique.[13]

The year 1904 was spent in Vienna with furious months of hard work in order to obtain his doctorate and thus fulfill a promise which he had made to his parents. He chose a discussion of Taine for his thesis and within a few months received his Degree with honorable mention. Thereafter he was free to live as he saw fit and, driven by a desire to learn everything possible in the shortest possible time, he chose Paris as his port of call.[14] He took up residence at the small Hotel Beaujolais in the Palais Royal in the immediate vicinity of the Bibliothèque Nationale and the Louvre, directly across from the former house of Marceline Desbordes-Valmore.[15] During this first extended stay in Paris he visited every nook and cranny of the city, one might say he literally breathed in the spirit of the French people. Through Verhaeren he met the leading artists of the new Impressionism – Bazalgette, Duhamel, Valéry, Rodin,[16] Renoir – and was accepted among them as one in a family circle. In no way and by no one was he regarded as a foreigner. That his love for France and especially Paris was so sincere and expansive is but natural under such circumstances.[17]

Zweig's first visit to England (1905) made a rather unfavorable impression upon him.[18] He missed the laughing gaiety and charm of the French. The English were far too reserved and, not understanding English too well, Zweig couldn't follow their clipped conversations which seemed to revolve incessantly around sports and politics. Most of his time was spent in the British Museum, studying the writings and drawings of William Blake or translating English works into German. He did, however, manage to purchase Blake's etching "King John" to add to his treasured collection of autographs.[19]

Between 1905 and the outbreak of the war in 1914 Zweig occupied himself wholly in traveling around the world and translating foreign works (especially Verhaeren) into German. In addition to his works previously mentioned, he published another volume of Novellen: *Erstes Erlebnis. Vier Geschichten aus Kinderland* (1911) and two dramas: *Das Haus am Meer* (1912) and *Der verwandelte Komödiant* (1913). He was horrified by the misery and poverty of the masses in India which he visited in 1912. The climate made him uncomfortable and the countryside grew monotonous. Even the riches of the temples seemed more strange than awesome to him.[20] His journey was not a complete loss to him, however, for he utilized every moment possible in studying the people – on the streets, in cabarets, in opium dens – and in absorbing the cults and doctrines of the "Land of Mystery."[21]

The first visit to America (1912) was an event of somewhat mixed reactions. Zweig was greatly impressed by the beauties of the Hudson Valley and the unheard of tolerance toward other races and religions. New York, too, was fascinating for a time.[22] In Philadelphia he saw some of his works on display, a fact which greatly flattered his ego and did much to enhance his disposition toward the New World. Before returning to his small apartment in Vienna, Kochgasse 8, which was to be his home until his removal to Salzburg, Zweig visited the final construction on the Panama Canal,[23] the impressions of which he crystalized in his essay: "Die Stunde zwischen zwei Ozeanen."[24]

When World War I broke out Zweig was working on his literary-historical essay about Dostoyevsky. He had planned a trip to Russia to acquaint himself personally with the Russian people and atmosphere but the outbreak of hostilities put an immediate end to his projected trip.[25] After the War such conflicting reports were received about Russia that he couldn't make up his mind to go there. It wasn't until 1928 that he finally visited Russia and then as an invited delegate to celebrate the Tolstoy centenary.[26] He closely observed the enthusiasm of the masses, the educational system, and the technological advances; he was greatly impressed. The journey was not without its somber note, however, in spite of the cordial reception given him. Just before leaving the country he found a note in his pocket, written in French, warning him not to be deceived by appearances, all was not as progressive as one might suppose, freedom was being sacrificed to technology and the people were slowly being imprisoned in their own homeland.[27]

Friendships were always a decisive influence on Zweig – two in particular, with Verhaeren and Romain Rolland. As mentioned above, Zweig first met Verhaeren in 1902 through the mediation of the Belgian sculptor van der Stappen. Between 1902 and 1910 Zweig translated Verhaeren's complete works and even arranged a lecture tour in Germany for him, having previously aided in the staging of some of Verhaeren's lyric-dramas, though to be sure not without some misgiving concerning their reception by the public – an anxiety, however, which proved to be totally unfounded. The two friends saw each other for the last time in the spring of 1914, the war preventing Zweig from visiting Verhaeren in Belgium and, long before the armistice was signed, Verhaeren was dead, having been run over by a train in 1916. One of the greatest sadnesses in Zweig's life was a direct result of Verhaeren, who in 1915 published his *La Belgique Sanglante*, a work in which he poured out all the penned up hatred in his heart for Germany and its people who had wrought such havoc on Europe and occupied his beloved Belgium. To Zweig such scathing bitterness, such unadulterated hatred seemed a desertion of the cause of international brotherhood which Zweig had first experienced so poignantly through Verhaeren. Though disappointed that even Verhaeren should succumb to the mass hatred so rampant in Europe, Zweig could not help but love him dearly to the end, as his tribute "Erinnerungen an Emile Verhaeren" so eloquently testifies.[28]

The other great friendship that contributed so much to Zweig's mental and emotional development was that with Romain Rolland.[29] While in Paris (1913), just by chance Zweig read Rolland's "L'Aube" in the periodical *Cahiers de la Quinzaine*. Inquiring about the author, Verhaeren informed him that he was primarily known as a musicologist through his essay on Beethoven. A meeting of the two was arranged by Verhaeren and from their first encounter they both were aware of the harmony of mind and spirit which they shared – a harmony which served as the basis for an intimate, brotherly friendship which was to endure some forty years.

In August, 1914, Rolland published his essay *Au-dessus de la mêlée* in which he sought to combat the hatred and fanaticism of the intellectuals from whom alone a spiritual fraternity could flow.[30] Shortly thereafter (September 19, 1914) Zweig published his "Abschiedsbrief an die Freunde im Ausland" in the *Berliner Tageblatt* wherein he bid a temporary farewell to his foreign friends, promising not to forget them and begging them to work with him again after the war to reconstruct European culture.[31] Most of Zweig's German friends began to avoid him, feeling him to be unpatriotic and Zweig himself would have wanted to be classed as a conscientious objector. He lacked, however, the strength to face the consequences of such flagrant anti-national sentiment and soon took a position in the War Archives. Though isolated in his native Vienna, Zweig was not "alone" for very long – soon letters from Rolland began to reach him, urging him to aid in organizing a congress of intellectuals to meet in Switzerland, whose primary aim would be to work for peace and international understanding. Neither Zweig nor Rolland found much support, the time was still premature, the invigorating effects of the night before hadn't had quite enough time to transform into the nausea of the morning after.[32]

The war was another decisive factor in Zweig's life. He fought the war-mania with all the powers at his command and in his effort to oppose the unreasonableness of sheer force he raised the tragic defeat of the conquered to a poetic principle.[33] His opposition to the war was based primarily on intellectual, humane grounds, not on an understanding of the economic causes which had aided the explosion at Serajevo. Zweig saw his task in the propagation of anti-war thought (a position in which he was greatly encouraged by Rolland), a task which he fulfilled in his essays, his prose works and above all in his drama *Jeremias*. Early in the war he wrote reviews of such anti-military works as *Le Feu* (1916) by Henri Barbusse[34] and the *Die Waffen nieder* (Novel, 2 volumes, 1889) of Bertha von Suttner, the founder of the Pacifist Movement who had persuaded Alfred Nobel to establish his Peace Prize. Zweig's later Novellen "Der Zwang" (1920), "Episode am Genfersee" (1918) and "Buchmendl" (1929) are stirring protests against the senselessness and barbarism of war.

During the Spring of 1915 Zweig was sent to Galicia to collect Russian posters for the State Archives. The dirt, filth and suffering that surrounded him on every side revolted him and he decided to combat such conditions directly and vigorously.[35] The immediate outcome of his decision was the drama *Jeremias*, a symbolic impassioned plea for peace which, though clothed in the biblical garb of the prophet Jeremiah, sought to expose the crimes of warmongers and the tragic consequences of their wars. He represented the suffering of the people and attempted to point out a spiritual-moral path for the future – an unbroken brotherhood of all peoples. The drama first appeared in 1917 during the Easter season and almost overnight 20,000 copies were sold. The director of the Züricher Theater proposed to produce the play and in February, 1918, *Jeremias* enjoyed an overwhelmingly successful première with Zweig attending the performance.[36]

While in Switzerland Zweig met and worked again with most of the influential, anti-war intellectuals of Europe who had emigrated to neutral territory: Romain Rolland, Masereel, Leonhard Frank, Franz Werfel, among others. It was a period of furious activity for all of them, all with but one objective: peace.[37] Zweig lectured and wrote article after article for the periodicals *La Feuille* and *Demain*.[38] An article he wrote in 1917 entitled "Das Herz Europas" describes in terms of admiration the selflessness and devotion of Rolland in his voluntary services in the Red Cross agency for the repatriation and solace of war prisoners. Though written primarily in honor of Rolland, his idealism and self-sacrifice can easily be applied to the group as a whole.[39] With the signing of the armistice in 1918 the group as such broke up, each returning to his respective country with but one thought in mind – to rebuild Europe as a united whole and to establish international brotherhood and peace.[40]

In 1912 Zweig had met a certain Frau Friderike von Winternitz (née Burger, born 1882), the wife of Felix von Winternitz and the mother of two small daughters. In the course of two years the two fell in love and Friderike left her husband. They moved near to one another at Baden, Austria, and then together to Rodaun in 1916. In 1920 their life together was legalized by a new Austrian law which allowed divorced Catholics to remarry. From the end of World War I to their divorce on December 25, 1938, the two were inseparable companions and help-mates, of one mind and body.[51] In 1917, while in Salzburg, Stefan saw a vacant house, an abandoned hunting lodge, on the Kapuzinerberg, just above the city. The site provided everything one could desire – quietude, gardened landscape, a beautiful view, everything – and miracle of miracles, it was for sale. Stefan decided immediately in favor of buying it and his wife completed negotiations for its purchase.[42] With the signing of the armistice Zweig decided to return immediately to Austria, in spite of the misery and deplorable conditions the war had left in its wake. The house on the Kapuzinerberg was almost in ruins and, with the scarcity of building materials, it was months before the house was really habitable.[43] The years Zweig spent in Salzburg (1919-1934) were the happiest and most productive of his life. The city itself was an ideal setting – a romantic blend of German Gothic and Baroque with Italian Renaissance, picturesque natural surroundings, within easy reach of the leading European capitals, and, for a few years at least, a harbor of quiet and rest.[44] It was only then that the Salzburg Festival grew to monstrous proportions, and during the Mozart Season his home became the gathering place of the world's great: Max Reinhardt, Thomas Mann, Franz Werfel, Emil Ludwig, Arturo Toscanini,[45] Bruno Walter,[46] Richard Strauss, Albert Einstein, Duhamel, Ravel, Hermann Bahr, [47] Albert Schweitzer, [48] Gustav Mahler[49] and of course Rolland and Masereel,[50] to mention but a few.[51] Had he been able to foresee the future importance of the city with the resultant loss of his own seclusion Zweig undoubtedly would never have purchased the house. For a time Zweig almost buried himself in Salzburg except for a few side excursions to Italy and France. The signs of rising Fascism in Italy and Germany and the assassination of Walter Rathenau were disturbing, but on the whole life was rather normal.[52] By 1933 he had published over 50 books, Novellen and essays and was asked by the Insel Verlag, a distinguished publishing company, to be allowed to publish all his works. His writings were soon translated into almost every European language and Chinese, with introductions by such famous authors as Maxim Gorki and Romain Rolland. It was estimated by a committee of the League of Nations that by 1930 he was the most translated author in the world.[53] It was during this period that Zweig's most famous works appeared, among them *Drei Meister* (1920), the Novellen, *Der Zwang* and *Angst* (both 1920), *Romain Rolland* (1921), the Novellen collection, *Amok* (1922), *Der Kampf mit dem Dämon* (1925), *Verwirrung der Gefühle* (1927), *Sternstunden der Menschheit* (1927), *Drei Dichter ihres Lebens* (1928),

Joseph Fouché (1929), *Die Heilung durch den Geist* (1931) and *Marie Antoinette* (1932) .[54] In November, 1931, Zweig celebrated his 50th birthday, a birthday which was remembered throughout the world, for from every corner of the globe best wishes and congratulations poured into Salzburg, feelings which were perhaps most fittingly summed up in an article of praise and affection written for the *Neue Rundschau* by Otto Zarek.[55] The following year Zweig was approached by Richard Strauss who asked him to write the libretto to an opera he had planned, *Die schweigsame Frau.* Zweig gladly accepted, not only because of the literary pleasure such a task would provide but in part flattered that Strauss had asked him to assume a position which had been the exclusive prerogative of Austria's literary esthete, Hugo von Hofmannsthal, until his death in 1929.[56]

Zweig was not only internationally famous and revered but equally loved and respected by the people of Salzburg with whom he would spend a few evenings a week in "his café," reading the newspapers and listening to the radio (having banned such disturbing elements from his house). All in all life was very pleasant and then January, 1933, Hitler seized power in Germany!

Life changed almost over night. With the burning of the Reichstag the signal for an all out persecution of the Jews began. Not only were their personal liberties abrogated and their human dignity degraded but their works proscribed almost *in toto.* A film based on Zweig's "Brennendes Geheimnis" was suppressed, the opera, *Die schweigsame Frau,* was banned after only one performance and his works were publicly burned and forbidden either to be sold, read or kept in a public or private collection. Zweig was not alone, however, for this "literary exile" from Germany was shared equally by the majority of the best writers of the German language (Th. Mann, Brecht, Brod, Kafka, Remarque, Schnitzler, Beer-Hofmann, Freud, etc., etc., etc.), but one which completely annihilated German literature from 1933 until the collapse of the "Tausendjähriges Reich" twelve years later.[57]

In order to watch the progress of things at a distance, Zweig went to London via Switzerland (October ,1933). At that time he had no thought of permanently leaving Salzburg.[58] The calmness of the life in England had a soothing effect on him and soon he was at work again. The result of this short sojurn was his biography of Mary Stuart.[59] By January, 1934, he was back in Vienna, but it was only too obvious that the situation on the continent was in no sense getting better. On the contrary, even his former friends and acquaintances in Salzburg avoided him.[60] It was at this time that Zweig decided to leave Austria and set up housekeeping in London. Not wishing to leave her aging mother-in-law alone, Mrs. Zweig remained in Austria. Realizing, however, that Zweig could not carry on his research alone,

Mrs. Zweig procured for him a young Jewish secretary, Miss Lotte Altmann, who five years later became the second Mrs. Zweig.[61] A Congress of the International Pen-Club was held in 1936 in Buenos Aires to which Zweig was invited as a guest speaker. Hoping to escape his fears as to the future of Europe, fears and pessimistic premonitions which insisted on invading his thoughts and his works, he willingly accepted the proffered invitation. The warm reception given him and the beauty of South America did lighten his mind, enough so that he was able to see some hope for the future.[62] In his works on Brazil he praised her for her warm welcome, her glorious past and her burning hope for the future.[63] His return to England (via a lecture tour of the U.S.A.)[64] found the international situation even more sinister. He flew to Vienna for the last time to visit his mother and to give most of his library and autograph collection away – most of his materials being given either to the Viennese National Library or the National Library at Jerusalem. What property he did not give away or send out of the country was immediately confiscated when Hitler annexed Austria.

Two of Zweig's biographies written during the years 1933-1939 are worthy of particular note for they both reflect his thought and in a veiled manner Zweig himself – they are his *Triumph und Tragik des Erasmus von Rotterdam* (1934) and *Castellio gegen Calvin* (1936). Both works seem to preach the same doctrine of humanism and tolerance but whereas *Erasmus* foreshadows the defeat of the individual, *Castellio* attempts to portray an example of resistance against brutal suppression. The former, a rather accurate portrait of Zweig as he was, the latter of him as he wished he could have been. Both, however, represent the struggle of individual freedom against force, of the one against the overpowering many, a struggle in which might seems to triumph. This triumph, however, is mere illusion, for the "ideal" lives on indefinitely. Man is at his best, is most noble only when he willingly sacrifices his own selfish ambitions to serve as an instrument of this ideal, as a tireless warrior in defense of peace and tolerance, a champion of the humanities and the spirit.[65]

The outbreak of World War II caused a complete change in Zweig's life. The house which he purchased in Bath became a regular home for refugees, among them Zweig's beloved friend Sigmund Freud, who, being forced to leave his native Austria, had come to England to accept a Chair of Honor which the British Royal Society of Science had extended to him.[66] During the Spring of 1940 Zweig lectured in Paris where he had gone primarily to see his first wife, desperately in need of the spiritual strength and mental equilibrium which she alone seemed to possess and from whom alone he could draw the courage needed to continue. Upon his return to England he found another letter from South America requesting that he undertake a second lecture tour. He gladly accepted. The tour was a triumph beyond all expectation. Until January, 1941, he remained in Brazil and then moved to New York to be near the facilities of the Yale University library and be near Friderike, who alone could furnish him with much of the material he needed for his autobiography which was already in preparation. To be able to see her daily, he rented a house in Ossining, New York, where he remained until August, 1941. The summer, however, proved too strenuous for both Stefan and his second wife who was failing rapidly. Fearing that Lotte couldn't survive another winter in the North, they returned to Brazil again, where they rented a house, a miniature replica of Zweig's Salzburg retreat on the Kapuzinerberg, in Petropolis, a small city not far distant from Rio de Janeiro.[67] That Fall Zweig finished his autobiography, all but completed his monumental study of Balzac[68] and wrote his last Novelle, "Schachnovelle," written in somewhat the same spirit as his *Castellio*, a masterpiece in the genre and by many considered to be the finest Novelle he ever wrote. On the morning of February 23, 1942, Zweig and his wife were found in their bedroom, lying side by side, two empty glasses on the night stand. Before freely ending his life Zweig wrote one last message to those whom he loved and was now leaving, a message of thanks to the country of Brazil for the obvious affection which it had tendered him, and a prayer of hope that those who still fought on would soon see the dawn of victory and peace. He, however, could no longer wait, his strength was gone, his usefulness ended here. Assuredly though he would wait for them beyond.[69]

To discuss the suicide of a human being and to attempt to judge its full import is tantamount to treading upon ground to which none but the Divine has right. Therefore, the comments which follow seek neither to condone nor to condemn Zweig's death, but rather to explain its causes. Although we can not read the thoughts of another and consequently can never attain absolute surety that our judgments are correct, we can, and should, seek to understand the most obvious reasons which would drive a man to will calmly and rationally the destruction of that life force within him, which by instinctive nature demands its own preservation.

Comparatively speaking Zweig had little reason to end his own life. Brazil was a quiet, beautiful country which had offered him not only refuge but love. He had sufficient time (perhaps too much?) to work on his "Balzac" manuscript and to revive his interest in Montaigne. He had been driven from his home, that is true, but his lot was for the most part far better than that of the hundreds of thousands who lost everything in their flight from the advancing Nazi hordes or those thousands who didn't escape in time. Zweig at least had some money, reputation, friends and to a great extent personal liberty. Viewed strictly externally, Zweig's position was better than most. But even here all was not what it seemed – his work on Brazil, although generally acclaimed, was most unfavorably criticized in Nazi controlled newspapers and Zweig himself was openly flaunted by Nazi agitators. The country was quiet and restful, but unfortunately too much so. Zweig was accustomed to activity and people and suddenly there was neither. Although the requisite time for working on his manuscripts was provided in excess, he was deprived access to primary source materials and even believed his beloved "Balzac" manuscript lost during the Blitz over England.[70] It should also be remembered that his whole life had been spent in luxury and security, now almost everything was swept away.[71] Through predisposition he desired a private, well ordered life and now he was forced to flee around the world, exposed to conditions which, though normal to most people, were disastrous to him. Too, he was in no sense of the word a business-minded individual. Any decision concerning financial or legal transactions had been left up to his first wife, and now he was left totally to his own devices.[72]

As bearing upon his suicide as these exterior circumstances might be, the very nature of his character preponderates in explaining his final act of resignation. As Zweig grew older the attacks of morbid depression and pessimism to which he was subject became increasingly more frequent and severe. Toward the end of his life he felt himself hunted, homeless and persecuted as a Jew. As a Humanist he saw only terror and force unleashed throughout the world. Even his mother tongue was denied him – he saw his final works appear only in translation, and with whom was he to converse in German, except his wife? To be forced to think and express oneself in a foreign language at his age seemed too great a strain (the language of Brazil, his last refuge, is Portuguese, a language Zweig did not speak). He was just plain tired. Impatient by nature, living far from his home and his friends (both of which constituted the core of his life), lacking sufficient strength to control his basically passionate nature and seeing nothing but destruction and hatred in a world in which he had endeavored to propagate peace and brotherhood, Zweig's resistance was broken. He was literally driven into the next world ahead of his friends for whom he was too impatient to wait.

Since 1942 a great many articles have appeared attempting to interpret and/or explain Zweig's death. Some commentators see in his suicide an act of martyrdom, a protest against Nazi barbarism.[73] Others consider it an act of treason and cowardice, springing from personal despair, a decided betrayal of those millions who looked to him for comfort and guidance. In his article "Réflexions sur le suicide de Stefan Zweig" Paul Beaulieu contends that such censure of contemporary intellectuals supports the view which forbids suicide on moral grounds.[74] According to this view we are all bound one to another and all to God. Thus our freedom is limited by our obligations. In the realm of theory this is true but in practical application it fails to take into consideration subjective elements which usually outweigh speculative arguments.[75]

As a Jew Zweig was not reared in the Christian tradition of "love thy neighbor as thyself." His God was more probably the deistic God of the Enlightenment and not the personal God of Christianity. The kenotic being worshipped in Christ by His followers had little or no significance for him. Zweig's humanism was based on intellectual principles of mutual understanding, not on Christian principles of mutual love. Even the desired ends differ – Zweig's humanism would establish cultural refinement and international peace as its final goal; the goal of Christian Humanism being an eternal and direct union with God, affected through love.

As a man Zweig was physically more delicate than most human beings, his sensibilities more refined. By nature somewhat egocentric Zweig was controlled by his ideas and ideals. Once these had been destroyed his life lost its meaning. His temperament demanded immediate contact with friends, perceptible signs of affection. The abstract concept of devotion given by the mysterious "masses" could hardly be considered a substitute.

As an individual Zweig repeatedly asserted that he was no hero – he didn't even want to be one. His natural inclination toward suicide can be gleaned through a psychological interpretation of his Novellen where the tendency toward resignation and death is usually a prime factor. His desire for personal freedom became almost an obsession with him, it was literally the highest good on earth. This meant that he was bound first to himself, to himself he must therefore be true. Zweig lived for and served an "idea." Individuals he loved and aided wherever and whenever possible, but the concept "masses" meant far less to him directly than the concept "humanity." Zweig's greatness flows from his psychological mastery and penetrating insight into the human soul, but this gift was likewise the source of his weakness. A realist in the realm of the psyche, Zweig remained to the end an idealist, an utopian in the macrocosm of political-social problems.[76] Zweig's Humanism is truly admirable, but he was actually driven to his death, broken by the world he loved.

> ... seduit par Montaigne au point de s'identifier avec sa pensée, il a abandonné la vie victime lointaine de la guerre qu'il avait cru pouvoir fuir.[77]

PRIMARY WORKS

Editions and Translations Thereof

I. COLLECTED WORKS

GERMAN

1. *Ausgewählte Werke* (Teilsamml.). Vol. I/II. Düsseldorf: Deutscher Bücherbund, 1960.

ITALIAN

2. *Opere Scelte*. Vol. I/II. Tr. Lavinia Mazzucchetti. Milano: Mondadori, 1961.

PORTUGUESE

3. *Obras Completas*. Vol. I/XX. Tr. Aurélio Pinheiro *et al*. Rio de Janeiro: Delta, 1953.

RUSSIAN

4. *Izbrannye Proizvedenija*. Vol. I/II. Tr. P. Bernštejn *et al*. Moskva: Goslitizdat, 1956; (Reprinted 1957).
5. — Kiev: Goslitizdat Ukrainy, 1957.
6. — Kujbysev: Kn. izd., 1957.
7. — Minsk: Goslitizdat BSSR, 1960.
8. *Sobranie Sochineniy Stefana Tsveyga*. Avtorizovannoe izdanie s predisloviem M. Gor'kogo i kritiko-biograficeskim ocerkom Richarda Spechta (Collected Works of Stefan Zweig. Authorized edition with foreword by M. Gorki and a critical biographical essay by Richard Specht). Leningrad: Vremya, 1928-1930.
       I. *Zhguchaya Tayna. Pervye Perezhivanija* (*Brennendes Geheimnis. Erstes Erlebnis*).
      II. *Amok. Novelly* (*Amok. Novellen*).
      III. *Smjatenie Chuvsto* (*Verwirrung der Gefühle*).
      IV. *Nezrimaja Kollekcija* (*Die unsichtbare Sammlung et al.*).
      V. *Rokovyemgnovenija* (*Sternstunden der Menschheit et al.*).
      VI. *Tri Pevca svoej Zhizni* (*Drei Dichter ihres Lebens*).
      VII. *Tri Mastera* (*Drei Meister*).
      VIII. *Marselina Debord-Val'more* (*Marceline Desbordes-Valmore*).
      IX. *Zhosef Fushe* (*Joseph Fouché*).
      X. *Bor'ba s Bezumiem* (*Kampf mit dem Dämon*).
9. Moskva: Izdatel'stvo Pravda, 1963.
      I. *Novelly* ("V Sumerkakh" ("Geschichte in der Dämmerung"), "Guvernantka" ("Die Gouvernante"), "Zhguchaya Tayna" ("Brennendes Geheimnis"), "Amok" ("Amok"), "Strakh" ("Angst")).
      II. *Neterpenie Serdtsa* (*Ungeduld des Herzens*); *Legendy* (*Legenden*).

1

III. *Zvezdnye Chasy Chelovechestva. Istoricheskie Miniatyury (Sternstunden der Menschheit)*; *Maggelan (Magellan)*; *Amerigo (Amerigo)*.
IV. *Mariya Styuart (Maria Stuart)*; *Zhosef Fushe (Joseph Fouché)*.
V. *Bal'zak (Balzac)*.
VI. *Frants Anton Mesmer (Franz Anton Mesmer)*; *Gel'derlin (Hölderlin)*; *Genrich fon Kleyst (Heinrich von Kleist)*; *Stendal' (Stendhal)*; *Marselina Debord Val'mor (Marceline Desbordes-Valmore)*; *Dikkens (Dickens)*.
VII. *Romen Rollan (Romain Rolland)*; *Vospominaniya ob Emile Verkharne (Erinnerungen an Emile Verhaeren)*; *Vstrechi s Liud'mi, Gorodami, Knigami (Begegnungen mit Menschen, Städten und Büchern)*.

SPANISH

10. *Obras Completas*. Vol. I/II. Estudio crítico por Carlos Soldevila. Barcelona: Juventud, 1952, 1953. (Contains: Vol. I: "La Piedad Peligrosa (Impaciencia del Corazón)" (*Ungeduld des Herzens*), "Calidoscopio" (*Kaleidoskop*), "Conocimiento Casual de un Oficio" ("Unvermutete Bekanntschaft mit einem Handwerk"), "Leporella" ("Leporella"), "Miedo" ("Angst"), "Ardiente Secreto" ("Brennendes Geheimnis"), "Novela Veraniega" ("Sommernovellette"), "La Institutriz" ("Die Gouvernante"), "Buchmendel" ("Buchmendel"), "El Refugio" ("Episode am Genfer See"), "La Colección Invisible" ("Die unsichtbare Sammlung"), "Noche Fantástica" ("Phantastische Nacht"), "La Calle del Claro de Luna" ("Die Mondscheingasse"), "Sendas Equívocas" ("Verwirrung der Gefühle"), "Carta de una Desconocida" ("Brief einer Unbekannten"), "El Jugado de Ajedrez" ("Schachnovelle"), "Una Carta" ("Vierundzwanzig Stunden aus dem Leben einer Frau"?), "El Candelabro Enterrado" ("Der begrabene Leuchter"), "Los Ojos del Hermano Eterno" ("Die Augen des ewigen Bruders"), "Jeremias" (*Jeremias*). Vol. II: "Maria Antonieta" (*Marie Antoinette*), "Tres Maestros: Balzac, Dickens, Dostoiewski" (*Drei Meister*), "Magallanes" (*Magellan*), "Americo Vespucio" (*Amerigo*), "Tres Poetas de su Vida: Casanova, Stendhal, Tolstoi" (*Drei Dichter ihres Lebens*)).
11. *Obras de Stefan Zweig*. Vol. I/II. Barcelona: José Janés; Madrid: Ediciones Castilla (s.a.), 1958. "Colección Maestros de Hoy" (Contains: "Stefan Zweig," por Fridcrike Maria Zweig. Tr. Alfredo Cahn; "Americo Vespucio" (*Amerigo*). Tr. Alfredo Cahn; "Tres Poetas de su Vida" (*Drei Dichter*) and "La Lucha contra et Demonio" (*Kampf mit dem Dämon*). Tr. Joaquin Verdaguer; "La Curación por Espíritu" (*Die Heilung durch den Geist*). Tr. Francisco Payarols; "Balzac" (*Balzac*). Tr. Aristides Gamboa).

II. POETRY IN BOOK FORM

12. *Ausgewählte Gedichte*. Leipzig: Insel, 1931 (Insel-Bücherei, No. 422, 1931: 1.-10. Tsd.; 1934: 11.-20. Tsd.)
13. — Wiesbaden: Insel, 1950. (Insel-Bücherei, No. 174, 1950: 21.-29. Tsd.; 1953: 30.-39. Tsd.).
14. *Die frühen Kränze*. Leipzig: Insel, 1906 (1906: 1.-2. Tsd.; 1917: 3.-4. Tsd.; 1920: 5.-6. Tsd.).
15. *Die gesammelten Gedichte*. Leipzig: Insel, 1924.
16. *Silberne Saiten*. Berlin-Leipzig: Schuster und Loeffler, 1901.

III. SINGLE POEMS

17. "Abendklänge," *Ge*, 16.J., II: 4 (1900), 236.
18. "Abendwolken," *DD*, XXXI (Oct., 1901 - Mar., 1902), 286.

2

19. "Abschied," *DD*, XXX (Apr.-Sept., 1901), 174.
20. "Am Abend," *DD*, XXVI (Apr.-Sept., 1899), 147.
21. "Bäume im Frühling," *Tag*, p. 120.
22. "Ballade von einem Traum," *NR*, XXXIV: 2 (1923), 716-722 (Reprinted in *Europäer*, pp. 157-162).
23. "Der Bildner (Meudon, Haus Rodin, 1913)," *In*, V : 1 (1924), 42-46 (cf. *Gesammelte Gedichte*, pp. 87-91; *Begegnungen*, pp. 74-77; *In*, XIII : 1 (Christmas, 1931), 15-16).
24. "Eine blaue Flamme," *DD*, XXXI (Oct., 1901 – Mar., 1902), 181.
25. "Bruges" (English tr. of "Brügge"), *CGP*, p. 191 (French tr. cf. *ALA*, pp. 392-395).
26. "Brügge," *ÖR*, VIII : 94-95 (Aug.-Oct., 1906), 126.
27. "The Dark Butterfly" (English tr. of "Der dunkle Falter), *CGP*, p. 190.
28. "Deutsche Stadt (Konstanz), "*ÖR*, VIII : 94-95 (Aug.-Oct., 1906), 128.
29. "Die Dinge, die die Abende erzählen...," (from "Die Lieder des Abends" in *Die frühen Kränze*), from Paul Zech's review of this book as quoted in *DLE*, 17.J.: 3 (Nov. 1, 1914), 171-172.
30. "Der Dirigent. In memoriam Gustav Mahlers," *InA* (1923), 95-99 (Reprinted in *Begegnungen*, pp. 123-126).
31. "Dostojewski" (French tr. of "Der Märtyrer"), *ALA*, pp. 396-405.
32. "Dunkle Sehnsucht," *Spiegelungen*, p. 22.
33. "Ein dunkler Weg," *DD*, XXXI (Oct., 1901 – Mar., 1902), 263.
34. "Das Einleitungsgedicht zu dem neuen Novellenbande: 'Verwirrung der Gefühle'," *In*, VII: 4 (1926), 277.
35. "Einsamkeit," *DD*, XXIX (Oct., 1900 – Mar., 1901), 57.
36. "Erkenntnis," *DD*, XXX (Apr.-Sept., 1901), 194.
37. "Erstes Ahnen," *Ge*, 16.J., II : 3 (1900), 182.
38. "Die Frage," *Z*, XLVII (June 18, 1904), 456.
39. "Das fremde Lächeln," *ÖR*, V : 57 (Nov., 1905 – Jan., 1906), 222.
40. "Frühlingssegen," *DD*, XXVIII (Apr.-Sept., 1900), 262.
41. "Gefangen," *DD*, XXVII (Oct., 1899 – Mar., 1900), 135.
42. "Hand in Hand," *Spiegelungen*, p. 22.
43. "Die Hände," *Liliencron*, p. 79.
44. "Herbst," *Europäer*, pp. 11-12.
45. "Herbstmorgen," *DD*, XXVII (Oct., 1899 – Mar., 1900), 159.
46. "Herbstsonette," *InA* (1911), 63-64 (Reprinted in *Tag*, pp. 120-121).
47. "Hymnus an die Reise," *In*, XIII : 1 (Christmas, 1931), 12-13.
48. "Im Feld," *DD*, XXIX (Oct., 1900 – Mar., 1901), 288.
49. "Im Glück," *DD*, XXVII (Oct., 1899 – Mar., 1900), 88.
50. "In den Tag hinein," *DD*, XXVIII (Apr.-Sept., 1900), 28.
51. "In der Kirche," *DD*, XXVI (Apr.-Sept., 1899), 267.
52. "In der Sternennacht," *DD*, XXIX (Oct., 1900 – Mar., 1901), 93.
53. "Indischer Spruch," *Tag*, p. 119.
54. "Kinder im Dorfe," *DD*, XXXI (Oct., 1901 – Mar., 1902), 233.
55. "Das Leben," *DD*, XXX (Apr.-Sept., 1901), 111.
56. "Liebeslied," *DD*, XXVI (Apr.-Sept., 1899), 77 (Reprinted in *Tag*, pp. 119-120).
57. "Lied des Einsiedlers," *In*, XIII : 1 (Christmas, 1931), 14-15.
58. "Linder schwebt der Stunden Reigen," *SZG*, p. 43 (Reprinted in *Europäer*, p. 33; *Leben-Werk*, p. 110; cf. below "Der Sechzigjährige dankt").
59. "Das Mädchen," *DD*, XXX (Apr.-Sept., 1901), 71.
60. "Der Märtyrer" (Poem about Dostojewski, Dec. 22, 1849), *InA* (1913), 26-34.
60a. "Matkowskys Othello (Geschrieben bei der Nachricht seines Todes 1909), *ADV* (1920).
61. "Meine Brust...," *DD*, XXV (Oct., 1898 – Mar., 1899), 258.
62. "Meine Saat," *DD*, XXXII (Apr.-Sept., 1902), 122.
63. "Morgenlicht," *DD*, XXVII (Oct., 1899 – Mar., 1900), 234.
64. "Die Mutter," *DD*, XXIX (Oct., 1900 – Mar., 1901), 145.

3

65. "Die Nacht der Gnaden," *Z*, XLIV (Sept. 12, 1903), 424-426.
66. "Nacht im Gebirge," *DD*, XXIX (Oct., 1900 – Mar., 1901), 168.
67. "Neue Fülle," *In*, XIII : 1 (Christmas, 1931), 11.
68. "Rauher Frühling," *DD*, XXIX (Oct., 1900 – Mar., 1901), 241.
69. "Reifes Glück," *DD*, XXX (Apr. – Sept., 1901), 86.
70. "Regentage," *DD*, XXIX (Oct., 1900 – Mar., 1901), 17.
71. "Rosenknospen," *DD*, XXV (Oct., 1898 – Mar., 1899), 123.
72. "Die Sängerin," *InA* (1914), 165-169.
73. "Der Sechzigjährige dankt" (Zweig's last poem), *Europäer*, p. 33 (Photocopy of same opposite p. 337; cf. "Linder schwebt der Stunden Reigen").
74. "Singede Fontäne," *InA* (1912), 103-105.
75. "Sommernächte am Komersee," *ÖR*, VIII : 94-95 (Aug.–Oct., 1906), 127.
76. "Sommerwende," *DD*, XXX (Apr.–Sept., 1901), 218.
77. "Sonnenaufgang in Venedig," *ÖR*, VIII : 94-95 (Aug.-Oct., 1906), 126.
78. "Spätsommer," *DD*, XXVII (Oct., 1899 – Mar., 1900), 18.
79. "Spinoza," *Spiegelungen*, p. 23.
80. "Sternengedanke," *DD*, XXIX (Oct., 1900 – Mar., 1901), 264.
81. "Stille Insel (Bretagne)," *ÖR*, VIII : 94-95 (Aug.-Oct., 1906), 127.
82. "Stimmen im Walde," *DD*, XXVIII (Apr.-Sept., 1900), 212.
83. "Der Sucher," *Z*, XLVI (Jan. 23, 1904), 146-147.
84. "Thautropfen," *DD*, XXVI (Apr.-Sept., 1899), 164.
85. "Ile Tranquille (Bretagne)," *ALA*, pp. 395-396.
86. "Ein Traum," *DD*, XXXI (Oct., 1901 – Mar., 1902), 109.
87. "Der verlorene Himmel. Eine Elegie," *InA* (1917), 152-155.
88. "Der Verschmähte," *DD*, XXXI (Oct., 1901 – Mar., 1902), 135.
89. "Verse in ein Stammbuch" (Poem dedicated to Anton Kippenberg on his 60th birthday), *Europäer*, p. 128 (Cf. *Leben-Werk*, p. 70).
90. "Weihnacht," *Spiegelungen*, p. 23.
91. "Werden," *DD*, XXXI (Oct., 1901 - Mar., 1902), 165.
92. "Winterabend im Zimmer," *DD*, XXVIII (Apr.-Sept., 1900), 52 (Reprinted in *Spiegelungen*, p. 22).
93. "Die Zärtlichkeiten," *DeB*, p. 90.

IV. DRAMAS

94. *Die Flucht zu Gott* (Ein Epilog zu Leo Tolstois unvollendetem Drama *Das Licht scheinet in der Finsternis*). Berlin: Bloch, 1927.
95. — (Bühnenmanuskript). *NT*, 1.J. : 2 (Dec., 1928), 34-55. (Premiere: Vereinigtes Städtisches Theater Kiel, Sept. 5, 1928).
96. *Das Haus am Meer. Ein Schauspiel in zwei Teilen.* Leipzig: Insel, 1912 (Premiere: Hofburgtheater Wien, Oct. 26, 1912).
97. *Jeremias. Eine dramatische Dichtung in neun Bildern.* Leipzig: Insel, 1917 (Uraufführung: Stadttheater Zürich, Feb. 27, 1918).
    1917 – 2. ed.
    1918 – 3. „
    1919 – 4. „ (9.-13 Tsd)
    1920 – 5. „ (14.-18. Tsd)
    1922 – 6. „ (19.-21. Tsd)
    1923 – 7. „ (22.-25. Tsd)
    1928 – 8. „ (26.-28. Tsd).
98. — Stockholm: Bermann-Fischer, 1939; Amsterdam: de Lange, 1939.
99. *Jeremias. Eine dramatische Dichtung in sieben Bildern.* Ed. L. Wery. Zwolle: W. E. J. Tjeenk Willink, 1940 (Neue deutsche Bibliothek, No. 23).
100. Dutch. *Als de Schaduwen Lengen* (Fragment uit *Jeremias*). Tr. J. Haantjes. Utrecht: Vrijzinnig Christelijke Jeugdcentrale, 1938.

4

101.   *Jeremias. Treurspel in negen Deelen.* Tr. Josef Boon.Antwerpen: P. Vink, 1934.
102.   English. "The Everlasting Road" (Adaptation from *Jeremiah*). *A Golden Treasury of Jewish Literature* (Sec. "Plays of a Changing World"). Sel. and ed. Leo W. Schwarz. New York-Toronto: Farrare, Rinehart, 1937, pp. 411-426.
103.   *Jeremiah. A Drama in Nine Scenes.* Tr. Eden and Cedar Paul. New York: Seltzer, 1922; new ed. New York: Viking, 1929; London: Allen and Unwin, 1929 (Preface by author in both 1929 editions).
104.   — New York: Viking, 1939 (A new preface by the author to mark the first American production by the New York Theater Guild, Feb. 3, 1939).
105.   French. *Jérémie.* Tr. Louis Charles Boudouin. Paris: Rieder, 1929 (Judaïsme, No. 10).
106.   Hebrew. *Yirmiyahu.* Tr. Avigdor Ha-meiri. Jerusalem: Dept. de la Jeunesse de l'Organisation Sioniste Mondiale, 1950 (This edition contains a critical essay about the play by the translator).
107.   Polish. *Jeremiasz. Poemat Dramatyczny w Dziewieciu Obrazach.* Tr. Melanja Wassermann. Warszawa: Hoesick, 1926.
108.   Portuguese. *Jeremias.* Tr. Cándido de Carvalho. Porto (Portugal): Livro Civilização, 1957 (4th ed.).
109.   Spanish. *Jeremias.* Tr. Alfredo Cahn. Barcelona: Hispano-Americana de Ediciones, 1945 (Col. Cumbre).
110.   — Tr. Alfredo Cahn. Buenos Aires: Espasa-Calpe, 1956.
111.   Yiddish. *Jirmijahu. Dr'am'atis'e Diktung 'in nein Bild'er.* Tr. Br'aq'azs. W'ars'e: Tur'em, 1929.
112. *Das Lamm des Armen.* Leipzig: Insel, 1929 (Simultaneous premiere Lobetheater Breslau, Städtisches Schauspielhaus Hannover, Stadttheater Lübeck, Neues Deutsches Theater Prag, Mar. 15, 1930).
113.   French. *Un Caprice de Bonaparte. Pièce en trois Actes.* Tr. Alzir Hella. Paris: Grasset, 1952.
114.   Spanish. *El Cordero de Pobre. Tragi-Comedia en tres Actos.* Tr. Alfredo Cahn. Buenos Aires: Editorial Claridad, 1942.
115. *Legende eines Lebens. Ein Kammerspiel in drei Aufzügen.* Leipzig: Insel, 1919 (1923 - 3.-4. Tsd.) (Premiere: Deutsches Schauspielhaus Hamburg, Dec. 25, 1918).
116.   Russian. *Legenda odnoj Zhizni. P'esa v trech Dejstvijach.* Foreword by A. G. Hornfeld. Tr. I. B. Mandelstam. Moskva-Petrograd: Gosudarstvennoe Izdatel'stvo, 1923.
117. *Quiproquo. Komödie.* Wien: n.p., 1928 (Written in conjunction with Alexander Lernet-Holenia, under the pseudonym Clemens Neydisser).
118. *Die schweigsame Frau. Komische Oper in drei Aufzügen frei nach Ben Jonson.* Berlin: Adolph Fürstner, 1935 (piano-vocal score Richard Strauss, Op. 80).
119.   English. *The Silent Woman. A Comic Opera in Three Acts.* Tr. Herbert Bedford. New York: Program Publishing, n.d.
120.   Italian. *La Donna Silenziosa. Opera Comica in tres Atti.* Tr. Ottone Schanzer. Milano: Sonzogno, 1936.
121. *Tersites. Trauerspiel in drei Aufzügen.* Leipzig: Insel, 1907 (1919, 2. rev. ed.) (Simultaneous premiere: Hoftheater Kassel and Dresden, Nov. 26, 1908).
122. *Der verwandelte Komödiant. Ein Spiel aus dem deutschen Rokoko.* Berlin: Bloch, 1912.
123.   — Leipzig: Insel, 1913 (1920, 2. ed.; 1923 - Reclam Bibliothek, No. 6374; reprinted 1926, 1928) (Premiere: Lobetheater Breslau, May 5, 1912).
124.   Swedish. *Komedianten. Ett Spel fran Tyska Rokokon.* Tr. Anders de Wahl. Stockholm: Albert Bonniers, 1919.
125. *Volpone. Eine lieblose Komödie in drei Akten* (nach Ben Jonson frei bearbeitet von Stefan Zweig). Berlin: Bloch, 1925 (Stage manuscript; Premiere: Burgtheater Wien, Nov. 11, 1926).
126.   — Potsdam: Kiepenheuer, 1926 (1927, 2. ed., 6.-8. Tsd.).
127.   — Frankfurt am Main: Fischer, 1950.
128.   — Leipzig: Insel, 1959 (2. ed., Reclams Universal-Bibliothek, No. 8359).

5

129.	English. *Volpone. A Loveless Comedy in Three Acts* (by Ben Jonson, freely adapted by Stefan Zweig). Tr. Ruth Langner. London: Allen and Unwin, 1928.
130.	— New York: Viking, 1928 (Reprinted 1956; Premiere of the English version in New York in the Guild Theatre, April 9, 1928).
131.	— *Twenty Best European Plays on the American Stage.* New York: Crown Publishing Co., 1957, pp. 401-442.
132.	French. *Volpone. Comédie en cinq Actes* (d'après Ben Jonson par Jules Romains et Stefan Zweig). Paris: Arthème Fayard et Cie, 1929.
133.	— *Théâtre de Jules Romains.* Vol. 5. Paris: Librairie Gallimard, 1929.
134.	— Paris: Paris-Théâtre, 1955 (Paris-Théâtre, No. 95).
135.	Spanish. *Volpone. Comedia en cinco Actos* (de Ben Jonson para Jules Romain y Stefan Zweig). Tr. Artemio Precioso and Rafael Sánchez Guerra. Madrid: Editorial Colón, 1930.

V. PROSE FICTION

136. *Amok. Novellen einer Leidenschaft.* Leipzig: Insel, 1922 (Contains "Der Amokläufer," "Die Frau und die Landschaft," "Phantastische Nacht," "Brief einer Unbekannten," "Die Mondscheingasse").

    1923 – 2. ed. (11.-21. Tsd.)
    1924 – 3. „ (22.-32. Tsd.)
    1925 – 4. „ (33.-45. Tsd.)
    1927 – 5. „ (46.-50. Tsd.)
    1928 – 6. „ (51.-60. Tsd.)
    1929 – 7. „ (61.-65. Tsd.)
    1930 – 8. „ (66.-70. Tsd.)
    1931 – 9. „ (71.-74. Tsd.)
    From here on in the series "2-Mark-50-Bücher"
    1931 – 1. ed. (75.-125. Tsd.)
    1931 – 2. „ (126.-150. Tsd.)

137. — Stockholm: Bermann-Fischer, 1946 (1.-10. Tsd.);
Frankfurt am Main: Fischer, 1950 (11.-20. Tsd.);
Frankfurt am Main: Fischer, 1956 (21.-40. Tsd.).
(Contains: "Der Amokläufer," "Brief einer Unbekannten," "Vierundzwanzig Stunden aus dem Leben einer Frau," "Buchmendel," "Episode am Genfer See," "Phantastische Nacht," "Verwirrung der Gefühle," "Die unsichtbare Sammlung").

138. *Angst. Novelle.* Berlin: H. S. Hermann, 1920 (Der kleine Roman. Illustrierte Wochenschrift, No. 19).

139. — Leipzig: Reclam, 1925 (Shortened version; Epilogue by Erwin H. Rainalter; Reclams Universal Bibliothek, No. 6540; Reprinted: 1927, 1928, 1929, 1930, 1931).

140. — Stuttgart: Reclam, 1947 (Epilogue by Alexandra Carola Grisson; Reprinted 1954).

141. — Wien: Humbolt, 1947 (Epilogue by Gottfried Ippisch; Kleine Hand-Bibliothek, No. 104).

142. *Die Augen des ewigen Bruders. Eine Legende.* Leipzig: Insel, 1922 (Insel-Bücherei, No. 349).

    1922 – 1. ed. (1.-10. Tsd.)
    1924 – 2. „ (11.-20. Tsd.)
    1925 – 3. „ (21.-30. Tsd.)
    1926 – 4. „ (31.-40. Tsd.)
    1927 – 5. „ (41.-60. Tsd.)
    1928 – 6. „ (61.-80. Tsd.)

		1929 – 7. ed. (81.-100. Tsd.)
		1929 – 8. „ (101.-120. Tsd.)
		1930 – 9. „ (121.-140. Tsd.)
		1932 – 10.„ (141.-170. Tsd.)
		1950 – 11.„ (171.-180. Tsd.)

143. — Wiesbaden: Insel, 1950 (Insel-Bücherei, No. 349).

    1950 – 12. ed. (181.-190. Tsd.)
    1952 – 13. „ (191.-200. Tsd.)
    1953 – 14. „ (201-210. Tsd.)
    1954 – 15. „ (211.-220. Tsd.)
    1955 – 16. „ (221.-240. Tsd.)
    1956 – 17. „ (241.-255. Tsd.)
    1958 – 18. „ (256.-265. Tsd.)
    1959 – 19. „ (266.-283. Tsd.)

144. — Frankfurt am Main: Insel, 1961 (Insel-Bücherei, No. 349). 1961 – 20. ed. (284.-303. Tsd.).

145. — Wien: 39. Avalun-Druck, 1924 (250 copies signed by author).

146. — Ed. J. G. Steersma. Amsterdam: Meulenhoff, 1939 (Meulenhoffs Sammlung deutscher Schriftsteller, No. 751; Intro. J. G. Steersma; Includes notes and vocabulary).

    1948 – 2. ed.
    1951 – 3. „
    1955 – 4. „

147. — *Wie sie es sehen.* (Sel. and ed., Harry Zohn *et al.*) New York: Henry Holt, 1952, pp. 131-171 (School edition).

148. *Ausgewählte Novellen.* Stockholm: Bermann-Fischer, 1946 (1.-5. ed.; Contains: "Amok," "Brief einer Unbekannten," "Vierundzwanzig Stunden aus dem Leben einer Frau," "Buchmendel," "Episode am Genfer See," "Phantatische Nacht," "Die Mondscheingasse," "Verwirrung der Gefühle," "Leporella," "Die unsichtbare Sammlung").

149. *Ausgewählte Prosa.* Ed. W. Kuiper. Amsterdam: Meulenhoff, 1952 (2. ed.; Meulenhoffs Sammlung deutscher Schriftsteller, No. 93).

150. *Der begrabene Leuchter.* Wien: Reichner, reprinted 1937 (Illustrations by Berthold Wolpe; 500 numbered copies; Frankfurt am Main: Fischer, 1963).

151. *Brennendes Geheimnis.* Leipzig: Insel, 1913 (Insel-Bücherei, No. 22).

    1916 – 2. ed.
    1917 – 3. „
    1918 – 4. „
    1918 – 5. „
    1922 – 6. „ (46.- 55. Tsd.)
    1924 – 7. „ (56.- 65. Tsd.)
    1926 – 8. „ (66.- 75. Tsd.)
    1927 – 9. „ (76.- 90. Tsd.)
    1928 – 10. „ (91.-110. Tsd.)
    1929 – 11. „ (111.-120. Tsd.)
    1930 – 12. „ (121.-140. Tsd.)
    1931 – 13. „ (141.-150. Tsd.)
    1932 – 14. „ (151.-170. Tsd.)

152. — Ed. Eva C. Wunderlich. New York: Farrar, Rinehart, 1938 (Intro. and vocabulary Eva C. Wunderlich).

153. *Brennendes Geheimnis und andere Erzählungen.* Berlin: Fischer, 1954 (Contains: "Brennendes Geheimnis," "Die Gouvernante," "Die Frau und die Landschaft," "Die Mondscheingasse," "Unerwartete Bekanntschaft mit einem Handwerk," "Leporella," "Untergang eines Herzens," "Angst").

154. *Brennendes Geheimnis und andere Erzählungen.* Frankfurt am Main: Büchergilde Gutenberg, 1957 (For members only).

7

155. "Brief einer Unbekannten," *Deutsche Dichterhandschriften*. Ed. Hanns Martin Elster. Dresden: Lehmannsche Verlagsbuchhandlung, 1922 (Contains facsimile of the second manuscript and an autobiography of the author).
156. "Buchmendel" (Die Novelle wurde dem Bergischen Bibliophilen-Abend als erste Jahresgabe vom Verfasser zur Veröffentlichung überlassen. Sie erschien von der Officina Serpentis in der Walbaum-Fraktur gedruckt im Jahre 1930).
157. *Episode am Genfer See* (*der Flüchtling*). Leipzig: Insel, 1927.
158. — *Aus unserer Zeit*. Ed. I. and C. Loran and Leland R. Phelps. New York: Norton, 1956 (School edition).
159. — *Bul*, 10 (Oct., 1962), 7-10.
160. — *InA* (1920), 170-179.
161. — *Krl*, III : 18 (1960) (With a drawing by Erich Behrend).
162. *Erstes Erlebnis. Vier Geschichten aus Kinderland*. Leipzig: Insel, 1911 (Contains: "Geschichte in der Dämmerung," "Die Gouvernante," "Brennendes Geheimnis," "Sommernovellette").
    1917 – 2. ed.
    1919 – 3. „
    1920 – 4. „ (8.-11. Tsd.)
    1922 – 5. „ (12.-15. Tsd.)
    1923 – 6. „ (16.-19. Tsd.)
    From here on subtitle "Die Kette. Ein Novellenkreis. Der erste Ring":
    1925 – 7. ed. (20.-22. Tsd.)
    1926 – 8. „ (23.-27. Tsd.)
    1927 – 9. „ (28.-32. Tsd.)
    1928 – 10. „ (33.-40. Tsd.)
    1930 – 11. „ (41.-46. Tsd.)
163. *Fragment einer Novelle*. Wien: Verlag der Internationalen Stefan Zweig Gesellschaft, 1961 (Special publication No. 2 of the Stefan Zweig Gesellschaft; Ed. Erich Fitzbauer; With four Lithographs by Hans Fronius).
164. *Gesammelte Erzählungen*. Wien-Leipzig-Zürich: Reichner, 1936 ("Die Kette," "Kaleidoskop").
164a. "Die Gouvernante," *Literatur für den Deutschunterricht. Erste Stufe*. Ed. Bernard Rechtschaffen, Conrad P. Homberger and Victor Bobetsky. New York: American Book Co., 1964, pp. 14-29 [School ed.].
164b. "Im Schnee," *JüAl* (1902) [Reprinted as the third Special Publication of the International Stefan Zweig Society. Wien: Im Verlag der Internationalen Stefan Zweig Gesellschaft, 1963; Drawings by Fritz Fischer].
165. *Kaleidoskop*. Wien-Leipzig-Zürich: Reichner, 1936 (Contains: Tales: "Unvermutete Bekanntschaft mit einem Handwerk," "Leporella," "Die unsichtbare Sammlung," "Episode am Genfer See," "Buchmendel," "Angst"; Legends: "Rahel rechtet mit Gott," "Die Augen des ewigen Bruders," "Die begrabene Leuchter," "Die Legende der dritten Taube," "Die gleich-ungleichen Schwestern"; Sternstunden der Menschheit: "Die Weltminute von Waterloo," "Die Marienbader Elegie," "Die Entdeckung Eldorados," "Heroischer Augenblick," "Der Kampf um den Südpol," "Die Eroberung von Byzanz," "Georg Friedrich Händels Auferstehung").
166. *Die Kette. Ring I und II*. Leipzig: Insel, 1922 -1924.
    (*Erstes Erlebnis*, 1922, 12.-15. Tsd. *Amok*, 1922-1924, 1.-32. Tsd.).
167. *Die Kette. Ring I, II und III*. Leipzig: Insel, 1925-1927 (*Erstes Erlebnis, Amok, Verwirrung der Gefühle*).
168. — Wien-Leipzig-Zürich: Reichner, 1936.
169. *Kleine Chronik*. Leipzig: Insel, 1929 (Insel-Bücherei, No. 408; Contains: "Die unsichtbare Sammlung," "Episode am Genfer See," "Leporella," "Buchmendel").
    1929 – 1. ed. (1.-30. Tsd.)
    1929 – 2. „ (31.-60. Tsd.)
    1930 – 3. „ (61.-100. Tsd.)

8

170. *Kleine Chronik. Drei Erzählungen.* Leipzig: Insel, 1951 (Without "Episode am Genfer See"; Epilogue by Fritz Adolf Hünich; 111.-130. Tsd.).
171. "Die Legende der dritten Taube," *Aus Nah und Fern.* Ed. Lore B. Foltin. Boston: Houghton and Mifflin, 1950, pp. 155-159 (School edition).
172. *Legenden.* Stockholm: Bermann-Fischer, 1945 (Contains: "Rahel rechtet mit Gott," "Die Augen des ewigen Bruders," "Der begrabene Leuchter," "Die Legende der dritten Taube," "Die gleich-ungleichen Schwestern"; Reprinted 1948, 1959).
173. *Legenden. Eine Auswahl.* Ed. Oskar Maar. Frankfurt am Main: Fischer, 1952 (Fischer-Schulausgaben; Contains: "Rahel rechtet mit Gott," "Die Augen des ewigen Bruders," "Die Legende der dritten Taube").
174. — Wien: Fischer, 1952.
175. *Legenden. Eine Teilsammlung.* Berlin-Darmstadt-Wien: Deutsche Buchgemeinschaft, 1959 (For members only).
176. *Die Liebe der Erika Ewald.* Berlin: Egon Fleischel, 1904 (Contains: "Die Liebe der Erika Ewald," "Der Stern über dem Wald," "Die Wanderung," "Das Wunder des Lebens").
177. *Meisternovellen. Eine Teilsammlung.* Gütersloh: Bertelsmann Lesering, 1962 (For members only).
178. *Menschen-Novellen.* Stuttgart-Zürich-Salzburg: Europäischer Buchklub, 1962 (Contains: Intro. by Wilhelm Schlösser, "Verwirrung der Gefühle," "Vierundzwanzig Stunden aus dem Leben einer Frau," "Leporella," "Episode am Genfer See," "Phantastische," "Der Zwang," "Sommernovellette," "Brennendes Geheimnis," "Schachnovelle," "Die unsichtbare Sammlung," Epilogue by Wolf R. Lang; For members only).
179. "Die Mondscheingasse," *Grf*, 1. J., XI : 10 (July, 1914), 319-335.
180. *Phantastische Nacht. Vier Erzählungen.* Frankfurt am Main-Hamburg: Fischer, 1954 (Fischer-Bücherei, No. 45; Reprinted 1955, 1956, 1957; Contains: "Phantastische Nacht," "Brief einer Unbekannten," "Vierundzwanzig Stunden aus dem Leben einer Frau," "Untergang eines Herzens").
181. "Phantastische Nacht," *RoR*, 2 (1929), 52-119 (With five woodcuts by Otto R. Schatz; Cf. "Der Zwang" below).
182. *Rahel rechtet mit Gott.* Berlin: Aldus Druck, 1930.
183. — *Der goldene Schnitt. Grosse Erzähler der Neuen Rundschau* 1890-1960. Ed. Christoph Schwerin. Frankfurt am Main: Fischer, 1960, pp. 347-358.
184. — *In A* (1929), 112-132.
185. — *Neue deutsche Erzähler* (Stefan Zweig, Franz Werfel, Jakob Wassermann, Carl Zuckmayer, *et al.*). Berlin: Francke, 1930, pp. 393-410.
186. — *NR*, 38. J., I (Mar., 1927), 260-273.
187. *Schachnovelle.* Buenos Aires: Pigmalion, 1942 (250 numbered copies).
188. — Stockholm: Bermann-Fischer, 1943 (Reprinted 1945, 1951, 1954).
189. — Wien: Bermann-Fischer, 1949 (With drawings by Hans Fronius).
190. — Frankfurt am Main: Fischer, 1951 (Reprinted 1957, 1959, 1960, 1961).
191. — Ed. J. H. Schouten. Amsterdam: Meulenhoff, 1950, (Meulenhoffs Sammlung deutscher Schriftsteller, No. 92; Reprinted 1952, 1954, 1960).
192. — Ed. A. Werner. København: Hirschsprung, 1950 (Deutsche Texte für das dänische Gymnasium, No. 4).
193. — Ed. Harry Zohn. New York: Norton, 1960 (School edition).
194. — Ed. Kristian Langlo and Margit Rogne. Oslo: Aschehoug, 1951.
195. *Schachnovelle und andere Erzählungen.* Wien: Buchgemeinschaft Donauland, 1961.
196. *Scharlach. ÖR*, XV : 5 (Apr.-June, 1908), 336-356, XV : 6 (Apr.-June, 1908), 415-432.
197. *Ungeduld des Herzens. Roman.* Stockholm: Bermann – Fischer, 1939. Amsterdam: Albert de Lange, 1939. New York-Toronto: Longmans, Green, Alliance Book Corp., 1939.
198. — Wien: Bermann-Fischer, 1949, Amsterdam: Querido, 1949 (24.-34. Tsd.).

9

199. — Wien: Büchergilde Gutenberg, 1953 (For members only).
200. — Frankfurt am Main: Fischer, 1954 (Die Bücher der Neunzehn; Reprinted: 1955, 1958, 1963).
201. — Berlin-Darmstadt: Deutsche Buchgemeinschaft, 1956 (For members only).
202. — Zürich: Buchclub Ex Libris, 1957 (For members only).
203. — Stuttgart-Hamburg: Deutscher Bücherbund, 1961 (For members only).
204. *Die unsichtbare Sammlung. Eine Episode aus der deutschen Inflation.* Berlin: Sonderdruck, n.p., 1927 (Hergestellt für die Mitglieder und Freunde des Berliner Bibliophilen-Abends beim Stiftungsfest am 8. Feb., 1927; 250 mit der Hand numerierte Exemplare).
205. — Maastricht: Halayon-Presse, 1933.
206. — Maastricht: Stols, 1933.
207. — Wien: Reichner, 1933.
208. — Amsterdam: Nederlandsche Vereniging voor Druk- en Boekkunst, 1951 (Illustrated by Harry Prenen).
209. "Die unsichtbare Sammlung," *Auf höherer Warte.* Ed. F. E. Coenen. New York: Holt, 1941 (School edition).
210. — *Helles und Dunkles.* Ed. Roy Temple House and Johannes Malthaner. Boston: Ginn, 1948 (School edition).
211. — *InA* (1927), 91-108.
212. — *VZ*, May 31, 1925.
213. *Verwirrung der Gefühle.* Leipzig: Insel, 1927 (Contains: "Vierundzwanzig Stunden aus dem Leben einer Frau," "Untergang eines Herzens," "Verwirrung der Gefühle").

       1927 – 1. ed. (1.-20. Tsd.)
       1927 – 2. „ (21.-30. Tsd.)
       1927 – 3. „ (31.-40. Tsd.)
       1927 – 4. „ (41.-60. Tsd.)
       1928 – 5. „ (61.-75. Tsd.)
       1929 – 6. „ (76.-85. Tsd.)
       1931 – 7. „ (86.-90. Tsd.).

214. — Frankfurt am Main: Fischer, 1960.
215. *Vier Novellen.* Ed. (with notes and introduction) Harold Jensen. London (*et al.*): Harrap, 1955 (Contains: "Buchmendel," "Episode am Genfer See," "Die unsichtbare Sammlung," "Unvermutete Bekanntschaft mit einem Handwerk"; School edition).
216. *Vierundzwanzig Stunden aus dem Leben einer Frau.* Gütersloh: Bertelsmann, 1958 (Kleine Bertelsmann-Lesering-Bibliothek, Vol. 14; For members only).
217. "Die Wanderung," *NFP*, Morgenblatt, April 11, 1902, pp. 1-2 (Reprinted in *Die Liebe der Erika Ewald* (1904)).
218. "Das Wunder des Lebens," *Meister-Novellen neuerer Erzähler.* Vol. I. Ed. Richard Wenz. Leipzig: Hesse and Becker, 1926, pp. 95-204.
219. *Der Zwang. Eine Novelle.* Leipzig: Insel, 1920 (With 10 woodcuts by Frans Masereel).
220. "Der Zwang," *RoR*, 2 (1929), 1-51 (With 10 woodcuts by Frans Masereel; Original title of this work according to the manuscript version was "Der Refractor," cf. *Blätter*, 3 (Oct., 1958), 7; Cf. also "Phantastische Nacht" above).

ALBANIAN

221. *Njëzetekatër orë nga jeta e një gruaje* ("Verwirrung der Gefühle"). Tr. Enver Fico. Tiranë: Ndërmarrja Shtetërore e Botimeve, 1958.

BULGARIAN

222. *Amok. Roman.* Tr. Stefan Pejkov. Pecatnica: "Stopansko Razvitie," n.d. (Translated

from the French; Appeared in the series "Izbranie Sucinenija," Vol. IX, No. 5 of the "Ikonomija i Domakinstvo").
223. *Dvadeset i cetiri casa ot zivota na zenata* ("Vierundzwanzig Stunden aus dem Leben einer Frau"). Tr. Metodi Vecerov. Sofija: Pravo, n.d. (Appeared in the "Library of Pearls of World Literature," No. 33).
224. *Ocite na vecnija brat. Indijskaja legenda* ("Die Augen des ewigen Bruders"). Tr. S. Manolova. Sofija: Knigoizdatelstvo Vuzrazdane, 1930.

CATALAN

225. *Amok* (sequit "Vint-i-quatre Hores de la Vida d'una Dona") ("Amok" and "Vierundzwanzig Stunden aus dem Leben einer Frau"). Tr. Ernest Martínez Ferrando. Badalona: Edicions Proa, 1929 (Appeared in the series "Biblioteca a tot Vent").

CZECH

226. *Dobrodruzství Zivota. Novely Vásne* (Contains: "Erstes Erlebnis," "Amok", "Verwirrung der Gefühle"). Tr. Otto F. Babler, Rudolf Cerny, Egon Hostovsky. Praha: Nakladatelstvi Melantrich, 1931.
227. *Kaleidoskop.* Tr. Jaroslava Votrubová Koutecká. Praha: Mladá Fronta, 1958.
228. *Knihomol.* ("Der Bücherwurm"). Tr. Luba and Rudolf Pelarovi. Praha: Cs. spisovatel, 1957.
229. *Neviditelná Sbirka. Episoda z Inflace v Nemecku* ("Die unsichtbare Sammlung"). Tr. Otto F. Babler. Olomouc: n.p., 1930.
230. *Tri Novelly* (Contains: "Putovani" ("Die Wanderung"), "Zazraky Zivota" ("Das Wunder des Lebens"), "Povidka za Soumraku" ("Geschichte in der Dämmerung")). Tr. Otto Klein. Praha: Vydal J. Otto, 1912.

DANISH

231. *Den begravede Lysestage (Der begrabene Leuchter).* Tr. Clara Hammerich. København: Jespersen and Pio, 1960.
232. *Braendende Hemmelighed.* ("Brennendes Geheimnis"). Tr. Jørgen Budtz-Jørgensen. København: Gyldendal, 1957 (3. ed.).
233. *Den evige Broders Øjne. En Legende.* ("Die Augen des ewigen Bruders"). Tr. Erik Nander. København: Hasselbalch, 1950 (4. ed., 1959).
234. *Eros. Tre erotiske Noveller.* ("Angst," "Geschichte in der Dämmerung," "Die Frau und die Landschaft"). Tr. Clara Hammerich. København: Hirschsprung,1953 (3. ed.).
235. *En Fantastisk Nat* ("Phantastische Nacht"). Tr. Helge Kjaergaard. København: Jespersen and Pio, 1958.
236. — København: Ti danske Forlaeggeres Bogklub, 1960 (2. ed.).
237. *Følelsernes Vildveje. Noveller.* Tr. Erik Nander. Aalborg: Frede and Lauritzen, 1949.
238. — København: Jespersen and Pio. 1953 (3. ed.).
239. *Et Hjertes Undergang* ("Der Untergang eines Herzens"). Tr. Helge Kjaergaard. København: Jespersen and Pio, 1957 (Sel. from *Kaleidoskop*; 2. ed., 1959).
240. *Hjertets Utaalmodighed (Ungeduld des Herzens).* Tr. Helge Kjaergaard. København: Jespersen and Pio, 1949 (3. ed., 1958).
241. *Kaleidoskop. Udvalgte Noveller.* Tr. Helge Kjaergaard. København: Jespersen and Pio, 1950.
242. *Legender (Legenden).* Tr. Clara Hammerich. København: Jespersen and Pio, 1951.
243. *Skaknovelle (Schachnovelle). Leporella.* Tr. Harald Engberg. København: Aschehoug, 1948 (3. ed., 1950; 5. ed., 1953; 6. ed., 1955; 8. ed., 1958).

244. *Spørg ikke* ("Brennendes Geheimnis"). Tr. Jørgen Budtz-Jørgensen. København: n.p., 1936.
245. — København: Gyldendal, 1951 (Cf. new ed. above *Braendende Hemmelighed*).

DUTCH

246. *Amok.* Tr. Reinier P. Sterkenburg. Amsterdam: Van Ditmar, 1947.
247. *Amok. Novellen van Hartstocht.* Tr. Reinier P. Sterkenburg. Zeist: Ploegsma, 1929.
248. *De begraven Kandelaar. Een Legende (Der begrabene Leuchter).* Amsterdam: de Lange, 1937.
249. *Brandend Geheim. Vier Verhalen van Jeugdleven (Erstes Erlebnis).* Tr. Mien Labberton. Zeist: Ploegsma, 1929.
250. — Amsterdam: Wereldbibliotheek, 1939 (2. and 3. ed.).
251. *Deernis en Liefde (Ungeduld des Herzens).* Tr. Guy Vanhamme. Hoogstraten (Belgium): Moderne Uitgeverij, 1946.
252. *Dwang* ("Der Zwang"). Tr. Reinier P. Sterkenburg. 's-Gravenhage: Prometheus, 1923 (Woodcuts by Frans Masereel).
253. *De Legende van de derde Duif* ("Die Legende von der dritten Taube"). Tr. Paul Huf. Amsterdam-Antwerpen: Wereldbibliotheek-Vereniging, 1952 (3. ed., 1953).
254. *Het Onberaden Medelijden (Ungeduld des Herzens).* Tr. Reinier P. Sterkenburg. Amsterdam: de Lange, 1939.
255. *De Oogen van den eeuwigen Broeder* ("Die Augen des ewigen Bruders"). Tr. Reinier P. Sterkenburg. Huis ter Heide: De Tijdstroom, 1925 (2. ed., 1933).
256. *Een Schaaknovelle (Schachnovelle).* Tr. Paul Huf. Amsterdam: Keesing, 1949.

ESTONIAN

257. *Malenovell (Schachnovelle).* Tr. N. Andresen. Tallin: Gaz.-zurn, 1957.

ESPERANTO

258. *Brulanta Sekreto kai aliaj Rakontoj (Brennendes Geheimnis und andere Erzählungen).* Tr. Kathe R. and Paul E. Schwerin. Rickmansworth: Esperanto Publishing Co., 1949 (2. ed., 1950).

ENGLISH

259. *Amok.* Tr. Eden and Cedar Paul. New York: Viking, 1931.
260. — London: Cassell, 1932.
261. "Amok," *Doctors' Choice. Sixteen Stories about Doctors and Medicine* (selected by famous physicians). Ed. Phyllis M. and Albert P. Blaustein. Intro. Walter C. Alvarez. New York: Funk and Wagnalls, 1957.
262. — *Great German Short Novels and Stories.* Ed. Bennett Alfred Cerf. New York: Modern Library, 1933.
263. — *Panorama of Modern Literature Contributed by 31 Great Modern Writers.* Intro. Christopher Morley. New York: Doubleday, 1934.
264. *Beware of Pity (Ungeduld des Herzens).* Tr. Phyllis and Trevor Blewitt. New York: Viking, 1939; London: Cassell, 1939 (Reprinted 1952, 1953, 1954).
265. "Book-Mendel" ("Buchmendel"), *MJ*, XX (July, 1932), 118-122, 198-206.
266. — *Men at War. Best Short Stories of All Time.* Intro. Ernest Hemingway. New York: Crown, 1942.
267. — *Book of Contemporary Short Stories.* Ed. Dorothy Brewster. New York: Macmillan, 1936.

268. — *Jewish Caravan. Great Stories of 25 Centuries.* New York: Rinehart, 1935.
269. *The Buried Candelabrum (Der begrabene Leuchter).* Tr. Eden and Cedar Paul. Illus. Berthold Wolpe. New York: Viking, 1937.
270. — Oxford: Phaidon Press, 1944.
271. *The Burning Secret* ("Brennendes Geheimnis"). New York: Scott and Seltzer, 1919 (Author listed as Stephen Branch (pseud.) – cf. *DLE*, 22.J.: 14 (Apr. 15, 1920), 892-893 for Zweig's rejection of this translation and the use of a pseudonym as unauthorized).
272. — London: Allen and Unwin, 1921.
273. *Conflicts: Three Tales.* (Contains: "Twentyfour Hours in the Life of a Woman" ("Vierundzwanzig Stunden aus dem Leben einer Frau"), "A Failing Heart" ("Untergang eines Herzens"), "Episode in the Early Life of Privy Councillor D." ("Verwirrung der Gefühle"). Tr. Eden and Cedar Paul. New York: Viking, 1927.
274. — London: Allen and Unwin, 1928.
275. "Confusion of Sentiment" ("Verwirrung der Gefühle"), 21 *Variations on a Theme.* Ed. Donald Webster Cory (pseud.). New York: Greenberg, 1953.
276. *Invisible Collection* ("Die unsichtbare Sammlung"). Illus. Joseph Malay. New York: Pynson Printers, 1926 (First printing cf. *VZ*, May 31, 1925).
277. "Invisible Collection," *Art of Modern Fiction.* Ed. Ray Benedict West and Robert Wooster Stallman. New York: Rinehart, 1949.
278. — *Best of Modern European Literature – Heart of Europe. An Anthology of Creative Writing in Europe 1920-1940.* Ed. Klaus Mann and Hermann Kesten. Intro. Dorothy Canfield Fisher. New York: L. B. Fischer, 1943 (Reprinted 1945).
279. — *Greatest Stories of all Times.* Ed. William Somerset Maugham. Garden City (New York): Garden City Pub. Co., 1943.
280. — *Great Short Stories.* Ed. Wilbur Lang Schramm. New York: Harcourt, 1950.
281. — *Tellers of Tales; 100 Short Stories from the United States, England, France, Russia and Germany.* Ed. William Somerset Maugham. New York: Doubleday, 1939.
282. *GB,* XIX (June, 1934), 641-649.
283. — *LA,* CCCXXVI: 4230 (Aug. 1, 1925), 255-262.
284. — *PCQ,* XXVI (Dec., 1939), 425-443.
285. "Jupiter," *Golden Book of Dog Stories.* Ed. Era Zistel. Chicago: Ziff Davis, 1947.
286. — *Famous Dog Stories.* Ed. Page Cooper. New York: Doubleday, 1948.
287. — *C,* CXXII (July, 1943), 30.
288. *Kaleidoscope. 13 Stories and Novellettes.* Tr. Eden and Cedar Paul. New York: Viking, 1934; London: Cassell, 1934 (Contains: "Book Mendel" ("Buchmendel"), "The Burning Secret" ("Brennendes Geheimnis"), "Fear" ("Angst"), "The Governess" ("Die Gouvernante"), "Impromptu Study of a Handicraft" ("Unvermutete Bekanntschaft mit einem Handwerk"), "The Invisible Collection" ("Die unsichtbare Sammlung"), "Leporella" ("Leporella"), "Letter from an Unknown Woman" ("Brief einer Unbekannten"), "Moonbeam Alley" ("Mondscheingasse"), "Rahel Arraigns God" ("Rahel rechtet mit Gott"), "The Runaway" ("Episode am Genfer See"), "Transfiguration" ("Phantastische Nacht"), "Virata" ("Die Augen des ewigen Bruders")).
289. *Kaleidoscope I.* Tr. Eden and Cedar Paul. London: Cassell, 1949 (2. ed., 1955).
290. *Kaleidoscope II.* Tr. Eden and Cedar Paul. London: Cassell, 1951 (2. ed., 1959).
291. "Leporella," *Crimes of Passion.* Ed. Herbert J. Solomon. Intro. David Partridge (pseud.). New York: Garden City Books, 1947.
292. *Letter from an Unknown Woman* ("Brief einer Unbekannten"). Tr. Eden and Cedar Paul. New York: Viking, 1932.
293. — London: Cassell, 1933.
294. "Moonbeam Alley," Tr. Eden and Cedar Paul. *Stories of Scarlet Women.* New York: Avon, 1955, pp. 54-70.
295. — *A World of Great Stories.* Ed. Hiram Haydn and John Cournos. New York: Crown, 1947, pp. 431-443.

13

296. *The Old-Book Peddler and Other Tales for Bibliophiles*. Tr. Theodore W. Koch. Evanston (Ill.): Northwestern University Press, The Charles Deering Lib., 1937 (Contains: "Books are the Gateway to the World" ("Das Buch als Eingang zur Welt"), "The Old Book Peddler" ("Buchmendel"), "The Invisible Collection" ("Die unsichtbare Sammlung"), "Thanks to Books" ("Dank an die Bücher")).

297. *Passion and Pain*. Tr. Eden and Cedar Paul. London: Chapman and Hall, 1924; New York: Richards, 1925 (Contains: "Compulsion" ("Der Zwang"), "Fowler Snared" ("Sommernovellete"), "The Governess" ("Die Gouvernante"), "Letter from an Unknown Woman" ("Brief einer Unbekannten"), "The Runaway" ("Episode am Genfer See"), "Transfiguration" ("Phantastische Nacht"), "Virata" ("Die Augen des ewigen Bruders")).

298. *The Royal Game*. Tr. B. W. Huebsch. New York: Viking, 1944; London: Cassell, 1945 (Contains: "The Royal Game" ("Schachnovelle"), "Amok" ("Amok"), "Letter from an Unknown Woman" ("Brief einer Unbekannten")).

299. — New York: Viking, 1961 (Compass Books, No. C99).

300. "The Royal Game," *WHC*, VII (Mar., 1944), 22-23.

301. "The Runaway" ("Episode am Genfer See"), *Adventures in Modern Literature*. Ed. Ruth Matilda Stauffer, William Hayes Cunningham and Catherine J. Sullivan. New York: Harcourt, 1951 (3. ed.).

302. *Stories and Legends*. Tr. Eden and Cedar Paul and Constantine Fitz Gibbon. London: Cassell, 1955 (Contains: "24 Hours from the Life of a Woman" ("Vierundzwanzig Stunden aus dem Leben einer Frau"), "Failing Heart" ("Der Untergang eines Herzens"), Episode in the Early Life of Privy Councillor D." ("Verwirrung der Gefühle"), "The Buried Candelabrum" ("Der begrabene Leuchter"), "The Legend of the Third Dove" ("Die Legende der dritten Taube"), "Dissimilar Doubles" ("Die Legende der gleichungleichen Schwestern")).

303. "Unseen Collection," *Yisröel. The First Jewish Omnibus*. Ed. Joseph Leftwich. New York: Heritage, 1933 (Rev. ed. New York: Beechhurst Press, 1952).

FINNISH

304. *Malttamaton Sydän. Romaanie (Ungeduld des Herzens)*. Tr. Lauri Hirvensalo. Porvoo: Werner Söderström, 1951 (2. ed.).

305. *Shakkitarina. Pienoisromaani (Schachnovelle)*. Tr. Aina Oksala. Jyväskylä: Gummerus, 1951.

FRENCH

306. *Amok ou le Fou de Malaisie* ("Amokläufer"). Tr. Alzir Hella and Olivier Bournac. Pref. Romain Rolland. Paris: A. Fayard, 1952 (Le Livre de Demain, No. 28).

307. — *Dictionnaire des Oeuvres de tous les Temps et de tous les Pays*. I (1952), 83. Paris: Laffont-Bompiani/Stock.

308. *Amok ou le Fou de Malaisie* ("Amokläufer"); *Lettre d'une Inconnue* ("Brief einer Unbekannten"); *La Ruelle au Clair de Lune* ("Die Mondscheingasse"). Tr. Alzir Hella and Olivier Bournac. Pref. Romain Rolland. Paris: Stock, 1930 (2. ed.); Bruxelles: Les Lettres latines, 1930 (2. ed.).

309. — Paris: Ferenczi et Fils, 1939 (Woodcuts by Michel Jacquot; Le Livre Moderne Illustré, No. 308).

310. — Paris: Delamain et Boutelleau, 1948 (97. ed.; Bibliothèque Germanique).

311. *Amok ou le Fou de Malaisie* ("Amokläufer"); *Lettre d'une Inconnue* ("Brief einer Unbekannten"); *Les Yeux du Frère Eternel* ("Die Augen des ewigen Bruders"). Tr. Alzir Hella and Olivier Bournac. Pref. Romain Rolland. Paris: Stock, 1927 (Le Cabinet Cosmopolite, No. 13).

312. *Brûlant Secret* ("Brennendes Geheimnis"); *Conte Crépusculaire* ("Geschichte in der

Dämmerung"); *La Nuit Fantastique* ("Phantastische Nacht"); *Les Deux Jumelles* ("Die gleich-ungleichen Schwestern"). Tr. Alzir Hella. Paris: Grasset, 1945 (Romans étrangers).

313. — Bruxelles-Paris-Amsterdam: "La Concorde," 1947.

314. *Le Chandelier Enterré. Légende (Der begrabene Leuchter).* Tr. Alzir Hella. Paris: Grasset, 1937 (13. ed.; Romans étrangers).

315. *La Confusion des Sentiments. Notes intimes du Professeur R. de D.* ("Verwirrung der Gefühle"). Tr. Alzir Hella and Olivier Bournac. Paris: Stock, 1929.

316. — *Dictionnaire des Oeuvres de tous les Temps et de tous les Pays.* I (1952), 509. Paris: Laffont-Bompiani/Stock.

317. *Destruction d'un Cœur* ("Untergang eines Herzens"); *La Gouvernante* ("Die Gouvernante"); *Le Jeu dangereux* ("Sommernovellette"?). Tr. Alzir Hella and Olivier Bournac. Paris-Neuchâtel: Attinger, 1931 (Reprinted 1946).

318. *Le Jouer d'Echecs (Schachnovelle).* Tr. Jacqueline Des Gouttes. (Neuchâtel-Paris: Delachaux et Niestlé, n.d. (2. ed.).

319. *La Peur* ("Angst"). Tr. Alzir Hella. Paris: Grasset, 1935 (18. ed.; Romans étrangers).

320. — Tr. Alzir Hella and Manfred Schenker. Paris: Ferenczi and Fils, 1937 (Le Livre Moderne Illustré, No. 271).

321. — N. 1.: L'Amitié par le Livre, 1946 (Imprimé en Belgique).

322. "La Peur," *APL,* CVI (Sept. 10, 1935), 238-241 (Résumé by M. Renier).

323. *La Pitié dangereuse (Ungeduld des Herzens).* Tr. Alzir Hella. Paris: Grasset, 1939.

324. — Paris: Club français du livre, 1951.

325. *La Ruelle au Clair de Lune* ("Die Mondscheingasse"); *La Gouvernante* ("Die Gouvernante"). Tr. Alzir Hella and Olivier Bournac. Paris: Snell, 1930 (Illustrated by Pierre Louchet).

326. *Vingt-quatre Heures de la Vie d'une Femme* ("Vierundzwanzig Stunden aus dem Leben einer Frau"). Tr. and Intro. Alzir Hella and Olivier Bournac. Paris-Neuchâtel: Attinger, 1929 (Reprinted 1932, 1944, 1947).

327. — Paris: Fayard, 1952 (Le Livre de Demain. Série étrangère, No. 36; Reprint 1953).

328. — Lausanne: La Guilde du Livre ,1960 (La petite Ourse, No. 39).

329. — Lausanne: La Guilde du Livre, 1962 (Supplément au Bulletin de la Guilde," May, 1962; Frontispice Claudine Frochause).

330. "Vingt-quatre Heures de la Vie d'une Femme," *Dictionnaire des Oeuvres de tous les Temps et de tous les Pays.* IV (1954), 705. Paris: Laffont-Bompiani/Stock.

GEORGIAN

31. *Amok* ("Amokläufer"). Tr. Leli Dzapharidzis. Tphilisi: Phroma, 1927.

332. *Phiphi* ("Angst"). Tr. Leli Dzapharidzis. Tphilisi: Phroma, 1927.

GREEK

333. *Abussos Aisthematon* ("Verwirrung der Gefühle"). Tr. A. Trikolonios. Athenai: Kerameos, 1950.

334. *Amok* ("Amokläufer"). Tr. S. Karagiannes. Athenai: Kerameos, 1951.

335. — Tr. G. Meranaios. Athenai: Daremas, 1954.

336. — Tr. T. Konstas. Athenai: Atlantis, 1958.

337. *Amok* ("Amokläufer"); *To Gramma mias Agnostes* ("Brief einer Unbekannten"). Tr. Al. Karrer. Athenai: Kerameos, 1948.

338. — Athenai: Gkobostes, 1951.

339. *Anypomoni Cardia* ("Untergang eines Herzens"). Tr. M. Cranaki. Athenai: K. M., 1953.

340. *Bradino Eidillio* ("Phantastische Nacht"). Tr. Al. Karrer. Athenai: Kerameos, 1948 (Reprinted 1949).

15

341. *Eicossi Tesseres Thores Apo Ti Zoi Mias Ghynaicas* ("Vierundzwanzig Stunden aus dem Leben einer Frau"). Tr. G. Semeriotes Athenai: Maris, 1948 (Reprinted 1954).
342. — Tr. L. Castanakis.Athenai: Govosti, n.d.
343. *E Katastrophe mias Kardis* ("Unterangang eines Herzens"). Tr. M. Loulis. Athenai: Kerameos, 1948.
344. *E Katastrophe mias Kardis* ("Untergang eines Herzens"); *Sto Pheggarolousto Dromaki* ("Die Mondscheingasse"). Tr. K. Meranaios and G. Semeriotes. Athenai: Maris, 1948.
345. *Ena Axechasto Epeissodio* ("Unerwartete Bekanntschaft mit einem Handwerk"). Tr P. Vovolinis. Athenai: Keramefs, n.d.
346. — Tr. B. Papanastassiou. Athenai: Lagoussis-Chryssochou, 1949.
347. *Epikindune Sumponia (Ungeduld des Herzens)*. Tr. P. Spilotopoulos. Athenai: Govostis, 1949.
348. *Ho Tan Xupnoun Ta Niata* ("Phantastische Nacht"); *He Gkoubernanta* ("Die Gouvernante"); *To Thanasimo Mustike* ("Brennendes Geheimnis"). Tr. Al. Karrer. Athenai: Kerameos, 1949.
349. *I Proti Apocalypsi* (German original unknown). Tr. N. Constantinidis. Athenai: Loghotechniki, Ghonia, n.d.
350. *Leporella* ("Leporella"). Tr. A. Trikolonios. Athenai: Kerameos, 1951.
351. *Mantel* (German original unknown). Tr. P. Papanastassiou. Athenai: Pelargos, 1950.
352. *O Phobos* ("Angst"). Tr. A. Trikolonios. Athenai: Kerameos, 1951.
353. — Tr. Sp. Levantis. Athenai: Govostis, 1954.
354. *Rachel* ("Rahel rechtet mit Gott"). Tr. K. L. Meranaios. Athenai: Maris-Kordakis, 1948.
355. *Sugchuse Aisthematon* ("Verwirrung der Gefühle"). Tr. Al. Karrer. Athenai: Govostis, 1949.
356. *To Fovero Mystico* ("Brennendes Geheimnis"). Tr. D. Dimitriou. Athenai: Loghotechniki, n.d.
357. *To Thameno Cantileri* ("*Der begrabene Leuchter*").Tr. G. Meranaios. Athenai: Daremas, 1954.
358. *To Nissi Me Tis Ghynaiko* ("Die Frau und die Landschaft"). Tr. K. L. Meranaios. Athenai: Maris, 1948.
359. — Tr. P. Vovolinis. Athenai: Keramefs, n.d.
360. *To Vassilico Paichnidi (Schachnovelle)*. Tr. A. Ghion. Athenai: Keramefs, n.d.
361. *1res Omorphes Histories* (German originals unknown). Tr. A. Trikolonios. Athenai: Kerameos, 1949.
362. *Virata* ("Die Augen des ewigen Bruders"). Tr. K. Meranaios. Athenai: Maris, 1948.

HEBREW

363. *Essim We-Arba Shoot Be-Hayeha Shel Isha. Sippurim* (Tales, German originals unknown). Tr. A. Cohn, D. Kimhi *et al.* Tel Aviv: Masada, 1954.
364. *Ha-R'Hov L'Or Ha-Yareah* (Tales, German originals unknown). Tel Aviv: Masada, 1949.
365. *Hisamer Min Ha-Rahamin (Ungeduld des Herzens)*. Tr. Elyaqim Weinberg. Tel Aviv: Masada, 1948 (Published in two volumes).
366. *Kovshey Olam* (German original unknown). Tr. Emil Feuerstein. Tel Aviv: Yavneh, 1950.
367. *Mishaq Ha-M'Lahim* ("Schachnovelle," "Untergang eines Herzens," "Verwirrung der Gefühle"). Tr. Pesah Lipovetzki. Tel Aviv: Leihman-Pales, 1949.

HUNGARIAN

368. *Amok. A Szenvedely Könyve* ("Amokläufer"). Tr. L. Ujvary Lajos. Budapest: Genius-Kiadas, 1929.

16

369. *Az Érzések Zürzavara* ("Verwirrung der Gefühle"). Tr. Kiss Dezsö. Budapest: Franklin-Társulat Kiadása, 1928.
370. *Égő Titok. Válogatott Elbeszélesek (Die Kette. Kaleidoskop* (Extracts thereof)). Tr. Anna Dániel, Mme. Pal Fodor *et al.* Budapest: Európa, 1957.
371. *Elsö Élmény (Erstes Erlebnis).* Tr. Dormándi László and Sandor Imre. Budapest: Pantheon, 1927.
372. *Három Legenda* (Three Legends – German originals unknown). Tr. Ferenc Góth. Budapest: Európa, 1957.
373. Huszonnégy Óra Egy Asszony Életéböl ("Vierundzwanzig Stunden aus dem Leben einer Frau"). Tr. Kiss Dezsö. Budapest: Lampel, 1926.
374. *A Láthatatlan Gyüjtemény* ("Die unsichtbare Sammlung"). Tr. György Káldor. Budapest: Terra, 1957.
375. *Rettegés Es Egyéb El-Beszélések* ("Angst" and Tales, German originals unknown). Tel Aviv: Alexander, 1952.
376. *Rettegés. Regény* ("Angst.Novelle"). Tr. Péter Bukovinszky. Budapest: Legszebb Könyvek Tára, 1928.
377. *Sakknovella (Schachnovelle).* Tr. Péter János. Bukarest: A Stünta si Tehnica Folyóirat Kiadása, 1957.
378. — Tr. Iván Fónagy. Budapest: Európa, 1959.

LANGUAGES OF INDIA

BENGALI

379. *Ajantiar Chithi* ("Brief einer Unbekannten"). Tr. Vidhayek Bhattacharya. Calcutta: Grantham, 1959.
380. *Antarjvala* ("Brennendes Geheimnis"). Tr. Shantiranjan Banerji. Calcutta: Sankar Sahitya Samsad, 1955.
381. *Godhulir Gan* ("Amokläufer"). Tr. Shantiranjan Banerji. Calcutta: Calcutta Publishers, 1953 (Translation of the English edition).
382. *Karuna Korona (Ungeduld des Herzens).* Tr. Shantiranjan Banerji. Calcutta: Nababharati, 1960.
383. *Priyatamesu* ("Brief einer Unbekannten"). Tr. Shantiranjan Bandy-Opadhyay. Barrackpur: Sabita Dasgupta, 1957 (2. ed.; Translation from the English edition).
384 *Priyatameshu* ("Brief einer Unbekannten"). Tr. Shantiranjan Banerji. Calcutta: Triveni Prakashan, 1960.
385. *Rajasuya (Schachnovelle).* Tr. Shantiranjan Banerji. Calcutta: T. K. Banerji, n.d.
386. *Sei Ascarya Rat* ("Phantastische Nacht"). Tr. Shantiranjan Bandy-Opadhyay. Calcutta: Bengal Publishers, 1955.
387. *Setubandha* ("Angst"). Tr. Shantiranjan Bandy-Opadhyay. Calcutta: Ghosh Brothers, 1956 (Translation of the English edition).
388. *Stefan Zweig'er Galpa Sangraha* (Collected Tales, German originals unknown). Tr. Dipak Chaudhuri. Calcutta: Rupa, 1960.

HINDI

389. *Aparchita Ka Patra* ("Brief einer Unbekannten"). Serialized in the New Delhi Weekly *Saptahik Hindustan* in 1958, exact dates unknown.
390. *Bujadil (Ungeduld des Herzens).* Tr. Shivadanasimha Chauhan and Vijaya Chauhan. Delhi: National Publishing House, n.d. (Contains an Introduction by the translators on Zweig and his works).
391. *Shatranj Ka Khel (Schachnovelle* and other tales, German originals thereof unknown). Tr. Shri S. C. Joshi. Girgaon, Bombay: Hindi Granth Ratnakar, 1949.
392. *Stefan Zweig Ki Mahan Kahaniyan* ("Novellen", German originals unknown). Tr.

17

Shivadanasingli Chauhan and Vijaya Chauhan. Delhi: Ranjit, 1957 (Contains an Introduction by the translators).
393. *Virata* ("Die Augen des ewigen Bruders"). Tr. Yashpal Jain. New Delhi: Sasta Sahitya Mandal, 1958 (2. ed.).

ORIYA

394. *Aparichitara Patra* ("Brief einer Unbekannten"). Tr. Lakshminarayana Mahanit. Cuttack: Lipikalaya, 1953 (Translation from the English edition).

MALAYALAM

395. *Neela Thattavum Velutha Pookkalum* ("Brief einer Unbekannten"). Tr. Mavelikkara Ascutan. Ernakulam: Sahitya Parishat, 1959.

TELUGU

396. *Aparichitalekha* ("Brief einer Unbekannten"). Tr. Abburi Chayadevi. Hyderabad: Sadhanaprakasan, 1956.

IRANIAN

397. *Namehe Yek Zane Nashenas* ("Brief einer Unbekannten"). Tr. Hassan Ali Nasr. Tehran: n.p., 1958.

ITALIAN

398. *Adolescenza. Quattro Storia del Paese dell'Infanzia* (*Erstes Erlebnis. Vier Geschichten aus Kinderland*). Tr. Marcella Dreyfus. Milano: Sperling and Kupfer, 1933.
399. *Amok* ("Amokläufer"). Tr. Enrico Rocca. Milano: Sperling and Kupfer, 1930.
400. *Caleidoscopio* (*Kaleidoskop*). Milano: Sperling and Kupfer, 1945 (Contains: "Lettera di una Sconosciuta" ("Brief einer Unbekannten"), "Leporella" ("Leporella"), "Amok" ("Amokläufer"), "Le Oro Siderati" (from *Sternstunden der Menschheit*)).
401. *Eventi e Raconti* (Contains: "La Paura" ("Angst"), "Adolescenza" (*Erstes Erlebnis*)). Milano: Sperling and Kupfer, 1945.
402. *Leggende* (*Legenden*). Tr. Anita Rho. Milano: Sperling and Kupfer, 1937 (Contains: "La Legenda della terza Colomba" ("Legende der dritten Taube"), "Il Candelabro Sepalto" ("Der begrabene Leuchter"), "Gli Occhi dell'eterno Fratello" ("Die Augen des ewigen Bruders"), "Rachele contende con Dio" ("Rahel rechtet mit Gott"); Reprinted 1945).
403. *Lettera di una Sconosciuta* ("Brief einer Unbekannten"). Tr. Berta Burgio Ahrens. Milano: Sperling and Kupfer, 1932 (Reprinted 1937).
404. *La Paura* ("Angst"); *Episodio sul Lago di Ginevra* ("Episode am Genfer See"); *Mel il Bibliofilo* ("Buchmendel"); *La Collezione Invisibile* ("Die unsichtbare Sammlung"); *Conoscenzi con un Mestiere* ("Unvermutete Bekanntschaft mit einem Handwerk"). Milano: Sperling and Kupfer, 1938.
405. *Sovvertimento dei Sensi* ("Verwirrung der Gefühle"). Tr. Berta Burgio Ahrens. Milano: Corbaccio, 1931.
406. *Ventiquattro Ore della Vita di una Donna* ("Vierundzwanzig Stunden aus dem Leben einer Frau"). Tr. Cristina Baseggio. *Lettera di una Sconosciuta* ("Brief einer Unbekannten"). Tr. Berta Burgio Ahrens. *Leporella* ("Leporella"). Tr. Berta Burgio Ahrens. *Amok* ("Amokläufer"). Tr. Enrico Rocca. Milano: Sperling and Kupfer, 1938.

JAPANESE

407. *Aishu No Monte Carlo* ("Vierundzwanzig Stunden aus dem Leben einer Frau"). Tr. Hikaru Tsuji. Tokyo: Kadokawa Shoten, 1953.
408. *Aiyoku No Umi* ("Amokläufer *et al.*). Tr. Yoshitaka Kawasaki. Tokyo: Kawade Shobo, 1956 (Contains: "Amokläufer," "Brief einer Unbekannten," *Fouché*).
409. *Aru Kokoro No Hametsu (Novellen)*. Tr. Yoshitaka Kawasaki. Tokyo: Kadokawa Shoten, 1953 (Contains: "Untergang eines Herzens," "Brennendes Geheimnis," "Die unsichtbare Sammlung").
410. *Irene – Fujin No Himitsu* ("Angst" *et al.*). Tr. Yoshimoto Nishi. Tokyo: Kadokawa Shoten, 1957 (Contains: "Angst," "Schachnovelle," "Leporella," "Buchmendel").
411. *On'na No Niju-yo-Jikan* ("Vierundzwanzig Stunden aus dem Leben einer Frau"). Tr. Kenji Takahashi. Tokyo: Shinchosha, 1950.
412. *Kokoro No Shoso (Ungeduld des Herzens)*. Tr. Kazuo Okubo. Tokyo: Keiyusha, 1950.
413. *Saisho No Taiken (Erstes Erlebnis)*. Tr. Yoshitaka Kawasaki. Tokyo: Hakusuisha, 1953.
414. *Ummei No Kake* ("Schachnovelle"); *Appaku* ("Der Zwang"); *Pari No Suri* ("Unvermutete Bekanntschaft mit einem Handwerk"). Tr. Kazuo Okubo. Tokyo: Misuzu Shobo, 1951 (Nos. 1 and 3 translated from the French version).
415. *Wasureji No Omokage* ("Brief einer Unbekannten"). Tr. Kazuo Okubo. Tokyo: Mikasa Shobo, 1956.

KOREAN

416. *Eoneu Yeoin Eui Isiba Sigan* ("Verwirrung der Gefühle"). Tr. Choe Hyeog-sun. Seoul: Daedongdang, 1960.
417. *Gam'jeong Eui' Hon'ran* ("Verwirrung der Gefühle"). Tr. Bag Changi. Seoul: Yang' mun'sa, 1959.

LATVIAN

418. *Valija Brutäne* ("Brennendes Geheimnis"). Riga: Gramatu Draugs, 1935 (Gramatu Drauga Romanu Serija, No. 74).
419. *Vinas Vestule* (German original unknown). Tr. B. Z. Riga: Mali, 1929.

LITHUANIAN

420. *Baime* ("Angst"). Tr. K. Karnauskas. Kaunas: V. Remigijus, 1929.

NORWEGIAN

421. *Amokløper* ("Amokläufer"); *Brennende Hemmelighet* ("Brennendes Geheimnis"). Tr. Barbara Ring. Oslo: Aschehoug, 1928.
422. *Den evige Brors Øyne* ("Die Augen des ewigen Bruders"). Tr. G. H. Carlsen. Berge : J. W. Eides Boktr., 1959.
423. *Farspjarta* ("Brennendes Geheimnis"). Tr. Severin Eskeland. Oslo: Olaf Norli, n.d.
424. *Leporella* ("Leporella"). Tr. Ursula Monsen. Oslo: Aschehoug, 1956 (Also contains a translation of "Buchmendel").
425. *Sjakknovelle (Schachnovelle)*. Oslo: Aschehoug, 1951.

POLISH

426. *Amok. Nowele Szalu* ("Amokläufer"). Tr. Zofija Tadeuszowa Rittnerowa. Lwow-Warszawa: Panteon, 1925 (Introductory poem translated by Leon Koppens).
427. *24 Godziny z Zycia Kobiety i inne Opowiadania* ("Vierundzwanzig Stunden aus dem Leben einer Frau" and other tales). Tr. Izabella Czermakowa, Zofija Rittnerowa and Maria Wislowska. Warszawa: Panstw. Instytut Wydawn., 1957 (Reprinted 1958).
428. *24 Godziny z Zycia Kobiety w Odmecie Uczuc* ("Vierundzwanzig Stunden aus dem Leben einer Frau" and other tales). Tr. Melanja Wassermann. Warszawa: Instytut Wydawniczy "Renaissance," 1927.
429. — Wien: n.p., 1928.
430. *Legendy (Legenden)*. Tr. Melanja Wassermann. Warszawa: Nakladem Tow. Wydawniczego "Roj", 1930 (Contains: Stefan Zweig – Biographische Notiz, "Rachela Prawuje Sie z Panem" ("Rahel rechtet mit Gott"), "Oczy Wiecznego Brata" ("Die Augen des ewigen Bruders"), "Legenda o Podobnych acz Roznych Blizniaczkach" ("Die Legende der gleich-ungleichen Schwestern"), "Legenda o Trzeciej Golebidy" ("Legende der dritten Taube"), "Wieza Babel" ("Der Turm zu Babel")).
431. *Pierwsze Przezycie (Erstes Erlebnis)*. Tr. Melanja Wassermann. Warszawa: Towarzystwo Wydawnicze "Roj," 1928.
432. — Tr. Maria Wislowska. Warszawa: Panstw. Instytut Wydawn., 1959.
433. *Wyborowe Dziela* (Selected works; German originals unknown). Warszawa-Krakow-Wien: n.p., 1929.

PORTUGUESE

434. *A Corrente. Novelas da Adolescencia, Novelas de Sofrimento (Erstes Erlebnis)*. Tr. Odilon Gallotti and Sylvio Aranha de Moura. Rio de Janeiro: Civilização Brasileira, 1960.
435. *Amok. O Doids da Malacia* ("Amokläufer"). Tr. Alice Ogando. Porto: Civilização, 1956(11. ed., 1958).
436. *As Três Paixôes. Três Novelas de Stefan Zweig* (Contains: "Divida Traiamente Paga" ("Die spät bezahlte Schuld"), "Seria ele?" ("War er es?"), "A Partida de Xadrex" (*Schachnovelle*)). Tr. Odilon Gallotti and Elias Davidovich. Rio de Janeiro: Guanabara, 1949 (Vol. XVI of Zweig's collected works; Novellen 1 and 2 are not available in the German originals).
437. *Caleidoscopio (Kaleidoskop)*. Tr. Alice Ogando. Porto: Civilização, 1943 (2. ed.; Reprinted 1952, 1957).
438. *O Candelabro Sagrado (Der begrabene Leuchter)*. Tr. Alice Ogando. Porto: Civilização, 1956(4. ed.; 5. ed., 1958).
439. *Confusão de Sentimentos* ("Verwirrung der Gefühle"). Tr. Alice Ogando. Porto: Civilização, 1957(8. ed.).
440. *Um Coração Destroçado* ("Untergang eines Herzens"). Tr. Campos Monteiro Filho. Porto: Civilização, 1957 (8. ed.).
441. *O Medo* ("Angst"). Tr. Alice Ogando. Porto: Civilização, 1956 (8. ed.; 9. ed., 1958).
442. *Noite Fantástica* ("Phantastische Nacht"). Tr. Alice Ogando. Porto: Civilização, 1953 (6. ed.; 7. ed., 1958).
443. *O Caso de um Coração* ("Untergang eines Herzens"); *Noite Fantástica* ("Phantastische Nacht"). Tr. Aurelio Pinheiro. Rio de Janeiro: Irmaõs Porgetti, 1941.
444. *Um Segredo Ardente* ("Brennendes Geheimnis"). Tr. Alice Ogando. Porto: Civilização, 1955(7. ed.; 8. ed., 1958).
445. *Vinte e quatro Horas de uma Mulher* ("Vierundzwanzig Stunden aus dem Leben einer Frau"). Tr. Alice Ogando. Porto: Civilização, 1955 (10. ed.; 11. ed., 1957; 12. ed., 1959).

20

446. Lis Ogls dal Frer Etern ("Die Augen des ewigen Bruders"). Tr. Clementina Gilli. Tusan-Stamp: Roth, 1948 (Chasa Paterna, No. 57).

447. *Amok* ("Amokläufer"). Tr. B. Madeleine. Bucureşti: Adeverul, 1929 (Biblioteca Dimineata, No. 107).
448. *Jucatorul de Şah (Schachnovelle)*. Tr. J. Popper. Bucureşti: Editata de Revista Stiinta si Tehnica, 1957.
449. *Leporella* ("Leporella"). Tr. B. Madeleine. Bucureşti: Adeverul, n.d.
450. *Ochii Fratelui Veşnic* ("Die Augen des ewigen Bruders"). Tr. Joachim Botez. Bucureşti: Adeverul, n.d. (Lectura Biblioteca, No. 216).
451. *Scrisoarea unei Necunoscute* ("Brief einer Unbekannten"). Tr. Sarina Cassvan-Pas. Bucureşti: Adeverul, 1929 (Biblioteca Dimineata, No. 119; A fragment of this Novelle appeared as No. 43 of the Lectura. Floarea Literaturilar Straine (Bucureşti: Adeverul) under the title "Adoratie" (Tr. F. Aderca); The same issue also contained "Strada Lunii" ("Die Mondscheingasse")).
452. *Simturi Ratacite* ("Verwirrung der Gefühle"). Tr. S. Paul. Bucureşti: Ciornei, 1929 (Contains: "Simturi Ratacite" ("Verwirrung der Gefühle"), "Donazeci si patru Ore din Viata unei Femei" ("Vierundzwanzig Stunden aus dem Leben einer Frau"); This latter Novelle also appeared in the Lectura. Floarea Literaturilar Straine, No. 115 (Bucureşti: Adeverul)).
453. *Spaima. Romanul unui Adulter* ("Angst"). Tr. E. Marghita. Bucureşti: Adeverul, 1928.

454. *Amok. Novelly (Amok)*. Tr. D. M. Gorfinkel and I. B. Mandelstam. Leningrad: Vremja, 1926 (Contains: "Amokläufer" and "Brief einer Unbekannten"; 2 ed., 1928; 3. ed., 1929).
455. *Dvadcat' chetyre Chasa iz Zhizni Zhenshchiny* ("Vierundzwanzig Stunden aus dem Leben einer Frau"). Tr. L. Vol'fson. Moskva: Goslitizdat, 1955.
456. *Fantasticheskaya Noch. Novelly* ("Phantastische Nacht" and other Novellen). Riga: Knigoizdatel'stvo Gramatu Draugs, 1928 (Contains: "Geschichte in der Dämmerung," "Die Gouvernante," "Sommernovellette," "Phantastische Nacht," "Vierundzwanzig Stunden aus dem Leben einer Frau").
457. *Gibel' Serdca. Novelly* ("Untergang eines Herzens" and other Novellen). Riga: Knigoizdatel'stvo Gramatu Draugs, 1927 (Contains: "Untergang eines Herzens," "Verwirrung der Gefühle," "Brennendes Geheimnis," "Brief einer Unbekannten").
458. *Glaza Ubitogo* ("Die Augen des ewigen Bruders"). Tr. L. N. Wsewolodskaja. n.l.; Izdatel'stvo Solnce, 1925.
459. *Nezrimaja Kollekcija* ("Die unsichtbare Sammlung"). Tr. P. S. Bernstein, I. E. Charodschinskaja. Leningrad: Vremja, 1928 (Contains: "Die unsichtbare Sammlung," "Leporella," "Der Zwang," "Episode am Genfer See," "Angst," "Das Geheimnis Byrons"; Each work also appeared individually; 2. ed., 1929).
460. *Novelly (Novellen*; German originals unknown). Tr. P. S. Bernstein *et al.* Moskva: Goslitizdat, 1959.
461. *Prichudy Serdca* ("Vierundzwanzig Stunden aus dem Leben einer Frau"). Tr. O. Brosniowskaja, L. Weissenberg, W. Velskij, D. Gorfinkel, B. A. Sukkan and M. Zeiner. Leningrad: Biblioteka Vsemirnoj Literatury, 1927.
462. *Rokovyemgnovenija* ("Sternstunden"). Tr. P. S. Bernstein, D. M. Gorfinkel, B. A. Sorgenfrei and M. Losinski. Leningrad: Vremja, 1928 (Contains: "Die Le-

gende von den gleich-ungleichen Schwestern," "Die Augen des ewigen Bruders," "Episode in Lyon," *Sternstunden der Menschheit*; Each work also appeared separately).

463. *Smjatenie Chusto* ("Vierundzwanzig Stunden aus dem Leben einer Frau" and "Verwirrung der Gefühle"). Tr. P. S. Bernstein and S. Krasilschtschikov. Leningrad: Vremja, 1927 (3. ed., 1929).

464. *Strach. Novella* ("Angst"). Tr. I. E. Charodschinskaja. Leningrad: Vremja, 1927 (2. ed.).

465. *Vtoraja Kniga Amoka. Novelly* ("Das zweite Buch des Amok"). Tr. I. B. Mandelstam. Leningrad: Atenej, 1924 (Contains: "Phantastische Nacht," "Die Mondscheingasse")).

466. *Zhguchaja Tajna. Pervye Perezhivanija* (*Brennendes Geheimnis. Erstes Erlebnis*). Tr. P. S. Bernštein, A. I. Kartuschanskaja. Leningrad: Vremja, 1925 (Contains: "Brennendes Geheimnis," Geschichte in der Dämmerung," "Die Gouvernante," "Sommernovellette"; 2. ed., 1928; 3. ed., 1929).

SERBO-CROATIAN

467. *Nestrpljivo Srce* (*Ungeduld des Herzens*). Tr. Kacusa Maletin-Avakumovic. Novi Sad: Maticasrpska, 1956 (Reprinted 1960).

468. *Novele* (*Novellen*; German originals unknown). Tr. Vladan Jojkic, Radivoj Kovacevic and Milan Tokin. Novi Sad: Maticasrpska, 1951.

469. *Pismo Nepoznate Zene i Druge Novele* (*Begegnungen mit Menschen, Büchern und Städten* and *Die Kette. Ein Novellenzyklus*). Tr. Vlatko Saric. Zagreb: Zora, 1957 (Reprinted 1959).

SLOVINIAN

470. *Tri Novele o Ljubezni* ("Drei Geschichten über Liebe"; German originals unknown). Tr. Herbert Grün. Ljubljana: Slovenski Knjizni Zavod, 1950.

SPANISH

471. *Amok* (*Amok*). Tr. Pedro Salazar Diaz. Buenos Aires: Tor, n.d. (Contains: "Amok" ("Amokläufer"), "Carta de una Desconocida" ("Brief einer Unbekannten"), "Una Noche Fantastica" ("Phantastische Nacht"), "La Mujer y el Paisaje" ("Die Frau und die Landschaft"), "La Callejuela a la Luz de la Luna" ("Die Mondscheingasse")).

472. — Tr. Koellen y Catalan. Madrid: Hoy, 1931.

473. *Ardiente Secreto. Novela* ("Brennendes Geheimnis"). Barcelona: Edita, 1952 (Illus. J. Narro).

474. *Calidoscopio. Novelas* (*Kaleidoskop*). Tr. José Lleonart. Buenos Aires-Barcelona: Juventud, 1941 (Contains: "Conocimiento Casual de un Oficio" ("Unvermutete Bekanntschaft mit einem Handwerk"), "Leporella" ("Leporella"), "Miedo" ("Angst"), "Ardiente Secreto" ("Brennendes Geheimnis"), "Novela Veraniega" ("Sommernovellette"), "La Institutriz" ("Die Gouvernante"), "Buchmendel" ("Buchmendel"), "El Refugiado" ("Episode am Genfer See"), "La Colección Invisible" ("Die unsichtbare Sammlung"), "Raguel Litiga Dios" ("Rahel rechtet mit Gott"), "Noche Fantastica" ("Phantastische Nacht"), "La Calle del Caro de Luna" ("Die Mondscheingasse"), "Los Ojos del Hermano Eterno" ("Die Augen des ewigen Bruders"), "La Leyenda de la tercera Paloma" ("Die Legende der dritten Taube"), "Las Hermanas Iguales y Desiguales" ("Die Legende der gleich-ungleichen Schwestern"); Reprinted 1945 (abridged), 1959, 1960, 1961).

22

475. *La Calle del Claro de Luna* ("Die Mondscheingasse"); *Leporella* ("Leporella"). Barcelona: Juventud, 1953 (Illus. Lorenzo Goñi).
476. *El Candelabro Enterrado* ("Der begrabene Leuchter"). Tr. Fernando Gutierrez and Diego Navarro. Barcelona: Lara, 1945.
477. — Barcelona: Germán Plaza, 1956 (Version Castellana).
478. — Barcelona: Janés, 1957 (Club de los Lectores).
479. *Carta de una Desconocida* ("Brief einer Unbekannten"). Tr. Rafael Ballester Escalas. Barcelona: Imperia, 1949.
480. *Carta de una Desconocida* ("Brief einer Unbekannten"); *Sendas Equívocas* ("Verwirrung der Gefühle"). Tr. Rafael Ballester Escalas and J. Farrán y Mayoral. Barcelona: Matéu, 1956 (Col. La Puma, No. 4; Reprinted 1960).
481. *Un Caso de Conciencia* (*Ungeduld des Herzens*). Tr. Alfredo Cahn. Cordoba (Argentina): Assandri, 1957.
482. *Celos y Confusion de Sentimientos* ("Verwirrung der Gefühle"). Tr. Alfredo Cahn. Buenos Aires: Anaconda, 1942.
483. *Impaciencia del Corazón* (*Ungeduld des Herzens*). Tr. Alfredo Cahn. Barcelona: Luis de Caralt, 1960 (Col. Gigante).
484. — Buenos Aires: Claridad, 1958 (2. ed.).
485. — Mexico: Drake, 1943.
486. — Mexico: Diana, 1960 (4. ed.).
487. "La Institutriz. Novela Corta" ("Die Gouvernante"), Tr. Octavio Méndez Pereira. *Biblioteca Selecta* (Panama), Feb., 1946, pp. 33-55.
488. *La Institutriz* ("Die Gouvernante"); *Buchmendel* ("Buchmendel"); *El Refugio* ("Episode am Genfer See"); *La Colección Invisible* ("Die unsichtbare Sammlung"). Barcelona: Juventud, 1953.
489. *Noche Fantástica* ("Phantastische Nacht"). Barcelona: Juventud, 1953.
490. *Novela Veraniega* ("Sommernovellette"); *Conocimiento Casual de un Oficio* ("Unerwartete Bekanntschaft mit einem Handwerk"). Barcelona: Juventud, 1953.
491. *Los Ojos del Hermano Eterno* ("Die Augen des ewigen Bruders"); *Miedo* ("Angst"). Tr. Mario Verdaguer. Barcelona: Apolo, 1953 (4. ed.; Biblioteca Freya).
492. — Barcelona: Juventud, 1957 (Col. "Z," No. 25; 2. ed., 1961).
493. *La Piedad Peligrosa* (*Ungeduld des Herzens*). Tr. Aristides Camboa. Barcelona: Hispano-Americana de Ediciones, 1946 (Col. "Z," No. 25; 2. ed., 1961).
493. *La Piedad Peligrosa* (*Ungeduld des Herzens*). Tr. Aristides Gamboa. Barcelona: Hispano-Americana de Ediciones, 1946 (Col. Cumbre; Reprinted 1955 (Club de los Lectores)).
494. — Barcelona: Germán Plaza, 1958 (Libros Plaza, Vol. 108).
495. *Sendas Equivocadas* ("Verwirrung der Gefühle"). Tr. J. Farran y Mayoral. Barcelona: Matéu, 1948 (Biblioteca Matéu, Vol. 2; Reprinted 1958).
496. *Veinticuatro Horas de la Vida de una Mujer* ("Vierundzwanzig Stunden aus dem Leben einer Frau"). Tr. Máximo Llorente. Prólogo de José Manuel Ripamonti. Buenos Aires: Tor, 1936.
497. *Voluntad Prodigiosa* (*Schachnovelle*). Barcelona: Edit. Cultural Ibérica, 1960.

SWEDISH

498. *Hjärtats Oro. Roman* (*Ungeduld des Herzens*). Tr. Hugo Hultenberg. Stockholm: Skoglund, 1943.
499. *Känslornas Irrväger. Tre Noveller* ("Verwirrung der Gefühle" and two other Novellen; German originals unknown). Tr. Fanny von Wilamowitz-Moellendorff. Stockholm: Wahlström and Widstrand, 1927.
500. *Kedjan* (*Die Kette*); *Amerigo* (*Amerigo*). Tr. Hugo Hultenberg. Stockholm: Skoglund, 1945.
501. *Den Outgrundliga Hemligheten. Romantiska och andra Berättelser* (*Kaleidoskop*). Tr. Hugo Hultenberg. Stockholm: Skoglund, 1954.

23

502. *Schack, Amok och andra Noveller* ("Schachnovelle, Amok and other Novellen"). Tr Hugo Hultenberg. Stockholm: Skoglund, 1943.

503. *Acimak (Ungeduld des Herzens)*. Tr. Samih Tiryakioglu. Istanbul: Varlik Yayinevi, 1958.
504. *Amok (Amok)*. Tr. Tahsin Yücel. Istanbul: Varlik Yayinevi, 1954 (2. ed., 1958).
505. *Bir Kalbin Ölümü* ("Untergang eines Herzens"); *Mürebbiye* ("Die Gouvernante"). Tr. Salah Birsel. Istanbul: Istanbul Yayinlari, 1954.
506. *Bir Kadmin Yirmi Dört Saati. Roman* ("Vierundzwanzig Stunden aus dem Leben einer Frau"). Tr. Samih Tiryakioglu. Istanbul: Varlik Yayinevi, 1957.
507. *Meçhul Kadinin Mektuplari* ("Brief einer Unbekannten"). Tr. Kemal Bekata. Ankara: Türkiye Matbaaclilik ve Gazetecilik, 1950.
508. *Ölünceye Kadar (Amok)*. Tr. Kemal Bekata. Ankara: Türkiye Matbaacilik ve Gazetecilik, 1950.
509. *Korku* ("Angst"). Tr. Behçet Necatigil. Istanbul: Varlik Yayinevi, 1960.
510. *Usta Isi Çeviren*. Tr. Tahsin Yücel ("Meisterwerke"; German originals unknown). Istanbul: Varlik Yayinevi, 1954.

511. *Amok (Amok)*. Tr. Vasil Bobynskyj. Kyiv: Zachidnja Ukraina, 1928.
512. *Lyst Neznajomoi* ("Brief einer Unbekannten"). Tr. Vasil Bobynskyj. Kyiv: Zachidnja Ukraina, n.d.
513. *Novely (Novellen)*. Tr. Galina Jara. Kyiv: Sjajvo, n.d. (Contains: "Geschichte in der Dämmerung," "Brief einer Unbekannten," "Die Mondscheingasse," "Die Frau und die Landschaft," "Phantastische Nacht," "Sommernovellette"; Intro. Oswald Burckhardt).
514. *Zbirnyk Tvariv (Novellen)*. Tr. Vasil Bobynskyj. Kyiv: Zachidnja Ukraina, 1929 (Contains: "Amokläufer," "Brief einer Unbekannten," "Verwirrung der Gefühle," "Die Mondscheingasse"; Intro. Dmitro Zagul).

515. *Am'oq. N'ow'eln fun 'a Leidnscha'ft (Amok. Novellen einer Leidenschaft)*. Tr. H. Br'aq' azsch. W'arsch'e: Tur'em, 1929.
516. *Di begrabene Menorah (Der begrabene Leuchter)*. Tr. Ch. Brakarz. Buenos Aires: n.p., 1942.
517. *D'erwakung (Erstes Erlebnis)*. Tr. H. Br'aq'azsch. W'arsch'e: Bzsch'oza, 1926.
518. *Der Plonter fun Gefiln* ("Verwirrung der Gefühle"). Tr. Ch. Brakarz. Buenos Aires: n.p., 1942.

VI. ESSAYS

519. *Abschied von Rilke*. Tübingen: Wunderlich, 1927 (Eine Rede öffentlich gesprochen beim Gedächtnisfeier Rilkes am 20. Feb., 1927 im Staatstheater zu München; Reprinted 1928).
520. — Tübingen-Stuttgart: Wunderlich, 1946 (Reprinted 1947, 1952).
521. "Abschied von Rilke," *Begegnungen*, pp. 59-73 (An excerpt appeared in *Von Juden in München. Ein Gedenkbuch*. München: n.p., 1958, p. 207).
522. *Arturo Toscanini. Ein Bildnis*. Wien-Leipzig-Zürich: Rechner, 1936 (This essay served originally as the Introduction to the book *Arturo Toscanini. Ein Lebensbild*. Wien: Reichner, 1935 by Paul Stefan-Gruenfeldt).

523. *Ausgewählte Prosa*. Ed. H. Wolf. Amsterdam: Meulenhoff, 1930 (Meulenhoff's Sammlung deutscher Schriftsteller, No. 53; Contains: "Stefan Zweig," "Die Weltminute von Waterloo," "Die Entdeckung Eldorados," "Der Kampf um den Südpol," "Die Episode am Genfer see," "Die unsichtbare Sammlung," *Joseph Fouché*, Chapter V; Reprinted 1935).
524. *Ausgewählte Prosa*. Ed. H. Wolf. Amsterdam: Meulenhoff, 1939 (Meulenhoff's Sammlung deutscher Schriftsteller, No. 66; Contains excerpts from *Erasmus*, *Maria Stuart* and *Marie Antoinette*).
525. *Ausgewählte Prosa*. Ed. W. Kuiper. Amsterdam: Meulenhoff, 1950 (Meulenhoff's Sammlung deutscher Schriftsteller, No. 93; Contains: "Die Weltminute von Waterloo," "Der Kampf um den Südpol," and excerpts from *Die Welt von gestern*, *Magellan* and *Marie Antoinette*).
526. *Begegnungen mit Menschen, Büchern, Städten*. Wien-Leipzig-Zürich: Reichner, 1937 (Contains: *Begegnungen mit Menschen*: "Erinnerungen an Emile Verhaeren" (1916), "Abschied von Rilke" (1927), "Auguste Rodin" (1913), "Arturo Toscanini" (1935), "Erinnerungen an Theodor Herzl" (1929), "Rede zu Ehren Maxim Gorkis" (1928), "Geburtstagsbrief an Hermann Bahr" (1923), "Busoni" (n.d.), "Unvergessliches Erlebnis. Ein Tag bei Albert Schweitzer" (1932), "Der Dirigent. Gustav Mahler" (n.d.), "Bruno Walter" (1936), "Frans Masereel" (1923), "Die Stimme. Josef Kainz" (n.d.), "Abschied von John Drinkwater" (1937). *Begegnungen mit der Zeit*: "Die Monotonisierung der Welt" (1925), "Besuch bei den Milliarden" (1932); *Worte Während des Krieges*: "Die schlaflose Welt" (1914), "Bei den Sorglosen" (1916), "Berta von Suttner" (1917), "Das Herz Europas" (1917), "Das Feuer" (1918), "Das Haus der tausend Schicksale" (1937), "Die moralische Entgiftung Europas" (1932). *Begegnungen mit Städten und Landschaften*: "Die Stunde zwischen zwei Ozeanen" (1912), "Ypern" (1918), "Benares: Die Stadt der tausend Tempel" (n.d.), "Das schönste Grab der Welt" (1928), "Der Rhythmus von New York" (1912), "Salzburg. Die Stadt als Rahmen" (n.d.), "Kleine Reise nach Brasilien" (1936). *Begegnungen mit Büchern*: "Das Buch als Eingang zur Welt" (n.d.), "Marceline Desbordes-Valmore" (1920), "Ernest Renan" (1923), "Dante" (1921), "Zu Goethes Gedichten" (1927), "Sainte-Beuve" (1925), "Anmerkung zu Joyces 'Ulysses'," (1928), "Hans Carossa" (1928), "Die unterirdischen Bücher Balzacs" (1920), "Arthur Rimbaud" (1907), "Sinn und Schönheit der Autographen" (1935), "Dank an die Bücher" (n.d.)).
527. — Berlin-Frankfurt am Main: Fischer, 1955 (Reprinted 1956).
528. *Durch Zeiten und Welten*. Intro. and sel. Erich Fitzbauer. Graz-Wien: Stiasny, 1961 (Stiasny Bücherei, No. 79; Contains: I. An der Schwelle der Neuzeit: "Grösse und Grenzen des Humanismus" (Aus *Triumph und Tragik des Erasmus von Rotterdam*), "Der grosse Augenblick" (Aus *Magellan*). II. "Das Antlitz Dostojewskis" (Aus *Baumeister der Welt*), "Tolstoi" (Aus *Baumeister der Welt*), "Nietzsches Doppelbildnis" (Aus *Baumeister der Welt*), "Der Dirigent. In memoriam Gustav Mahler" (Aus *Begegnungen*). III. Schicksale aus der Zeit: "Episode am Genfer See," "Die unsichtbare Sammlung." IV. Heimat Österreich: "Das Wien von gestern" (Aus *Zeit und Welt*), "Herbstwinter in Meran" (Aus *Fahrten*), "Salzburg: Die Stadt als Rahmen" (Aus *Begegnungen*). V. In der Fremde: "Sommer in Rio" (Aus *Brasilien*), "Abschiedsbrief (Petropolis, 22. II. 1942). VI. Lebenstafel. VII. Bibliographie: a) Werke Stefan Zweigs, b) Briefe Stefan Zweigs, c) Das wichtigste Schrifttum über Stefan Zweig in deutscher Sprache.
529. *Erinnerungen an Emile Verhaeren*. Wien: Christoph Reissers Söhne, 1917.
530. — Im Selbstverlag des Verfassers. Leipzig: Spamerschen Buchdruckerei, 1927.
531. — Salzburg: n.p., 1927.
532. "Erinnerungen an Emile Verhaeren," *Begegnungen*, pp. 9-58.
533. *Europäisches Erbe*. Ed. Richard Friedenthal. Frankfurt am Main: Fischer, 1960 (Contains: "Montaigne," "Chateaubriand," "Jaurès," "Léon Bazalgette,"

"Edmond Jaloux," "Romain Rolland," "Pour Ramuz!," "Lafcadio Hearn," "Jens Peter Jacobsens 'Niels Lyhne'," "Rabindranath Tagores 'Sadhána'," "Das Drama in Tausendundeiner Nacht," "E.T.A. Hoffmann," "Gustav Mahlers Wiederkehr," "Arthur Schnitzler. Zum 60. Geburtstag," "Jakob Wassermann," "Peter Rosegger," "Anton Kippenberg," "Vorbeigehen an einem unauffälligen Menschen – Otto Weininger," "Abschied von Alexander Moissi," "Walter Rathenau," "Rainer Maria Rilke," "Joseph Roth," "Die Tragik der Vergesslichkeit," "Ist die Geschichte gerecht?," "Der Turm zu Babel").

534. *Fahrten. Landschaften und Städte.* Leipzig-Wien-Zürich: Tal, 1919 (Contains: "Die ferne Landschaft," "Herbstwinter in Meran," "Schöner Morgen. Bozner Berge," "Abendaquarelle aus Algier," "Nächte am Comersee," "Frühlingsfahrt durch die Provence," "Sonnenaufgang in Venedig," "Hydepark," "Stille Insel. Bretagne," "Frühling in Sevilla," "Alpenglühen an Zürichsee," "Die Stadt der tausend Tempel," "Tai Mahal," "Gwalier," "Stadt am See. Konstanz," "Der Rhythmus von New York," "Brügge," "Die Stunde zwischen zwei Ozeanen," "Der verlorene Himmel. Elegie der Heimkehr"; Volksausgabe, 1922).

535. *Flüchtiger Spiegelblick.* Leipzig: Insel, 1927 (Promotion material).

536. *Das Herz Europas. Ein Besuch im Genfer Roten Kreuz.* Zürich: Rascher, 1918 (Cf. *Begegnungen*, pp. 194-207).

537. *Reise nach Russland.* Wien: Sonderdruck, 1928 (Cf. *Zeit und Welt*, pp. 203-245).

538. *Sinn und Schönheit der Autographen.* Wien: Sonderdruck, 1935.

539. *Worte am Grabe Sigmund Freuds.* London: Sonderdruck, 1939.

540. — Amsterdam: De Lange, 1939.

541. *Zeit und Welt.* Stockholm: Bermann-Fischer, 1943 (Contains: I. *Menschen und Schicksale*: "Lord Byron. Das Schauspiel eines grossen Lebens" (1924), "Marcel Prousts tragischer Lebenslauf" (1925), "Hugo von Hofmannsthal" (1929), "Worte am Sarge Sigmund Freuds" (1939), "Mater Dolorosa. Die Briefe von Nietzsches Mutter an Overbeck" (1937), "Tolstoi als religiöser und sozialer Denker" (1937), "Irrfahrt und Ende Pierre Bonchamps. Die Tragödie Philippe Daudets" (1924), "Legende und Wahrheit der Beatrice Cenci" (1926). II. *Länder und Landschaften*: "Die Gärten im Kriege" (1939), "Das Wien von gestern" (1940), "Dank an Brasilien" (1936), "Abendaquarelle aus Algier" (1908), "Brügge" (1904), "Die Kathedrale von Chartres" (1924), "Oxford" (1907), "Reise nach Russland" (1928). III. *Zeit und Welt*: "Das Geheimnis des künstlerischen Schaffens" (1938), "Geschichtsschreibung von morgen" (1939), "Der europäische Gedanke in seiner historischen Entwicklung" (1932), "1914 und heute" (1936), "Die Geschichte als Dichterin" (1939), "Thomas Mann: 'Lotte in Weimar'" (1939); Reprinted 1946).

DANISH

542. *Møde Med en Svunden Tid.* Tr. Karl Hornelund. København: Jespersen and Pio, 1958 (Excerpts from *Begegnungen* and *Zeit und Welt*).

FRENCH

543. *Le Cœur de l'Europe. Une Visite à la Croix-rouge Internationale de Genève* ("Das Herz Europas"). Genève-Paris: Editions du Carmel, 1918.

544. *Derniers Messages* (*Zeit und Welt*). Tr. Alzir Hella. Paris-Neuchatel: Attinger, 1949 (Contains: "L'Histoire de Demain" ("Geschichtsschreibung von morgen"), "La Pensée européenne dans son développement historique" ("Der europäische Gedanke in seiner historischen Entwicklung"), "La Vienne d'Hier" ("Das Wien von gestern"), "Le Secret de la Création artistique" ("Das Geheimnis des

26

künstlerischen Schaffens"), "L'Histoire, cette poétesse" ("Die Geschichte als Dichterin"), "Hugo von Hofmannsthal" ("Hugo von Hofmannsthal"), "Tolstoi" ("Tolstoi als religiöser und sozialer Denker"), "Légende et Vérité de Béatrice Cenci" ("Legende und Wahrheit der Beatrice Cenci"), "Lord Byron" ("Lord Byron. Das Schauspiel eines grossen Lebens"), "Mater Dolorosa. Die Briefe Nietzsches Mutter an Overbeck"), "1914 et Maintenant" ("1914 und heute")).

545. *Souvenirs et Rencontres (Begegnungen).* Tr. Alzir Hella. Paris: Grasset, 1951 (Contains: "Prologue," "Rencontre avec Emile Verhaeren" ("Erinnerungen an Emile Verhaeren"), "Frans Masereel" ("Frans Masereel"), "Arturo Toscanini" ("Arturo Toscanini"), "Adieu à Rilke" ("Abschied von Rilke"), "Hans Carossa" ("Hans Carossa"), "Maxime Gorki" ("Rede zu Ehren Maxim Gorkis"), "Notes sur 'Ulysse' de Joyce" ("Anmerkungen zu Joyces 'Ulysses'"), "Arthur Rimbaud" ("Arthur Rimbaud"), "Notes sur Goethe" ("Zu Goethes Gedichten"), "Ernest Renan" ("Ernest Renan"), "Sainte-Beuve" ("Sainte-Beuve"), "Dante" ("Dante"), "Marceline Desbordes-Valmore" ("Marceline Desbordes-Valmore")).

546. *Souvenirs sur Emile Verhaeren* ("Erinnerungen an Emile Verhaeren"). Tr. Hendrik Coopman. Intro. Franz Hellens. Bruxelles: Kryn, 1931.

GREEK

547. *Anamnisseis Kai Synantisseis (Begegnungen).* Tr. Ep. Cauris. Athenai: Moundjouridhis, 1956.
548. *To Mustiko tes Kallitechnikes Demiourgias* ("Das Geheimnis des künstlerischen Schaffens"). Tr. L. Pavlidis. Athenai: Kerameos, 1949.
549. *Teleftaia Minymata (Zeit und Welt).* Tr. N. Prionistis. Athenai: Atlas, 1954.

ITALIAN

550. *Arturo Toscanini* ("Arturo Toscanini"). Tr. Lavinia Mazzucchetti. Milano: Officina Tipografica Gregoriana, 1935.
551. *Incontri ed Amicizie* (Excerpts from *Begegnungen, Zeit und Welt* and *Marceline Desbordes-Valmore*). Tr. Anita Limentani. (Intro. Lavinia Mazzucchetti. Milano-Verona: Mondadori, 1950.

JAPANESE

552. *Asu no Rekishi* (Excerpts from *Zeit und Welt*). Tr. Nobuo Iizuka. Tokyo: Risô-sha, 1958.
553. *Waga Shi Waga Tomo* (Excerpts from *Begegnungen* and *Zeit und Welt*). Tr. Nobuo Iizuka. Tokyo: Risô-sha, 1958).

PORTUGUESE

554. *Encontros. Impressões sobre Livros e Escritores (Begegnungen).* Tr. Maria Henrique Oswald. Porto: Civilização, 1955 (3. ed.).

SPANISH

555. *El Arcano de la Creación Artística* ("Das Geheimnis des künstlerischen Schaffens"). Tr. Aristides Gregory and Alfredo Cahn. Buenos Aires: Espasa-Calpe Argentina, 1952.

556. *El Mundo Insomne. Ideas, Ciudades y Paisajes (Begegnungen)*. Tr. Sigfrido Krebs. Barcelona: Luis de Caralt, 1947 (Reprinted 1960).
557. *Países y Paisajes* ("Länder und Landschaften" from *Zeit und Welt*). Tr. Tristán de la Rosa. Barcelona: Apolo, 1952 (Contains: "La Viena de ayer" ("Das Wien von gestern"), "Jardines durante la Guerra" ("Die Gärten im Kriege"), "Acuarela vespertina de Argel" ("Abendaquarelle aus Algier"), "Brujás" ("Brügge"), "La Catedral de Chartres" ("Die Kathedrale von Chartres"), "Oxford" ("Oxford"), "Viaje a Rusia" ("Reise nach Russland"), "Gracias al Brasil" ("Dank an Brasilien")).
558. *Personas y Destinos* ("Menschen und Schicksale" from *Zeit und Welt*). Tr. Tristán de la Rosa. Barcelona: Apolo, 1952 (Contains: "Lord Byron" ("Lord Byron. Das Schauspiel eines grossen Lebens"), "La trágica Vida de Marcel Proust" ("Marcel Prousts tragischer Lebenslauf"), "Hugo von Hofmannsthal" ("Hugo von Hofmannsthal"), "Palabras junto al Féretro de Sigmund Freud" ("Worte am Sarge Sigmund Freuds"), "Mater dolorosa – la Madre de Nietzsche" ("Mater Dolorosa. Die Briefe von Nietzsches Mutter an Overbeck"), "Tolstoi" ("Tolstoi als religiöser und sozialer Denker"), "Odisea y Muerte de Pierre Bonchamps" ("Irrfahrt und Ende Philippe Daudets"), "Leyenda y Verdad de Beatriz Cenci" ("Legende und Wahrheit der Beatrice Cenci")).
559. *Tiempo y Mundo* ("Zeit und Welt" from *Zeit und Welt*). Tr. Tristán de la Rosa. Barcelona: Apolo, 1953 (Contains: "El Misterio de la Creación artística" ("Das Geheimnis des künstlerischen Schaffens"), "La Historia del Mañana" ("Geschichtsschreibung von morgen"), "El Desarrollo histórico del Pensamiento europeo" ("Der europäische Gedanke in seiner historischen Entwicklung"), "1914 y Hoy" ("1914 und heute"), "La Historia como Fuente de Poesia" ("Die Geschichte als Dichterin"), "Thomas Mann: Lotte in Weimar" ("Thomas Mann: 'Lotte in Weimar'")).
560. *Tiempo y Mundo. Impresiones y Ensayos. 1904-1940 (Zeit und Welt)*. Tr. Editorial Juventud. Texto revisado por el Richard Friedenthal. Barcelona: Juventud, 1959 (Reprinted 1960).

561. *Möten med Människor, Böcker och Städer (Begegnungen mit Menschen, Büchern und Städten)*. Tr. Hugo Hultenberg. Stockholm: Skoglund, 1943.
562. *Tiden och Världen. Samlade Essayer och Föredrag. 1904-1940 (Zeit und Welt)*. Tr. Hugo Hultenberg. Stockholm: Skoglund, 1944.

VII. BIOGRAPHICAL STUDIES

VIIA. AMERIGO VESPUCCIO

563. *Amerigo, die Geschichte eines historischen Irrtums*. Stockholm: Bermann-Fischer, 1944.
564. —— Frankfurt am Main: Fischer, 1954 (In the series "Fischers Schulausgaben moderner Autoren").

ENGLISH

565. *Amerigo. A Comedy of Errors in History*. Tr. Andrew St. James. New York: Viking, 1942 (Originally appeared serially in *Blue Book* under the title "The Mystery of America's Godfather"; Book edition contains an eight page facsimile of the 1504 Augsburg edition of the "Mundus Novus").

GREEK

566. *Americo Vespuci. I Historia mias historikis Planis.* Athenai: Caravias, 1953.

PORTUGUESE

567. *Americo Vespúcio.* Tr. José Francisco dos Santos. Lisbõa: Civilização, 1956 (4. ed.).

RUSSIAN

568. *Amerigo.* Tr. L. P. Lezhneva. Moskva: Geografgiz, 1960 (1. ed. 96 pp.; 3. ed., 1960, 159 pp.).

SPANISH

569. *Américo Vespucio.* Tr. Alfredo Cahn. Buenos Aires: Claridad, 1942.
570. — Barcelona: Lara, 1946.
571. — Barcelona: Germán Plaza, 1958 (Col. "Quién fué").
572. — Madrid: Dédalo, 1960.

SWEDISH

573. *Amerigo. Kedjan (Die Kette).* Tr. Hugo Hultenberg. Stockholm: Skoglund, 1945.

VII B. BALZAC

574. *Balzac. Der Roman seines Lebens.* Epilogue Richard Friedenthal, ed. Stockholm: Bermann-Fischer, 1946 (Reprinted 1947).
575. — Stockholm-Amsterdam-Wien: Bermann-Fischer, 1950.
576. — Hamburg-Berlin: Deutsche Hausbücherei, 1953 (For members only).
577. — Frankfurt am Main: Fischer, 1954.
578. — Zürich: Büchergilde Gutenberg, 1957 (For members only; Reprinted 1959). Frankfurt am Main: Büchergilde Gutenberg.
579. — Leipzig: Insel, 1958 (Ed. for East Germany).

BULGARIAN

580. *Romanát na Edin Zhivot Balzak.* Tr. Dimitár Stoevski. Sofija: Nar. Kultura, 1960.

CZECHOSLOVAKIAN

581. *Balzac.* Tr. Maria Klimová. Bratislava: Pravda, 1949.

DANISH

582. *Balzac. Hans Livs Roman.* Tr. Clara Hammerich. København: Hirschsprung, 1949.

DUTCH

583. *Balzac. De Roman van zijn Leven.* Tr. F. W. van Heerikhuizen. Amsterdam: De Lange, 1950.

ENGLISH

584. *Balzac*. Tr. William and Dorothy Rose. New York: Viking, 1946 (Reprinted 1948).

FINNISH

585. *Balzac. Suuren Kirkailijan Elämä*. Tr. Olli Nuorto. Jyväskylä: Gummerus, 1948.

FRENCH

586. *Balzac. Le Roman de sa Vie*. Tr. Fernand Delmas. Paris: Michel, 1950.

GREEK

587. *Mpalzak*. Tr. Ioannes Beratis. Athenai: Govostis, 1950.

HEBREW

588. *Balzac*. Tr. Uriel Shelah. Jerusalem: Karni, 1952.

HUNGARIAN

589. *Balzac*. Tr. Tamás Mátrai. Budapest: Bibliotheca, 1958.

ITALIAN

590. *Balzac. Il Romanzo della sua Vita*. Tr. Lavinia Mazzucchetti. Milano-Verona: Mondadori, 1950.

JAPANESE

591. *Balzac*. Tr. Akira Mizuno. Tokyo: Hayakawa-Shobo, 1959.

PORTUGUESE

592. *Balzac. O Romance da sua Vida*. Tr. Mário José Domingues. Porto: Civilização, 1951 (Reprinted 1956, 1960).

SERBO-CROATIAN

593. *Balzak*. Tr. Nika Milićević. Sarajevo: Narodna Prosvjeta, 1959 (Gama Biblioteka, No. 331).

SPANISH

594. *Balzac*. Tr. Arístides Gamboa. Barcelona: Hispano-Americana de Ediciones, 1948 (Club de los Lectores; Reprinted 1955).
595. — Tr. A. Gregory. Mexico: Cumbre, 1953.

30

SWEDISH

596. *Balzac. Romanen om en Diktares Liv.* Tr. Hugo Hultenberg. Stockholm: Skoglund, 1947.

VII C. CALVIN

597. *Castellio gegen Calvin oder ein Gewissen gegen die Gewalt.* Wien-Leipzig-Zürich: Reichner, 1936.
598. — Berlin-Frankfurt am Main: Fischer, 1954.

DANISH

599. *Samvittighed mod Magt. Castellio mod Calvin.* Tr. Aage Schiøttz-Christensen. København: Jespersen and Pio, 1959.

DUTCH

600. *Strijdrond een Brandstapel. Castellio tegen Calvijn.* Tr. Reinier P. Sterkenburg. Amsterdam: De Lange, 1936.

ENGLISH

601. *The Right to Heresy. Castellio against Calvin.* Tr. Eden and Cedar Paul. New York: Viking, 1936.
602. — Boston: Beacon Press, 1951.
603. — London: Cassell, 1951.

FRENCH

604. *Castellion contre Calvin ou Conscience contre Violence.* Tr. Alzir Hella. Paris: Grasset, 1946 (8. ed.; Cf. *Nef.*, 3.a. 21 (Aug., 1946), 42-54).

ITALIAN

605. *Castillio contro Calvino. Una Coscienza contro la Forza.* Tr. Albina Calendo. Napoli: Fiorentino, 1945.

PORTUGUESE

606. *Castélio contra Calvino. Uma Consciencia contra a Violencia.* Tr. Odillon Galloti. Porto: Civilização, 1957 (4. ed.).

SPANISH

607. *Castelión contra Calvino.* Tr. Ramón María Tenreiro. Barcelona: Juventud, n.d.
608. — Buenos Aires: Juventud, 1940.

SWEDISH

609. *Vald och Rätt. Castellio contra Calvin.* Tr. Hugo Hultenberg. Stockholm: Skoglund, 1942.

610. *Marceline Desbordes-Valmore. Das Lebensbild einer Dichterin.* Leipzig: Insel, 1920 (With translations from the French by Gisela Etzel-Kühn; Zweig's introductory essay to this volume is reprinted in *Begegnungen*, pp. 318-372).

611. — Leipzig: Insel, 1927.

FRENCH

612. *Marceline Desbordes-Valmore. Son Oeuvre.* Tr. Alzir Hella and Olivier Bournac. Paris: La Nouvelle Critique, 1928 (Document pour l'Histoire de la Littérature française; Reprinted 1945, 64 numbered copies).

POLISH

613. *Tragedja Kobiety. Powieść o Marcelinie Desbordes-Valmore.* Tr. R. Centnerszwerowa. Warszawa: Instytut Wydawniczy "Renaissance," 1929.

RUSSIAN

614. *Marselina Debord-Val'mor. Sud'ba Poetessy.* Leningrad: Vremja, 1930 (Vol. VIII of Zweig's collected works).

SPANISH

615. *La Tragedia de una Vida. Marcelina Desbordes-Valmore.* Tr. J. B. Thomas. Buenos Aires: Tor, 1936.

VII E. ERASMUS VON ROTTERDAM

616. *Triumph und Tragik des Erasmus von Rotterdam.* Wien-Leipzig-Zürich: Reichner, 1934 (Reprinted 1935).

617. — Frankfurt am Main: Fischer, 1950 (Reprinted 1958).

DANISH

618. *Erasmus fra Rotterdam. En Biografi.* Tr. Georg Rønberg. København: Jespersen and Pio, 1934 (Reprinted 1953).

DUTCH

619. *Triomf en Tragiek van Erasmus van Rotterdam.* Tr. Reinier P. Sterkenburg. Maastricht-Brussel: Stols, 1934.

620. — Amsterdam: Meulenhoff, 1959.

ENGLISH

621. *Erasmus of Rotterdam.* Tr. Eden and Cedar Paul. New York: Viking, 1934 (Reprinted as Viking Compass Book C-13, 1956, 1961).

622. —   Garden City (New York): Garden City Pub. Co., 1937.
623. —   London: Cassell, 1934 (Reprinted with *Calvin against Castellio. The Right to Heresy*, 1951).

FRENCH

624. *Erasme. Grandeur et Décadence d'une Idée*. Tr. Alzir Hella. Paris: Grasset, 1935.
625. —   Bruxelles: Editions du Frêne, 1945 (Illus. Alessandro Berretti).

GREEK

626. *Erasmos*. Tr. G. Mperates. Athenai: Govostis, 1950.

ITALIAN

627. *Erasmo da Rotterdam*. Tr. Lavinia Mazzucchetti. Milano-Verona: Mondadori, 1935 (Reprinted 1937; Reprinted 1950 in the series "Biblioteca Moderna Mondadori," No. 137 with Introduction by the Translator).

PORTUGUESE

628. *Triunfo e Infortúnio de Erasmo de Rotterdão*. Tr. Alice Ogando. Porto: Civilização, 1959 (6. ed.).

SERBO-CROATIAN

629. *Erazmo Roterdamski*. Tr. Nika Milićević. Sarajevo: Narodna Prosvjeta, 1957.

SPANISH

630. *Triunfo y Tragedio de Erasmo de Rotterdam*. Tr. Ramón M. Tenreiro. Barcelona: Juventud, 1935 (Col. "Z," No. 73; Reprinted 1951, 1961).

VII F. JOSEPH FOUCHÉ

631. *Joseph Fouché. Bildnis eines politischen Menschen*. Leipzig: Insel, 1929
      1930 – 2. ed. (21.-35. Tsd.)
      1930 – 3. „   (36.-40. Tsd.)
      1930 – 4. „   (41.-48. Tsd.)
      1932 – 5. „   (49.-53. Tsd.).
632. —   Wien-Leipzig-Zürich: Reichner, 1936.
633. —   Amsterdam-Stockholm: Bermann-Fischer, 1948 (Reprinted 1950).
634. —   Zürich: Büchergilde Gutenberg, 1951 (For members only).
635. —   Frankfurt am Main-Hamburg: Fischer, 1952 (Fischer Bücherei, No. 4).
636. —   Berlin: Fischer, 1956 (Reprinted 1960 (16.-18. Tsd.)).
637. —   Berlin-Darmstadt-Wien: Deutsche Buch-Gemeinschaft, 1960 (For members only).

CZECHOSLOVAKIAN

638. *Josef Fouché. Šarlatan Europy. Román politického Člověka*. Tr. Vaclav Beneš-Šumavský. Praha: Vilimek, 1930.

33

DANISH

639. *Kamaeleonen. Romanbiografi om Joseph Fouché.* Tr. Clara Hammerich. København: Hirschsprung, 1950.
640. — København: Ti danske Forlaeggeres Bogklub, 1960 (New ed.).

DUTCH

641. *Joseph Fouché. De Roman van een Gewetenlooze.* Tr. Reinier P. Sterkenburg. Utrecht: De Haan, 1930.
642. — Amsterdam: Van Ditmar, 1947 (Reprinted Amsterdam-Antwerpen: Van Ditmar, 1948).
643. — 's-Gravenhage: Succes, 1954.

ENGLISH

644. *Joseph Fouché.* Tr. Eden and Cedar Paul. New York: Viking, 1930.
645. — New York: Blue Ribbon Books, 1932.
646. — London: Cassell, 1930 (Reprinted 1934, 1948).

FINNISH

647. *Poliisimestari Fouché. Elämänkuvaus.* Tr. Martti Santavuori. Jyväskylä: Gummerus, 1953.

FRENCH

648. *Joseph Fouché. Un Ministre de la Police sous Napoléon.* Tr. Alzir Hella and Olivier Bournac. Paris: Grasset, 1930 (Reprinted 1931, 1951, 1957, 1959).
649. — Paris: Flammarion, 1935.
650. — Bruxelles: Editions du Frêne, 1946.
651. — Paris: Le Club du Meilleur Livre, 1957.

GREEK

652. *Joseph Fouché.* Tr. K. Meranaios. Athenai: O Cosmos tou Viveiou, 1956.

HEBREW

653. *Josef Fouché.* Tr. Yizhak Hirschberg. Tel Aviv: Beker, 1951.
654. — Tel Aviv: Ger'iney Zahav, 1958.

HINDI

655. *Raj Neta. Joseph Fouché.* Tr. C. D. Pandey. Maliwada, Delhi: Shri Y. D. Sharma, Sharma, Sasta Sahitya Prakashan, n.d.

HUNGARIAN

656. *A Rendörminiszter Fouché Élete.* Tr. Szinnai Tivadar. Budapest: Pantheon-Kiadás, 1930.

34

ITALIAN

657. *Fouché.* Tr. Lavinia Mazzucchetti. Milano: Mondadori, 1930 (6. ed., 1937).

JAPANESE

658. *Joseph Fouché.* Tr. Teiji Takahashi and Hideo Akiyama. Tokyo: Iwanami Shoten, 1951.
659. *Joseph Fouché et al.* Tr. Kôkichi *et al.* Tokyo: Kawade Shobô, 1956 (Besides *Fouché* this book contains: *Sekai Bungaku Zenshû* (German original unknown, author Hans Carossa), *Malte no Shuki* (Rilke's *Aufzeichnungen des Malte Laurids Brigge*), *Duine Nohika* (Rilke's *Duineser Elegien*), *Kamisama no Hanashi* (Rilke's *Geschichten vom lieben Gott*), *Utisukushiki Madoi no Toshi* (Carossa's *Das Jahr der schönen Täuschungen*)).

NORWEGIAN

660. *Joseph Fouché. Portrett av et politisk Menneske.* Tr. Constance Wiel Schram. Oslo: Aschehoug, 1930.

POLISH

661. *Józef Fouché. Powieść Biograficzna.* Tr. R. Centnerszwerowa. Warszawa: Instytut Wydawniczy "Renaissance," n.d.

PORTUGUESE

662. *José Fouché.* Tr. Alice Ogando. Porto: Civilização, 1956 (Reprinted 1960, 8. ed.).

RUSSIAN

663. *Zhosef Fushe. Portret politicheskogo Dejatelja.* Tr. P. S. Bernstein. Leningrad: Vremja, 1931 (Vol. IX of his collected works; Foreword by Prof. A. Kudrjavcev, 7-12).

SPANISH

664. *Fouché. Retrato de un Político.* Tr. Máximo José Kahn and Miguel Pérez Ferrero. Madrid: Espasa-Calpe, 1930.
665. *Fouché, el Genio Tenebroso.* Barcelona: Juventud, 1935 (Reprinted 1954, 1956, 1958; Col. "Z," Vol. 21 – Grandes Biografias).
666. *Joseph Fouché.* Tr. Medeiros y Alburquerque. Rio de Janeiro: Guanabara, 1949.
667. *Fouché, Retrato de un Político.* Tr. Máximo José Kahn and Miguel Pérez Ferrero. Mexico City: Editorial Latino-Americana, 1957.
668. — Mexico City: Editora de Periódicos, 1960 (Populibros La Prensa, No. 39).

SWEDISH

669. *Fouché, Hertig d'Orrante. En Politikers Porträtt.* Tr. Hugo Hultenberg. Stockholm: Norstedt and Söners, 1930.
670. — Stockholm: Skoglund, 1948.

671. *Magellan. Der Mann und seine Tat.* Wien-Leipzig-Zürich: Reichner, 1938.
672. — Frankfurt am Main: Fischer, 1938 (Reprinted 1953, 1961).
673. — Zürich: Buch-Gemeinschaft "Ex Libris," 1951 (For members only).

CZECHOSLOVAKIAN

674. *Magellan. Muž a Jeho Čin.* Tr. Josef Nemeček. Epilogue, Vera Macháčková. Praha: NV, 1959 (In the Series "Khihovna Vojáka," No. 127).

DANISH

675. *Jorden er Rund. Magellans Eventyrlige Bedrift.* Tr. Clara Hammerich. København: Hirschsprung, 1951.

ENGLISH

676. *Conqueror of the Seas. The Story of Magellan.* Tr. Eden and Cedar Paul. New York: Viking, 1938.

ESTONIAN

677. *Magalhâes.* Tr. Karin Reinla. Tallin: Estgosizdat, 1960.

FRENCH

678. *Magellan.* Tr. Alzir Hella. Paris: Grasset, 1938.
679. — Bruxelles: Editions du Frêne, 1946.

GREEK

680. *Magellanos.* Tr. G. Lampsa. Athenai: Bergadi, 1953.
681. — Athenai: K. M., 1956.

HEBREW

682. *Magellan. Ha-ish u-foolo.* Tr. Yizhak Hirschberg. Tel Aviv: Beker, 1951.

HUNGARIAN

683. *Magellan Ferdinand. A Föld elsö Körülhajózása.* Tr. Zoltán Horváth. Budapest: Táncsics Kiado, 1957 (Reprinted 1958, 1960).

ITALIAN

684. *Magellano.* Tr. Lavinia Mazzucchetti. Milano-Verona: Mondadori, 1938.

36

JAPANESE

685. *Magellan.* Tr. Yoshitaka Kawasakai. Tokyo: Kawade Shobô, 1956.
686. — Tr. Teiji Takahashi and Toshiak Feijii. Tokyo: Kadokawa Shoten, 1958.

MACEDONIAN

687. *Magelan. Čovek i Delo.* Tr. Lazo Aleksov. Skopje: Kočo Racin, 1956.

MOLDAVIAN

688. *Epopeja luj Maželan.* Tr. A. Gromov. Kišinev: Kartja Moldovenjaske, 1959.

POLISH

689. *Magellan.* Tr. Zofia Petersowa. Warszawa: Ksiązka i Wiedza, 1951.

PORTUGUESE

690. *Fernão de Magalhães.* Tr. Maria de Castro Henriques Oswald. Porto: Civilização, 1956 (8. ed.; 9. ed., 1960).

RUMANIAN

691. *Magellan. Omul si Fapta sa.* Bucuresti: Editura Tineretului, 1956 (2. ed., 1959).

RUSSIAN

692. *Podvig Magellana.* Tr. A. S. Kulisher. Moskva: Gosud. Izd.-vo Geografichiskvi Literatury, 1956.
693. *Magellan et al.* Tr. A. P. Gelovani and Š. N. Buačidze. Tbilisi: Codna, 1959 (Also contains: *Amerigo. Pobeg v Bessmertie. Bor'ba za Južnyj Poljus*).

SERBO-CROATIAN

694. *Magellan.* Tr. Boško Petrović. Novi Sad: Matica Srpska, 1949.
695. — Sarajevo: Narodna Prosvjeta, 1956.

SLOVENIAN

696. *Magellan.* Tr. Pavle Flerè. Ljubljana: Mladinska Knijiga, 1956.

SPANISH

697. *Magellanes. El Hombre y su Gesta.* Tr. Alfredo Cahn. Buenos Aires: Claridad, 1942.
698. — Barcelona: Juventud, 1954 (Reprinted 1955, 1957 in Col. "Z," No. 33).
699. *Magellanes. La Aventura más Audaz de la Humanidad.* Mexico City: Editora de Periódicos, 1959 (Populibros La Prensa, No. 33).

37

700. *Marie Antoinette. Bildnis eines mittleren Charakters.* Leipzig: Insel, 1932.
701. — Wien: Reichner, 1936.
702. — Amsterdam: De Lange, 1939.
703. — Amsterdam: Querido, 1939.
704. — Wien: Bermann-Fischer, 1948.
705. — Berlin: Suhrkamp, 1949.
706. — Amsterdam: Bermann-Fischer and Querido, 1949.
707. — Wien: Büchergilde Gutenberg, 1951 (For members only).
708. — Zürich: Buchgemeinschaft "Ex Libris," 1952 (For members only).
709. — Frankfurt am Main: Fischer, 1948 (Reprinted in Fischer in Frankfurt-Hamburg, 1951, 1953, 1954, 1959, 1961).
710. — Berlin-Darmstadt-Wien: Deutsche Buch-Gemeinschaft, 1959 (For members only).

DANISH

711. *Marie Antoinette. Et Gennemsnitsmenneskes Portraet.* Tr. Kirstine Jespersen. København: Jespersen and Pio, 1933 (Reprinted 1951, 1952, 1953, 1954).

DUTCH

712. *Marie Antoinette. Portret van een Middelmatig Karakter.* Tr. G. J. Werumeus Buning-Ensink. Amsterdam: De Lange, 1933 (Reprinted 1936, 1939, 1949, 1954, 1956).

ENGLISH

713. *Marie Antoinette. The Portrait of an Average Woman.* Tr. Eden and Cedar Paul. New York: Viking, 1933.
714. — Garden City (New York): Garden City Pub., Co., 1935.
715. — London: Cassell, 1933 (Reprinted 1935, 1952, 1953).

FRENCH

716. *Marie Antoinette.* Tr. Azlir Hella. Paris: Grasset, 1933 (Reprinted 1934, 1952, 1958).
717. — Bruxelles: Editions du Frêne, 1948.
718. — Bruxelles: Editions Biblis, 1954 (Col. "Figures de l'Histoire," No. 2. Sélection des Lettres).
719. — Paris: Club des Libraires de France, 1954.
720. — Paris: Librairie Générale Française, 1959 (Col. "Livre de Poche. Série historique").

GREEK

721. *Maria Antouaneta.* Tr. Ioannes Asteriadis. Athenai: Govostis, 1950.
722. — Tr. J. Kouchtsoglou. Athenai: K.M., 1953.
723. — Tr. I. Androulidakis. Athenai: Romantso, 1954.

ITALIAN

724. *Maria Antonietta. Una Vita Involontariamente Eroica.* Tr. Lavinia Mazzucchetti. Milano-Verona: Mondadori, 1933 (4. ed., 1937).

725. *Marie Antoinette*. Tr. Teiji Takahashi and Hideo Akiyama. Tokyo: Mikasashobo, 1950 (Reprinted 1951, 1953).
726. — Tr. Hajime Yamashita. Tokyo: Kadokawa Shoten, 1958 (Reprinted 1959).

LATVIAN

727. *Marija Antuanete. Karalienea Tragiskas Dzwes Romas Tulkoijis*. Tr. Valdemara Karklins. Riga: Gramatu Draugs, 1933.

POLISH

728. *Maria Antonina*. Tr. Zofia Petersowa. Warszawa: J. Przeworski, 1948.

PORTUGUESE

729. *Maria Antonieta*. Tr. Alice Ogando. Porto: Civilização, 1958 (9. ed.).

SPANISH

730. *María Antonieta*. Mexico City: Editorial Drake, 1942.
731. *María Antonieta. Una Vida Involuntariamente Heroica*. Tr. Ramón María Tenreiro. Buenos Aires: Juventud, Argentina, 1948.
732. — Barcelona: Juventud, 1951 (Reprinted 1953, 1954, 1956, 1958, 1961).
733. — Mexico City: Editorial Latino-Americana, 1957.

SWEDISH

734. *Marie Antoinette. En Olycklig Drattnings Historia*. Tr. Erland Radberg. Stockholm: Forum, 1946 (Reprinted 1953, 1959).

VII J. MARIA STUART

735. *Maria Stuart*. Wien-Leipzig-Zürich: Reichner, 1935.
736. — Amsterdam: De Lange and Querido, 1939 (Forum Bücherei).
737. — Amsterdam-Wien: Bermann-Fischer and Querido, 1949.
738. — Frankfurt am Main: Fischer, 1951 (Reprinted 1954).
739. — Wien: Österreichische Buchgemeinschaft, 1951 (Vols. 68-69).
740. — Berlin-Darmstadt: Deutsche Buch Gemeinschaft, 1954 (For members only).
741. — Zürich: Buchclub "Ex Libris," 1958 (For members only).
742. — Frankfurt am Main-Hamburg: Fischer, 1959 (Fischer Bücherei, No. 279).
743. — Düsseldorf: Deutscher Bücherbund, 1959 (For members only).
744. — Stuttgart: Stuttgarter Hausbücherei, 1959 (For members only).

BULGARIAN

745. *Marija Stjuart*. Tr. Dimitar Stoevski. Sofija: Nar. Kultura, 1957.

DANISH

746. *Maria Stuart.* Tr. Georg Rønberg. København: Jespersen and Pio, 1936 (Reprinted 1953, 1954).

DUTCH

747. *Maria Stuart.* Tr. Reinier P. Sterkenburg. Amsterdam: De Lange, 1935 (Reprinted 1950).

ENGLISH

748. *Mary, the Queen of Scots.* Tr. Eden and Cedar Paul. New York: Viking, 1935.
749. — London: Cassell, 1935 (Reprinted 1950).

FINNISH

750. *Maria Stuart. Elämäkerta Romaani.* Tr. Elina Vaara Jyväskylä: Gummerus, 1938 (3. ed., 1955).

FRENCH

751. *Marie Stuart.* Tr. Alzir Hella. Paris: Grasset, 1936 (Reprinted 1958 in the series "Le Livre de Poche historique," Nos. 337-338).
752. — Bruxelles: Editions du Frêne, 1947.
753. — Paris: Club des Libraires de France, 1954.

GREEK

754. *Maria Stouart.* Tr. J. Asteriadis. Athenai: Govostis, 1948.
755. — Tr. G. Codjioulas. Athenai: Romantso, 1956.

HUNGARIAN

756. *Stuart Mária.* Tr. Ference Kelen, Zoltán Horváth and György Rónay. Budapest: Gondolat, 1957.

IRANIAN

757. *Mari-Stuart.* Tr. Farhad. Tehran: n.p., 1958.

ITALIAN

758. *Maria Stuarda.* Tr. Lavinia Mazzucchetti. Milano-Verona: Mondadori, 1936 (2. ed.).

JAPANESE

759. *Maria Stuart.* Tr. Teiji Takahashi and Yoshiyuki Nishi. Tokyo: Shinchô-sha, 1953.

POLISH

760. *Maria Stuart.* Tr. Maria Wislowska. Warszawa: Pánstw. Instytut Wydawn., 1959.

PORTUGUESE

761. *Maria Stuart.* Tr. Alice Ogando. Porto: Civilização, 1955 (7. ed.; 8. ed. 1957).

RUSSIAN

762. *Marija Stjuart.* Tr. R. Gal'perinoj. Foreword, B. Suckova. Moskva: Izd. inostr. Lit., 1959 (Reprinted 1960).
763. — Sverdlovsk: Kn. izd., 1960.

SERBO-CROATIAN

764. *Marija Stjuart.* Tr. Nika Milicević. Sarajevo: Narodna Prosvjeta, 1956.

SPANISH

765. *María Estuardo.* Tr. Ramón María Tenreiro. Barcelona: Juventud, 1958 (Reprinted 1959; Col. "Z," Vol. 40).

SWEDISH

766. *Maria Stuart.* Tr. Hugo Hultenberg. Stockholm: Skoglund, 1936 (Reprinted 1949).

VII K. FRANS MASEREEL

767. *Frans Masereel .Der Mann und Bildner.* Berlin: Juncker, 1923 (Written in conjunction with Arthur Holitscher; In the series "Graphiker unserer Zeit," Vol. I).
768. *Frans Masereel.* Dresden: Verlag der Kunst, 1959 (With contributions by Stefan Zweig, Pierre Vorms, Gerhard Pommeranz-Liedtke and a bibliography by Hanns-Conon von der Gabelentz).

VII L. ROMAIN ROLLAND

769. *Romain Rolland. Der Mann und das Werk.* Frankfurt am Main: Rütter and Loening, 1921 (Reprinted 1923, 1926, 1929).

CHINESE

770. *Lo-man Lo-lan.* Tr. Yang Jen-piän. Shanghai: Communist Press, 1929 (Tr. from the English edition).

ENGLISH

771. *Romain Rolland. The Man and his Work.* Tr. Eden and Cedar Paul. New York: Seltzer, 1921.
772. — London: Allen and Unwin, 1921.

41

FRENCH

773. *Romain Rolland. Sa Vie, son Oeuvre.* Tr. Odette Richez. Bruxelles: Office de Publicité, 1929.
774. — Neuchâtel: Editions de la Baconnière, 1929 (Reprinted 1936).
775. — Paris: Editions Pittoresques, 1929.

GREEK

776. *Romain Rolland.* Tr. N. Vrettacos. Athenai: Vivliecdhotiki, 1954.
777. — Tr. Mina Zographon and C. Meranaios. Athenai: Ghalaxias, n.d.

HUNGARIAN

778. *Romain Rolland Élete. Négy Képpel.* Tr. Lanyi Viktor. Budapest: A kultura könyv-kiadó eś nyomda r.t. kiadása, 1923 (Contains only the section "Lebensbildnis" from the original).

JAPANESE

779. *Roman Rooran.* Tr. Riûtaro Hattori. Tokyo: Ars, 1925.
780. — Tr. Kazuo Okubo. Tokyo: Keiyû-sha, 1951 (Tr. from the French).
781. — Tokyo: Sôgen-sha, 1953.
782. *Jônetsu no Hito Romain Rolland.* Tr. Kazuo Okubo. Tokyo: Kadokawa Shoten, 1955.

RUSSIAN

783. *Romen Rollan'. Ego Zhizn i Tvorchestvo.* Tr. G. Henkel. Moskva-Petrograd: Gosudarstvennoc Izdatel'stvo, 1923.

SPANISH

784. *Romain Rolland. El Hombre y su Obra.* Tr. Alfredo Cahn. Buenos Aires: Claridad, 1936 (Reprinted 1942; Biblioteca de Obras Famosas, Vol. 74).
785. *La Lucha contra el Mundo. Romain Rolland.* Tr. G. Almagro Rodiera. Barcelona: A. G. Ivern, 1949.

YIDDISH

786. *R'om'en R'ol'an. Der M'entš 'un d'os W'erq.* Tr. I. B'aše'wis. W'arse': Q'oop'er'atiw "Bik'er," 1929 (2. ed.).

VII M. ÉMILE VERHAEREN

787. *Emile Verhaeren.* Leipzig: Insel, 1910 (2. ed., 1913).

ENGLISH

788. *Emile Verhaeren.* Tr. Jethro Bithell. Boston-New York: Houghton-Mifflin, 1914.
789. — London-Edinburgh: Constable, 1914.

42

790. *Emile Verhaeren. Sa Vie, son Oeuvre.* Tr. Paul Morisse and Henri Chernet. Paris: Mercure de France, 1910.

791. *Emile Verhaeren.* Tr. Mina Zographon and C. Meranaios. Athenai: Podakis, 1954.

792. *Emile Verhaeren.* Buenos Aires: Tor, 1942 (Also contains "Despedida de Rilke" ("Abschied von Rilke")).

VII N. PAUL VERLAINE

793. *Paul Verlaine.* Berlin-Leipzig: Schuster and Loeffler, 1905 (In the series "Die Dichtung. Eine Sammlung von Monographien." Ed. Paul Remer. Vol. XXX).

ENGLISH

794. *Paul Verlaine.* Tr. O. F. Theis. Boston-New York: Luce, 1913.
795. — Dublin-W.C.: Maunsel, 1913.

VII O. BAUMEISTER DER WELT

796. *Baumeister der Welt: Drei Meister – Der Kampf mit dem Dämon – Drei Dichter ihres Lebens.* Wien-Leipzig-Zürich: Reichner, 1935 (Reprinted 1936).
797. — Frankfurt am Main: Fischer, 1951 (Reprinted 1952, 1955, 1956, 1958).

ENGLISH

798. *Master Builders.* Tr. Eden and Cedar Paul. New York: Viking, 1939.

SERBO-CROATIAN

799. *Neimari Svijeta.* Tr. Isak Samokovlija, Miodrag Petrović *et al.* Sarajevo: Veselin Masleša, 1957.

TURKISH

800. *Usta isi.* Tr. Tahsin Uücel. Istanbul: Yayinevi, 1954.

VII P. DREI DICHTER IHRES LEBENS

801. *Drei Dichter ihres Lebens: Casanova – Stendhal – Tolstoi.* Leipzig: Insel, 1928 (2. ed. 1928 (13.-20. Tsd.)).
802. — Frankfurt am Main: Fischer, 1961 (Fischer-Bücherei, No. 42).

DANISH

803. *Liv og Digt*. Tr. Clara Hammerich. København: Jespersen and Pio, 1957.

ENGLISH

804. *Adepts in Self-Portraiture*: *Casanova – Stendhal – Tolstoy*. Tr. Eden and Cedar Paul. New York: Viking, 1928.
805. — London: Allen and Unwin, 1929.
806. — London: Cassell, 1952 (Reprinted 1954)

FRENCH

807. *Casanova*. Tr. Alzir Hella and Olivier Bournac. Paris-Neuchâtel: Attinger, 1930 (9. ed.).
808. *Tolstoi*. Tr. Alzir Hella and Olivier Bournac. Paris: Attinger, 1928 (Reprinted 1946).
809. (*Essai sur*) *Tolstoi*. Tr. J. Angelloz. Paris: Corréa, 1940.
810. *Trois Poètes de leur Vie*. *Introduction générale*: *Stendhal – Casanova – Tolstoi*. Tr. Alzir Hella. Paris: Delamain et Boutelleau, 1937 (6. ed.; Reprinted 1950).
811. — Paris: Stock, 1937/1938.

GREEK

812. *Kasanobas*. Tr. Mina Zographon and Kostas Meranaios. Athenai: Maris, 1950.
813. *Stendhal*. Tr. A. Pangalos. Athenai: Govostis, 1954.
814. *Tolstoj*. Tr. K. Meranaios. Athenai: Nea Loghotechnia, 1956.

HUNGARIAN

815. *Tolsztoj*. Tr. Sajó Aladár. Budapest: Franklin-Társulat, 1928.

ITALIAN

816. *Tre Poeti della propria Vita*. Tr. Enrico Rocca. Milano: Sperling and Kupfer, 1930 (Reprinted 1931, 1945).

JAPANESE

817. *Stendhal*. Tr. Mizuho Aoyagi. Tokyo: Shinchô-sha, 1951.
818. *Tolstoi*. Tr. Teiji Takahashi. Tokyo: Kôbundô, 1950.

POLISH

819. *Homo eroticus*: *Casanova*. Tr. R. Centnerszwerowa. Wien: n.p., 1931.

RUSSIAN

820. *Pevec svoej Zhizni*. *Lev Tolstoj*. Tr. P. S. Bernstein. Leningrad: Vremja, 1928 (2. ed., 1929; Contains the essays on Casanova and Stendhal as well as the Tolstoy

44

study. It also contains a facsimile of the Foreword written by Zweig Sept. 14, 1928 while on a visit in Moscow. This forms volume VI of his collected works in Russian translation).

821. *Velikaja Zhizn. Lev Tolstoj.* Tr. St. Wetkin. Leningrad: Izdatel'stvo Krasnaja Gazeta, 1928.

SPANISH

822. *Tolstoi.* Tr. Alfredo Gallard. n.l.: Proa, 1930.
823. — Buenos Aires: Tor, 1942.
824. *Tolstoi. Tres Aspectos de su Vida.* Tr. Joaquín Verdaguer. Barcelona: Apolo, 1951.
825. — Barcelona: Germán Plaza, 1958 (Reprinted 1959).

SWEDISH

826. *Liv som blev Dikt*: *Casanova-Stendhal-Tolstoj.* Tr. Hugo Hultenberg. Stockholm: Skoglund, 1947.

VII Q. DREI MEISTER

827. *Drei Meister*: *Balzac-Dickens-Dostojewski.* Leipzig: Insel, 1920.
        1920 – 1. ed. (1.- 3. Tsd.)
        1921 – 2. „ (4.- 8. Tsd.)
        1922 – 3. „ (9.-12. Tsd.)
        1923 – 4. „ (13.-15. Tsd.)
        1925 – 5. „ (16.-20. Tsd.)
        1927 – 6. „ (21.-25. Tsd.)
        1929 – 7. „ (26.-30. Tsd.).
828. — Frankfurt am Main-Hamburg: Fischer, 1958 (Fischer Bücherei, No. 192).

DANISH

829. *To Portraetter*: *Dostojevski og Nietzsche.* Tr. Clara Hammerich. København: Jespersen and Pio, 1955.

ENGLISH

830. *Three Masters*: *Balzac-Dickens-Dostoeffsky.* Tr. Eden and Cedar Paul. New York: Viking, 1930; London: Allen and Unwin, 1930.

FRENCH

831. *Deux grands Romanciers du XIXe Siècle*: *Balzac-Dickens.* Tr. Alzir Hella and Olivier Bournac. Paris: Simon Kra, 1927.
832. *Dostoievski.* Tr. Henri Bloch. Paris: Rieder, 1928-1929.
833. *Trois Maîtres*: *Dostoievski-Balzac-Dickens.* Tr. Henri Bloch and Alzir Hella. Paris: Grasset, 1949 (3. ed.).

GREEK

834. *Balzac - Dickens.* Tr. K. L. Meranaios. Athenai: Maris-Kordakis, 1948.
835. *Pheontor Ntostogiebski.* Tr. Yannis Beratis. Athenai: Govostis, 1950.

HUNGARIAN

836. *Három Mester. Balzac-Dickens-Dostojevskij.* Tr. Térey Sándor. Budapest: Franklin-Társulat, 1926.

ITALIAN

837. *Tre Maestri: Balzac-Dickens-Dostojevski.* Tr. Berta Burgio Ahrens. Milano: Sperling and Kupfer, 1932 (Reprinted 1938).
838. — Tr. Enrico Rocca. Milano: Sperling and Kupfer, 1945.

JAPANESE

839. *Dostoevskii.* Tr. Teiji Takahashi. Tokyo: Kôbundô, 1950.

PORTUGUESE

840. *Tres Mestres.* Tr. Alice Ogando. Porto: Civilização, 1959 (5. ed.).

RUSSIAN

841. *Tri Mastera: Bal'zak-Dikkens-Dostoevskij.* Tr. G. A. Sukkau, B. A. Sorgenfrei, P. S. Bernstein. Leningrad: Vremja, 1929 (Vol. VII of collected works).

SERBIAN

842. *Dostojevski.* Tr. Miodrag Petrović. Beograd: Kñizarnica Svetlost, 1931.
843. *Graditelji Svijeta: Balzak-Dickens-Dostojevski.* Tr. Isak Samokovlija, Miodrag Petrović. Sarajevo: Veselin Masleša, 1955.

SPANISH

844. Balzac, Honoré de. *Eugenia Grandet.* Biographical study of Balzac by Stefan Zweig. Madrid: Siglo XX, 1949.
845. Dickens, Charles. *Oliverios Twist.* Biographical study of Dickens by Stefan Zweig. Tr. E. L. V. Madrid: Siglo XX (José Ruiz Alonso), 1949.
846. *Dostoiewski.* Barcelona: Juventud, 1959 (Col. "Z," No. 53).
847. *Stendhal.* Buenos Aires: Tor, n.d.
848. — Tr. Joaquín Verdaquer. Barcelona: Germán Plaza, 1958 (Col. Quién fué).
849. *Tres Maestros: Balzac-Dickens-Dostoiewski.* Tr. and Intro. Wenceslas Roces Suárez. Madrid: Cenit, 1929.

SWEDISH

850. *Tre Mästre: Balzac-Dickens-Dostojevskij.* Tr. Hugo Hultenberg. Stockholm: Skoglund, 1944.

46

VII R. DER KAMPF MIT DEM DÄMON

851. *Der Kampf mit dem Dämon*: *Hölderlin-Kleist-Nietzsche*. Leipzig: Insel, 1925
    1925 – 1. ed. (1.-10. Tsd.)
    1925 – 2. „ (11.-22. Tsd.)
    1928 – 3. „ (23.-27. Tsd.)
    1929 – 4. „ (28.-32. Tsd.)
    1933 – 5. „

FRENCH

852. *Le Combat avec le Démon*: *I - Hölderlin*. Tr. Alzir Hella and Olivier Bournac. Paris: Stock, 1928.
853. *Le Combat avec le Démon*: *II – Nietzsche*. Tr. Alzir Hella and Olivier Bournac. Paris: Stock, 1930.
854. *Le Combat avec le Démon*: *Hölderlin-Kleist-Nietzsche*. Tr. Alzir Hella. Paris: Stock, 1936.
855. — Paris: Delamain and Boutelleau, 1937.
856. — Bruxelles: Editions du Frêne, 1945.

GREEK

857. *O Aghonas me to Daimona*. Tr. G. Jiannacopoulos. Athenai: K.M., 1956.
858. *Oi Dhianooumenoi Brosta sti Dhynami*. Tr. G. Stavropoulos. Athenai: Loghotechniki Ghonia, 1956.
859. *Frederic Nietzsche*. Tr. K. L. Meranaios. Athenai: Maris, 1948.
860. *Frederic Nietzsche. O Paidagogos tes Leuterias*. Tr. P. Spiliotopoulos. Athenai: Govostis, 1948.

ITALIAN

861. *La Lotta col Demone*: *Hölderlin-Kleist-Nietzsche*. Tr. A. Overdorfer. Milano: Sperling and Kupfer, 1930 (Reprinted 1933, 1945).

JAPANESE

862. *Mashin tono Tatakai*. Tr. Hideo Akiyama. Tokyo: Kadokawa Shoten, 1958.

PORTUGUESE

863. *Os Constructores do Mundo. O Combate com o Demónio*: *Hölderlin-Kleist-Nietzsche*. Tr. Alice Ogando. Porto: Civilização, 1955 (4. ed.; 5. ed., 1959).

SPANISH

864. *La Lucha contra el Demonio*: *Hölderlin*. Tr. Joaquín Verdaquer. Barcelona: Apolo, 1951.
865. — Barcelona: Germán Plaza, 1959 (Col. Quién fué, Vol. 30).
866. *La Lucha contra el Demonio*: *Kleist*. Tr. Joaquín Verdaquer. Barcelona: Apolo, 1951.
867. — Barcelona: Germán Plaza, 1959 (Col. Quién fué, Vol. 34).
868. *La Lucha contra el Demonio*: *Nietzsche*. Tr. Joaquín Verdaquer. Barcelona: Apolo, 1951.

869. —   Barcelona: Germán Plaza, 1958 (Col. Quién fué, Vol. 8).
870. *La Lucha contra el Demonio*: *Hölderlin-Kleist-Nietzsche*. Tr. Joaquín Verdaquer. Barcelona: Apolo, 1934 (Reprinted 1946).
871. —   Barcelona: Plaza and Janés, 1961.

VII S. HEILUNG DURCH DEN GEIST

872. *Die Heilung durch den Geist*: *Franz Anton Mesmer-Mary Baker-Eddy-Sigmund Freud*. Leipzig: Insel, 1931.
873. —   Wien-Leipzig-Zürich: Reichner, 1936.
874. —   Frankfurt am Main-Wien: Fischer, 1952.

DANISH

875. *Sjaelens Laegedom.* Tr. Clara Hammerich. København: Hirschsprung, 1936.

DUTCH

876. *Genezing door den Geest*: *Sigmund Freud*. Tr. Reinier P. Sterkenburg. Arnhem: Van Loghum Slaterus, 1932 (Kleine Bibliotheek van hedendaagsch Cultuursleven, No. 7).

ENGLISH

877. *Mental Healers.* Tr. Eden and Cedar Paul. New York: Ungar, 1932 (Reprinted 1962).
878. —   London: Cassell, 1933.
879. —   Garden City (New York): Garden City Pub. Co., 1934.

FRENCH

880. *La fantastique Existence de Mary Baker-Eddy.* Tr. Alzir Hella and Juliette Pary. Paris: Stock, 1932 (9. ed.).
881. *La Guérison par l'Esprit*: *Sigmund Freud*. Tr. Alzir Hella and Juliette Pary. Paris: Stock, 1932.
882. *La Guérison par l'Esprit*: *Franz Anton Mesmer-Mary Baker-Eddy-Sigmund Freud*. Tr. Alzir Hella and Juliette Pary. Paris: Stock, 1934.

GREEK

883. *Franz Anton Mesmer.* Tr. G. Mperates. Athenai: Govostis, n.d.
884. *Stokhasmoi kai Oramata.* Tr. M. Lillis. Athenai: Prometheus, 1950.

ITALIAN

885. *L'Anima che guarisce.* Tr. Lavinia Mazzucchetti. Milano: Sperling and Kupfer, 1931 (Reprinted 1937).

NORWEGIAN

886. *Helbredelse ved Aand*: *Franz Anton Mesmer-Mary Baker-Eddy-Sigmund Freud*. Tr. Constance Wiel Schram. Oslo: Aschehoug, 1931.

48

887. *Mary Baker-Eddy*. Tr. L. Belmont. Wien: n.p., 1931.

888. *A Cura pelo Espírito*: *Franz Anton Mesmer-Mary Baker-Eddy*. Tr. Alice Ogando. Porto: Civilização, 1957 (5. ed.).

889. *La Curación por el Espiritu*: *Sigmund Freud*. Tr. Francisco Payarols. Barcelona: Apolo, 1934 (Reprinted 1949).
890. *La Curación por el Espiritu*: *Mary Baker-Eddy*. Tr. Francisco Payarols. Barcelona: Apolo, 1951.
891. *La Curación por el Espiritu*: *Mary Baker-Eddy-Sigmundo Freud*. Tr. Alfredo Cahn. Buenos Aires: Espasa Calpe, 1953.
892. *Franz Anton Mesmer*. Tr. Francisco Payarols. Barcelona: Germán Plaza, 1959 (Col. Quién fué, No. 12).
893. *Sigmund Freud*. Tr. Francisco Payarols. Barcelona: Germán Plaza, 1959 (Col. Quién fué, No. 24).
894. *La Curación por el Espiritu*. Tr. Francisco Payarols. Barcelona: Plaza and Janés, 1961.

895. *Själslig Läkekonst*: *Franz Anton Mesmer-Mary Baker-Eddy-Sigmund Freud*. Tr. Hugo Hultenberg. Stockholm: Skoglund, 1945.

VII T. STERNSTUNDEN DER MENSCHHEIT

896. *Georg Friedrich Händels Auferstehung. Eine historische Miniatur*. Wien-Leipzig-Zürich: Reichner, 1937 (350 numbered copies).
897. *Heroischer Augenblick. Dostojewski, Petersburg, Semenowskplatz. 22. Dez. 1849*. Leipzig: Staatliche Akademie für graphische Künste und Buchgewerbe, n.d. (25 numbered copies).
898. *Kampf um den Südpol. Kapitän Scott. 90. Breitengrad, 16. Jan. 1912*. Hannover: H. Nannen (Cf. Alpha Verlag), 1948 (Ill. Heinz Fehling; "Die bunten Hefte," No. 1).
899. *Sternstunden der Menschheit. Drei historische Miniaturen*. Ed. with notes by Dr. Robert Pick, Academy of Commerce, Vienna-London. London: G. Bell and Sons, 1930 (Special Intro. written by Stefan Zweig for this ed.; Contains: "Die Weltminute von Waterloo," "Die Entdeckung Eldorados," "Der Kampf um den Südpol").
900. *Sternstunden der Menschheit. Fünf historische Miniaturen*. Leipzig: Insel, 1927 (Contains: "Die Weltminute von Waterloo," "Die Marienbader Elegie," "Die Entdeckung Eldorados," "Heroischer Augenblick," "Der Kampf um den Südpol"; School edition).
    1927 – 20. Tsd. ((Leipzig)
    1928 – 30. Tsd. („)
    1929 – 200. Tsd. („)
    1931 – 300. Tsd. („)

1935 – 320. Tsd. (Leipzig)
1948 – 335. Tsd. („   )
1949 – 355. Tsd. (Wiesbaden)
1950 – 365. Tsd. (Leipzig)
1950 – 375. Tsd. (Wiesbaden)
1951 – 395. Tsd. („   )
1952 – 403. Tsd. („   )
1952 – 417. Tsd. (Leipzig)
1952 – 436. Tsd. (Wiesbaden)
1953 – 456. Tsd. (Leipzig)
1957 – 553. Tsd. (Wiesbaden)
1961 – 615. Tsd. (Frankfurt am Main)
(The Leipzig editions appearing since 1952 do not include the foreword written by Zweig for the original edition).

901. — Ed. with Intro., notes, German questions and vocabulary by Felix Wittner and Theodore Geissendörfer. New York: Prentice Hall, 1931 (School edition).

902. *Sternstunden der Menschheit. Zwölf historische Miniaturen.* Stockholm: Bermann-Fischer, 1945 (Contains: "Flucht in die Unsterblichkeit," "Die Eroberung von Byzanz," "Georg Friedrich Händels Auferstehung," "Das Genie einer Nacht," "Die Weltminute von Waterloo," "Die Marienbader Elegie," "Die Entdeckung Eldorados," "Heroischer Augenblick," "Das erste Wort über den Ozean," "Die Flucht zu Gott," "Der Kampf um den Südpol," "Der versiegelte Zug").
1943 – Stockholm: Bermann-Fischer (1.-9. ed.)
1947 – Stockholm: Bermann-Fischer (10.-16. ed.)
1949 – Berlin-Frankfurt am Main: Fischer
1950 – Wien: Fischer
1951 – Frankfurt am Main: Wien Büchergilde Gutenberg
1951 – Frankfurt am Main: Fischer (Reprinted 1953, 1956, 1958).

DANISH

903. *Stjernestunder.* Tr. Clara Hammerich. København: Jespersen and Pio, 1950 (Reprinted 1954).

DUTCH

904. *Georg Friedrich Händel's Opstanding.* Tr. Reinier P. Sterkenburg. Amsterdam: Wereldbibliotheek, 1939 (2. ed. Amsterdam-Antwerpen: Wereldbibliotheek, 1953).
905. *Lotswendingen.* Tr. Reinier P. Sterkenburg. Amsterdam: Wereldbibliotheek, 1939 (2. ed., 1946; Contains: "Die Eroberung von Byzanz," "Flucht in die Unsterblichkeit," "Das Genie einer Nacht," "Der versiegelte Zug").
906. *Noodlotsuren der Mensheid. Vijf historische Miniaturen.* Tr. Reinier P. Sterkenburg. Zeist: Ploegsma, 1931.
907. — Amsterdam: Wereldbibliotheek, 1950 (2. ed.; 3. ed., 1951).
908. — Antwerpen: Wereldbibliotheek, 1954 (4. ed.).

ENGLISH

909. *Twelve Historical Miniatures.* Tr. Eden and Cedar Paul. New York: Viking, 1940 (Reprinted London: Cassell, 1955; Contains: "The Head Upon the Rostrum, Cicero's Death. Dec. 7, 43 BC," "The Conquest of Byzantium. May 29, 1453," "Flight into Immortality, Núñez de Balboa Discovers the Pacific Ocean. Sept. 25, 1513," "The Lord Gave the Word, Handel's Messiah. Aug. 21, 1741," "The Decisive Hour at Waterloo. June 18, 1815," "The Genius of

one Night, the 'Marseillaise.' April 25, 1792," "The Marienbad Elegy –
Goethe's Last Love. Sept. 5, 1823," "El Dorado – the Gold of California.
Jan. 12, 1848," "The First Word Across the Atlantic – Cyrus Field's Cable.
Aug. 5, 1858," "Quest of the South Pole – Scott Reaches the Pole. Jan. 16,
1912," "The Sealed Train – Lenin Leaves Zürich. April 9, 1917," "Wilson's
Failure. Mar. 15, 1919").

FINNISH

910. *Ihmiskunnan Tähtihetkiä. Yksitoista historiallista Pienoiskuvaa.* Tr. J. A. Hollo. Porvoo-
Helsinki: Söderström, 1953.

FRENCH

911. *Les Heures étoilées de l'Humanité.* Tr. Alzir Hella. Paris: Grasset, 1928 (Reprinted
1939; Contains: "La Prise de Byzance," "La Fuite dans l'Immortalité," "La
Résurrection de Georges Frédéric Haendel," "Le Génie d'une Nuit," "La
Minute mondiale de Waterloo," "L'Elégie de Marienbad," "La Découverte de
l'Eldorado," "Instant historique. Dostoiewsky, Saint Pétersbourg, Place
Semenov 22.12.1849," "La Lutte pour le Pôle de Sud").
912. — Extracts ed. Fernand Delmas. Paris: Hachette, 1954.

GREEK

913. *Oi Meghales Ores tis Anthropotitos.* Tr. A. Karrer. Athenai: Rodaki-Pavlov, 1948.
914. — Tr. S. Patatzis. Athenai: n.p., n.d. (1956?).

HEBREW

915. *Sheot Horat Goral.* Tr. Edna Kornfeld. Tel Aviv: Gar'iney Zahav, 1957/58.

ITALIAN

916. *Momenti Eccelsi. Cinque Miniature Storiche.* Tr. Berta Burgio Ahrens. Milano: Sperling
and Kupfer, 1935.
917. *La Resurrezione di Händel.* Tr. Marcella Gorra. Milano: Sperling and Kupfer, 1935.

JAPANESE

918. *Lenin no Fûinressha* ("Der versiegelte Zug"). Tr. Teiji Takahashi. Tokyo: Kôbundô,
1951.
919. *Ummei no Hoshi. Kagayaku Toki.* Tr. Mayumi Haga. Tokyo: Kadokawa Shoten,
1956/57.

POLISH

920. *Gwiazdy Ludzkości. Opowiadania biograficzne.* Tr. Zofia Petersowa. Warszawa:
Wiedza, 1948.

RUMANIAN

921. *Lupta pentru Polul Sud* ("Der Kampf um den Südpol"). Tr. Aurel B. Luca. Bucureşti: Adeverul, 1928.

SPANISH

922. "Balboa o la Fuga a la Immortalidad," *BibS*, II : 17 (May, 1947), 25-26.
923. *El Genio de una Noche y otras Narraciones*. Buenos Aires: Anacorda, 1941 (Contains: "El Genio de una Noche," "El Tren precintado," "La Cabeza sobre la Tribuna," "El Fracaso de Wilson," "Fuga a la Immortalidad," "La Conquista de Bizancio," "La primera Palabra a través de Oceáno").
924. *Momentos estelares de la Humanidad. Doce Miniatures históricas*. Tr. Mario Verdaquer and Fernando Trías Beristain. Barcelona: Apolo, 1956 (Club de los Lectores, No. 33).
925. — Barcelona: Juventud, 1956 (Reprinted 1958; Col. "Z," Vol. 17).
926. *Nuevos Momentos estelares de la Humanidad*. Tr. Alfredo Cahn. Santiago de Chile: Ercilla, 1940 (2. ed.; Contains: "Resurrección de Jorge Federico Händel," "El Genio de una Noche," "Fuga a la Immortalidad," "La Conquista de Bizancio," "La primera Palabra a través del Oceáno").
927. *Voluntad prodigosa. Biografía de G. F. Händel*. Barcelona: Cultural Ibérica, 1960.

SWEDISH

928. *Odödliga Ögonblick i Mänsklighetens Historia*. Stockholm: Skoglund, 1947.

TURKISH

929. *Insanlik Tarihinde Yildizin Parladigi Anlar*. Tr. Burhan Arpad. Istanbul: Istanbul Matbaasi, 1954 (Reprinted 1956).

VIII. BRASILIEN

930. *Brasilien. Ein Land der Zukunft*. Stockholm: Bermann-Fischer, 1941.

DUTCH

931. *Brazilie, Het Land der Toekomst*. Tr. Johan Winkler. Amsterdam: De Boer, 1953.

ENGLISH

932. *Brazil, Land of the Future*. Tr. Andrew St. James. New York: Viking, 1941.
933. — London-Toronto: Cassell, 1942.

FRENCH

934. *Le Brésil, Terre d'avenir*. Tr. Jean Longeville. New York: Edition de la Maison française, 1942.
935. — Paris: Michel, 1949.

936. *Brasilia, I Chora tous Mellontos.* Tr. V. Rodapoulos. Athenai: Ecdhosseis, 1955

PORTUGUESE

937. *Brasil, País do Futuro.* Tr. Odilon Gallotti. Rio de Janeiro: Guanabara, 1941.
938. — Porto: Civilização, 1959.

SPANISH

939. *Brasil, Tierra del Futuro.* Tr. Alfredo Cahn. Buenos Aires: Espasa Calpe Argentina, 1941 (Reprinted 1942, 1943).

SWEDISH

940. *Brasilien, Framtidslandet.* Tr. Hugo Hultenberg. Stockholm: Skoglund, 1945.

IX. DIE WELT VON GESTERN

941. *Die Welt von gestern. Erinnerungen eines Europäers.* Stockholm: Bermann-Fischer, 1944 (Reprinted 1947, 1948).
942. — London: Hamilton (In conjunction with Bermann-Fischer), 1945.
943. — Frankfurt am Main: Suhrkamp, 1947.
944. — Wien: Bermann-Fischer, 1948.
945. — Berlin-Frankfurt am Main: Suhrkamp, 1949.
946. — Sel. and Intro. Jef. Jefsen. København: Schultz, 1949.
947. — Wien: Fischer, 1952.
948. — Frankfurt am Main-Hamburg: G. B. Fischer, 1953 (Grosse Romane der Zeit).
949. — Berlin-Frankfurt am Main: S. Fischer, 1955 (Reprinted 1958).
950. — Zürich: Buchklub "Ex Libris," 1959 (For members only).
951. — Gütersloh: Bertelsmanns Lesering, 1960 (For members only).

DANISH

952. *Verden af i Gaar. En Europaeers Erindringer.* Tr. Helge Kjaergaard. København: Jespersen and Pio, 1948 (Reprinted 1949, 1953, 1954).

DUTCH

953. *De Wereld van gisteren. Herinneringen van een Europeaan.* Tr. F. W. van Heerikhuizen. Amsterdam: De Lange, 1948.

ENGLISH

954. *The World of Yesterday.* Tr. Eden and Cedar Paul. New York: Viking, 1943 (Zweig Bibliography, pp. 443-445).
955. — London: Cassell, 1953.

FRENCH

956. *Le Monde d'hier. Souvenirs d'un Européen.* Tr. Jean Paul Zimmermann. Paris: Michel, 1948 (Nouv. Sér., No. 23).

GREEK

957. *O Chthessinoscosmos. Anamnisseis enos Evropaiou.* Tr. M. Zographon and K. Meranaios. Athenai: Synchroni Loghotechnia, 1956.
958. — Athenai: Dhiethneis Ecdhasseis, n.d. (1956?).

ICELANDIC

959. *Veröld sem var. Sjálfsaevisaga.* Tr. Halldór J. Jónsson and Ingólfur Pálmason. Reykjavík: Bókautgáfa Menningarjóds, 1958.

NORWEGIAN

960. *Verden av i gar. En Europeers Eindringer.* Tr. Inger and Anders Hagerup. Oslo: Aschehoug, 1948.

POLISH

961. *Swiat w Czorajszy.* Tr. Maria Wislowska. Warszawa: Panstwowy Instytut Wydawniczy, 1958.

PORTUGUESE

962. *O Mundo de Ontem. Memórias de un Europeu.* Tr. Manuel Rodrigues. Porto: Civilização, 1953 (3. ed., 1958).
963. *O Mundo que eu vi. Minhas Memórias.* Tr. Odilon Gallotti. Rio de Janeiro: Guanabara, 1943.

SERBO-CROATIAN

964. *Jučerašnji Svet. Seúanje Jednog Evropejca.* Tr. Aleksandar Tišnia. Novi Sad: Matica Srpska, 1952.

SLOVENIAN

965. *Včerajšnji Svet. Spomeni Evropejca.* Tr. Angela Vodè. Ljubljana: Cankarjeva Zalozba, 1958.

SPANISH

966. *El Mundo de ayer. Autobiografía.* Tr. Alfredo Cahn. Buenos Aires: Claridad, 1942.
967. — Barcelona: Hispano-Americana, 1947 (Reprinted 1955, 1956).
968. — Mexico: n.p., 1949.

SWEDISH

969. *Världen av i gar. En Europés Minnen.* Tr. Hugo Hultenberg. Stockholm: Skoglund, 1945.

YIDDISH

970. *Di Velt fun Nekhtn. Zikhroynes fun an Eyropeyer.* Tr. Hayim Brakzgh. Buenos Aires: Yikdukh, 1959.

X. CORRESPONDENCE IN BOOK-FORM

971. *Briefwechsel: Stefan Zweig-Friderike Maria Zweig.* 1912-1942. Bern: Scherz, 1951.

ENGLISH

972. *Stefan Zweig and Friderike Maria Zweig: Their Correspondence.* Tr. Henry G. Alsberg and Erna MacArthur. New York: Hastings House, 1954.

SPANISH

973. *Correspondencia de Stefan y Friderike Maria Zweig (Seleccionada y Recopilada por Friderike Maria Zweig).* Tr. Fernando Trías Beristain. Barcelona: AHR, 1957.
974. *Richard Strauss – Stefan Zweig. Briefwechsel.* Frankfurt am Main: Fischer, 1957.
975. *Unbekannte Briefe aus der Emigration an eine Freundin.* Ed. Gisella Selden-Goth. Wien-Stuttgart-Basel: Hans Deutsch, 1963.

XI A. LETTERS TO OR FROM ZWEIG IN BOOKS

976. *Alfred Kubin. Leben-Werk-Wirkung.* Ed. Paul Raabe. Hamburg: Rowohlt, 1957 (Letters to Kubin: Oct. 15, 1909 and April, 1937).
977. *Briefwechsel: Rainer Maria Rilke-André Gide.* 1909-1926. Tr. Wolfgang A. Peters. Stuttgart: Deutsche Verlagsanstalt; Wiesbaden: Insel, 1957 (Includes letters from Zweig to Rolland and Rolland to Zweig in 1916).
978. *Correspondence: Rainer Maria Rilke-André Gide.* 1909-1926. Intro. and Commentaires Renée Lang. Paris: Corrêa, 1952 (Complétée par quelques lettres de Rilke et de Gide á divers correspondants, par des lettres de Romain Rolland, Stefan Zweig et Marie de Tour et Taxis et par des extraits du Journal de Gide).
979. Dehmel, Richard. *Ausgewählte Briefe.* 1902-1920. 2 Vols. Berlin: Fischer, 1923 (Seven letters to Zweig between 1902 and 1917).
980. *Erich Ebermayer. Buch der Freunde.* Ed. Peer Baedeker and Karl Lemke. Lohhof bei München: Lemke, 1960 (33 letters written by Zweig and Ebermayer between 1924 and 1939).
981. Freud, Sigmund. *Briefe: 1873-1939.* Frankfurt am Main: Fischer, 1960 (Eight letters from Freud to Zweig between 1908 and 1938).
982. Rolland, Romain. *Journal des Années de Guerre.* 1914-1919. Paris: Michel, 1952 (Includes innumerable letters and excerpts thereof written by Rolland and Zweig).
983. Starr, William Thomas. *Romain Rolland and a World at War.* Evanston (Ill.): Northwestern University Press, 1956 (Includes some ten letters or parts thereof written by Rolland to Zweig).
984. Wildgans, Anton. *Ein Leben in Briefen, Manuskripten und Bildern.* Ed. Lilly Wildgans. 3 Vols. Wien: Frick, 1947 (Includes many letters from Wildgans to Zweig between 1910 and 1930 and innumerable references to Zweig in other letters).

985. "Abschiedsbrief an die Freunde," *Europäer*, p. 43 (Photocopy of same p. 44; Cf. *Leben-Werk*, pp. 116-117 and *Durch*, p. 120).

986. "Brief an die Redaktion," *DLE*, 22.J : 14 (April 15, 1920), 892-893 (Letter from Zweig to the effect that the English version of "Das brennende Geheimnis" published by Scott and Seltzer (New York, 1920) with Stephan Branch as its author was not authorized by him or by the Insel Verlag. Zweig decidedly rejects the use of an English version of his name merely to facilitate the sale of his book in America).

987. "Briefe Zweigs an Jean Schorer," *Blätter*, 13/14 (April, 1962), 7 (Quote: "17 Briefe und eine Karte von Stefan Zweig an Jean Schorer sind von Schorer der Zweig Gesellschaft überlassen. Es handelt sich um die gesamte Korrespondenz, die Zweigs Buch *Castellio gegen Calvin. Ein Gewissen gegen die Gewalt* betrifft...").

988. "Briefe Zweigs an verschiedene Korrespondenten," *Spiegelungen*, pp. 19-21, 74-77, 86-93 (Letters to Karl Emil Franzos, Karl Klammer, Kurt Frieberger, Rudolf Kayser, Alfred Wolfenstein, Felix Braun, Guido Fuchs).

989. "Cartas de Stefan Zweig a Jules Romain, 1940-1942," *Cuadernos Americanos* (Mexico), Jan.-Feb., 1943, p. 52-72.

990. "Correspondencia inédita de Stefan Zweig," *Correio da Manha* (Rio de Janeiro), April 15, 1945.

991. Dehmel, Richard. "Two Letters to Stefan Zweig (Nov. 1, 1909 and Sept. 7, 1917)," *Blätter*, 8/10 (Oct., 1960), 23-25.

992. "Lettre de Stefan Zweig à Charles Du Bos: 1er septembre 1929," *Cahiers Charles Du Bos* (Société des Amis de Charles Du Bos), June, 1961, p. 35-36.

993. "Letter to the Editor," *Adam*, XV: 167-168 (Feb.-Mar., 1947) (This letter by Zweig to the editor of the periodical *Adam* concerns his article "The Mission of the Intellectuals" which appeared in this periodical, III : 152 (Sept., 1941), 2).

994. McClain, William H. "Soviet Russia Through the Eyes of Stefan Zweig and Romain Rolland," *MLN*, LXIX : 1 (Jan., 1954), 11-17 (Excerpts from the unpublished Zweig-Rolland correspondence to be found in the archives of the "Association des Amis de Romain Rolland" in Paris).

995. McClain, William and Harry Zohn. "Stefan Zweig and Romain Rolland: The Literary and Personal Relationship," *Germ R*, XXVIII : 4 (Dec., 1953), 262-281 (Excerpts from the unpublished Zweig-Rolland correspondence to be found in the "Association des Amis de Romain Rolland" archives in Paris).

996. Oechler, William F. "Reception of Emile Verhaeren in Germany. Some unpublished Letters of Stefan Zweig," *MLN*, LXII (Apr., 1947), 226-234.

997. Romains, Jules. "Derniers Mois et dernières Lettres de Stefan Zweig," *RP*, 62. a. (Feb., 1955), 3-23 (Letters of Zweig to Romains between 1940 and Feb. 19, 1942).

998. "Stefan Zweigs letzter Brief an Felix Braun," *Blätter*, 4/5 (Apr., 1959), 10.

999. Zohn, Harry. "Stefan Zweig and Contemporary European Literature. In Memoriam Stefan Zweig," *GLL*, N.S., V : 3 (Apr., 1952), 202-212 (Excerpt from a letter of Zweig to Julius Bab on page 206).

1000. Zohn, Harry. "Stefan Zweig's Last Years: Some Unpublished Letters," *MfDU*, XLVIII : 2 (Feb., 1956), 73-77 (Excerpts from Zweig's correspondence with Mme. Selden-Goth from June, 1935 to Christmas, 1941).

1001. Zohn, Harry and Jean-Pierre Barricelli. "Music in Stefan Zweig's Last Years – Some Unpublished Letters," *JulR*, III : 2 (Spring, 1956), 3-11 (Excerpts from Zweig's correspondence with Alfred Einstein and with Mme. Selden-Goth).

XII. EXCERPTS OF ZWEIG'S WORKS APPEARING IN PERIODICALS, NEWSPAPERS AND BOOKS

ABSCHIED VON RILKE:

1002. *DL*, XXIX : 6 (1926-1927), 346.
1003. *Juden*, p. 207.
1004. *MNN*, No. 52, Feb. 22, 1927.
1005. *NFP*, Feb. 20, 1927.

BALZAC:

1006. *NLAS*, 29.a.: 1184 (1950), 1-2 ("Le Mariage de Balzac").

BRASILIEN. EIN LAND DER ZUKUNFT:

1007. *Journeys*, pp. 381-402.
1008. *LA*, CCCLI (Jan., 1937), 384-392 ("Brazilian Diary"; Tr. from the German by R. Norden).
1009. *PL*, Oct. 17/21, 1936.
1010. *RP*, 56.a.: 7 (July, 1949), 36-50 ("Brésil").

CALVIN:

1011. *Nef*, 3.a.: 21 (Aug., 1946), 42-54 ("Castellion contre Calvin").
1012. *PL*, April 5, 1936 ("Sebastian Castellio: ein Gewissen gegen die Gewalt").

DREI DICHTER (Casanova):

1013. *DLW*, IV : 2 (1929), 3 ("Casanova, homo eroticus").
1014. *In*, IX : 2 (Spring, 1928), 120-125 ("Casanova").
1015. *NFP*, Jan. 21, 1928 ("Casanova: die Heldenzeit der Abenteurer").

DREI DICHTER (Stendhal):

1016. *Bd*, May 27, 1928 ("Stendhals Bildnis").
1017. *BT*, Mar. 25, 1928 ("Stendhals Bildnis").
1018. *DFR*, II (1929), 269-274 ("Lügenlust und Wahrheitsfreude bei Stendhal").
1019. *DLW*, IV : 17 (1929), 3 ("Stendhal als Psycholog").
1020. *Isb*, I : 12 (Oct., 1954), 21-23 ("Yalan söylemek zevki ve hakikat aşki: M. Henry Beyle Stendhal hakkinda" ("Les Plaisirs du Mensonge et l'Amour de la Vérité – à propos de Henry Beyle Stendhal"); Tr. in Turkish by Muzaffer Esen).
1021. *KZ*, Mar. 29, 1928 ("Stendhal der Individualist").
1022. *MZ*, July 28, 1928 ("Lügenlust und Wahrheitsfreude bei Stendhal").
1023. *NFP*, Mar. 1/4, 1928 ("Stendhals Lebensbildnis").
1024. *RHb*, 46.a.: 11 (1937-1938), 391-412 ("Poètes de leur Vie: Stendhal").

DREI DICHTER (Tolstoi):

1025. *DLW*, IV : 11 (1929), 3 ("Tolstoi der Künstler").
1026. *HaN*, Jan. 25, 1929 ("In Tolstois Heim").

1027.   *In*, IX : 4 (Fall, 1928), 249-260 ("Ein Tag aus dem Leben Tolstois").
1028.   *KZ*, Nov. 8, 1927 ("Das Bildnis Tolstois").
1029.   *LA*, CCCXXXIV (Jan. 1, 1928), 56-62 ("Day from Tolstoi's Life").
1030.   *NFP*, Nov. 19, 1927 ("Das Bildnis Tolstois").
1031.   *NZZ*, Nov. 16, 1927 ("Tolstois 'Rasputin',").
1032.   *SchM*, Nov. 8, 1927 ("Tolstoi: die Tragödie eines Gewissens").
1033.   *V*, Nov. 20, 1927 ("Tolstoi, Schtschegolew, Piscatur: 'Rasputin',").

DREI MEISTER (Dostojewski):

1034.   *BT*, Feb. 23, 1914 ("Dostojewski: der Sinn seines Schicksals").
1035.   *DWr*, III (Feb., 1914), 92-108 ("Dostojewski: die Tragödie seines Lebens").
1036.   *In*, I : 4 (1920), 195-197 ("Dostojewskis Antlitz").
1037.   *ÖR*, XL : 3 (July-Sept., 1914), 199-203 ("Dostojewski: der Kampf um die Wahrheit").

ERASMUS:

1038.   *NFP*, Dec. 30, 1933 ("Triumph und Tragik des Erasmus von Rotterdam").
1039.   *RB*, LXXIII (Mar. 16, 1935), 194-198 ("Erasme et sa Mission").
1040.   *RH*, 60.a., CLXXVI (1935), 98 ("Erasme").
1041.   *WuW*, 6.J. (1951), 18-19 ("Dulce bellum inexpertiis – aus 'Erasmus von Rotterdam',").

FAHRTEN:

1042.   *DgD*, 8.J.: 40 (1956), 5 ("Sevilla-Spaniens Lächeln").
1043.   *DZfS*, VI : 114 (1923), 2 ("Frühling in Sevilla").
1044.   *FuS*, II (1928), 161 ("Die Kathedrale von Chartres").
1045.   *InA* (1921), 130-132 ("Drei Landschaften: 'Alpenglühen am Zürichsee,' 'Taj Mahal', 'Schöner Morgen: Bozner Berge',").
1046.   *NFP*, Mar. 4, 1924 ("Die Kathedrale von Chartres").

FOUCHÉ:

1047.   *Cht*, Jan. 31, 1931.
1048.   *En*, May 15, 1931 ("Une Évolution de Fouché").
1049.   *In*, X : 4 (Fall, 1929), 269-273 ("Fouchés Votum").
1050.   *InA* (1930), 159-168 ("Fouchés Kampf mit Robespierre").
1051.   *NFP*, May 19, 1929 ("Joseph Fouché, Herzog von Otranto. Der Endkampf mit Napoleon").
1052.   *REI*, X (1930), 199-237 ("Fouché contre l'Empereur").
1053.   *RHb*, Oct. 4, 1930 ("Fouché contre l'Empereur").

HEILUNG DURCH DEN GEIST:

1054.   *NR*, XLII : 2 (1931), 258-270 ("Die Heilung durch den Geist").
1055.   *SM*, IV (1931), 121-132 ("Die Heilung durch den Geist").
1056.   *SSA*, III : 10279.

HEILUNG DURCH DEN GEIST (Mesmer):

1057.   *Hy*, X (Feb., 1932), 130-134 ("Mesmerism minus Mesmer").
1058.   *InA* (1931), 11-18 ("Franz Anton Mesmer").
1059.   *KZ*, Feb. 5, 1931 ("Mesmers Nachfolger").
1060.   *NFP*, July 13, 15, 17, 20, 27 and Aug. 3, 7, 8, 10, 17, 1930 ("Mesmer").
1061.   *VZ*, Feb. 17, 1931 ("Bildnis Franz Anton Mesmers").

HEILUNG DURCH DEN GEIST (Mary Baker Eddy):

1062.   *APL*, XCVIII (May-June, 1932), 367-373, 415-421, 459-466 ("La Vie merveil-
        leuse de Mary Baker Eddy"; Tr. A. Hella and J. Pary).
1063.   *NR*, XLI : 1 (1930), 610-641, 770-799 and XLI : 2 (1930), 14-60 ("Das Leben
        und die Lehre des Mary Baker Eddy").
1064.   *RC*, 12.a.: 9/10 (1932-1933), 11-17 ("La Vie merveilleuse de Mary Baker Eddy").

HEILUNG DURCH DEN GEIST (Freud):

1065.   *HK*, Jan. 31, 1931 ("Die Entdeckung der Hypnose").
1066.   *In*, XII : 2 (Easter, 1931), 94-105 ("Abendlicher Blick ins Weite").
1067.   *NFP*, Dec. 10, 1930 ("Sigmund Freud als Charakter").
1068.   *NFP*, Dec. 25, 1930 ("Freuds Technik der Psychoanalyse").
1069.   *NLZ*, Jan. 31, 1931 ("Ein Bildnis Freuds").
1070.   *PB*, III (1931), 5-18 ("Sigmund Freud und die Situation der Jahrhundert-
        wende").
1071.   *RA*, 5.a. (1931), 1089-1099; Cont. 6.a. (1932), 47-60 ("Sigmund Freud").
1072.   *VZ*, Dec. 19, 1930 ("Ein Bildnis Freuds").

KAMPF MIT DEM DÄMON:

1073.   *In*, VI : 2 (Easter, 1925), 123-136 ("Der Kampf mit dem Dämon: Hölderlin-
        Kleist-Nietzsche"; This article serves as the Intro. to Zweig's book by the
        same name).
1074.   *RHb*, 45.a.: 10 (1937-1938), 391-402 ("Le Combat avec le Démon").

KAMPF MIT DEM DÄMON (Hölderlin):

1075.   *BU*, II (1927), 653-667 ("Hölderlin").
1076.   *DH*, I (1924), 14 ("Die heilige Schar: Vorklang zu einem Hölderlin Bildnis").
1077.   *DL*, 27.J.: 3 (1924), 131-135 ("Hölderlin: Phaethon oder die Begeisterung").
1078.   *Kt*, 38.J.: 7 (1925), 8-15 ("Hölderlin und Weimar").
1079.   *NA*, CCLXV (May 1, 1929), 68-71 ("La santa Schiera"; Tr. from the German
        by G. Gentilli; Cf. *DH* above).
1080.   *NFP*, Nov. 11, 1924 ("Hölderlins Untergang").
1081.   *PJ*, CXCIX (1925), 26-46 ("Hölderlins drei gestaltiges Werk").

KAMPF MIT DEM DÄMON (Kleist):

1082.   *BBM*, June 24, 1925, p. 21 ("Kleistens Lebensplan").
1083.   *DL*, 26.J.: 10 (1924), 581-583 ("Kleist der Erzähler").
1084.   *DRa* (1925-1926), 68 ("Heinrich von Kleist, der Gejagte").

1085.	*In A* (1925), 118-133 ("Die Pathologie des Gefühls bei Kleist").
1086.	*Kt*, July, 1924, pp. 143-147 ("Das Drama zum Drama bei Kleist").
1087.	*NFP-Jb* (1925), 33-40 ("Kleists Untergang").

KAMPF MIT DEM DÄMON (Nietzsche):

1088.	*BBM*, Mar., 1925 ("Nietzsche als Erzieher zur Freiheit").
1089.	*GR*, CXXXIV (1930), 200-207 ("Nietzsche et la Danse au dessus de l'
	Abîme").
1090.	*LA*, CCCXXV (Apr. 18, 1925), 142-148 ("Nietzsche's Evensong").
1091.	*LNL*, July 19, 1930 ("L'Influence du Sud sur Nietzsche").
1092.	*RB*, LXVIII (Nov. 1, 1930), 641-646 ("Frédéric Nietzsche et la Maladie").

MAGELLAN:

1093.	*Journeys*, pp. 54-67 ("Great Moments from 'Conqueror of the Seas: the Story
	of Magellan'").
1094.	*RD*, XXXII (1938), 111-127 ("Conqueror of the Seas: the Story of Magellan";
	Tr. by Eden and Cedar Paul).

MARCELINE DESBORDES-VALMORE:

1095.	*DLE*, XXII: 4 (Nov. 15, 1919), 209-214 ("Die Dichterin Marceline Desbordes-
	Valmore").
1096.	*DLE*, 23.J.: 24 (Sept. 15, 1921) 1476-1479 (Franz Strunz, "Notre Dame des
	Pleurs – Marceline Desbordes-Valmore").
1097.	*In*, VIII: 4 (Fall, 1927), 282-285 ("Menschlichkeit").
1098.	*NFP*, Nov. 7/9, 1918 ("Marceline Desbordes-Valmore. Das Lebensbild einer
	Dichterin").

MARIE ANTOINETTE:

1099.	*Crumbs*, pp. 67-85 ("Marie Antoinette").
1100.	*In*, XIII : 4 (Fall, 1932), 193-207 ("Königin des Rokoko").
1101.	*In A* (1933), 153-166 ("Ein Kind wird verheiratet").
1102.	*NR*, XLIII : 1 (Mar., 1932), 300-324 ("War er es? war er es nicht? Fersen und
	Marie Antoinette").
1103.	*NYT*, 13 (April 1, 1933), 5 ("Marie Antoinette. The Story of an Average
	Woman").
1104.	*PB*, IV (1932), 100-112 ("Das eheliche Missgeschick Marie Antoinettes").
1105.	*RB*, CI (Nov. 3/17, 1933), 498-503, 527-530, 556-560 ("Marie Antoinette";
	Tr. Alzir Hella).
1106.	*RHb*, 42.a.: 11 (1936), 139-166, 285-313, 437-473 ("Marie Antoinette, Königin
	von Frankreich: Martyre de la Reine Marie- Antoinette").

STERNSTUNDEN:

1107.	*Diktate*, p. 74 ("Kapitän Scott"), p. 130 ("Der Kampf um die Erde").
1108.	*DMfC*, 8./9.J. (1929), 424-432 ("Die Entdeckung Eldorados. J. A. Suter,
	Kalifornien, Jan., 1848").
1109.	*DNSch*, 20.J. (1959), 62-64, 102-105 ("Georg Friedrich Händels Auferste-
	hung").

1110.   *DuZ*, pp. 61-69 ("Die Entdeckung Eldorados").
1111.   *DWk*, 11.J. (1931), 107-110 ("Die Entdeckung Eldorados").
1112.   *EdD*, pp. 10-21 ("Der Kampf um den Südpol").
1113.   *Geistesleben* ("Die Weltminute von Waterloo").
1114.   *GB*, XV (April, 1932), 330-334 ("Goethe's Last Love Affair"; Tr. of "Die Marienbader Elegie" by Eden and Cedar Paul).
1115.   *GB*, XV (Feb.-Mar., 1932), 116-124 ("Weltminute von Waterloo"), 231-237 ("Die Entdeckung Eldorados").
1116.   *InA* (1928), 108-127 ("Die Weltminute von Waterloo").
1117.   *Karussell*, pp. 147-163 ("Der Kampf um den Südpol").
1117a.   *Negen Vuurmakers*, pp. 124-134 (Abbreviated form of "Der Kampf um den Südpol").
1118.   *NFP*, Jan. 28/29, 1914 ("Kapitän Scotts letzte Fahrt").
1119.   *PL*, Dec. 24, 1928 ("Die Weltminute von Waterloo").
1120.   *RB*, CXIII (Jan. 10, 1939), 12-15 ("Le Messie de Haendel").
1121.   *RdO*, XXXII (1930-1932), 27-35, 217-235 ("El Minuto universel de Waterloo. Napoléon, 18.6.1815").
1122.   *RP*, CCLVII : 24 (Dec., 1936), 789-808 ("Résurrection de Georges Haendel").
1123.   *RP*, 45.a.: 21 (Nov., 1938), 179-201 ("Prise de Byzance").

VERHAEREN:

1124.   *In*, I : 2 (Dec., 1919), 78-87 ("Verhaerens Sommer").
1125.   *In*, VIII : 1 (Christmas, 1926), 69-73 ("Stunden mit Emile Verhaeren").

WVG (WELT VON GESTERN):

1126.   *CJR*, VII (April, 1944), 205 ("Die Welt von gestern").
1127.   *DdG*, pp. 52-54 ("Der junge Hofmannsthal").
1128.   *Hofmannsthal*, pp. 63-64 (Excerpt from *WvG*, 1955 ed., pp. 55-57 ("Die Schule im vorigen Jahrhundert")).
1129.   *Merian*, XVII : 1 ("Salzburg") (Jan., 1964), 57 (Cf. *WvG*, 1955 ed., pp. 269-270).
1129a.   *Spectrum*, pp. 7-9 (Cf. *WvG*, 1955 ed., pp. 13-16).
1130.   *ZdZ*, IV (1961), 29-32 (Cf. *WvG*, 1955 ed., pp. 13-16; *ZdZ* also appeared in one volume form; The above quote is to be found therein on pages 432-436).

XIII. ARTICLES AND LECTURES BY ZWEIG

1131.   "Abendaquarella aus Algier" (1908) (Reprinted in *Zeit und Welt*, pp. 161-168).
1132.   "Abschied von Alexander Moissi," Lecture in Milan, June 5, 1935 (Reprinted in *Europäisches Erbe*, pp. 227-231).
1133.   "Abschied von John Drinkwater" (1937) (Reprinted in *Begegnungen*, pp. 148-151).
1134.   "A la Mémoire d'Alfred Fried," *AL*, 3.a.: 6 (June ,1921).
1135.   "Alberta von Puttkammer," *DLE*, 8.J.: 12 (Mar. 15, 1906), 836-841, 846-849.
1136.   "Alessandro Poerio. Ein Italiener bei Goethe," *NFP*, Sept. 18, 1918.
1137.   "Alfred H. Fried," *NFP*, May 13, 1921.
1138.   "Alfredo Canciani-Bildhauer," *VFZM*, 22.J.: 24 (1903).
1139.   "A mes Frères français," *D*, II (1916-1918), 125-128.
1140.   "An den Genius der Verantwortlichkeit," *NR*, XXXVI : 6 (June, 1925), 624-626.
1141.   "An Detlev von Liliencron," *Liliencron* (1904).
1142.   "An die Freunde in Fremdland," *BT*, Sept. 19, 1914 (Reprinted in *Mann-Werk*, pp. 63-70).

1143. "An Karl Kraus," *Kraus*, pp. 38-39.
1144. "Anmerkung zum 'Ulysses'," *NR*, XXXIX : 10 (Oct., 1928), 477-479 (Reprinted in *Begegnungen*, pp. 418-421).
1145. "Anthologie: Aufmarsch der Jugend (Anthologie jüngster Prosa)," *MP*, Jan. 2, 1929.
1146. "Anton, Friend of all the World," *RD*, XXXV (Oct., 1939), 69-72.
1147. "Anton Kippenberg," *DBK*, X-XI (1924), 46-52 (Cf. also *FZ*, May 22, 1924; *Kippenberg* (1924); *Europäisches Erbe*, pp. 214-222).
1148. "An Wilhelm Schmidtbonn," *Schmidtbonn*, pp. 9-10.
1149. "Arthur Rimbaud," *Z*, LVII (1907), 300-305 (Reprinted in *InA* (1908), 84-96; *Begegnungen*, pp. 432-440; This article also serves as the Introduction to *Arthur Rimbaud. Leben und Dichtung*. Leipzig: Insel, 1907).
1150. "Arthur Schnitzler - Narrateur," *RA*, 6.a. (1932), 387-398.
1151. "Arthur Schnitzler zu seinem 6osten Geburtstage," *NR*, 33.J.: 1 (1922), 510-513 (Reprinted in *Europäisches Erbe*, pp. 183-187).
1152. "Aufruf zur Geduld," *DTb*, I : 1 (Jan., 1920), 7-10.
1153. "Aus Romain Rollands Kindheit," *DRa*, 1-17 (1924-1925), 197.
1154. "Autobiographische Skizze," *DLE*, XVII : 4 (Nov. 15, 1914), 199-202.
1155. "Das Autographensammeln," *VZ*, Sept. 14, 1913.
1156. "Die Autographensammlung als Kunstwerk," *DBK*, II (1914), 44-50 (Reprinted in *Spiegelungen*, pp. 44-51).
1157. "Balzacs Codices vom eleganten Leben," *DLE*, XIV : 9 (Feb. 1, 1912), 613-616.
1158. "Bei Albert Schweitzer," *In*, XIV : 2 (1933), 73-83 (Reprinted in *Begegnungen*, pp. 113-122; *Schweitzer*, pp. 7-19).
1159. "Bei den Franzosen in Kanada," *FZ*, Mar. 25, 1911.
1160. "Bei den Sorglosen" (1916) (Reprinted in *Begegnungen*, pp. 181-186).
1161. "Benares: Stadt der tausend Tempel," *NFP*, Mar. 23, 1909 (Reprinted in *Begegnungen*, pp. 254-261.)
1162. "Ben Jonson," *NFP*, Nov. 4, 1926 (Cf. also *FTb* (1927-1928), 189).
1163. "Ben Jonsons 'Volpone' in Deutschland, *"LNN*, May 7, 1927.
1164. "Berta von Suttner" (1917) (Reprinted in *Begegnungen*, pp. 187-194).
1165. "Besuch bei den Milliarden" (1932) (Reprinted in *Begegnungen*, pp. 163-174).
1166. "Bildnis Busonis," *In*, VI : 1 (1924), 54-56 (Reprinted in *Begegnungen*, pp. 111-112).
1167. "Brief an einen französischen Freund," *Carossa* (Dec. 15, 1928), pp. 186-192 (Reprinted in *Begegnungen*, pp. 422-426).
1168. "Brief an Romain Rolland," *BT*, Dec. 22, 1912 (This letter was reprinted in French translation as a preface to Rolland's open letter to Gerhardt Hauptmann in the *JdG*, Sept. 2, 1914).
1169. "Brief eines deutschen Malers aus Italien," *InA* (1909), 128-132.
1170. "Brügge: das nördliche Venedig," *VFZM*, 23.J.: 3 (1902) (Altered version reprinted in *Zeit und Welt*, pp. 169-179).
1171. "Bruno Walter: Kunst der Hingabe," Paul Stefan Gruenfeldt, *Bruno Walter*. Wien: Reichner, 1936 (Reprinted in *Begegnungen*, pp. 127-129).
1172. "Das Buch als Eingang zur Welt," *PL*, Aug. 15, 1931 (Cf. also *SNT*, Nov. 28/29, 1931; *KT*, Dec. 6, 1931; *Begegnungen*, pp. 309-317).
1173. "Das Buch als Weltbild," *Un*, 45.J.: 1 (1928) (Cf. also *KHZ*, Mar. 22, 1929).
1174. "Bücherladen in London: Bermondsey Bookshop," *FVb*, III (1928), 301.
1175. "Bücher und der Krieg," *DBK*, IV (Jul.-Dec., 1915), 37.
1176. "Byroniana," *FZ* (Lit. Beil.), No. 602 (Cf. *DLE*, XXXII : 4 (1929-1930), 222; Cf. also "Max Brod," *DLz*, XVI (1929), 55-59).
1177. "Camille Lemonnier," *NFP*, Oct. 12, 1902.
1178. "Cäsar und Napoleon," *NR*, XXXVI : 5 (May, 1925), 521-525.
1179. "Eine Charakteristik von Paul Verlaine," *FZ*, 51 (1905).
1180. "Charles Baudelaire," *DD*, XXXII (Apr.-Sept., 1902), 65-68 (Reprinted in *MfL*, LXXII (May 15, 1903), 66-70).
1181. "Charles Baudelaire und Paul Verlaine in deutschem Gewande," *WZ*, 20178 (1903).

1182. "Charles Dickens," *Z*, LXX (Jan.-June, 1910), 249-264 (This article also serves as the Introduction to Dicken's *Ausgewählte Romane und Novellen*. Leipzig: Insel, 1910; Appeared in English translation by Kenneth Burke in *Di*, LXXIV (Jan., 1923), 1-24 (Picture of Zweig on page 16 by Henri le Fauconnier)).

1183. "Charles Theodor H. de Coster: 'Uilenspiegel,'" *MNN*, Dec. 29, 1910.

1184. "City Without a Heart: Chartres," *Tr*, LV (June, 1930), 28-30 (Tr. from the German by F. Ladislas).

1185. "Constant Meunier," *VFZM*, 22.J.: 9 (1902).

1186. "Crommelynck," *NR*, XIX : 4 (1908), 1852-1853.

1187. "Dank an die Bücher," *DBa*, 1 (1949), 1 (Reprinted in *Begegnungen*, pp. 449-450).

1188. "Dank an Romain Rolland," *PL*, Jan. 26, 1936.

1189. "Dante," *In*, III : 1 (Oct., 1921), 1-13 (Reprinted in *NFP*, Sept. 11, 1921 and *Begegnungen*, pp. 387-396).

1190. "Demokratische Menge und ihre Dichter," *Gwt*, 14 (Jan.-June, 1910).

1191. "Denkwürdiger Tag – Zum 100sten Geburtstag der 'Marienbader Elegie'," *In*, IV : 4 (1923), 243-253 (Reprinted in *NFP*, Sept. 2, 1923; Cf. also *Sternstunden der Menschheit*).

1192. "Deutsche Bücherei," *NFP*, Sept. 14, 1916.

1193. "Ein deutscher Dichter: Hermann Hesse," *KöT*, Oct. 24, 1915.

1194. "Le Dieu Pan," *E*, XVII (1930), 321-327.

1195. "Das Drama Verhaerens," *DSch*, 39 (June-Dec., 1910).

1196. "Die drei Meyer-Sammlungen," *BT*, June 17, 1924.

1197. "Echte und falsche Autographen," *ARsch*, VII (1926), 115.

1198. "Edmond Jaloux" (1931) (Reprinted in *Europäisches Erbe*, pp. 99-101).

1199. "Effects of War on the Future of Writing," *NYT*, VI (July 28, 1940), 2; VI (Aug. 25, 1940), 2.

1200. "Emil Ludwig at Fifty," *LA*, CCCXL (Apr., 1931), 163-167.

1201. "Emil Ludwig zum 50sten Geburtstag," *NFP*, Jan. 25, 1931.

1202. "Emile Verhaeren," *DLE*, V : 14 (Apr. 15, 1903), 972-978.

1203. "Emile Verhaeren – ein Dichter des Universums," *Ze*, Mar. 2, 1910.

1204. "E. M. Lilien," *MfL*, LXXII : 14 (Nov., 1903), 439-446; LXXII : 16 (Dec., 1903), 506-513 (This article serves as the Introduction to the book *E. M. Lilien. Sein Werk*. Berlin-Leipzig: Schuster and Loeffler, 1903).

1205. "Ernst Lissauer," *CVZ*, XI (1932), 501.

1206. "Ernst Renan," *NFP*, Feb. 25, 1923 (Reprinted in *Begegnungen*, pp. 373-386).

1207. *Europa – America latino* (Articles by Alcides Arquedas, E. Diez Canedo, Georges Duhamel, W. J. Entwistle, Joan Estelrich, F. de Fiqueiredo, P. Henriquez-Urena, C. Ibarguren, Conde Keyserling, Emil Ludwig, Jacques Maritain, R. H. Mottram, Afranio Peixoto, Louis Piérard, Alfonso Reyes, Carlos Reyles, Jules Romains, Francisco Romero, B. Sanin Cano, Juan B. Teran, G. Ungaretti, Stefan Zweig). Tr. E. M. S. Danero. Buenos Aires: Comision Argentina de Cooperacion Intelectuel, 1937.

1208. "Ex libris: Moderne Deutsche und ihre Künstler," *VFZM*, 22.J.: 2 (1902).

1209. "F. A. Brockhaus: Beschwerde gegen einen Verleger (Casanova betr.)," *BT*, June 29, 1926.

1210. "Das Feuer" (1918) (Reprinted in *Begegnungen*, pp. 207-218).

1211. "Fishermen on the Seine," *HM* CLXXXII (Feb., 1941), 273-275.

1212. "Flauberts Nachlass," *BT*, Jan. 11, 1911 (Cf. also *DLE*, XIII : 12 (Mar. 15, 1911), 879-881).

1213. *Flüchtiger Spiegelblick*. Leipzig: Insel, 1927 (Promotion material).

1214. "Flug und Wort," *BT*, Aug. 23, 1913.

1215. "Frans Masereel," *Masereel* (Cf. the 1923 article "Frans Masereel. Der Mann und Bildner" reprinted in *Begegnungen*, pp. 130-139).

1216. "Franz Karl Ginskey zum 60sten Geburtstag des Dichters am 8.9.1931," *PL*, Sept. 6, 1931 (Cf. also *ÖR*, 17.J. (June-Dec., 1931), 845; *Un*, 49 (1931)).

1217. "Für Jacob Wassermann (by Thomas Mann, Stefan Zweig, Hermann Hesse and

Alfred Döblin)," *NR*, XLIV : 3 (Mar., 1933), 357-361 (Cf. also *DL*, XXXV : 8 (1932-1933), 468).

1218. "Die Gärten im Kriege" (1939) (Reprinted in *Zeit und Welt*, pp. 121-125).

1219. "Galiziens Genesung," *NFP*, Aug. 31, 1915.

1220. "Geburtstagsgruss an Schalom Asch," *DLW*, VI : 43 (1930), 1.

1221. "Dem Gedächtnis Jacob Julius Davids," *DIDÖ* (Feb., 1906), 1-3 (Cf. also *ÖR*, IX : 3 (Nov.-Dec., 1906), 217-219 and *Blätter*, 4/5 (April, 1959), 5-7).

1222. "Die gefangenen Dinge: Brüsseler Weltausstellung," *NFP*, Aug. 17, 1910.

1223. "Das Geheimnis der Beatrice Cenci," *MZ*, May 1, 1927 (Cf. *NFP*, Dec. 2, 1926 and *Zeit und Welt*, pp. 103-115).

1224. "Das Geheimnis des künstlerischen Schaffens," Lecture given in America, 1938 (Reprinted in *Zeit und Welt*, pp. 251-274).

1225. "Der geistige Aufbau der neuen Generation," *NFP*, Nov. 20, 1932.

1226. "Die Geschichte als Dichterin,"A lecture destined to be delivered at the International P.E.N. Club in Stockholm, Sept., 1939 before the outbreak of World War II intervened (Reprinted in *Zeit und Welt*, pp. 337-360).

1227. "Geschichtsschreibung von morgen," Lecture in America before the outbreak of World War II (Reprinted in *Zeit und Welt*, pp. 275-298).

1228. "G. Falke: Stadt mit den goldenen Türmen. Falke zu seinem 6osten Geburtstag," *BT*, Jan. 7, 1913.

1229. "Ghetto Stimmungen," *DLE*, 10. J. (1908), 1344-1349 (Contributions by St. Zweig, L. Adelt and P. Neuburger).

1230. "Great Lesson from a Great Man: Rodin," *CW*, CLI (Aug., 1940), 599-601 (Printed simultaneously in *RD*, XXXVII (Aug., 1940), 26-28; Cf. also *WE*, 2.J.: 5 (1947-1948), 48-50).

1231. "Gustav Mahlers Wiederkehr," *NFP*, April 25, 1915 (Reprinted in *Europäisches Erbe*, pp. 172-182).

1232. "Gwalior: die indische Residenz," *BT*, Mar. 20, 1909.

1233. "Hans Carossa," *BT*, Nov. 8, 1928 (Reprinted in *Begegnungen*, pp. 422-426).

1234. "Hans Franck," *MNN*, July 30, 1929.

1235. "Hartrott and Hitler," *FW*, IV (Dec., 1942), 234-235.

1236. "Das Haus der tausend Schicksale" (London, 1937) (Reprinted in *Begegnungen*, pp. 219-222).

1237. "H. Benzmann," *F* 29 (1903).

1238. "Heimkehr zu Goethe," *NR*, XXII : 9 (Sept., 1921), 1007.

1239. "Heinrich Lammasch," *BT*, Jan. 20, 1920.

1240. "Herbstwinter in Meran," *Blätter*, 6/7 (Oct., 1959), 14-18 (First printing of this essay in *Fahrten* (1919; 2. ed. 1922); Cf. Joseph Maurer, "Über Zweigs Aufsatz 'Herbstwinter in Meran'," *Blätter*, 6/7 Oct., 1959), 18-19).

1241. "Hermann Bahr. Zu seinem 6osten Geburtstag," *NFP*, July 19, 1923 (Reprinted in *Begegnungen*, pp. 106-110).

1242. "Das Herz Europas. Ein Besuch im Genfer Roten Kreuz" (Dec., 1917) (Reprinted in *Begegnungen*, pp. 194-207).

1243. "Hommage à Romain Rolland," *Com*, III : 31 (Mar., 1936), 789-801 (Tribute to Rolland's 7oth birthday).

1244. "Honoré de Balzac," *HN* (Beilage), 15 (1906) (Cf. also *Z*, LXIV (1908), 53-62, 100-111).

1245. "Hugo von Hofmannsthal. Gedächtnisrede zur Trauerfeier im Wiener Burgtheater" (1929) (Reprinted in *Zeit und Welt*, pp. 33-48).

1246. "Die indische Gefahr für England," *NFP*, July 13, 1909.

1247. "Internationalismus oder Kosmopolitanismus," *DLW*, II : 27 (1929), 1.

1248. "Irrfahrt und Ende Pierre Bonchamps'. Die Tragödie Daudets," *NFP*, Mar. 28, 1926 (Reprinted in *Zeit und Welt*, pp. 89-102).

1249. "Isolde Weisshand," *NR*, XX : 3 (1909), 1229-1230.

1250. "Ist die Geschichte gerecht?" *DK*, I : 2 (1952-1953), 3 (Cf. *WaM*, June 9, 1952; Reprinted in *Blätter*, 3 (Oct., 1958), 1-2; *Europäisches Erbe*, pp. 271-273).

1251. "Jacob Wassermann," *NR*, 33.J.II: 8 (1912), 1131-1145 (Reprinted in *Europäisches Erbe*, pp. 187-208).
1252. "Jean Christophe," *LF*, 11 (Mar., 1913), 481-543 (Articles and replies concerning Rolland's novel *Jean Christophe* by Stefan Zweig, Georges Duhamel, Charles Lemonnier, Emile Verhaeren *et al.*).
1253. "Jeremias Gotthelf und Jean Paul," *BT*, May 14, 1924.
1254. "Johannes Schlaf," *DLE*, IV : 20 (July, 1902), 1377-1388 (Also contains a Zweig portrait).
1255. "Joseph Roth," Eulogy at funeral services in Paris, 1939 (Reprinted in *Europäisches Erbe*, pp. 251-264).
1256. "Juden in einem allgemeinen politischen Leben," *OS*, 1 (April, 1939), 103-105.
1257. "Jüngste Generation der deutschen Lyriker," *DLW*, III : 10 (1929), 4.
1258. "Karl Haushofer," *ZfG*, 26.J. (1955), 768-769.
1259. "Karl Loewe, der Dichter," *NFP*, Feb. 18, 1912.
1260. "Die Kathedrale von Chartres" (1924) (Reprinted in *Zeit und Welt*, pp. 183-190).
1261. "Kleine Reise nach Brasilien" (Fall, 1936) (Reprinted in *Begegnungen*, pp. 274-305).
1262. "König der Juden," *Herzl*, pp. 55-57 (Cf. also "Erinnerungen an Theodor Herzl," *Begegnungen*, pp. 88-95).
1263. "Die Kunst des Briefes," *Blätter*, 15 (Jan., 1963), 8-9 (First printed as an epilogue to Otto Heuschele's *Briefe aus Einsamkeiten*, Berlin: n.p., 1922).
1264. "Kunst und Wirklichkeit. Bermerkungen zum Drama 'Lord Byron kommt aus der Mode'," *PTb* (1930), 59 (Cf. *DLz*, XVI (1929), 55-59 and *DL*, XXXII : 4 (1929-1930), 222).
1265. "Laukhard der Landstörtzer," *NR*, XIX : 3 (1908), 1389-1391.
1266. "Legende und Wahrheit der Beatrice Cenci," *NFP*, Dec. 2, 1926 (Reprinted in *Zeit und Welt*, pp. 103-115; Cf. also *MZ*, May 1, 1927).
1267. "Die Lektion, die mir Auguste Rodin erteilt hat," *WE*, 2.J.: 5 (1947-1948), 48-50 (Cf. "Great Lesson from a Great Man: Rodin," *CW*, CLI (Aug., 1940), 599-601 and *RD*, XXXVII (Aug., 1940), 26-28).
1268. "Lemonniers 'L'Homme en Amour'," *MfL*, LXXII : 13 (Oct., 1903), 407-409 (First printed as the Introduction to the German translation of this work. Tr. Paul Adler. Leipzig: Rothbarth, 1903).
1269. "Leo Feld, Gedächtnis eines Freundes," *NFP*, May 16, 1925.
1270. "Léon Bazalgette" (1927) (Reprinted in *Europäisches Erbe*, pp. 95-98).
1271. "Lettres allemandes," *RE*, Jan., 1929.
1272. "Os Livros subterrâneos de Balzac," Tr. Milton Araryo. *Balzac. Historia dos treze...* Rio de Janeiro, 1952 (Original version appeared as "Die unterirdischen Bücher Balzacs," *In*, II : 2 (1920), 71-77; Reprinted in *Begegnungen*, pp. 427-431).
1273. "Lob des deutschen Verlegers," *VZ*, Nov. 9, 1912.
1274. "Lord Byron," *In*, V : 3 (July, 1924), 147-156 (Reprinted in *Zeit und Welt*, 9-20).
1275. "The Lord gave the Word," Tr. Eden and Cedar Paul. *PR*, XXXVIII (Dec., 1936), 12-13 (Excerpt from the Paul translation of "Händel's Messiah" in *Twelve Historical Miniatures*. New York: Viking, 1940).
1276. "Die Lyrik um Stefan George," *DLE*, VI : 3 (Nov. 1, 1903), 169-172.
1277. "Der lyrische Nachwuchs," *VFZM*, 22.J.: 11 (1903) (Eleven literary portraits).
1278. "Marcel Prousts tragischer Lebenslauf," *MfL*, 4 (1953), 1, 6 (Cf. *NFP*, Sept. 27, 1925; *PL*, Feb. 22, 1931; *Ze*, 9.J.: 3 (1954), 6; Entire article reprinted in *Zeit und Welt*, pp. 21-31).
1279. "Mater Dolorosa. Die Briefe von Nietzsches Mutter an Overbeck" (1937) (Reprinted in *Zeit und Welt*, pp. 55-64).
1280. "Max Brod," *DLz*, XVI (1929), 55-59 (This article concerns Brod's drama *Lord Byron kommt aus der Mode*. Wien: Zsolnay, 1929; Cf. also *DL*, XXXII : 4 (1929-1930), 222; *PTb* (1930), 59 and *Wi*, I/II (1929), 124).
1281. "Max Brod. Zu seinem 50sten Geburtstag," *Brod* (1934).
1282. "Max Hermann-Neisse. Kleine Festrede an einen deutschen Dichter in der Emigration zum 50sten Geburtstag," *PL*, May 31, 1936.

1283. "Max Hermann-Neisse zum Gedächtnis," *Au(NY)*, Apr. 18, 1941 (Reprinted as a postscript to Hermann-Neisse's book of poems *Erinnerung und Exil*. Zürich: Oprecht, 1946; Cf. also *Blätter*, 11/12 (Oct., 1961), 13-15).
1284. "Maxim Gorki zu seinem 60sten Geburtstag," *NFP*, Mar. 25, 1928 (Cf. also *VQR*, 5 (Oct., 1929), 492-501 and *Begegnungen*, pp. 96-105).
1285. "Meine Autographensammlung," *Ph*, III : 7 (1930), 279-289.
1286. "The Mission of the Intellectuals," *AIR*, XIII : 152 (Sept., 1941), 2 (Cf. *AIR*, XV : 167/168 (Feb.-Mar., 1947) for a reproduction of Zweig's letter to the Editor in Chief of the periodical concerning this article).
1287. "Moissi im Gespräch," *Moissi*, pp. 56-57.
1288. "Die Monotonisierung der Welt," *NFP*, Jan. 31, 1925 (Reprinted in *FuS*, II (1928), 65-69 and *Begegnungen*, pp. 155-162).
1289. "Montaigne," *NR*, XI (1948), 257-265 (Entire article reprinted in *Europäisches Erbe*, pp. 7-81).
1290. "Die moralische Entgiftung Europas," Lecture before the Academia di Roma, 1932 (Reprinted in *Begegnungen*, pp. 223-236).
1291. "Moskauer Theater," *HaN*, Jan. 11, 1929.
1292. "Musset und Baudelaire in deutscher Übertragung," *FZ*, June 1, 1924.
1293. "Nach einem Jahr – deutsch-französische Gesellschaft," *DFR*, II (1929), 1-5.
1294. "Das neue Belgien," *AZ*, 43 (1909).
1295. "Neue Lyrik," *F*, VI : 3 (1904), 49-51.
1296. "Neue Napoleon Manuskripte," *Ph.*, II (1929), 246.
1297. "Das neue Pathos," *DLE*, XI : 24 (Sept. 15, 1909), 1701-1707.
1298. "1914 und heute. Anlässlich des Romans von Roger Martin du Gard 'Eté 1914'" (1936) (Reprinted in *Zeit und Welt*, pp. 329-336).
1299. "Nietzsche und der Freund," *InA* (1919), 111-123 (Originally printed in *NFP*, Dec. 21, 1917).
1300. "Der Orient: Drama in Tausendundeiner Nacht," *NFP*, Jan. 30, 1917.
1301. "Oskar A. H. Schmitz," *Schmitz* (1923).
1302. "Ostende, Saisontage," *VFZM*, 22.J.: 2 (1902).
1303. "Oskar Březina," *ÖR*, XIX : 6 (June, 1909), 444-450 (Discussion of the German version of Březina's *Hände*, translated from the Czech by Emil Saudek. Wien: Moritz Frisch, 1908; Reprinted in *Karel Ločak v Praze*. Tr. Zdenek Doležil).
1304. "Oxford" (1907) (Reprinted in *Zeit und Welt*, pp. 193-202).
1305. "Paul Verlaine," *MfL*, LXXI : 40 (Oct. 4, 1902), 313-315.
1306. "Peter Rosegger. Zum Tod des Dichters," *Nz*, June 26, 1918 (Reprinted in *Europäisches Erbe*, pp. 209-213).
1307. "Le Poésie de Goethe," *LNL*, XX (Oct., 1949), 6 (Cf. *Begegnungen*, pp. 397-405).
1308. "Pour Ramuz," *Ramuz* (1938) (Cf. *Europäisches Erbe*, pp. 122-126).
1309. "Ein Prager Dichter," *PT*, XXVII (1903), 141 (About Paul Leppin).
1310. "Profit from my Experience," *RD*, XXXIX (July, 1941), 39-43.
1311. "Prolog und Epilog zu Shakespeares 'Sturm,' Quasi una Phantasia," *InA* (1926), 68-75.
1312. "Proust Himself," *AM*, CXLVI (Nov., 1930), 606-610 (Cf. 1278).
1313. "Provisorisches über Rudolf Pannwitz," *DLE*, XXIV : 16 (May 15, 1922), 982-984.
1314. "Un pur Poète: Rainer Maria Rilke," *RE* (Jan., 1929), 1394-1401.
1315. "Rabindranath Tagores 'Sadhâna'. Ein zeitgemässes Gespräch," *DLE*, XXIV : 1 (Oct. 1, 1921), 1-6 (Cf. *Europäisches Erbe*, pp. 148-156).
1316. "Rainer Maria Rilke," *MNN*, Feb. 22, 1927 (Cf. "Abschied von Rilke" (1927), reprinted in *Begegnungen*, pp. 59-73; Cf. also *DSlb*, II (1946), 170).
1317. "Rainer Maria Rilke," Lecture in London, 1936 (Reprinted in *Europäisches Erbe*, pp. 244-250).
1318. "Rainer Maria Rilke in Paris," *Erz*, 2.J.: 7 (1948), 3-6.
1319. "Rathenau Reflexionen: der Kaufmann und der Künstler," *NFP*, Sept. 18, 1908.
1320. "Reconnaissance," *Hommage*, pp. 86-91.

1321. "Reise nach Russland," *NFP*, Oct. 23, 26, 28, 1928 (Reprinted in *KHZ*, Nov. 29, 1928 and *Zeit und Welt*, pp. 203-245).
1322. "R. H. Francé als Bildner," *Francé*, p. 35.
1323. "Der Rhythmus von New York," *SP*, Dec. 7, 1913 (Reprinted in *DA*, Dec. 8, 1913 and *Begegnungen*, pp. 264-270).
1324. "Romain Rolland," *LJZ*, 7 (1926).
1325. "Romain Rolland," Lecture in Berlin, Meistersaal, Jan. 29, 1926 (Reprinted in *Europäisches Erbe*, pp. 102-121).
1326. "Romain Rolland after the War," *Di*, LXXVI (May, 1924), 445-448.
1327. "Romain Rolland, el Hombre y la Obre," *Ud*, I : 3 (April, 1936), 5-6.
1328. "Romain Rolland und 'Jean Christophe'," *NFP*, Mar. 20, 1914, pp. 1-4.
1329. "Romain Rolland und der Ruhm," *NFP*, Mar. 20, 1914.
1330. "Die Romantik der Bourgeoisie," *InA* (1911), 112-123.
1331. "Rousseau, der Erzieher zu einer neuen Gesellschaft," *DAZ*, Dec. 8, 1918 (Reprinted in *WZ*, Mar. 23, 1921).
1332. "Rückkehr zum Märchen," *NFP*, Dec. 14, 1913.
1333. "Sainte-Beuve," *NFP*, May 6, 1923 (This article also serves as the Intro. to the German version of Sainte-Beuve's *Literarische Portraits aus dem Frankreich des XVII-XIX. Jahrhunderts*. Frankfurt am Main: Frankfurter Verlagsanstalt, 1923; Reprinted in *Begegnungen*, pp. 406-417.)
1334. "Salzburg: Die Stadt als Rahmen," *Herz* (1935) (Reprinted in *Begegnungen*, pp. 271-273 und *Blätter*, 2 (July, 1958), 1-4).
1335. "Die Sammlung Morrison," *VZ*, Sept. 6, 1917 (Reprinted in *DBK*, VI (1918), 73).
1336. "Die schlaflose Welt," *NFP*, Aug., 1914 (Reprinted in *Begegnungen*, pp. 175-180).
1337. "Schnitzler und die Jugend," *M*, May 15, 1912 (Schnitzler Geburtstagssondernummer, zu seinem 50sten Geburtstag) (Reprinted in *Blätter*, 13/14 (April, 1962), 10-12).
1338. "Das schönste Grab der Welt: Tolstois Grab," Excerpt from 'Eine Russlandreise'" (1928) (Reprinted in *Begegnungen*, pp. 262-263).
1339. "Die Schweiz als Hilfsland Europas," *Do*, II (1918), 832-834).
1340. "Selbstanzeige: Gedichte von Paul Verlaine," *Z*, XL (Sept. 27, 1902), 536.
1341. "Shakespeare," *FTb* (1927-1928), 173.
1342. "Sigmund Freud, der Siebzigjährige," *DLW*, II : 19 (1929), 1.
1343. "Sigmund Freuds 75ster Geburtstag," *CVZ*, X (1931), 237.
1344. "Sigmund Freud zum 80sten Geburtstag," *PL*, May 3, 1936.
1345. "Sinn und Schönheit der Autographen," *DNSch*, 19.J. (1958), 118 (Original version was a lecture given at a book exhibition of the *London Sunday Times* (1935); Reprinted in *Begegnungen* (1937 ed.), pp. 469-476; *Begegnungen* (1955 ed.), pp. 441-448; An excerpt of this lecture is used as an Intro. to the volume *Lyrische Handschriften unserer Zeit* (50 Gedichthandschriften deutscher Lyriker der Gegenwart). Ed. Hartfrid Voss. Ebenhausen bei München: Hartfrid Voss, 1958, p. 5).
1346. "Soyka," *NR*, XXII : 2 (1911), 1638-1640.
1347. "Stefan Georges Stellung im deutschen Geistesleben," *DLE*, IV : 28 (July 13, 1928) (Autobiographical notes from Walter Benjamin, Bert Brecht, Martin Buber, Willy Hellpach, Friedrich Muckermann, Josef Ponten, Franz Rosenzweig, Wilhelm Schäfer, Ruth Schaumann, P. Expeditus Schmidt, Oscar A. H. Schmitz, Ina Seidel. Reminiscenses from French contemporaries: Albert Saint-Paul, André Gide, Francis Vielé Griffin. Friedrich Sternthal: "Zu Georges Politeia." Reproduction of the manuscript of "Ein Angelico" with a dedication to Albert Saint-Paul and a picture of him in his youth. *DLE*, IV : 29 (July 20, 1928) – further contributions by Frank Thiess, Paul Wiegler, Karl Wolfskehl, Stefan Zweig. Cf. also Max Rychner, "Zeitgenossen über Stefan George," *NSchR*, XXI : 34 (1928), 561-563).
1348. "Stefan Zweig über Henri Barbusse. Nachwort zum Roman 'Die Schutzflehenden',"

   Blätter, 13/14 (April, 1962), 14-15 (Cf. also the essay "Das Feuer," *Begegnungen*, pp. 207-218 concerning Barbusse's antiwar novel 'Le Feu').

1349. "Standhals deutsche Wiederkehr," *FZ*, Dec. 6, 1921.

1350. "Die Stimme. In memoriam Josef Kainz," *Begegnungen*, pp. 140-147.

1351. "Die Stunde zwischen zwei Ozeanen – der Panama Kanal," *NFP*, July 6, 1911 (Reprinted in *Begegnungen*, pp. 239-247).

1352. "Der Suez Kanal," *NFP*, Nov. 18, 1914.

1353. "Das Tagebuch des jungen Flauberts," *Pan* (Jan.-June, 1911), 181-188, 226-234.

1354. "Das Tagebuch eines halbwüchsigen Mädchens," *AdP* (1926), 140-145.

1355. "Thanks to Books," Tr. Theodore W. Koch. *Lib*, XXXV (Mar., 1930), 113-114 (Reprinted in *Librarians*, pp. 3-4; *SRL*, XLI (Feb. 8, 1958), 24; *WLB*, XXXII (Mar., 1958), 477-478; Cf. also original "Dank an die Bücher," reprinted in *Begegnungen*, pp. 449-450).

1356. "Theresa Feodor Ries," *VFZM*, 21.J. :21 (1902).

1357. "Thomas Mann: 'Lotte in Weimar'" (1939) (Reprinted in *Zeit und Welt*, pp. 363-366; Tr. into English in *The Stature of Thomas Mann. Anthology of Critical Essays*. Ed. Charles Neider, New York: New Directions, 1947; London: Owens, 1951, pp. 188-190).

1357a. "Thomas Mann zum 50sten Geburtstag," *BT*, May 31, 1925, p. 5 (Messages of congratulations from Hermann Bahr, Rudolf Binding, Waldemar Bonsels, Herbert Eulenberg, Jakob Wassermann, Stefan Zweig, Alfons Paquet, Walter von Molo, Wilhelm von Scholz, Wilhelm Schäfer).

1358. "Tolstoi als religiöser und sozialer Denker" (1937) (Reprinted in *Zeit und Welt*, pp. 67-88).

1359. "Tolstois Lehre," *Gewalt*, pp. 227-232.

1360. "Die Tragik der Vergesslichkeit" (1919) (Reprinted in *Europäisches Erbe*, pp. 265-270).

1361. "Der Turm zu Babel," *VZ*, May 8, 1916 (Reprinted in *PL*, Jan. 1, 1930 and *Europäisches Erbe*, pp. 274-279; Appeared as "La Tour de Babel" in *LC* (April-May, 1916); This article was translated into English by Eden and Cedar Paul as "The Workers Dread Nought," cf. Charles Baudouin, *Contemporary Studies*. Tr. Eden and Cedar Paul. London: Allen and Unwin, 1924, p. 283).

1362. "Überschätzung der Lebenden," *ARsch*, 7.J.: VII (1926), 19.

1363. "Um Jaurès," *NFP*, Aug. 6, 1916 (Reprinted in *V*, Aug. 29, 1916 and *Europäisches Erbe*, pp. 85-94).

1364. "Die unterirdischen Bücher Balzacs," *DBib*, V (1916), 48-52 (Reprinted in *In*, II: 2 (Dec., 1920), 71-77 and *Begegnungen*, pp. 427-431).

1365. "Unvergessliches Erlebnis. Ein Tag bei Albert Schweitzer," *Schweitzer*, pp. 7-19 (Cf. *In*, XIV : 2 (1933), 73-83).

1366. "Verlaine," *DDi*, III (1905).

1367. "Die Vernachlässigten" (Antworten auf die Rundfrage von F. W. Bischoff, B. Diebold, H. Eulenberg, O. Flake, M. Hermann-Neisse, H. Hesse, H. Kasack, C. Köppen, Th. Mann, G. Pohl, E. M. Remarque, W. von Scholz, H. Sochaczewer, Stefan Zweig), *DLe*, III (1930), 1-2 (Cf. also *DL*, XXXII : 10 (1929-1930), 593).

1368. "Verse eines Gottsuchers," *DN*, XXIII (1905-1906), 571 f.

1369. "Die Verstümmelten," *NR*, XXXIV : 11 (Nov., 1923), 1054-1055.

1370. "Victor Hugo als Lyriker," *MfL*, LXXI : 11 (Mar. 15, 1902), 81-83.

1371. "Vom österreichischen Dichter. Ein Wort zur Zeit," *DLE*, XVII : 5 (Dec., 1914), 263-265.

1372. "Vom Sinn unseres Jahrhunderts," *Abz*, Sept. 6, 1932.

1373. "Von den Bäumen," *Kt*, 24.J. (June-Dec., 1911), 42.

1374. "Vorbeigehen an einem unauffälligen Menschen – Otto Weininger," *BT*, Oct. 3, 1926 (Reprinted in *Europäisches Erbe*, pp. 223-226).

1375. "Walter Rathenau," Written immediately after his assassination on June 24, 1922 (Reprinted in *Europäisches Erbe*, pp. 232-243).

1376. "Walt Whitman," *NFP*, May 28, 1919.
1377. "Warum meine Bücher Erfolg hatten," *RvB*, 29 (1949), 20-21.
1378. "Warum nur Belgien, warum nicht auch Polen? Eine Frage an die Neutralen," *NFP*, Apr. 14, 1915.
1379. "Wedekind, der Unbürgerliche," *Wedekind*, pp. 242-244.
1380. "Der Weg A.T. Wegners," *BT*, Dec. 15, 1921.
1381. "Der Weg Hermann Hesses," *NFP*, Feb. 6, 1923, pp. 1-3.
1382. "Die Welt der Autographen," *DBK*, 12./13.J. (1927), 70-77 (Cf. *JDB*, XII/ XIII (1925-1926), 70-77).
1383. "Where France Hoards Gold," *LA*, CCCXLII (May, 1932), 214-220.
1384. "Das Wien von gestern," Lecture in Paris, 1940 (Reprinted in *Zeit und Welt*, pp. 129-150).
1385. "Wilhelm Holzamer," *MfL*, LXXI : 38 (Sept. 20, 1902), 297-298.
1386. "Wille zur Universalität," *Kippenberg*, pp. 154-161.
1387. "Worte am Sarge Sigmund Freuds," Delivered at the Crematorium in London, Sept. 26, 1939 (Reprinted in *Zeit und Welt*, pp. 51-54).
1388. "Würdigung Ödön von Horvaths," *BdTG*, 67 (1954-1955).
1389. "Ypern," *BT*, Sept. 16, 1928 (Reprinted in *Begegnungen*, pp. 248-253).
1390. "Zu Emil Luckas 50sten Geburtstag," *KZ*, May 12, 1927.
1391. "Zum 70sten Geburtstag von Sigmund Freud," *MNN*, May 5, 1926 (Reprinted in *AdP* (1937)).
1392. "Zur Entstehung des 'Volpone'," *NZZ*, Sept. 28, 1927.
1393. "Zur Geschichte des europäischen Gedankens," *Abz*, Jan. 29, 1933 (Cf. *Zeit und Welt*, pp. 299-326).
1394. "Zur modernen Lyrik," *KdöL*, XVII (July-Dec., 1901), 38-40.
1395. "Zur Physiologie des dichterischen Schaffens. Ein Fragebogen," *DLW*, 39 (1928), 3-4; 40 (1928), 3; 41 (1928), 3-4.
1396. "Zur Schutzfristfrage," *BdBh*, May 7, 1927.
1397. "Zutrauen zur Zukunft," *Frau*, pp. 7-17.
1398. "Zu Verhaerens 10ten Todestag," *DLW*, II : 48 (1926), 4.
1399. "Zwei Aphorismen," *DD*, XXVIII (Apr.-Sept., 1900), 240.
1400. "Zwei Aphorismen," *DD*, XXVIII (Apr.-Sept., 1900), 299.

XIV. TRANSLATIONS BY ZWEIG

1401. Barbusse, Henri. *Die Schutzflehenden. Der Roman einer Vorkriegsjugend.* Zürich-Leipzig-Stuttgart: Rascher and Cie, 1932 (Tr. and epilogue by Zweig).
1402. Baudelaire, Charles. *Die Blumen des Bösen.* Berlin: Oesterheld, 1921 (Tr. of eight poems).
1403. — *Gedichte in Vers und Prosa.* Leipzig: Hermann Seemann Nachfolger, 1902 (Tr. with Camill Hoffmann; Introductory essay by Zweig entitled "Charles Baudelaire", pp. 7-20).
1404. — "Der Albatros" (poem), *DD*, XXX (Apr.-Sept., 1901), 246.
1405. — "La Beauté" (poem), *MfL*, LXXII : b (May 15, 1903), 65.
1406. — "La Beauté" (poem), *Weltdichtung*, p. 161.
1407. — "Le Chat" (poem), *MfL*, LXXII : b (May 15, 1903), 65.
1408. — "Don Juan aux Enfers" (poem), *MfL*, LXXII : b (May 15, 1903), 65.
1409. — "Der Duft" (poem), *DD*, XXX (Apr.-Sept., 1901), 247.
1410. — "L'irreparable" (poem), *DD*, XXX (Apr.-Sept., 1901), 289.
1411. — "Harmonien" (poem), *DD*, XXX (Apr.-Sept., 1901), 246.
1412. — "Herbstlied" (poem), *DD*, XXX (Apr.-Sept., 1901), 248 (Reprinted in *Spiegelungen*, p. 32).
1413. — "Die Katze" (poem), *DD*, XXX (Apr.-Sept., 1901), 247.
1414. — "Der Mensch und das Meer" (poem), *DD*, XXX (Apr.-Sept., 1901), 246.

1415. — "Die Musik" (poem), *DD*, XXX (Apr.-Sept., 1901), 248.
1416. — "Noch heute" (poem), *DD*, XXX (Apr.-Sept., 1901), 246).
1417. — "Der Rahmen" (poem), *DD*, XXXI (Oct., 1901 - Mar., 1902), 50.
1418. — "Die Riesin" (poem), *DD*, XXXI (Oct., 1901 - Mar., 1902), 50.
1419. — "Die Seele des Weins" (poem), *DD*, XXXI (Oct., 1901 - Mar., 1902), 25.
1420. — "Semper eadem" (poem), *DD*, XXX (Apr.-Sept., 1901), 247.
1421. — "Spleen" (poem), *DD*, XXX (Apr.-Sept., 1901), 266.
1422. — "Was sagst Du heute..." (poem), *DD*, XXX (Apr.-Sept., 1901), 247.
1423. — "Der Wein des Einsamen" (poem), *DD*, XXX (Apr.-Sept., 1901), 248.
1424. — "Der Wiederkehrende" (poem), *DD*, XXX (Apr.-Sept., 1901), 248.
1425. Browning, Elizabeth Barrett. "Blasse Liebe" (poem), *DD*, XXXI (Oct., 1901 - Mar., 1902), 96.
1426. Camoens. "Weh, wieviel Not und Fährnis auf dem Meere" (poem), *Europäer*, p. 13 and p. 369 (Cf. also *Leben-Werk*, p. 89 and *Spiegelungen*, p. 102).
1427. Edman, Irwin. *Ein Schimmer Licht im Dunkel*. Stockholm: Bermann-Fischer, 1940 (Tr. by Stefan Zweig and Richard Friedenthal).
1428. Hugo, Victor. "Juninacht" (poem), *DD*, XXXI (Oct., 1901 - Mar., 1902), 254.
1429. Keats, John. "Sonett" (poem), *Spiegelungen*, p. 34 (Zweig's rendition of Keats' last sonnet).
1430. Lemonnier, Camille. "Alte Leutchen," *Ze*, 486 (1904), 37-38, 47-48.
1431. de Lentino, Jacopo. "Sonett" (poem), *FrA* (1923).
1432. Marx, Madeline. *Weib. Roman*. Basel: Rhein Verlag, 1920 (Tr. by Stefan and Friderike Maria Zweig).
1433. Pirandello, Luigi. *Man weiss nicht wie* (Drama: *Non si sa come*). Wien: Reichner, 1935.
1434. Rolland, Romain. *Clerambault. Geschichte eines freien Gewissens im Kriege*. Frankfurt am Main: Rütten and Loening, 1922 (Reissued in München: Kindler and Schiermeyer, 1960).
1435. — *Den hingerichteten Völkern* (*Aux peuples assassinés*). Zürich: Rascher, 1918.
1436. — *Die Zeit wird kommen* (*Le Temps viendra*). Wien-Leizpig: Tal, 1919 (Reissued in Leipzig-Zürich: Rotapfel, 1921 and Zürich: Hofmann, 1945).
1437. Russell, Archibald B. H. *Die visionäre Kunstphilosophie des William Blake*. Leipzig: Julius Zeitler, 1906.
1438. Silvestre, Armand. "Kennst Du...?" (poem), *DD*, XXVII (Oct., 1899 - Mar., 1900), 220.
1439. — "Zärtliche Verse" (poem), *DD*, XXVII (Oct., 1899 - Mar., 1900), 188.
1440. Suarès, André. *Cressida*. Wien: Tal, 1920 (Tr. by Stefan Zweig and Erwin Rieger).
1441. Symons, Arthur. "Die Schönheit spricht" (poem), *Spiegelungen*, p. 33.
1442. Verhaeren, Emile. *Ausgewählte Gedichte*. Berlin: Schuster and Loeffler, 1904.
1443. — *Ausgewählte Gedichte*. Leipzig: Insel, 1910 (Forms Vol. II of Zweig's translation of Verhaeren's "Ausgewählte Werke"; Reprinted 1913, 1923).
1444. — *Drei Dramen: Helenas Heimkehr – Philipp II – Das Kloster*. Leipzig: Insel, 1910 (2. ed., 1914; Vol. III of the "Ausgewählte Werke").
1445. — *Helenas Heimkehr*. Leipzig: Insel, 1909 (Unpublished ms. of the original translation; Première Stuttgarter Hoftheater, Oct. 13, 1910).
1446. — *Helenas Heimkehr. Drama in Vier Akten*. Leipzig: Reclams Universalbibliothek, 1928 (No. 6850).
1447. — *Hymnen an das Leben*. Leipzig: Insel, 1911 (Reprinted 1912, 1919, 1931; Intro. by Zweig; Inselbücherei, No. 5).
1448. — *Rembrandt*, Leipzig: Insel, 1912 (Reprinted 1918, 1920, 1923).
1449. — *Rubens*. Leipzig: Insel, 1913 (Reprinted 1917, 1920, 1922).
1450. — "Abendstimmung" (poem), *InA* (1914), 128-130.
1451. — "An meine Augen" (poem), *In*, VIII : 1 (Christmas, 1926), 65-68.
1452. — "Die Arbeit" (poem), *Lyrik*, p. 537 (Translation of the poem by Zweig, Rilke and Stefan George).
1453. — "Der Baum" (poem), *InA* (1910), 18-21.
1454. — "Der Baum" (poem) *RRh*, 6.a.: 8/9 (May-June, 1926), 27-29.

1455. — "Die Bäume" (poem), *Lyrik*, p. 588 (Translation of the poem by Zweig, Rilke and Stefan George).
1456. — "Dialog" (poem), *DSt*, I (1911-1912), 92-94.
1457. — "Eines Abends" (prose tr. of a poem), *InA* (1921), 26-28.
1458. — "Die Freude" (poem), *NR*, III : 19 (1908), 1371-1372.
1459. — "Die Freude" (poem), *RRh*, I : 3 (1920-1921), 149.
1460. — "Hymnen an das Leben" (poem), *Antlitz*.
1461. — "Die Ideen" (poem), *InA* (1914), 123-125.
1462. — "Die kleinen Städte" (prose tr. of a poem), *InA* (1921), 24-26.
1463. — "Die letzte Sonne" (poem), *Spiegelungen*, pp. 34-35.
1464. — Neun Gedichte, *Franz. Dichter*, pp. 197-209 (Tr. Erna Heinemann-Grautoff and Stefan Zweig).
1465. — "Rings um mein Haus" (poem), *In*, VIII : 1 (Christmas, 1926), 63-65.
1466. — "Die Singspielhallen" (poem), *DSt*, I (1911-1912), 90-92.
1467. — "Die Ströme" (poem), *InA* (1914), 125-128.
1468. — "Tanz der Greise und Greisinnen" (poem), *InA* (1913), 168-172.
1469. — "Die Toten" (poem), *Lyrik*, p. 536 (Translation of the poem by Zweig, Rilke and Stefan George).
1470. — "Die Träume" (poem), *RRh*, I : 3 (1920-1921), 149-150.
1471. — "Die Wege" (poem), *InA* (1921), 23-24.
1472. — "Das Wort" (poem), *InA* (1911), 69-73.
1473. — "Zwei Menschen" (poem), *RRh*, I : 3 (1920-1921), 150.
1474. Verlaine, Paul. *Eine Anthologie der besten Übersetzungen.* Ed. Stefan Zweig. Berlin: Schuster and Loeffler, 1902 (Zweig translated six poems in this anthology: "Mondschein," "Die Unverdorbenen," "Regenlied," "Das linde Lied," "Intérieur," "Einst war ich gläubig").
1475. — "Einst war ich gläubig" (poem), *DD*, XXXII (Apr.-Sept., 1902), 178.
1476. — "Il pleure dans mon coeur" (poem), *Weltdichtung*, p. 167.
1477. — "Intérieur" (poem), *Spiegelungen*, pp. 32-33.
1478. — Siebzehn Gedichte, *Franz. Dichter*, pp. 167-183 (Tr. Richard von Schaukal, Georg von der Vring, Richard Dehmel, Ernst Hardt, Wolf Graf Kalckreuth, Stefan Zweig, Otto Hauser, Rainer Maria Rilke, Robert Faesi, Felix Braun).
1479. — "Der Tod" (Verlaine's last poem), *In*, I : 3 (Feb., 1920), 128.
1480. — Zwanzig Gedichte, *Franz. Lyrik*, pp. 226-265 (Tr. Hermann Hesse, Franz von Rexroth, Stefan Zweig, Paul Zech, Richard von Schaukal, Felix Braun, Walter Hasenclever, Rainer Maria Rilke).

XV. FOREWORDS AND EPILOGUES WRITTEN BY ZWEIG

1481. Ambrosi, Gustinus. "Trente ans de surdité," *RdV*, IX : 9 (Sept., 1935), 1425-1430 (Zweig wrote an Intro. for this article which was translated into French by L. Halberstam).
1482. Anderson, Erica. *Die Welt Albert Schweitzers. Ein Photobuch.* Berlin-Frankfurt am Main: Fischer, 1955 (Foreword and picture titles by Zweig; Cf. "Unvergessliches Erlebnis: Ein Tag bei Albert Schweitzer," *Begegnungen*, pp. 113-122. English version, *The World of Albert Schweitzer*, tr. Walter Hasenclever).
1483. Bahr, Hermann. *Die schöne Frau. Novellen.* Leipzig: Reclam, 1924 (Epilogue by Zweig; Reclams Universal-Bibliothek, No. 6451).
1484. Balzac, Honoré. *Balzac. Sein Weltbild aus den Werken.* Stuttgart: Lutz, 1908 (Intro. by Zweig; "Aus der Gedankenwelt grosser Geister," Vol. II. Gen. ed. Lothar Brieger-Wasservogel).
1485. Baum, Oskar. *Nacht ist umher. Erzählung.* Leipzig: Reclam, 1929 (Epilogue by Zweig).
1486. Bianche, Renzo. *Semblanza de Arturo Toscanini* (Toscanini, intimo autógrafos de

Wagner y Verdi). Montevideo: C. Garcia and Cía, 1940 (Foreword by Zweig; Cf. "Arturo Toscanini," *Begegnungen*, pp. 78-87).

1487. Bloch, Jean Richard. *Vom Sinn unseres Jahrhunderts*. Tr. from the French by Paul Amann. Berlin-Wien-Leipzig: P. Zsolnay, 1932 (Intro. by Zweig).

1488. Brod, Max. *Tycho Brahes Weg zu Gott*. Berlin: Herbig, 1927 (Epilogue by Zweig; Reprinted Berlin: Herbig, 1955).

1489. Casanova, Giacomo, Chevalier de Seingalt. *Mémoires*. Amsterdam: G. W. Breughel, 1950 (Foreword tr. into Dutch by C. J. Kelk (Cf. "Casanova," *Drei Dichter ihres Lebens*; *Mémoires* tr. into Dutch by J. A. Sandfort).

1490. Chateaubriand, François René Auguste Vicomte de. *Romantische Erzählungen*. Wien-Leipzig-München: Rikola, 1924 (Ed. with Intro. by Zweig).

1491. Dickens, Charles. *Ausgewählte Romane und Novellen*. Vol. I-XII. Leipzig: Insel, 1910 (Intro. by Zweig, "Charles Dickens," Vol. I, pp.v-xxx; Cf. later "Dickens" in *Drei Meister*).

1492. Dostojevsky, Feodor Mikailovich. *La Voce sotterranea*. Tr. from the Russian by Wanda Kruscinska and S. Catalano. Milano: Delia, 1928 (Foreword by Zweig from his "Dostojewski," *Drei Meister*).

1493. Dostojewski, Fedor Michailowitsch. *Sämtliche Romane und Novellen*. Tr. from the Russian by H. Röhl and K. Nötzel. Vol. I-XXV. Leipzig: Insel, 1921 (Intro. by Zweig, Vol. I, pp. vii-cxxxvi; Cf. "Dostojewski," *Drei Meister*).

1494. Errante, Vincenzo. *Lenau. Geschichte eines Märtyrers der Poesie*. Mengen: H. Heine, 1949 (Intro. by Zweig in the form of a letter to Errante, Feb. 2, 1937).

1495. Ginzkey, Franz Karl. *Brigitte und Regine und andere Dichtungen*. Leipzig: Reclam, 1924 (Epilogue by Zweig; Reclam Universal-Bibliothek, No. 6453).

1496. — *Franz Karl Ginzkey. Dem Dichter und Freunde zum 50sten Geburtstag*. Wien: Wiener Literarische Anstalt, 1921 (Epilogue by Zweig).

1497. Goethe, Johann Wolfgang von. *Goethes Gedichte. Eine Auswahl*. Leipzig: Reclam, 1927 (Ed. and Intro. by Zweig; This Intro. was reprinted in *Begegnungen*, pp. 397-405; Poems newly printed 1948, 1949, 1951, 1952, 1953, 1955).

1498. Goll, Claire. *My Sentimental Zoo*. Tr. from the French by May de Huyn. Mount Vernon, New York: Peter Pauper Press, 1942 (Intro. by Zweig).

1499. Gorki, Maxim. *Erzählungen*. Tr. from the Russian by Arthur Luther. Leipzig: Insel, 1931 (Intro. by Zweig, pp. 5-16; Reprinted 1948).

1500. Hearn, Lafcadio. *Das Japanbuch. Eine Auswahl aus Lafcadio Hearns Werken*. Tr. from the English by Berta Franzos. Frankfurt am Main: Ruetten and Loening, 1911 (Intro. by Zweig, pp. 1-12).

1501. Hellens, Franz (pseud. for Friedrich van Ermengem). *Bass-Bassina-Bulu. Roman*. Berlin: Axel Juncker, 1922 (Intro. by Zweig, pp. 1-6).

1502. Herrmann-Neisse, Max. *Erinnerung und Exil. Gedichte*. Zürich: Oprecht, 1946 (Epilogue by Zweig).

1503. Heuschele, Otto. *Briefe aus Einsamkeiten. Drei Kreise*. Berlin: Juncker, 1924 (Epilogue by Zweig entitled "Die Kunst des Briefes"; Reprinted in *Blätter*, 15 (Jan., 1963), 8-9).

1504. Hoffmann, E. T. A. *Princesse Brambilla*. Tr. from the German by Alzir Hella and Olivier Bournac. Paris-Neuchâtel: Attinger, 1929 (In the series "Romantiques allemands," No. 1; Intro. by Zweig).

1505. Jacobsen, Jens Peter. *Niels Lyhne*. Tr. from the Danish by Ottomar Enking. Leipzig: Paul List, 1925 (Epilogue by Zweig; Reprinted 1948).

1506. Latzko, Andreas. *De Achterhoede*. Tr. from the German by A. M. de Jong. Amsterdam: Wereldbibliotheek, 1946 (Intro. by Zweig tr. into Dutch by Nico van Suchtelen).

1507. — *Le dernier Homme*. Genève: Edition du Sablier, 1920 (Intro. by Zweig; 11 woodcuts by Franz Masereel).

1508. Leftwich, Joseph. *What Will Happen to the Jews?* London: P. S. King and Sons, 1936 (Intro. by Zweig, pp. ix-xii; Further quotes from Zweig, pp. 143, 202).

1509. Lemonnier, Camille. *Die Liebe im Menschen*. Tr. from the French by Paul Adler.

Leipzig: Rothbarth, 1903 (Intro. by Zweig; 11th ed. 1909; Reprinted Leipzig: Wigand, 1920).

1510. — *Warum ich Männerkleider trug. Erlebnisse einer Frau.* Tr. from the French by P. Cornelius. Berlin: Juncker, 1910 (Intro. by Zweig).

1511. Leppin, Paul. *Prager Rhapsodie. Erstes Buch.* Prag: Stil Verlag, 1938 (Intro. by Zweig).

1512. (*E.M.*) *Lilien. Sein Werk.* Berlin-Leipzig: Schuster and Loeffler, 1903 (Intro. by Zweig, pp. 9-29).

1513. Lind, Emil. *Albert Schweitzer. Leven en Werk.* Tr. from the German by Jan Poortenaar. Naarden: In den Toren, 1949 (Intro. by Zweig; 3. ed. 1955).

1514. Mann, Klaus and Willi Fehse. *Anthologie jüngster Lyrik.* Hamburg: Gebrüder Enoch, 1927 (Intro. by Zweig).

1515. Mayer, Paul. *Wunden und Wunder. Gedichte.* Heidelberg: Saturn, 1913 (Intro. by Zweig).

1516. Mércereau, Alexander. *Worte vor dem Leben.* Tr. from the French by Paul Friedrich. Leipzig: Insel, 1914 (Epilogue by Zweig, pp. 149-154).

1517. Mozart, Wolfgang Amadeus. *Ein Brief von Wolfgang Amadeus Mozart an sein Augsburger Bäsle.* Wien-Leipzig-Zürich: Reichner, 1931 (Intro. by Zweig).

1518. Prager, Hans. *Die Weltanschauung Dostojewskis.* Hildesheim: Borgmeyer, 1925 (Intro. by Zweig).

1519. Relgis, Eugen. *Muted Voices.* Tr. from the Spanish by Rose Freeman-Ishill. Berkeley Heights, New Jersey: Oriole Press, 1938 (Intro. by Zweig; German version of this introduction reprinted in *Blätter*, 8/10 (Oct., 1960), 25).

1520. Renan, Ernest. *Jugenderinnerungen.* Tr. from the French by Hannah Szass. Frankfurt am Main: Frankfurter Verlags Anstalt, 1925 (Intro. by Zweig, pp. 5-27; Cf. 526).

1521. Rimbaud, Arthur. *Gedichte.* Tr. from the French by K. L. Ammer (pseud. for Karl Klammer). Wiesbaden: Insel, 1954 (Intro. by Zweig; Insel-Bücherei, No. 592; Cf. 526).

1522. — *Leben und Dichtung.* Tr. from the French by K. L. Ammer (pseud. for Karl Klammer). Leipzig: Insel, 1907 (Intro. by Zweig).

1523. Robakidse, Grigol. *Das Schlangenhemd. Ein Roman des georgischen Volkes.* Jena: Diederichs, 1928 (Intro. by Zweig).

1524. Rolland, Romain. *Liber amicorum Romain Rolland.* Zürich-Leipzig: Rotapfel, 1926 (Zweig was an editor and contributor to this work; Reprinted in French Paris: Michel, n.d.).

1525. Rose, William and G. Craig Houston. *Rainer Maria Rilke. Aspects of his Mind and Poetry.* London: Sidgwick and Jackson, 1938 (Intro. by Zweig, pp. 1-9).

1526. Rousseau, Jean Jacques. *Emil oder über die Erziehung.* Postdam: Gustav Kiepenheuer, 1919 (Intro. by Zweig, pp. 7-16).

1527. Sainte-Beuve, Charles Augustin. *Literarische Portraits aus dem Frankreich des XVII.-XIX. Jahrhunderts.* 2 Vol. Frankfurt am Main: Frankfurter Verlags Anstalt, 1923 (Intro. by Zweig, Vol. I, pp. 5-25; Reprinted 1925; Calw: Hatjè, 1947 (Reprinted 1949); Wien: Verkauf, 1947 (Reprinted 1949). St. Gallen: Zollikofer, 1949).

1528. Soulie, Gaston. *Plus jamais ça!* Paris: Debresse, 1937 (Preface in the form of letters by Romain Rolland and Zweig).

1529. Specht, Richard. *Florestan Kestners Erfolg. Eine Erzählung aus den Wiener Märztagen.* Leipzig: Reclam, 1929 (Epilogue by Zweig; Reclam Universal-Bibliothek, No. 7038-7039).

1530. Stefan-Gruenfeldt, Paul. *Arturo Toscanini.* Tr. from the German by Eden and Cedar Paul. New York: Viking, 1936 (Intro. by Zweig; Reprinted New York: Blue Ribbon Books, 1938).

1531. — *Arturo Toscanini. Ein Lebensbild.* Wien: Reichner, 1936 (Intro. by Zweig; Reprinted as "Arturo Toscanini. Ein Bildnis" in *Begegnungen*, pp. 78-87).

1532. Stonehill, Charles Archibald, ed. *The Jewish Contribution to Civilization.* Birmingham,

England: Frank Juckes Press, 1940 (Intro. by Zweig, pp. 5-7; Minor Zweig Bibliography, pp. 195-196).

1533. Tolstoy, Leo. *De levende Gedachten van Tolstoi* (verzameld door Stefan Zweig). Tr. Frank de Vries. Den Haag: Servire, 1939 (Levende Gedachten. Eerste Reeks, No. 3).

1534. — (*Stefan Zweig Presents the*) *Living Thoughts of Tolstoy*. Greenwich, Conn.: Fawcett Publications, Inc., 1960 (In "The Living Thoughts Series – A Premier Book"; Tr. of the Tolstoy essay (1937) from the German by Barrows Mussey; Intro. essay, pp. 9-32).

1535. — *Nusus Mukhtaroh nun Tolstoy*. Tr. Shukry Muhammed 'Ayyad. al-Qahirah: dar al-Qalam, 1960 (Selected texts from Tolstoy; Intro. by Zweig).

1536. — *Les Pages immortelles de Tolstoi*. Paris: Corréa, 1939 (Intro. essay by Zweig, tr. into French by J. Angelloz).

1537. Verhaeren, Emile. *Hymnen an das Leben*. Leipzig: Insel, 1911 (Intro. and tr. by Zweig).

1538. Verlaine, Paul. *Anthologie der besten Übertragungen der Gedichte Verlaines*. Berlin: Schuster and Loeffler, 1902 (Ed. and Intro. by Zweig with six Zweig translations; 2. ed. 1907; 3. ed. 1911).

1539. — *Gedichte. Eine Auswahl der besten Übertragungen*. Leipzig: Insel, 1927 (Sel. and epilogue by Zweig, pp. 69-70; Reprinted in 1929, 1938; Insel-Bücherei, No. 394).

1540. — *Gesammelte Werke*. Ed. Stefan Zweig. Leipzig: Insel, 1922 (Intro. to Vol. II, pp. 5-21 entitled "Paul Verlaines Leben"; Vol. I includes the following Zweig translations: "Mondschein," p. 45, "Die Unverdorbenen," p. 49, "Regenlied," p. 93, "Das linde Lied," p. 130, "Intérieur," p. 170, "Einst war ich gläubig..," p. 291).

1541. Voss, Hartfrid, ed. *Lyrische Handschriften unserer Zeit*. Ebenhausen bei München: Voss, 1958 (Intro. by Zweig).

1542. Zodykow, Maxim. *Stimme aus dem Dunkel*. Berlin: Lehmann, 1931 (Intro. by Zweig).

XVI. BOOK REVIEWS BY STEFAN ZWEIG

1543. Bahr, Hermann, *O Mensch. Roman*. Berlin: Fischer, 1910 (Rev.: *BT*, Sept. 28, 1910).

1544. Baumberg, Antonie. *Kleine Erzählungen und Skizzen*. Wien: Konegen, 1902 (Rev.: *DLE*, 5.J.: 11 (Mar. 1, 1903), 744-748 ("Skizzen-und Novellenbücher")).

1545. Blumenthal, Hermann. *Der Weg der Jugend. Roman*. Berlin: Marquardt, 1907 and *Knabenalter. Roman*. Berlin: Marquardt, 1908 (Rev.: *DLE*, 10.J.: 19 (Jul. 1, 1908), 1348).

1546. Buddha, Gotamo. *Reden*. German tr. Karl Eugen Neumann. München: Piper, 1919 (Rev.: *NFP*, No. 19787, Sept. 26, 1919, pp. 1-3 ("Erhabenes Vermächtnis")).

1547. Dahm, Paula. *Gedichte*. Dresden: Pierson, 1902 (Rev.: *DLE*, 4.J.: 14 (April, 1902), 974 ("Neue Frauenlyrik")).

1548. D'Annunzio, Gabriele. *Römische Elegien*. German tr. Eugen Gugeia. Wien: Stern, 1903 (Rev.: *DLE*, 5.J.: 18 (June 15, 1903), 1258).

1549. Dostoevskaja, Anna Grigorevna. *Die Lebenserinnerungen der Gattin Dostojewskis*. German tr. Dmitri Umanskij. Ed. René Fülöp-Miller and Friedrich Eckstein. München: Piper, 1925 (Rev.: *DL*, XXVII : 10 (June, 1925), 581-583).

1550. Duimchen, Theodor. *Mittel und Wege*. Berlin: Johannes Räde, 1902 (Rev.: *DLE*, 5.J.: 11 (Mar. 1, 1903), 744-748 ("Skizzen und Novellenbücher")).

1551. Eck, Miriam. *Herbst*. Berlin: Schuster and Löffler, 1901 (Rev.: *DLE*, 4.J.: 14 (Apr., 1902), 972 ("Neue Frauenlyrik")).

1552. Eisenschitz, Fritz. *Ja wir!* Berlin: Jung-Deutschland Verlag, 1901 (Rev.: *DLE*, 3.J.: 18 (June, 1901), 1291 ("Neue Skizzen- und Novellenbücher")).

1553. Finckl, Ludwig. *Rosen*. Stuttgart-Leipzig: Deutsche Verlagsanstalt, 1906 (Rev.: *ÖR*, IX : 2 (Nov.-Dec., 1906), 147).

1554. Flakes, Otto. *Ruland*. *Roman*. Berlin: Fischer, 1922 and *Die Simona*. *Roman*. Berlin: Fischer, 1922 (Rev.: *NR*, XXXIV : 3 (Mar., 1923), 285-287).

1555. Flaubert, Gustave. *Herodias*. German tr. Dr. Paul Adler. Leipzig: Seemann, 1903 (Rev.: *DLE*, 6.J.: 24 (Sept. 15, 1904), 1737-1738).

1556. — *Ein schlichtes Herz*. German tr. Ernst Hardt. Leipzig: Insel, 1904 (Rev.: *DLE*, 6.J.: 24 (Sept. 15, 1904), 1737-1738).

1557. — *Die Schule der Empfindsamkeit*. German tr. Luise Wolf. Minden in Westfalen: Bruns, 1904 (Rev.: *DLE*, 7.J.: 24 (Sept. 15, 1905), 1793-1795).

1558. — *Die Versuchung des heiligen Antonius*. German tr. F. P. Greve. Minden in Westfalen: Bruns, 1905 (Rev.: *DLE*, 9.J.: 6 (Dec. 15, 1906), 474-475).

1559. Forbes-Mosse, Irene. *Mezza voce*. Berlin: Schuster and Löffler, 1901 (Rev.: *DLE*, 4.J.: 14 (Apr., 1902), 972 ("Neue Frauenlyrik")).

1560. Franck, Hans. *Godiva*. München: Delphin, 1919 (Rev.: *DLE*, 22.J.: 11 (Mar. 1, 1920), 644-646 (Pp. 646-650 contain excerpts from the drama *Godiva*)).

1561. Frei, Leonore. *Lebensflut*. *Gedichte*. Berlin: Dümmler, 1899 (Rev.: *DLE*, II : 8 (Jan. 15, 1900), 579-580).

1562. Gelber, A. 1001 *Nacht, der Sinn der Erzählungen der Scheherezade*. Wien: Perles, 1917 (Rev.: Wien, 1917; Reprinted in *Europäisches Erbe*, pp. 157-168 ("Das Drama in Tausendundeiner Nacht")).

1563. Gerhardt-Amytor, Dagobert von. *Röntgenstrahlen*. and *Das Amselnest*. Breslau: Schottländer, 1902 (Rev.: *DLE*, 5.J.: 11 (Mar. 1, 1903), 744-748 ("Skizzen- und Novellenbücher")).

1564. Greiner, Leo. *Das Tagebuch*. *Gedichte*. München-Leipzig: Georg Müller, 1906 (Rev.: *ÖR*, VIII : 102/103 (Aug.-Oct., 1906), 420).

1565. Gundolf, Friedrich. *Heinrich von Kleist*. Berlin: Georg Bondi, 1922 (Rev.: *FZ*, Feb. 2, 1923).

1566. Günther, Christian. *Strophen*. Sel. and ed. with Intro. by Wilhelm von Scholz. Leipzig: Diederichs, 1902 (Rev.: *MfL*, LXXI : 50 (Dec. 13, 1902), 398-399 ("Eine neue Ausgabe Christian Günthers")).

1567. Guth, Alfred. *Vom letzten Tag*. Berlin: Hugo Steinitz, 1901 (Rev.: *DLE*, 3.J.: 18 (June, 1901), 1292 ("Neue Skizzenbücher")).

1568. Heijermans, Herman. *Sabbath*. German tr. R. Ruben. Pössneck in Th.: Bruno Feigenspann, 1904 (Rev.: *DLE*, 7.J.: 8 (Jan. 15, 1905), 594).

1569. Heine, Heinrich. *Deutschland, ein Wintermärchen*. Ed. Friedrich Hirth. Berlin: Lehmann, 1915 (Rev.: *DLE*, XVIII : 13 (Apr. 1, 1916), 795-798 ("Eine Faksimileausgabe von Heines 'Deutschland, ein Wintermärchen'")).

1570. de Herédia, José Maria. *Trophäen*. German tr. Emil von Gebsattel. München: Weber, 1909 (Rev.: *DLE*, 13.J.: 3 (Nov. 1, 1910), 219).

1571. Hesse, Hermann. *Blick ins Chaos*. Bern: Seldwyla, 1920 (Rev.: *BN*, July 27, 1922 ("Selbstbesinnungsschriften von Künstlern")).

1572. — *Musik des Einsamen*. *Gedichte*. Heilbronn: Salzer, 1915 (Rev.: *BN*, Feb. 28, 1915, p. 1).

1573. — *Peter Camenzind*. Berlin: Fischer, 1904 (Rev.: *F*, VI : 14 (1904), 270).

1574. Hochstetter, Sophie. *Geduld*. *Roman*. Berlin: P. Letto, 1904 and *Er versprach ihr einst das Paradies*. *Novelle*. Berlin: Gebr. Paetel, 1904 (Rev.: *DLE*, 8.J.: 2 (Oct. 15, 1905), 137-139).

1575. Hofmannsthal, Hugo von. *Elektra*. Berlin: Fischer, 1903 (Rev.: *MfL*, LXXII : 17 (Dec., 1903), 528-530).

1576. Holzamer, Wilhelm. *Der arme Lukas*. Leipzig: Seemann, 1903 (Rev.: *DLE*, 5. J.: 12 (Mar. 15, 1903), 854-855).

1577. Hönigsberg, Margret. *Rot und andere Gedichte*. Dresden-Leipzig: Pierson, 1899 (Rev.: *DLE*, 1.J.: 23 (Sept. 1, 1899), 1498-1499).

1578. Janitschek, Maria. *Esclarmonde. Ihr Leben und Leiden*. Stuttgart: Deutsche Verlagsanstalt, 1906 (Rev.: *DLE*, 9.J.: 1 (Oct. 1, 1906), 67).

1579. Knorr, Josephine von. *Gedichte*. Berlin-Leipzig: Cotta, 1901 (Rev.: *DLE*, 4.J.: 14 (Apr., 1902), 971 ("Neue Frauenlyrik")).
1580. Kurowski, Ludwig. *Menschenbilder*. Wien: Selbstverlag, 1901 (Rev.: *DLE*, 3.J.: 18 (June, 1901), 1292 ("Neue Skizzenbücher")).
1581. Laforgue, Jules. *Sagenhafte Sinnspiele*. German tr. Paul Wiegler. Stuttgart: Juncker, 1905 (Rev.: *DLE*, 7.J.: 23 (Sept. 1, 1905), 1716-1718).
1582. Lent, Gertrud. *Im Sommer*. Berlin: Harmonie, 1903 (Rev.: *DLE*, 5.J.: 11 (Mar. 1, 1903), 744-748 ("Skizzen- und Novellenbücher")).
1583. Liebish, Rudolf. *Der zerbrochene Krug und andere Geschichten*. Dessau: Dünnhaupt, 1903 (Rev.: *DLE*, 5.J.: 11 (Mar. 1, 1903), 744-748 ("Neue Skizzen- und Novellenbücher")).
1584. Lucka, Emil. *Dostojewski*. Stuttgart-Berlin: Deutsche Verlagsanstalt, 1924 (Rev.: *DLE*, XXVI : 7 (Apr.-Sept., 1924), 436).
1585. — *Winland. Novellen und Legenden*. Wien: Deutsch-Österreichischer, 1912 (Rev.: *DLE*, 14.J.: 20 (July 15, 1912), 1447-1448).
1586. Maeterlinck, Maurice. *Gedichte*. German tr. R. Ammer and Friedrich von Oppeln-Bronikowski. Jena: Diederichs, 1906 (Rev.: *DLE*, 10.J.: 20 (July 15, 1908), 1464-1465).
1587. Mann, Thomas. Foreword to *Rede und Antwort*, dated München, Apr., 1921; First book printing in *Rede und Antwort*. Berlin: Fischer, 1922 (Rev.: *NR* (Berlin), XXXII : 2 (1921), 1315-1321 ("Thomas Manns 'Rede und Antwort'")).
1588. Meier-Gräfe, Julius. *Dostojewski, der Dichter*. Berlin: Rowohlt, 1926 (Rev.: *DL*, XXVIII : 8 (1925-1926), 461-462).
1589. Mell, Max. *Das bekränzte Jahr. Gedichte*. Berlin: Juncker, 1911 (Rev.: *NR*, XXIII : 1 (1912), 598-599 ("Schöne Verse")).
1590. Michel, Wilhelm. *Friedrich Hölderlin*. Weimar: E. Lichtenstein, 1925 (Rev.: *DL*, XXVIII : 4 (1925-1926), 245).
1591. Moore, George. *Aus toten Tagen*. German tr. Max Meyerfeld. Berlin: Fleischel, 1907 (Rev.: *DLE*, 11.J. : 23 (Sept. 1, 1909), 169).
1592. Netto, Hadrian Maria. *Sibylle und der Papagei. Eine Salzburger Idylle*. Dresden: Sibyllen-Verlag, 1921 (Rev.: *DLE*, 24.J.: 9 (Feb. 1, 1922), 561).
1593. Orzeszko, Helene. *Der starkere Simson und Anderes*. Berlin: Siegfried Cronback, 1903 (Rev.: *DLE*, 5.J.: 11 (Mar. 1, 1903), 744-748 ("Skizzen- und Novellenbücher")).
1594. Perfall, Anton von. *Die Hexen von Nordehoog*. München: Langen, 1902 (Rev.: *DLE*, 5.J.: 11 (Mar. 1, 1903), 744-748 ("Skizzen- und Novellenbücher")).
1595. — *Die Landstreicherin*. Leipzig: Müller-Mann, 1903 (Rev.: *DLE*, 5.J.: 11 (Mar. 1, 1903), 744-748 ("Skizzen- und Novellenbücher")).
1596. — *Die Molschule*. München: Langen, 1901 (Rev.: *DLE*, 5.J.: 11 (Mar. 1, 1903), 744-748 ("Skizzen- und Novellenbücher")).
1597. Pruschanski, N. *Ein Blatt aus der Chronik unserer Stadt*. Berlin: Cronbach, 1903 (Rev.: *DLE*, 6.J.: 19 (July 1, 1904), 1378-1379).
1598. Rafael, L. (pseud. for Hedwig Kiesekamp). *Abendgluten*. Leipzig: Brietkopf and Härtel, 1901 (Rev.: *DLE*, 4.J.: 14 (Apr., 1902), 973 ("Neue Frauenlyrik")).
1599. Raff, Helene. *Modellgeschichten*. Berlin: Gebr. Pietel, 1902 (Rev.: *DLE*, 5.J.: 11 (Mar. 1, 1903), 744-748 ("Skizzen- und Novellenbücher")).
1600. Reinfels, Peter von. *Flammen der Liebe*. Leipzig: Pierson, 1900 (Rev.: *DLE*, 5.J.: 11 (Mar. 1, 1903), 744-748 ("Skizzen- und Novellenbücher")).
1601. Reischl, Friedrich and Luigi Kasimir. *Das Buch von der schönen Stadt Salzburg*. Wien: Hugo Heller, 1923 (Rev.: *DLE*, XXVI: 7 (Apr.-Sept., 1924), 437).
1602. Rice, Muriel. *Von zwei Ufern. Gedichte*. German tr. Theodor Lessing. Göttingen: Hapke, 1909 (Rev.: *DLE*, 12.J.: 9 (Feb. 1, 1910), 666-667).
1603. Rilke, Rainer Maria. *Neue Gedichte*. Leipzig: Insel, 1905 (Rev.: *DLE*, 11.J.: 6 (Dec. 15, 1908), 416-418).
1604. Rössler, Arthur. *Es gibt solche Menschen*. München: August Schupp, 1901 (Rev.: *DLE*, 3.J.: 18 (June, 1901), 1291 ("Neue Skizzenbücher")).

1605. Sachs, Erich. *Ein Lebensmorgen.* Berlin: Ebering, 1900 (Rev.: *DLE*, 3.J.: 18 (June, 1901), 1292 ("Neue Skizzenbücher")).
1606. Salus, Hugo. *Novellen des Lyrikers.* Berlin: Fleischel, 1903 (Rev.: *DLE*, 6.J.: 5 (Dec. 1, 1903), 366-367).
1607. Samain, Albert. *Gedichte.* German tr. Lucy Abels. Berlin: Borngräber, 1911 (Rev.: *DLE*, 13.J.: 12 (Mar. 15, 1911), 914-915).
1608. Schäfer, Wilhelm. *Gottlieb Mangold.* Berlin: Schuster and Loeffler, 1901 (Rev.: *DLE*, 3.J.: 18 (June, 1901), 1291 ("Neue Skizzenbücher")).
1609. Schlaf, Johannes. *Maeterlinck.* Berlin: Marquardt, 1906 (Rev.: *DLE*, 9.J.: 11 (Mar. 1, 1907), 907).
1610. Schmitz, Oskar A. H. *Haschisch.* Frankfurt am Main: Südwestdeutscher Verlag, 1902 (Rev.: *DLE*, 5.J.: 11 (Mar. 1, 1903), 744-748 ("Skizzen- und Novellenbücher")).
1611. Schullern, Heinrich von. *Neues Skizzenbuch.* Linz: Österreichische Verlagsanstalt, 1901 (Rev.: *DLE*, 3.J.: 18 (June, 1901), 1290-1291 ("Neue Skizzenbücher")).
1612. Schwarz, Heinrich. *Salzburg und das Salzkammergut.* Wien: Anton Schroll, 1926 (Rev.: *DL*, XXVIII : 7 (1925-1926), 443).
1613. Semmig, Jeanne Bertha. *Enzio.* Berlin: Georg Heinrich Meyer, 1901 (Rev.: *DLE*, 4.J.: 14 (Apr., 1902), 973 ("Neue Frauenlyrik")).
1614. Soederberg, Eduard. *Gassenlieder.* German tr. Max Bamberger. Strassburg: Josef Singer, 1902 (Rev.: *DLE*, 5.J.: 20 (July 15, 1903), 1442).
1615. Stendhal (pseud. for Henri Beyle). *Bekenntnisse eines Egoisten.* German tr. Artur Schurig. Jena: Diederichs, 1905 (Rev.: *DLE*, 8.J.: 22 (Aug. 15, 1906), 1623).
1616. Strassburger, Egon H. *Firlefanz der Puppendoktor. Märchen.* Berlin: Heinemann, 1921 (Rev.: *DLE*, 24.J.: 6 (Dec. 15, 1921), 370-371).
1617. Suttner, Bertha von. *Die Waffen nieder.* Dresden: Pierson, 1889 (Rev.: *NFP*, June 21, 1918, pp. 1-4).
1618. Theodor, Josef. *Aus Tag und Traum.* Breslau: Schottländer, 1902 (Rev.: *DLE*, 5.J.: 11 (Mar. 1, 1903), 744-748 ("Skizzen- und Novellenbücher")).
1619. Thoma, Ludwig. *Assessor Karlchen.* München: Langen, 1901 (Rev.: *DLE*, 3.J.: 18 (June, 1901), 1290 ("Neue Skizzenbücher")).
1620. Verlaine, Paul. *Gedichte.* German tr. Otto Hauser. Berlin: Concordia, 1899 (Rev.: *DLE*, 2.J.: 23 (Sept. 1, 1900), 1661).
1621. Wegner, Arnim T. *Fünf Finger über Dir.* Stuttgart: Deutsche Verlagsanstalt, 1930 (Rev.: *DL*, XXXII : 4 (1929-1930), 235).
1622. Zech, Paul. *Rimbaud. Querschnitt durch sein Leben und Werk.* Leipzig: Wolkenwanderer, 1927 (Rev.: *Tb*, VIII : 6 (1927), 225-227).

XVII A. ARTICLES AND BOOK REVIEWS OF WORKS BY STEFAN ZWEIG

POETRY

Ausgewählte Gedichte. Leipzig: Insel, 1931 (or later editions).

1623.   *NL*, 33.J. (1931), 84 (J. Demmering).
1624.   *RCC*, 36.a.: 1 (1936-1937), 553-557 (R. Pitrou).

"Der Bildner" (Rodin).

1625.   *DF*, XXV : 640/648 (Jan., 1924), 49-52 (Karl Kraus).

Die frühen Kränze. Leipzig: Insel, 1906 (or later editions).

1626.   *Bb*, 20 (1907), 621-622 (W. Unus).

1627. *BT*, 40 (Paul Zech: "Zeitgeist") (Cf. *DLE*, 17.J.: 3 (Nov. 1, 1914), 171-172, contains the poem "Die Dinge, die die Abende erzählen" from "Die Lieder des Abends").
1628. *DLE*, 9.J.: 14 (Apr. 15, 1907), 1089-1092 (Leo Greiner: "Neue Lyrik" – Zweig's *Frühe Kränze et al.*).
1629. *Z*, XVI (1907), 437-441 (Alberta von Puttkamer).
1630. *Z*, XVI (1908), 13 (Alberta von Puttkamer) (Cf. *DLE*, 10.J.: 9 (Feb. 1, 1908), 652; *DLE*, IX (1906-1907), 109).

Die gesammelten Gedichte. Leipzig: Insel, 1924.

1631. *DL*, XXVII : 1 (Oct., 1924 – Mar., 1925), 6-7 (Ernst Lissauer: "Zur Lyrik der Gegenwart" – Zweig's *Gedichte et al.*).
1632. *DLZ*, June 21, 1924 (H. W. Keim) (Cf. *DL*, XXVI : 2 (Apr.-Sept., 1924), 736).
1633. *PJ*, CXCV (1924), 303 (K. Busse).

Silberne Saiten. Berlin: Schuster and Löffler, 1901.

1634. *DLE*, III : 13 (Apr., 1901), 937 (R. M. Werner).

DRAMAS

Das Haus am Meer. Ein Schauspiel. Leipzig: Insel, 1912.

1635. *DLE*, 15.J.: 9 (Feb. 1, 1913), 613-615 (Walter von Molo: "Die Persönlichkeit im Drama").
1636. *MNN*, Dec. 9, 1912 (R. Elchinger: "Zweigs 'Haus am Meer'").
1637. *PL*, Oct. 27, 1912 (F. Salten: "Stefan Zweigs 'Das Haus am Meer,' ein Schauspiel").
1638. *Ze*, Oct. 27, 1912 (L. Feld: "Zweigs 'Haus am Meer'").

Jeremias. Leipzig: Insel, 1917 (or later editions).

1639. *AZJ*, LXXXIV (1920), 1 (J. B. Münz) (Cf. *DLE*, 22.J.: 10 (Feb. 15, 1920), 613).
1640. *BBC*, XI (1917), 17 (Ilse Reicke: "Historische Dichtung aus der Gegenwart") (Cf. *DLE*, 20.J.: 7 (Jan. 1, 1918), 411).
1641. *CVZ*, XIII : 40, 1. Beibl. (Oct. 5, 1934), 1-2 (Eva Reichmann-Jungmann: "Stefan Zweigs 'Jeremias.' Zur bevorstehenden Aufführung im Berliner Kulturbund").
1642. *CVZ*, XIII : 43, 3. Beibl. (1934), 2 (W. S. Matzdorff).
1643. *DDr*, 1.J. (1918), 358 (H. Pankow).
1644. *DIZ*, 105 (1920), 22-23 (L. H. Wolf).
1645. *DLE*, 21.J.: 6 (Dec. 15, 1918), 353 (Theodor Hampe).
1646. *DLE*, 22.J.: 6 (Dec. 15, 1919), 346-348 (Robert F. Arnold).
1647. *DNE*, IV (1920), 3 (P. Cornelius: "Stefan Zweig und sein 'Jeremias'") (Cf. *DLE*, 22.J.: 14 (Apr. 15, 1920), 865).
1648. *Je*, V (1925) 559-575 (A. Blau).
1649. *JR*, XXXIV : 81 (1934), 3 ("Stefan Zweigs 'Jeremias'. Première im jüdischen Kulturbund").
1650. *JR*, XXXIV: 84 (1934), 6 (R. Wischnitzer-Bernstein: "Bühnenlieder zum 'Jeremias'").

1651. *JR*, XXXIV (1934), 644 (E. Simon: "Zeittheater in Palästina? Stefan Zweigs 'Jeremias'").
1652. *M*, IX (1918), 9 (Eugen Kilian) (Cf. *DLE*, 20.J.: 18 (June 15, 1918), 1109).
1653. *NFP*, Sept. 28, 1917 (Paul Zifferer) (Cf. *DLE*, 20.J.: 4 (Nov. 15, 1917), 221-222).
1654. *NFP*, Oct. 10, 1919 ("Stefan Zweigs 'Jeremias,' das Trauerspiel der Pessimisten").
1655. *NZZ*, Sept. 2, 1917 (Paul Stefan) (Cf. *DLE*, 20.J.: 2 (Oct. 15, 1917), 103).
1656. *Pb*, 1918, p. 273 (Fraedrich).
1657. *PL*, Mar. 9, 1918 (F. Berau).
1658. *PT*, 288 (Friedrich Hirth) (Cf. *DLE*, 20.J.: 6 (Dec. 15, 1917), 348).
1659. *RT*, I (1921), 44-45 (Kurt Felix: "Über Zweigs 'Jeremias'").
1660. *Soz*, 5.J. (1919), 244-246.
1661. *VZ*, Oct. 13, 1917 (Franz Servaes) (Cf. *DLE*, 20.J.: 4 (Nov. 15, 1917), 221-222)
1662. *W-Z*, June 13, 1918 (Eugen Kilian).

Jeremiah. Tr. Eden and Cedar Paul. New York: Viking, 1922 (or later editions).

1663. *BTr*, Dec. 2, 1922, p. 3.
1664. *CW*, CXLVIII (March, 1939), 731.
1665. *Cwl*, XXIX (Feb. 17, 1939), 469 (Vernon Grenville).
1666. *LT*, June 29, 1934, p. 14; 4/5 Star Ed., June 29, 1934, p. 14.
1667. *LT*, May 30, 1950, p. 6.
1668. *N*, CXLVIII (Feb. 18, 1939), 212.
1669. *NYHTB*, Jan. 14, 1923, p. 17 (A. D. Douglas).
1670. *NYTBR*, Dec. 24, 1922, p. 17 ("Drama for a Post-War World").
1671. *SRL*, VI (Sept. 28, 1929), 190 (Amelia von Ende: "A Zweig Drama").
1672. *T*, XXXIII (Feb. 13, 1939), 24.
1673. *TAM*, XXIII (Apr., 1939), 248.

Das Lamm des Armen. Leipzig: Insel, 1929.

1674. *DDr*, N.F. II (1930), 272.
1675. *DL*, XXXII : 8 (1929-1930), 476 (W. Müller).
1676. *DSL*, 31.J. (1930), 264 (Hallener).
1677. *Hw*, VII (1930), 282-285 (H. Fischer: "Uraufführung von 'Das Lamm des Armen' in Prag").
1678. *LNN*, Sept. 18, 1930 (E. Delpy: "Stefan Zweigs 'Das Lamm des Armen'; Erstaufführung in Leipzig").

Legende eines Lebens. Ein Kammerspiel. Leipzig: Insel, 1919 (or later editions).

1679. *DLE*, 21.J.: 10 (Feb. 15, 1919), 607-608 (Fritz Ph. Baader).
1680. *DZ*, Jan. 20, 1923 ("Stefan Zweigs 'Legende eines Lebens'").
1681. *Hg*, III/IV (1923), 85.
1682. *HN*, Dec. 27, 1919 ("Zweigs 'Legende eines Lebens' (Uraufführung)").
1683. *PJ*, CXCI (1923), 246-249 (H. Heynen).
1684. *WM*, CXXXIV (Mar., 1923), 96-97 (F. Düsel).
1685. *ZfB*, N.F. 11.J.: 2, Beibl. (1920), 513.

Die schweigsame Frau. Komische Oper in 3 Aufzügen. Berlin: Adolph Fürstner, 1935 (or other editions).

1686. *CVZ*, XIII : 31, 2. Beibl. (Aug. 2, 1934), 2 (Hans Reisiger: "Richard Strauss und Stefan Zweig").

1687. *LT*, July 21, 1934, p. 11; 4/5 Star Ed. July 21, 1934, p. 11. ("Herr Stefan Zweig's (Germany) Libretto for Strauss-Opera").
1688. *NA*, CCLXV (May 1, 1929), 53-67 (Enrico Rocca:"L'Opera di Stefan Zweig").
1689. *NK*, VIII : 48 (1957), 8 ("Stefan Zweig: Dzieje jednego libretta (Sprawa wystawienia opery R. Straussa 'Milcząca Kobieta')").
1690. *NYT*, July 18, 1934, p. 11 ("R. Strauss Attacked by *Der Stürmer* for Basing New Opera on Text Supplied by Zweig because He is Jewish").
1691. *NYT*, June 12, 1935, p. 9 ("Zweig's Libretto for Opera 'The Silent Woman', by Strauss, Incurs Nazi Disfavor").
1692. *NYT*, June 24, 1935, p. 12 ("Preview of Opera 'The Silent Woman'").
1693. *NYT*, June 25, 1935, p. 15 ("Premiere of 'The Silent Woman'").
1694. *NYT*, June 26, 1935, p. 19 ("Germany Hails Opera 'The Silent Woman'").

Tersites. Ein Trauerspiel. Leipzig: Insel, 1907; 2. Auflage (veränd.), 1919 (or later editions).

1695. *BT*, Nov. 27, 1908 ("Stefan Zweigs 'Thersites'").
1696. *BW*, XI (Oct., 1908 – Mar., 1909), 300 (Edgar Pierson).
1697. *DLE*, 11.J. : 1 (Oct. 1, 1908), 30-33 (L. Berg: "Die Tragödie des Neides").
1698. *DM*, 4.J. (Jan. 4, 1909).
1699. *DW*, XI (1908), 25 (Josef Lamm) (Cf. *DLE*, 11.J.: 20 (July 15, 1908), 1447).
1700. *HK*, Feb. 11, 1909 (F. Hartmann).
1701. *LNN*, Jan. 20, 1918 (E. Delpy: "Zweigs 'Tersites' (Erstaufführung)").
1702. *NFP*, 15725 (Alberta von Puttkamer) (Cf. *DLE*, 10.J.: 18 (June 15, 1908), 1288).
1703. *NZ*, 233 (Cf. *DLE*, 10.J.: 18 (June 15, 1908), 1288).

Der verwandelte Komödiant. Berlin: Felix Bloch Erben, 1912 (or later editions).

1704. *DB*, 5 (1947), 10 ("Stefan Zweigs 'Der verwandelte Komödiant'").
1705. *DB*, 10 (1947), 11 ("Stefan Zweigs 'Der verwandelte Komödiant' aufgeführt in Augsburg").
1706. *DLE*, 14.J.: 17 (June 1, 1912), 1226-1227 (Erich Freund).
1707. *DLE*, 16.J.: 11 (Mar. 1, 1914), 907-909 (Moritz Necker).

Volpone. Eine lieblose Komödie. Bearbeitung von Stefan Zweig nach Ben Jonson. Potsdam: Kiepenheuer, 1926 (or later editions).

1708. *DZ*, Dec. 24, 1926 (R. Biedrzynski: "Stefan Zweigs 'Volpone', Tanz ums Geld").
1709. *JDSG*, N.F. III/IV (1927), 183-190 (Helene Richter: "Ben Jonsons 'Volpone' und sein Erneuerer Stefan Zweig").
1710. *MZ*, Nov. 28, 1926 (B. Guillemin: "Stefan Zweigs 'Volpone'").
1711. *NFP*, Nov. 7, 1926 (Raoul Auernheimer: "Stefan Zweigs 'Volpone'").
1712. *S*, 3.J.: 23 (1948), 7 (W. Lenning: "Zwei Dichter und ein Regisseur: Ben Jonson – Stefan Zweig – 'Volpone'").
1713. *TR*, Dec. 24, 1926 (G. Manz: "Stefan Zweigs 'Volpone'").

Volpone. A Loveless Comedy in 3 Acts; by Ben Jonson, freely adapted by Stefan Zweig. Tr. Ruth Langner. London: Allen and Unwin, 1928 (or other editions).

1714. *Bl*, XXIV (July, 1928), 394.
1715. *Bm*, LXVII : 4 (June, 1928), 419-421 (Ernest Boyd: "Modernizing Ibsen and Ben Jonson").

1716.   *COS*, Sept., 1928, p. 100.
1717.   *CW*, CXXVII (July, 1928), 340-343.
1718.   *Di*, LXXXIV (June, 1928), 528.
1719.   *LT*, Nov. 9, 1926, p. 123.
1720.   *LT*, Nov. 24, 1928, p. 11.
1721.   *NRep*, LIV (Apr. 25, 1928), 295-296 (Stark Young).
1722.   *NSN*, XV (Jan. 29, 1938), 164-165.
1723.   *NYT*, Apr. 10, 1928, p. 32.
1724.   *NYT*, Apr. 22, 1928, p. 9 (J. Brooks Atkinson: "Rare Ben. How Zweig's Adaptation of 'Volpone' Transforms Jonson's Text").
1725.   *NYT*, Apr. 22, 1928, p. 9 (R. G. Noyes).
1726.   *NYT*, May 2, 1928, p. 16 (L. Shubert Banton and T. Holburn).
1727.   *NYT*, June 27, 1928, p. 29.
1728.   *O*, CXLVIII (Apr. 25, 1928), 665.
1729.   *PMB*, XXXIII (July, 1928), 405.
1730.   *PMLA*, XLVI (June, 1931), 605-607 (George W. Whiting: "Volpone, Herr von Fuchs and Les Héritiers Rabourdin").
1731.   *Sp*, CXLVIII (Jan. 30, 1932), 141 (P. Fleming).
1732.   *Sp*, CLX (Jan. 28, 1938), 132.
1733.   *SRL*, IV (Apr. 21, 1928), 782 (J. M. Brown).
1734.   *TAM*, XII (May, 1928), 368 (Rosamond Gilder).
1735.   *TAM*, XII (June, 1928), 387 (J. M. Brown).
1736.   *WLB*, XXIV (June, 1928), 189.

Volpone, de Ben Jonson, adapté par Jules Romains, d'après Stefan Zweig. Paris, Fayard et Cie, 1928 (or later edition).

1737.   *APL*, XCI (Dec. 15, 1928), 583 (Gérard Bauer).
1738.   *EN*, Dec. 1, 1928 (J. J. Bernard) (Cf. *DFR*, II (1928), 77).
1739.   *I*, LXXXVI : 2 (Dec. 8, 1928), 704.
1740.   *JD*, XXXVI : 2 (Aug. 30, 1929), 356-358 (H. Bidou).
1741.   *MF*, CCVIII (Dec. 15, 1928), 647-653 (Critile).
1742.   *MF*, CCLXXIX (Oct. 15, 1937), 364-367.
1743.   *NRF*, N.S. XXXII (1929), 126-128 (B. Crémieux).

FICTION

GERMAN

Amok. Leipzig: Insel, 1922.

1744.   *DLE*, 25.J.: 19-20 (July 1, 1923), 1036 (Hans Joachim Homann).
1745.   *NFP*, Dec. 3, 1922, pp. 34-35 (Erwin Rieger: "Stefan Zweigs neues Novellenbuch: 'Amok'").
1746.   *NR*, 34.J.: 2 (1923), 670 (Otto Zarek).
1747.   *Nz*, Dec. 9, 1922 (Otto Zarek) (Cf. *DLE*, 25.J.: 9-10 (Feb. 1, 1923), 526).

Angst. Leipzig: Insel-Reclam, 1925.

1748.   *VK*, 40.J.: 1 (1925), 231 (Karl Strecker).

Die Augen des ewigen Bruders. Leipzig: Insel, 1922 (or later editions).

1749.   *BBC*, No. 519 (Cf. *DLE*, 25.J.: 6 (Dec. 15, 1922), 358 (Ernst Lissauer)).
1750.   *NBL* (Kunst), No. 376 (Cf. *DLE*, 25.J.: 23-24 (Sept. 1, 1923), 1184 (Ernst Lissauer)).
1751.   *Nw*, 6.J. (1924), 281.

Brennendes Geheimnis. Erzählung. Leipzig: Insel, 1914 (or later editions).

1752.   *SS* (Lit. Beilage), 28.J. (1925), 28.

Erstes Erlebnis. Leipzig: Insel, 1911 (or later editions).

1753.   *Im*, I : 2 (May, 1912), 209-211 (Dr. Theodor Reik).
1754.   *Ja*, I-II (1912-1913), 141 (H. Friedrich).
1755.   *MF*, XCVI (1912), 867 (Henri Albert).
1756.   *NG*, IX : 7 (July 14, 1913), 379-381 (Helene Stöcker: "Vier Geschichten aus Kinderland").
1757.   *ÖR*, XXXII : 1 (July-Sept., 1912), 82-83 (Ludwig Ullmann).
1758.   *ZB*, N.F. IV : 2 (Oct.-Mar., 1912-1913), 466-467 (C.N.).

Fragment einer Novelle. Ed. Erich Fitzbauer. Wien: Verlag der Internationalen Stefan-Zweig-Gesellschaft, 1961 (or later editions).

1759.   *Blätter*, 13/14 (Apr., 1962), 4 (Robert Braun: "Vorgeahntes Schicksal").
1760.   *LT*, Oct. 27, 1961, p. 772.

Die Liebe der Erika Ewald. Berlin: Egon Fleischel, 1904.

1761.   *DLE*, 7.J.: 4 (Nov. 15, 1904), 291-292 (Hermann Hesse).
1762.   *F*, VI (1905), 51 (Camill Hoffmann) (Cf. *DLE*, 7.J.: 10 (Feb. 15, 1905), 712).

Verwirrung der Gefühle. Leipzig: Insel, 1927 (or other editions).

1763.   *BA*, I : 4 (Oct., 1927), 62 (Ernst Rose).
1764.   *BBB*, VII (1926), 22 (Hans Franck) (Cf. *DL*, XXIX : 9 (1926-1927), 534).
1765.   *CVZ*, 5.J. (1926), 667-668 (Ernst Lissauer).
1766.   *DL*, XXIX : 3 (1926-1927), 175-176 (Anselma Heine).
1767.   *NBL*, No. 495 (Leonhard Adelt) (Cf. *DL*, XXIX : 3 (1926-1927), 157).
1768.   *NFP*, Oct. 6, 1926 (Leonhard Adelt).

Vier Novellen. Ed. and Intro. Harold Jensen. London: Harrap, 1955.

1768a.   *GLL*, N.S. IX : 3 (April, 1956), 231-232 (W. Schlegelmilch).

DANISH

Spørg ikke (*Brennendes Geheimnis*). Tr. Jørgen Budtz-Jørgensen. København: Jespersen and Pio, 1936.

1769.   *BV*, 16.a. (1936-1937), 32.

Amok. Tr. Eden and Cedar Paul. New York: Viking, 1931.

1770.   *BTr*, July 18, 1931, p. 1 (W.E.H.).
1771.   *Fo*, LXXXVI (Aug., 1931), 10.
1772.   *NRep*, LXVII (July 15, 1931), 242.
1773.   *NYHTB*, June 14, 1931, p. 7 (Margaret C. Dawson: "A White Man Amuck").
1774.   *NYTBR*, June 14, 1931, p. 7 (Louis Kronenberger: "Zweig's Tale of Guilt").
1775.   *PMB*, XXXVI (Oct., 1931), 69.
1776.   *SR*, July 26, 1931, p. 7.
1777.   *SRL*, VII (July 11, 1931), 963.

Beware of Pity. Tr. Phyllis and Trevor Blewitt. New York: Viking, 1939.

1778.   *Bl*, XXXV (Apr. 1, 1939), 253.
1779.   *BTr*, Mar. 25, 1939, p. 1 (O. E. Schoen-Rene).
1780.   *COS*, June, 1939, p. 12.
1781.   *Cwl*, XXX (June 2, 1939), 164-165 (P. T. Hartung).
1782.   *LT*, May 5, 1939, p. 20 (J.S.).
1783.   *LT*, May 6, 1939, p. 263.
1784.   *MG*, May 5, 1939, p. 7 (Wilfred Gibson).
1785.   *N*, CXLVIII (Apr. 1, 1939), 381 (Maxwell Geismar: "Descent into Pity").
1786.   *Ne*, XIII (1939), 43.
1787.   *NSN*, XVII (May 20, 1939), 786 (John Mair).
1788.   *NY*, XV (Mar. 18, 1939), 85.
1789.   *NYHTB*, Mar. 19, 1939, p. 15 (Alfred Kazin: "Stefan Zweig's Novel").
1790.   *NYTBR*, Mar. 19, 1939, p. 6 (Louis Kronenberger: "Stefan Zweig's Brilliant Novel").
1791.   *PIQ*, Autumn, 1939, p. 29.
1792.   *PW*, CXXXV (1939), 791 (A. Hackett).
1793.   *Sp*, CLXII (May 12, 1939), 822 (Kate O'Brien).
1794.   *SR*, Mar. 26, 1939, p. 7 (R. W. N.).
1795.   *SRL*, XIX (Mar. 18, 1939), 10 (George Stevens: "Code of a Gentleman").
1796.   *T*, XXXIII (Mar. 27, 1939), 76.
1797.   *WLB*, XXXV (Apr., 1939), 66.

The Buried Candelabrum. Tr. Eden and Cedar Paul. New York: Viking, 1937.

1798.   *Bl*, XXXIV (Dec. 1, 1937), 130.
1799.   *CIW*, XXXI (1938), 180.
1800.   *ILN*, CXCII (1936-1937), 202.
1801.   *LT*, Dec. 11, 1937, p. 945.
1802.   *NRep*, XCIII (Dec. 15, 1937), 179 (Harry Thornton Moore: "Light of Israel").
1803.   *NYHTB*, Nov. 7, 1937, p. 14 (Alfred Kazin: "Parable for Wandering Jews").
1804.   *NYTBR*, Oct. 17, 1937, p. 8 (Harold Strauss: "Stefan Zweig's Legend of the Menorah").
1805.   *SR*, Oct. 17, 1937, p. 7 (F.G.B.).
1806.   *SRL*, XVI : 25 (Oct. 16, 1937), 22 (S. V. Benét: "The Voice of Israel: The Buried Candelabrum").
1807.   *T*, XXX (Oct. 25, 1937), 80.

The Burning Secret. London: Allen and Unwin, 1921.

1808.   *LT*, Apr. 7, 1921, 230 (L.S.).

Conflicts. Three Tales. Tr. Eden and Cedar Paul. New York: Viking, 1927; London: Allen and Unwin, 1928.

1809.   *LA*, CCCXXXIII (Nov. 1, 1927), 844.
1810.   *N*, CXXVI : 3262 (Jan. 11, 1928), 48-49 (Alter Brody: "Wanted, A Literary Tariff").
1811.   *NRep*, LIII (Jan. 4, 1928), 200-201.
1812.   *NYEP*, Oct. 29, 1927, p. 14 (Ruth Lechlitner).
1813.   *NYHTB*, Sept. 18, 1927, p. 5 (Babette Deutsch).
1814.   *NYTBR*, Oct. 9, 1927, pp. 8, 14 (Harry Salpeter: "Three Powerful Stories").
1815.   *NYW*, Oct. 16, 1927, p. 10 (Harry Salpeter).

Kaleidoscope. Thirteen Stories and Novelletes. Tr. Eden and Cedar Paul. New York: Viking, 1934; London: Cassell, 1934.

1816.   *Bl*, XXX (July, 1934), 353.
1817.   *BTr*, Apr. 21, 1934, p. 1 (F.M.).
1818.   *COS*, July, 1934, p. 16.
1819.   *Fo*, XCII (Jan., 1934), v. (Edith H. Walton).
1820.   *LT*, June 26, 1934, p. 19.
1821.   *LT*, July 12, 1934, p. 491.
1822.   *N*, CXXXVIII (May 16, 1934), 571 (Florence Codman: "Middle Europe").
1823.   *NRep*, LXXIX: 1022 (July 4, 1934), 216-217 (Barthold Fles: "Now as a Story Teller").
1824.   *NYHTB*, Apr. 1, 1934, p. 5 (F. L. Marsh: "Zweig, a Great European Story Teller").
1825.   *NYTBR*, Apr. 1, 1934, p. 8 (Louis Kronenberger: "Brilliant Tales by Stefan Zweig").
1826.   *SR*, May 13, 1934, p. 7.
1827.   *SRL*, X (Apr. 28, 1934), 661 ("Echoes of Events").
1828.   *Sp*, CLIII (July 13, 1934), 64 (Graham Greene).

Letter from an Unknown Woman. Tr. Eden and Cedar Paul. New York: Viking, 1932; London: Cassell, 1933.

1829.   *N*, CXXXV (July 20, 1932), 62.
1830.   *NSN*, V (1933), 264.
1831.   *NYHTB*, June 19, 1932, p. 3 (F. T. Marsh: "Unwavering Devotion").
1832.   *NYTBR*, June 19, 1932, p. 6 (Harold Strauss: "A Masterly Novelette by Stefan Zweig").
1833.   *SR*, June 17, 1932, p. 7.
1834.   *SRL*, VIII (June 18, 1932), 791 (Wm. Rose Benét: "L'Inconnu").

Passion and Pain. Tr. Eden and Cedar Paul. New York: B. G. Richards, 1925; London: Chapman and Hill, 1924.

1835.   *Di*, LXXX (Mar. 1, 1926), 252 (Gilbert Seldes).
1836.   *N*, CXXII (1926), 39.
1837.   *NYHTB*, Aug. 16, 1925, p. 5 (J. J. Smertenko).
1838.   *NYTBR*, Apr. 26, 1925, p. 8.
1839.   *NYTBR*, June 6, 1925, p. 9 (Elizabeth Sanderson).
1840.   *NYW*, May 3, 1925, p. 7.

The Royal Game. (The Royal Game – Amok – Letter from an Unknown Woman). Tr. Eden and Cedar Paul. New York: Viking, 1944; London: Cassell, 1945.

1841.   *BWk*, Apr. 16, 1944, p. 3 (Jack Conroy).
1842.   *K*, XII (Jan. 1, 1944), 7.
1843.   *LJ*, LXIX (Apr. 1, 1944), 304 (M. P. McKay).
1844.   *N*, CLVIII (May 6, 1944), 547 (Diana Trilling).
1845.   *NY*, XX (Apr. 15, 1944), 83.
1846.   *NYHTB*, Apr. 9, 1944, p. 5 (F. H. Bullock).
1847.   *NYTBR*, Apr. 9, 1944, p. 7 (Kenneth Fearing: "Chess Mad").
1848.   *SR*, May 14, 1944, p. 4 (L. S. Munn).
1849.   *SRL*, XXVII (Feb. 26, 1944), 5-7 (Christopher La Farge: "Say It With Fiction"; Zweig Portrait, p. 5).

FRENCH

Amok ou le Fou de Malaise. Tr. Alzir Hella and Olivier Bournac. Paris: Stock, 1927.

1850.   *RELV*, 44.a. (1927), 321 (Henri Loiseau).

La Confusion des Sentiments. Tr. Alzir Hella and Olivier Bournac. Paris: Stock, 1929.

1851.   *NRF*, N.S. XXXIV (1930), 585 (René Lalou).

Vingt-quatre Heures de la Vie d'une Femme. Tr. Alzir Hella and Olivier Bournac. Paris: Attinger, 1929.

1852.   *BU*, II (1929), 791 (Daniel Rops).

ITALIAN

Adolescenze (*Erstes Erlebnis*) Tr. Marcella Dreyfus. Milano: Sperling and Kupfer, 1933 (or later editions).

1853.   *ICS*, XVI (1933), 267.
1854.   *RN*, 3. sér., XIX (1936-1937), 227.

Leggende. Tr. Anita Rho. Milano: Sperling and Kupfer, 1937.

1855.   *NSB*, 4.a. (1938), 21.

Lettera d'una Sconosciuta ("Brief einer Unbekannten"). *Leporella.* Tr. Berta Burgio Ahrens. Milano: Sperling and Kupfer, 1932.

1856.   *ICS*, XVI (1933), 55.

La Paura ("Angst" *et al.*). Milano: Sperling and Kupfer, 1938.

1857.   *LI*, 4.a.: 2 (1939), 796.

Sovvertimento dei Sensi ("Verwirrung der Gefühle") Tr. Berta Burgio Ahrens, Milano: Corbaccio, 1931.

1858.   *ICS*, XV (1932), 211 (E. Palmieri).

POLISH

24 Godziny z Zycia Kobiety i Inne Opowiadania ("24 Stunden aus dem Leben einer Frau"). Warszawa, 1957.

1859.   *TL*, 213 (1957), 4 (Marceli Ranicki: "Dwaj Pisarze Niemieccy").

ESSAYS

GERMAN

Abschied von Rilke. Tübingen: Rainer Wunderlich, 1927 (or later editions).

1860.   *DT*, 20.-21.J. (1929), 390 (Otto Jancke).

Arturo Toscanini – Ein Bildnis. Wien: Reichner, 1936.

1861.   *CVZ*, 15.J.: 8, 2. Beilage (1936), 2.

Erinnerungen an Emile Verhaeren. Wien: Christoph Reissers Söhne, 1917; Leipzig: Selbstverlag des Verfassers, 1927 (or other editions).

1862.   *D*, 2.J. (1919), 265.
1863.   *JDB*, 7.J. (1920), 105.

Europäisches Erbe. Ed. Richard Friedenthal. Frankfurt am Main: Fischer, 1960.

1864.   *LT*, Jan. 6, 1961, p. 5.

Fahrten. Landschaften und Städte. Wien – Leipzig: Tal and Co., 1919 (or later editions).

1865.   *BüB*, III (1923), 42 (E. Ackerknecht).
1866.   *DLE*, 23.J.: 15 (May 1, 1921), 953 (Wilhelm Schmidtbonn).
1867.   *DLE*, 25.J.: 4 (Nov. 15, 1922), 250 (Herbert Johann Holz).
1868.   *ZB*, N.F., 12.J.: 2, Beilage (1920), 310.

Das Herz Europas. Zürich: Max Rascher, 1918.

1869.   *DLE*, 20.J.: 22 (Aug. 15, 1918), 1357-1360 (Kurt Martens: "Flugschriften über den Krieg").
1870.   *IAR*, 3.J.: 9-10 (1918), 7.
1871.   *WL*, 11.J.: 15 (1918), 93-94 (O. Volkart).

Sinn und Schönheit der Autographen. Wien: Sonderdruck des Verfassers, 1935.

1872.   *DS*, 2.J. (1936), 145.

86

ENGLISH

Amerigo, A Comedy of Errors in History. Tr. Andrew St. James. New York: Viking, 1942.

1873.   *A*, LXVI (Mar. 14, 1942), 635.
1874.   *AHR*, XLVIII (Oct., 1942), 86 (W. J. Wilson).
1875.   *Bl*, XXXVIII (May 1, 1942), 328.
1876.   *Cwl*, XXXV (Apr. 10, 1942), 628 (Max Fischer).
1877.   *LJ*, LXVII (Feb. 1, 1942), 131 (G. E. Brown).
1878.   *N*, CLIV (Feb. 21, 1942), 230 (Samuel Eliot Morrison: "Dr. Vespucci").
1879.   *NY*, XVIII (Feb. 28, 1942), 60.
1880.   *NYHTB*, Apr. 5, 1942, p. 19 (Henry Steele Connager: "Vespucci's New World").
1881.   *NYTBR*, Mar. 8, 1942, p. 3 (Philip Ainsworth Means: "How America Received Its Name").
1882.   *WLB*, XXXVIII (Apr., 1942), 68.

GERMAN

Balzac. Der Roman seines Lebens. Stockholm: Bermann-Fischer, 1946 (or later editions).

1883.   *NDL*, 7.J.: 11 (Nov., 1959), 45-46 (Kurt Böttcher: "Der Lebensroman des unerschöpflichen Balzac").
1884.   *W*, 15.J.: 692 (1947), 5 (F. Bondy: "Balzac der Mächtige").

ENGLISH

Balzac. Tr. William and Dorothy Rose. New York: Viking, 1946 (or later editions).

1885.   *Bl*, XLIII (Jan. 15, 1947), 154.
1886.   *BMCN*, Nov., 1946 (Henry Seidel Canby).
1887.   *BS*, VI (Dec. 1, 1946), 141-142 (Victor R. Yanitelli).
1888.   *BWk*, Nov. 24, 1946, p. 3 (Jex Martin).
1889.   *ILN*, CCXII (Jan. 31, 1948), 120 (John Squire: "A Great Creator Re-created").
1890.   *LJ*, LXXI (Nov. 1, 1946), 1541 (F. E. Hirsch).
1891.   *NRep*, CXV (Dec. 2, 1946), 730 ,732-733 (Harry Levin: "Grandeur and Decadence").
1892.   *NSN*, XXXIV (Dec. 20, 1947), 493-494 (Raymond Mortimer).
1893.   *NY*, XXII (Nov. 23, 1946), 120 (Hamilton Basso).
1894.   *NYHTB*, Nov. 17, 1946, p. 5 (Marvin Lowenthal).
1895.   *NYP*, Dec. 9, 1946, p. 31 (Matthew Josephson: "Stefan Zweig's 'Balzac' and the Human Comedy").
1896.   *NYTBR*, Nov. 24, 1946, p. 1 (Henri Peyre: "A Baffling, Superhuman Figure").
1897.   *SFC*, Dec. 26, 1946, p. 12 (George Snell).
1898.   *Si*, XXVI (Feb., 1947), 52 (Boniface Buckley).
1899.   *SRL*, XXIX (Dec. 14, 1946), 13 (Robert Pick: "One of Literature's Immortals").
1900.   *T*, XLVIII (Nov. 25, 1946), 116 ("Posthumous Portrait").

PORTUGUESE

Balzac. O Romance da sua Vida. Tr. Mario José Dominques. Porto: Civilização, 1951.

1901.   *Oc*, XL : 154 (1951), 107-108 (J. de Castro Osorio).

87

GERMAN

Castellio gegen Calvin; oder ein Gewissen gegen die Gewalt. Wien: Reichner, 1936 (or later editions).

1902.   *DSa*, 2.J. (1947), 598-600 (Pierre Bertrand: "Das Problem der Toleranz oder Castellion gegen Calvin"; This article first appeared in French in the *Tribune de Genève*, Apr. 21, 1947; German translation by Harold Mason).

DUTCH

Strijd Rond een Brandstapel. Castellio tegen Calvijn. Tr. Reinier P. Sterkenburg. Amsterdam: Albert de Lange, 1936.

1903.   *Bks*, 30.J. (1937), 469.

ENGLISH

The Right to Heresy. Castellio Against Calvin. Tr. Eden and Cedar Paul. New York: Viking, 1936; London: Cassell, 1936.

1904.   *Bl*, XXXIII (Dec., 1936), 106.
1905.   *CC*, LIII (Dec. 2, 1936), 1616 (John T. McNeill: "Prophet versus Reformer").
1906.   *Chm*, CLI (Jan. 1, 1937), 19 (A. L. Murray).
1907.   *Chr*, II (1937), 332-335 (C. H. Moehlman).
1908.   *COS*, Dec., 1936, p. 23.
1909.   *CW*, CXLIV (Jan., 1937), 499 (B.L.C.).
1910.   *LT*, Nov. 7, 1936, p. 910.
1911.   *MG*, Oct. 30, 1936, p. 7 (George Jackson).
1912.   *N*, CXLIII (Oct. 24, 1936), 488 (Alice Beal Parsons: "The Pitiless Christ").
1913.   *NRep*, LXXXIX (July 20, 1937), 362 (W. L. Sperry).
1914.   *NYHTB*, Oct. 25, 1936, p. 7 (Reinhold Niebuhr: "On the Arrogance of Minor Prophets").
1915.   *NYTBR*, Nov. 15, 1936, p. 9 (Lloyd W. Eshleman: "Stefan Zweig's New Parable of the Right to Heresy").
1916.   *RaE*, XXXIV (1936-1937), 235 (F. M. Powell).
1917.   *SP*, CLVII (Dec. 25, 1936), 1131 (A. L. Rowse).
1918.   *SR*, Nov. 22, 1936, p. 7 (F.G.B.).
1919.   *SRL*, XV (Nov. 28, 1936), 10 (Garret Mattingly: "Humanist versus Dictator").
1920.   *Tab*, CLXIX (Apr. 3, 1937), 485.

FRENCH

Castellion contre Calvin ou Conscience contre Violence. Tr. Alzir Hella. 8th ed. Paris: Grasset, 1936 (or later editions).

1921.   *LP*, May, 1948.
1922.   *MS*, June 10, 1947.
1923.   *PRO*, Sept. 15, 1947.
1924.   *Ré*, Apr. 12, 1947 (Roland de Pury).
1925.   *SC*, Apr., 1948.
1926.   *TrG*, Apr. 21, 1947 (Pierre Bertrand).
1927.   *VP*, May 16, 1947 (Jacques Courvoisier).
1928.   *VP*, June 13, 1947.

Marceline Desbordes-Valmore. Das Lebensbild einer Dichterin. Leipzig: Insel, 1920 (or later editions).

1929.	*BT*, Apr. 17, 1921 (F. Michael).
1930.	*DL*, XXX : 3 (1927-1928), 182 (Georg Ransohoff).
1931.	*DLE*, 23.J. (1921), 1475 (F. Strunz).
1932.	*DNS*, XXX (1922), 194 (W. Friedmann).
1933.	*Hl*, 18.J.: 2 (1922), 375-379 (F. Fuchs).
1934.	*LCfD*, 72.J. (1921), 521 (O. Hachtman).
1935.	*LH*, 64.J. (1927), 209 (L. Gausebeck-Dörper).
1936.	*PJ*, CLXXXIV (1921), 132 (W. Heynen).
1937.	*VV*, II (1922), 543 (Hermann Hesse).
1938.	*WL*, XIV (1921), 936 (C. Seelig).
1939.	*WM*, Sept., 1923, p. 105.
1940.	*ZB*, N.F., XIV : Lit. (1922), 193.

Triumph und Tragik des Erasmus von Rotterdam. Wien-Leipzig-Zürich: Herbert Reichner, 1934.

1941.	*BIG*, X (1934), 50 (Badt-Strauss).
1942.	*CVZ*, 13.J.: 30, 3. Beibl. (Oct. 5, 1934), 3 (Julius Bab).
1943.	*JR*, 40.J.: 20 (1935), 9 (Rosenkranz).
1944.	*Mo*, X (1935), 567 (Cohn).
1945.	*NFP*, Nov. 4, 1934.

Erasmus fra Rotterdam. Tr. G. Rønberg. København: Jespersen and Pio, 1934 (or later editions).

1946.	*BV*, 17.a. (1936-1937), 25.

Erasmus of Rotterdam. Tr. Eden and Cedar Paul. New York: Viking, 1934; London: Cassell, 1934 (or later editions).

1947.	*A*, LII (Nov. 10, 1934), 115 (H. H. Coulson: "Thomas More's Friend").
1948.	*AR*, IV (Dec., 1934), 246 (Charles F. Ronayne: "Two Portraits of Erasmus").
1949.	*Bl*, XXXI (Dec., 1934), 129.
1950.	*BTr*, Dec. 19, 1934, p. 3.
1951.	*CC*, LI (Dec. 19, 1934), 1626.
1952.	*CF*, XV (Mar., 1935), 236 (W. A. Breyfogle).
1953.	*Cwl*, XXI (Jan. 25, 1935), 379 (Paul Crowley).
1954.	*COS*, Jan., 1935, p. 3.
1955.	*CW*, CXL (Feb., 1935), 622 (R. J.S.H.).
1956.	*Fo*, XCIII (Feb., 1935), vi (E. H. Walton).
1957.	*JMH*, VII (1935), 365-366 (W. K. Ferguson).

1958.	*LM*, XXXI (1938), 180-181 (B. Dobrée).
1959.	*LT*, Feb. 14, 1935, p. 86.
1960.	*NRep*, LXXXI (Jan. 23, 1934), 314
1961.	*NSN*, VIII (Nov. 24, 1934), 759 (K. John).
1962.	*NYHT*, Nov. 3, 1934, p. 9 (Lewis Gannett).
1963.	*NYHTB*, Nov. 4, 1934, p. 3 (Preserved Smith: "A Brains Truster of Reformation Days").
1964.	*NYTBR*, Nov. 4, 1934, p. 5 (Percy Hutchinson).
1965.	*PIO*, Spring, 1935, p. 34.
1966.	*SAQ*, XXXIV (1935), 445-448 (R. Giese).
1967.	*SeR*, XLIII (1935), 236-240 (A. E. DuBois).
1968.	*Sp*, CLIII : Sup. 8, Nov. 23, 1934 (A. L. Rowse).
1969.	*SR*, Jan. 6, 1935, p. 7 (F.G.B.).
1970.	*SRL*, XI (Dec. 1, 1934), 328 (H.T.C.).
1971.	*Th*, XI (Sept., 1936), 301.
1972.	*WLB*, XXXI (Jan., 1935), 12.

FRENCH

Erasme. Grandeur et Décadence d'une Idée. Tr. Alazir Hella. Paris: Grasset, 1935 (or later editions).

1973.	*APL*, CII (May 10, 1935), 564 (A. Lang).
1974.	*CdS*, 22.a. (June, 1935), 517-518.
1975.	*EPCJ*, 72.a., CCXXIV (1935), 858 (J. Lecler).
1976.	*LLM*, 33.a. (1936-1937), 277.
1977.	*MF*, 46.a., CCLXII (1936-1937), 423-425 (J. E. Spenlée).
1978.	*Op*, XXVIII : 9 (1937-1938), 14 (Y. Clogenson).
1979.	*RdV*, 7.a. (1939), 1272-1273.
1980.	*RELV*, 53.a. (1936-1937), 365 (H. Chanchoy).
1981.	*RH*, 60.a., CLXXVI (1935), 98 (H. Hauser).
1982.	*RHEF*, XXII (1936-1937), 83-84 (P. Jourda).
1983.	*RHPR*, 15.a. (1935), 379 (H. Strohl).

ITALIAN

Erasmo da Rotterdam. Tr. Lavinia Mazzucchetti. Milano-Verona: Mondadori, 1935 (or later editions).

| 1984. | *BF*, 10.a. (1937-1938), 239-240 (E. Porena). |
| 1985. | *CM*, IX (1936-1937), 199 ff. (E. Cione). |

GERMAN

Joseph Fouché. Bildnis eines politischen Menschen. Leipzig: Insel, 1929 (or later editions).

1986.	*Abl*, V (1928-1929), 143 (O. Steinbrinck).
1987.	*BBZ*, Kunst, No. 257 (Peter Hamecher: "Der Mann ohne Gewissen") (Cf. *DL*, XXXII : 4 (1929-1930), 222).
1988.	*BT*, Jan. 7, 1930 (Heinrich Eduard Jacob) (Cf. *DL*, XXXII : 6 (1929-1930), 349).
1989.	*BüB*, 11.J.: 1/3 (1931), 131 (G. A. Narciss).
1990.	*DAZ*, Oct. 23, 1929 (Th. Böttiger).

1991. *DBu*, 9.J. (1929), 345.
1992. *DJZ*, VI (1928-1929), 296.
1993. *DL*, XXXII (1929-1930), 369-370 (C. F. W. Behl).
1994. *DLW*, V (1930), 41 (Willy Haas: "Die Staatspolizei") (*Cf. DL*, XXXII : 3 (1929-1930), 158).
1995. *DNN*, Sept. 17, 1929.
1996. *DR*, IV (1929), 47-50 (H. Kranz).
1997. *DRg*, II (1929), 963.
1998. *DRZ*, No. 296 (A. Baldus) (Cf. *DL*, XXXII : 6 (1929-1930), 349).
1999. *DT*, XXI : 9 (1929), 686-691 (H. Elbrechter: "Gesicht unserer Zeit") (Cf. *DL*, XXXII : 5 (1929-1930), 287).
2000. *EuG*, 7.J. VIII: Beilage (1929), 15 (H. Thieme).
2001. *FT*, Oct. 15, 1929 (W. Bolze).
2002. *G*, 9.J. (1930), 174 (Fränke).
2003. *Gr*, 24.J. (1930), 662 (I. Terhaar).
2004. *HFbl*, Oct. 5, 1929 (Joachim Maass: "Stefan Zweigs Bildnis eines politischen Menschen") (Cf. *DL*, XXXII : 3 (1929-1930), 155).
2005. *HK*, Sept. 29, 1929 (K. Voss).
2006. *HSFS*, 8.J. (1930), 112 (Radebeul).
2007. *JR*, 34.J. (1929), 694 (Rosenkranz).
2008. *KAZ*, Nov. 6, 1929.
2009. *KP*, No. 325 (Will Scheller: "Unheroische Biographie") (Cf. *DL*, XXXII: 5 (1929-1930), 283).
2010. *KVZ*, No. 809 (Heinrich Karl Köhler: "Ein Genie des Verrats") (Cf. *DL*, XXXII : 5 (1929-1930), 283).
2011. *KZ*, Sept. 21, 1930 (J. Kreutzer).
2012. *LH*, 66.J. (Sept., 1929), 216 (E. Alker).
2013. *MNN*, Nov. 11, 1929 (L. Adelt).
2014. *NR*, 1928, p. 829 (O. Flake).
2015. *NZZ*, No. 89 (H. A. Wyss) (Cf. *DL*, XXXII : 6 (1929-1930), 348).
2016. *PJ*, CCXX (1930), 298-306 (W. Heynen).
2017. *SchR*, 32.J. (1932), 648 (Chastonay: "Fouché und Talleyrand").
2018. *VZ*, Oct. 6, 1929 (Paul Wiegler: "Genie des Hintergrunds") (Cf. *DL*, XXXII: 3 (1929-1930), 155).
2019. *ZP*, XX (1930), 535-538 (Charmatz).

ENGLISH

Joseph Fouché. The Portrait of a Politician. Tr. Eden and Cedar Paul. New York: Viking, 1930; London: Cassell, 1930 (or later editions).

2020. *BA*, VI (1932), 301 (G. Mueller).
2021. *Bl*, XXVII (Jan., 1931), 206.
2022. *Bm*, LXXI (Aug., 1930), 555 (Margaret Wallace).
2023. *BTr*, Aug. 27, 1930, p. 2.
2024. *HO*, XXI : 5 (Dec., 1930), 395 (C. R. Hall).
2025. *LM*, XXII (Oct., 1930), 567 (Cl. Wilkinson).
2026. *LT*, Sept. 19, 1930, p. 15.
2027. *N*, CXXXI (Aug. 27, 1930), 226 (Eugene Loehrke: "Bloodless Biography").
2028. *NAR*, CCXXX (Oct., 1930), 506 (Herschel Brickell: "A Stefan Zweig Biography").
2029. *NRep*, LXV (Dec. 31, 1930), 200.
2030. *NS*, XXXVI (Oct. 18, 1930), 58.
2031. *NYHTB*, Aug. 10, 1930, p. 1 (M. M. Colum).
2032. *NYTBR*, Aug. 17, 1930, p. 9 (Alexander Nazaroff: "Fouché, Whom Napoleon Called 'the perfect Traitor'").

2033. *O*, CLV (Aug. 13, 1930), 586 (Allen W. Porterfield: "The Season's Greatest Story").
2034. *RR*, LXXXII (Sept., 1930), 12.
2035. *SRL*, XXVIII (Nov., 1930), 273.
2036. *SRL*, VII (Aug. 9, 1930), 36 (A. W. G. Randall).

FRENCH

Joseph Fouché. Tr. Alzir Hella and Olivier Bournac. Paris: Grasset, 1930 (or later editions).

2037. *E*, XXX (1932), 634-635 (P. Abraham).
2038. *GR*, 35.a. (Apr., 1931), 309-313 (J. Ernest-Charles).
2039. *JD*, XXXVII : 1 (Feb. 21, 1930), 318-320 (M. Muret: "Vie de Fouché").
2040. *P*, 3. sér. CLXXXI (1931), 207-208 (Geoffroy de Grandmaison).
2041. *RB*, LXIX : 13 (July 4, 1931), 403-407 (René Moulin: "Fouché, vu par Stefan Zweig").
2042. *REH*, 99.a. (1932), 448 (L. Miran).
2043. *RELV*, 47.a. (1930), 162-165 (C. Pitollet).
2044. *RP*, 42.a., V (1935), 458-462 (A. Albert-Petit: "Ministre de la police sous Napoléon: Fouché").
2045. *Ts*, Feb. 27, 1930 (A. Levinson).

ITALIAN

Fouché. Tr. Lavinia Mazzucchetti. Milano: Mondadori, 1930.

2046. *BF*, 5.a. (1930), 707-708 (G. Gabrielli).
2047. *ICS*, XIII (1930), 322 (E. Palmieri).

SPANISH

Fouché, el Genio Tenebroso. Tr. de la Editorial. Barcelona: Juventud, 1935 (or later editions).

2048. *U*, 14.a. (1937-1938), 592 (J. M. Castro y Calvo).

ENGLISH

Conqueror of the Seas. The Story of Magellan. Tr. Eden and Cedar Paul. New York: Viking, 1938 (or later editions).

2049. *A*, LVIII (Mar. 5, 1938), 526 (Mother Mary Lawrence).
2050. *As*, Mar., 1938, 203.
2051. *BA*, XIV (1940), 300 (Pieter H. Kollewijn).
2052. *Bl*, XXXIV (Feb. 15, 1938), 226.
2053. *BTr*, Feb. 5, 1938, p. 1 (Julius Adelberg).
2054. *CF*, XVIII (Aug., 1938), 155 (Eleanor Godfrey).
2055. *CH*, XLVIII (Apr., 1938), 2 (N. B. Cousins: "Magellan's Odyssey").
2056. *Cwl*, XXVII (Feb. 25, 1938), 501 (Lloyd W. Eshleman).
2057. *COS*, Mar., 1938, p. 6.
2058. *GJ*, XCII (1937-1938), 88.
2059. *ILN*, CXCII (1937-1938), 698 (J. Squire: "Magellan, Pioneer of the Pacific").
2060. *LT*, Apr. 12, 1938, p. 9 ("Magellan, Pioneer of the Pacific").

2061. *LT*, Apr. 16, 1938, p. 261.
2062. *MG*, Apr. 22, 1938, p. 7 (R. Brown).
2063. *N*, CXLVI (Feb. 5, 1938), 158 (Alan Villiers: "Conqueror of the Seas").
2064. *Ne*, XI (1938), 29 ("Stefan Zweig Eulogizes the First Man Ever to Make a Round-the-World Cruise").
2065. *NRep*, XCIV (Feb. 16, 1938), 55.
2066. *NYHTB*, Feb. 6, 1938, p. 3 (Charles J. Finger: "The Tale's the Thing; Here It's Nobly Told").
2067. *NYTBR*, Feb. 6, 1938, p. 3 (R. L. Duffus: "A Smooth-Sailing Narrative of Magellan and His Voyage").
2068. *SE*, II (Oct., 1938), 520.
2069. *SGM*, LIV (1937-1938), 254.
2070. *SR*, Feb. 6, 1938, p. 72 (F. G. Bratton).
2071. *SRL*, XVII (Feb. 5, 1938), 5 (Oliver La Farge).
2072. *T*, XXXI (Feb. 14, 1938), 67.
2073. *WLB*, XXXIV (Apr., 1938), 63.

ITALIAN

Magellano. Tr. Lavinia Mazzucchetti. Milano: Mondadori, 1938.

2074. *BF*, 13.a. (1939), 512-514 (N. Naldoni-Centenari).
2075. *NA*, CD (Nov. 1, 1938), 117-120 (Raolo Girosi: "Vita e Cultura Italiana nel Mondo – Un Pilota Liqure di Magellano Dimenticato da Stefano Zweig").
2076. *RdC*, 13.a. (1938-1939), 1013-1015 (N. Naldoni-Centenari).
2077. *RM*, 71.a. (1937-1938), 133.

POLISH

Magellan. Tr. Zofia Petersowa. Warszawa: Ksiązka i Wiedza, 1957.

2078. *NLW*, 9 (1957), 8 (Lucjan Wolanowski: "Przygoda która nazywa sie historia").

GERMAN

Marie Antoinette. Bildnis eines mittleren Charakters. Leipzig: Insel, 1932.

2079. *DL*, XXXV : 4 (1932-1933), 240 (C. F. W. Behl).
2080. *Fr*, 41.J. (1933), 61 (Spörri).
2081. *FZ*, Nov. 27, 1932.
2082. *Kr*, 1931-1933, p. 250 (Benninghoff).
2083. *KZ*, Oct. 23, 1932 (O. Doderer).
2084. *KZ*, No. 43 (D. H. Sarnetzki)(Cf. *DL*, XXXV : 3 (1932-1933), 149).
2085. *LCfD*, July, 1933, p. 1043 (J. Hohlfeld).
2086. *PL*, Nov. 4, 1932.
2087. *VZ*, No. 302 (Ernst Lissauer) (Cf. *DL*, XXXV : 4 (1932-1933), 213).

DANISH

Marie Antoinette. Et Gennemsnitsmenneskers Portraet. Tr. Kristine Jespersen. København: Jespersen and Pio, 1933 (or later editions).

2088. *BV*, 16.a. (1936-1937), 73.

Marie Antoinette. Portret van een Middelmatig Karakter. Tr. G. J. Werumeus Buning. Amsterdam: Albert de Lange, 1933.

2089.   *Bks,* 27.J. (1933-1934), 184.

Marie Antoinette. Portrait of an Average Woman. Tr. Eden and Cedar Paul. New York: Viking, 1933; London: Cassell, 1933.

2090.   *BA,* VII (1933), 466 (H. H.).
2091.   *Bl,* XXIX (May, 1933), 267.
2092.   *BTr,* Apr. 19, 1933, p. 2 (J. W. Maury).
2093.   *CDT,* Apr. 8, 1933, p. 18 (Fanny Butcher).
2094.   *COS,* Nov., 1933, p. 12.
2095.   *Cwl,* XX (May 4, 1934), 8.
2096.   *Fo,* LXXXIX (June, 1933), vii.
2097.   *LT,* Feb. 2, 1933, p. 69.
2098.   *MH,* XVIII (1934), 495-497 (B. Bunzel).
2099.   *N,* CXXXVI (Apr. 26, 1933), 478 (Catharine Young: "Portrait of Marie").
2100.   *NC,* CIX (1933), xv (J. Hayward).
2101.   *NRep,* LXXIV (May 10, 1933), 371 (Leo Gershoy).
2102.   *NRep,* LXXXIV (Sept. 25, 1935), 192 (Robert Morris Lovett: "A Pair of Queens").
2103.   *NSN,* VI (Oct. 14, 1933), sup., xviii.
2104.   *NYEP,* Apr. 8, 1933, p. 7 (William Soskin).
2105.   *NYHTB,* Apr. 9, 1933, p. 1 (Albert Guerard: "Marie Antoinette's Romantic Life and Death").
2106.   *NYTBR,* Apr. 2, 1933, p. 3 (Herbert Gorman).
2107.   *NYTBR,* May 7, 1933, p. 5.
2108.   *PA,* VI : 10 (1932), 489 (No. 3943) (A. B. Herrig: "Das eheliche Missgeschick Marie Antoinettes," in *PB,* IV (1932), 100-112).
2109.   *PIQ,* Autumn, 1933, p. 34.
2110.   *RR,* LXXXVII (May, 1933), 4.
2111.   *SG,* XXII (Oct., 1933), 528.
2112.   *Sp,* CLI (Sept. 29, 1933), 410 (James Laver).
2113.   *SR,* Apr. 23, 1933, p. 7 (R.R.C.).
2114.   *SRL,* IX (Apr. 1, 1933), 514 (Meade Minnigerode: "Portrait of a Queen").
2115.   *Th,* IX (June, 1934), 142-144.
2116.   *WLB,* XXIX (May, 1933), 137.

Marie Antoinette. Tr. Alzir Hella. Paris: Grasset, 1933.

2117.   *APL,* CII (May 25, 1934), 564 (A. Lang).
2118.   *CdS,* 21.a. (1934), 250-251 (G. Petit).
2119.   *JD,* XL : 2 (July 28, 1933), 149-152 (M. Muret).
2120.   *RA,* 7.a. (1931-1933), 1143.
2121.   *RB,* LXXII (1934), 197.
2122.   *RELM,* 51.a. (1934), 270-271 (H. Loiseau).
2123.   *RG,* 25.a. (1934), 280 (L. Brun).
2124.   *RQH,* 64.a. CXXV (1936-1937), 117-120.

Maria Antoinetta. Tr. Lavinia Mazzucchetti. Milano: Mondadori, 1933.

2125.   *ICS*, XVI (1933), 82 (E. Palmieri).
2126.   *L*, 4.a. (1933), 132-134 (M. Corra).
2127.   *NA*, CCCLXX (1933), 127-129 (A. Pompeati).

Maria Stuart. Wien-Leipzig-Zürich: Herbert Reichner, 1935.

2128.   *MO*, XI (1935), 136 (Silbergleist).
2129.   *NFP*, May 5, 1935 (J. Gregor).
2130.   *PL*, Apr. 25, 1935 (Otto Zarek).

Maria Stuart. Tr. Georg Rønberg. København: Jespersen and Pio, 1936.

2131.   *BV*, 19.a. (1936-1937), 44.

Maria Stuart. Tr. Reinier P. Sterkenburg. Amsterdam: Albert de Lange, 1935.

2132.   *Bks*, 29.J. (1936), 284-285.
2133.   *GN*, 1936, pp. 274-276 (Maart).

The Queen of Scots. Tr. Eden and Cedar Paul. New York: Viking, 1935; London: Cassell' 1935.

2134.   *A*, LIV (Oct. 19, 1935), 43 (Alfred G. Brickel: "The Catholic Queen").
2135.   *AB*, CLVI (Oct., 1935), 10 (Carl Van Doren).
2136.   *Bl*, XXXII (Oct., 1935), 41.
2137.   *BTr*, Aug. 28, 1935, p. 2 (Julius Adelburg).
2138.   *CDT*, Aug. 24, 1935, p. 9 (Fanny Butcher).
2139.   *CF*, XV (Nov., 1935), 374 (E.G.).
2140.   *CH*, XLIII (Oct., 1935), vii (John Chamberlin).
2141.   *COS*, Aug., 1935, p. 16.
2142.   *CW*, CXLII (Nov., 1935), 245 (P.C.).
2143.   *Fo*, XCIV (Nov., 1935), vii (E. H. Walton).
2144.   *LD*, CXX (Sept. 21, 1935), 24 (Sketch of Zweig included).
2145.   *LM*, XXXII (Sept., 1935), 505 (S. Spender).
2146.   *LT*, Oct. 10, 1935, p. 623.
2147.   *LT*, Oct. 15, 1935, p. 20.
2148.   *MB*, X (1935), 365.
2149.   *N*, CXLI (Sept. 11, 1935), 306-307 (C. G. Stillman).
2150.   *NRep*, LXXXIV (Sept. 25, 1935), 192 (Robert Morris Lovett: "A Pair of Queens").

2151.   *NSN*, X (Nov. 2, 1935), 652 (Renée Haynes).
2152.   *NYHTB*, Aug. 25, 1935, p. 3 (Mary Lamberton Becker: "The Most Readable and the Most Reliable").
2153.   *NYTBR*, Aug. 25, 1935, p. 1 (Peter Monro Jack); Dec. 1, 1935, p. 42.
2154.   *RR*, XCII (Oct., 1935), 4.
2155.   *Sp*, CLV : 2 (Oct. 18, 1935), 618 (A. L. Rowse).
2156.   *SR*, Sept. 8, 1935, p. 7 (F.G.B.).
2157.   *SRL*, XII (Aug. 31, 1935), 6 (J. E. Neale: "The Daughter of Debate").
2158.   *Th*, XII (Dec., 1936), 694 (F. H. Reynolds).
2159.   *WLB*, XXXI (July, 1935), 84.
2160.   *YR*, N.S. XXV (1936), 609-612 (C. Read).

FINNISH

Maria Stuart. Elämäkerta Romaani. Tr. Elina Vaara. Jyväskylä: Gummerus, 1938.

2161.   *Fk*, CXX (1938-1939), 61-66 (H. Hirn).

FRENCH

Marie Stuart. Tr. Alzir Hella. Paris: Grasset, 1936.

2162.   *CdS*, 23.a. (June, 1936), 514-516.
2163.   *EC*, V (1936-1937), 693 (C. Leclère).
2164.   *EPCJ*, 73.a. CCXXVII (1937-1938), 700 (J. Lecler).
2165.   *RELV*, 55.a. (1937-1938), 410 (H. Loiseau).
2166.   *RH*, CLXXX (1936-1937), 103-106 (R. Chauviré).

ITALIAN

Maria Stuarda. Tr. Lavinia Mazzucchetti. Milano: Mondadori, 1936.

2167.   *ICS*, 19.a. (1936-1937), 149 (G. A. Andriulli).
2168.   *NSB*, 2.a. (1936), 54.
2169.   *RN*, XXIV (1936-1937), 57 (M. L. Fiumi).

SWEDISH

Maria Stuart. Tr. Hugo Hultenberg. Stockholm: Skoglund, 1936.

2170.   *HT*, LVI (1936), 432.

GERMAN

Romain Rolland. Der Mann und das Werk. Frankfurt am Main: Ruetten and Loening, 1921 (or later editions).

2171.   *Bg*, 10.J.: 7 (1921), 79 (F. Castelle).
2172.   *Bib*, 13.J. (1931), 1402 (O. Jonsen).
2173.   *BT*, May 29, 1921 (J. Chapire).
2174.   *Büh*, II (1921), 95 (G. Morgenstern).

2175. *DNZ*, 39.J.: 1 (1921), 342 (I. Hift).
2176. *DT*, 13.J. (1921), 705 (E. Hoppe-Meyer).
2177. *Gr*, XX (1925-1926), 371-373.
2178. *HFbl*, Apr. 16, 1921 (H. Meyer-Bonfey).
2179. *LGRP*, 43.J. (1922), 187 (W. Friedmann).
2180. *LTb*, Dec. 1, 1921 (W. Friedmann).
2181. *LW*, 1926, p. 518 (Fr. Werner).
2182. *NBKL*, IV (1921), 5 (Martha Schiff).
2183. *NFP*, Mar. 11, 1923 (Ellen Key).
2184. *Nz*, Apr. 20, 1921 (Otto Zarek).
2185. *WAZ*, No. 12803 (Cf. *DLE*, 23.J.: 10 (Feb. 15, 1921), 613).
2186. *WL*, XIV (1920), 740 (Hermann Hesse).
2187. *WL*, XIV (1921), 936 (C. Seelig).
2188. *ZFEU*, XX (1921), 274 (H. Engel).
2189. *ZFEU*, XXVI : 1 (1927), 61 (C. Appel).

ENGLISH

Romain Rolland. The Man and His Work. Tr. Eden and Cedar Paul. New York: Seltzer, 1921.

2190. *Bm*, LXIII (Oct., 1922), 36.
2191. *BTr*, Nov. 2, 1921, p. 4 (E. F. Edgett).
2192. *Di*, LXXII (Jan., 1922), 92 (Kenneth Burke).
2193. *Fm*, IV (Nov. 30, 1921), 286.
2194. *LT*, Mar. 3, 1921, p. 145 (L. S.).
2195. *LT*, Dec. 15, 1921 (L. S.).
2196. *N*, CXIII (Nov. 16, 1921), 571 (Gregory Zilboorg: "The Apostle of Peace").
2197. *NRep*, XXVIII (Oct. 19, 1921), 222 (R. M. Lovett).
2198. *NYHTB*, Dec. 3, 1921, p. 225 (Ernest Boyd).
2199. *NYTBR*, Dec. 11, 1921, p. 14 ("Romain Rolland, the Idealist").
2200. *O*, XLIX : 1254 (Feb. 11, 1922), 116-117 (Newton Fuessle).
2201. *RR*, LXIV (Dec., 1921), 668.

FRENCH

Romain Rolland, sa Vie et son Oeuvre. Tr. O. Richey. Bruxelles: Office de Publicitè, 1929.

2202. *BU*, I (1930), 388-389 (E. Buenzod).
2203. *P*, CLXXXI (1931), 199-200 (M. Citoleux).

SPANISH

Romain Rolland, el Hombre y su Obra. Tr. Alfredo Cahn. Buenos Aires: Claridad, 1936.

2204. *Ud*, I : 3 (Apr., 1936), 5-6.

GERMAN

Emile Verhaeren. Leipzig: Insel, 1910.

2205. *DNS*, XIX (1911), 368-372 (L. Petry: "Stefan Zweig: Verhaeren. Verhaerens Gedichte").

2206.   *Gwt*, 40 (1911) (W. Wantoch: "Stefan Zweig: Verhaeren. Verhaerens Gedichte").
2207.   *NFP*, Feb. 19, 1911 (F. Servaes).
2207a.   *RRh*, 1.a.: 3 (Dec. 1, 1920), 149-150 (Dr. H. Krell: "Emile Verhaeren").
2208.   *WR*, 1911, p. 46 (E. W. Trojau: "Stefan Zweig: Verhaeren. Verhaerens Gedichte").

ENGLISH

Emile Verhaeren. Tr. Jethro Bithell. London-Edinburgh: Constable and Co., 1914; New York: Houghton Mifflin Co., 1914.

2209.   *A*, XII (Mar. 13, 1915), 542.
2210.   *An*, II (Nov. 28, 1914), 559.
2211.   *Bm*, XLVII (Dec., 1914), 77-78 (Francis Bickley).
2212.   *BTr*, Dec. 16, 1914, p. 27.
2213.   *MLN*, XXVII (Mar. 3, 1912), 117-119 (A. Schinz: "Modern French Poets").
2214.   *N*, XCIX (Dec. 24, 1914), 740.
2215.   *NYTBR*, Jan. 3, 1915, 2.
2216.   *YR*, N.S., V (1915), 197-198 (J. Erskine).

FRENCH

Emile Verhaeren, sa Vie, son Oeuvre. Tr. P. Morrise and H. Chernet. Paris: n.p., 1910.

2217.   *BMB*, 15.a. (1911), 29 (F. Masoin).

GERMAN

Baumeister der Welt: *Drei Meister – Der Kampf mit dem Dämon – Drei Dichter ihres Lebens*. Wien-Leipzig-Zürich: Herbert Reichner, 1935.

2218.   *CVZ*, 14.J.: 50, 4. Beibl. (1935), 2.

ENGLISH

Master Builders. A Typology of the Spirit. Tr. Eden and Cedar Paul. New York: Viking, 1939.

2219.   *BTr*, Nov. 11, 1939, p. 4 (H. M. Jones).
2220.   *Bl*, XXXVI (Nov. 15, 1939), 115.
2221.   *Cwl*, XXXI (Dec. 1, 1939), 141 (Euphemia van Rensselaer-Wyatt).
2222.   *Fo*, CII (Nov., 1939), 230 (Mary M. Colum: "Artists at Work").
2223.   *JNMD*, XCI (1939), 816.
2224.   *N*, CXLIX (Nov. 25, 1939), 584 (James Orrick: "Trilogy of Trilogies").
2225.   *NY*, XV (Sept. 23, 1939), 78.
2226.   *NYHTB*, Oct. 8, 1939, p. 20 (Albert Guerard: "Three Times Three Men").
2227.   *PIQ*, Winter, 1940, p. 22.
2228.   *SRL*, XXI (Nov. 25, 1939), 11 (Paul Rosenfeld: "An Analysis of Literary Genius").

GERMAN

Drei Dichter ihres Lebens: *Stendhal-Casanova-Tolstoi*. Leipzig: Insel, 1928.

2229.   *DG*, 5.J. (1929), 33 (F. Vogeler).
2230.   *DL*, XXX : 11 (1927-1928), 676 (Felix Braun).
2231.   *LGRP*, 50. J. (1929), 350-355 (Lerch).

ENGLISH

Adepts in Self-Portraiture: *Casanova, Stendhal, Tolstoy*. Tr. Eden and Cedar Paul. New York: Viking, 1928; London: Allen and Unwin, 1929.

2232.   *AH*, CXXII : 20 (Mar. 23, 1928), 707 (Franklin Gordon: "Stefan Zweig, Portrayer of Soul Conflicts").
2233.   *Bm*, LXIX (Mar., 1929), 101 (Lawrence S. Morris).
2234.   *BTr*, Nov. 10, 1928, p. 6 (J. W. Maury).
2235.   *COS*, Dec., 1928, p. 134.
2236.   *Di*, LXXXVI (June, 1929), 513-516 (Padraic Colum: "Studies in Personality").
2237.   *Fo*, LXXXI (Jan. 1, 1929), vi.
2238.   *LT*, Feb. 7, 1929, p. 93.
2239.   *N*, CXXVIII (Apr. 10, 1929), 431-432 (Angus Burrell: "Men in Masks").
2240.   *NS*, XXXII (Feb. 16, 1929), 604 (R. A. Scott-James).
2241.   *NYEP*, Nov. 10, 1928, p. 8 (Paul Eldridge).
2242.   *NYHTB*, Aug. 10, 1930, p. 1 (Mary M. Colum: "The Impulse to Biography").
2243.   *NYHTB*, Nov. 18, 1928, p. 4 (Eugen Löhrke: "Spiritual Surgery").
2244.   *NYTBR*, Nov. 11, 1928, p. 2 (Edwin Clark: "Three Great Egotists Portrayed by Stefan Zweig").
2245.   *NYW*, Dec. 16, 1928, p. 10 (Harry Salpeter).
2246.   *SLR*, XXVII (Feb., 1929), 59.
2247.   *SRL*, V (June 15, 1929), 1117.
2248.   *YR*, XIX (Sept., 1929), 163-166 (Albert Fuillerat: "Stendhal's Genius for Self-Analysis").

ITALIAN

Tre Poeti della Propria Vita: *Casanova-Stendhal-Tolstoi*. Tr. Enrico Rocca. Milano: Sperling and Kupfer, 1930.

2249.   *IC*, 12.a. (1931), 141-146 (R. Poggioli).
2250.   *ICS*, 14.a. (1931), 148.
2251.   *L*, 2.a. (Mar., 1931), 131-132 (Lavinia Mazzucchetti).

DANISH

Tolstoi – from *Drei Dichter ihres Lebens* (Danish version?).

2252.   *Fi*, 25.a. (1943), 302.

FRENCH

Casanova. Tr. Alzir Hella and Olivier Bournac. Paris: Attinger, 1930.

2253.   *P*, CLXXXI (1931), 121-122 (L. Mensch).
2254.   *RMd*, CCI (1936-1937), 80.

Tolstoi. Tr. Alzir Hella and Olivier Bournac. Paris: Attinger, 1928.

2255.   *APL,* XCI (Oct. 1, 1928), 305-306 (Benjamin Crémieux).
2256.   *BU,* II (1929), 906-907 (M. Beaufils).
2257.   *LNE,* 3.a. (1929), 493 (R. Rey Alvarez).
2258.   *MF,* 40.a. CCXI (1929), 470-474 (A. Chevalley).
2259.   *MF,* CCXVI (1931), 476-479 (J. E. Spenlée).
2260.   *NRe,* 4.sér. XCIX (1930), 157.
2261.   *RELV,* 45.a. (1928), 460 (H. Loiseau).

GERMAN

Drei Meister: Balzac-Dickens-Dostojewski. Leipzig: Insel, 1920.

2262.   *BT,* Nov. 7, 1920 (H. Sachaczewer).
2263.   *BüB,* I (1921), 60 (Homann).
2264.   *DLE,* 23.J.: 14 (Apr. 15, 1921), 842-845 (H. W. Keim).
2265.   *DNS,* July 12, 1930, p. 444.
2266.   *DTg,* Oct. 20, 1920 (H. Bieber).
2267.   *Kt,* June, 1921, pp. 166-168 (Fischer).
2268.   *LGRP,* 44.J. (1923), 378 (A. Streuber).
2269.   *LH,* 1921, p. 79 (Chr. Flaskamp).
2270.   *NFP,* Sept. 16, 1920 (O. Walzel).
2271.   *NR,* 1921, p. 669 (O. Flake).
2272.   *Nz,* Sept. 16, 1920 (Otto Zarek: "Ein notwendiges Buch") (Cf. *DLE,* 25.J.: 3 (Nov. 1, 1920), 162).
2273.   *ÖR,* LXV (1920), 282 (M. Pirker).
2274.   *VV,* I (1919-1920), 817 (Hermann Hesse).
2275.   *VZ,* Feb. 13, 1921 (Erich Marcus: "Der Romancier") (Cf. *DLE,* 23.J.: 13 (Apr. 1, 1921), 806).
2276.   *WZV,* 5 (1923), 90-92 (H. Keyserling).
2277.   *ZB,* N.F. 13.J.: 1 (1921), 181.

ENGLISH

Three Masters: Balzac, Dickens, Dostoeffsky. Tr. Eden and Cedar Paul. New York: Viking, 1930; London: Allen and Unwin, 1930.

2278.   *Bl,* XXVI (July, 1930), 395.
2279.   *Bm,* LXXI (June, 1930), 338-339.
2280.   *BTr,* June 28, 1930, p. 2.
2281.   *CW,* CXXXII (Nov., 1930), 241 (J. J. R.).
2282.   *LT,* June 26, 1930, p. 530.
2283.   *NRep,* LXIV (Sept. 3, 1930), 80 (Arthur Colton: "Three Novelists").
2284.   *NS,* XXXV (July 12, 1930), 445.
2285.   *NYHTB,* Apr. 27, 1930, p. 6 (Angel Flores: "Masters of the Novel").
2286.   *NYS,* Nov. 18, 1946, p. 21 (Wm. McFee: "Balzac and Dostoevsky are Subjects of Biography by Zweig and Troyat").
2287.   *NYTBR,* May 11, 1930, p. 2 (Louis Kronenberger).
2288.   *NYW,* June 1, 1930, p. 7.
2289.   *O,* CLIV (Apr. 30, 1930), 709 (F.L.R.).
2290.   *RX,* VI (July, 1930), 74-75 (S. P. Rudens).
2291.   *SLR,* XXVIII (Sept., 1930), 217.
2292.   *SRL,* CXLIX (June 28, 1930), 830.

Deux Grands Romanciers du XIXe Siècle: Balzac-Dickens. Tr. Alzir Hella and Olivier Bournac. Paris: Simon Kra, 1927.

2293.	*NRF*, N.S. XXX (1928), 863 (R. Fernandez).
2294.	*RAA*, V (1928), 368-370 (E. Famière).
2295.	*RELV*, 44.a. (1927), 321 (H. Loiseau).
2296.	*RG*, 18.a. (1927), 373 (R. Pitrou).

Dostoievski. Tr. Henri Bloch. Paris: Rieder, 1929.

2297.	*BU*, II (1929), 1415 (E. Buenzod).
2298.	*P*, 2. sér. CIX (1928-1929), 135 (P. Pisani).
2299.	*RG*, 19.a. (1929), 345 (A. Fournier).

ITALIAN

Tre Maestri: Balzac-Dickens-Dostojevski. Tr. Berta Ahrens. Milano: Sperling and Kupfer, 1932.

2300.	*IC*, 14.a. (1933), 45-50 (M. Robertazzi).
2301.	*ICS*, XVI (1933), 142 (E. Caprile).
2302.	*L*, 4.a. (1933), 252-254 (G. Zamboni).
2303.	*NA*, CCCLXX (1933), 129-131 (A. Pompeati).
2304.	*RN*, 55.a. 3. ser., XVIII (1933), 156.

GERMAN

Der Kampf mit dem Dämon: Hölderlin-Kleist-Nietzsche. Leipzig: Insel, 1925.

2305.	*BT*, No. 350 (Erich Everte) (Cf. *DL*, XXVII : 12 (Apr.-Sept., 1925)).
2306.	*BüB*, VI (1926), 211 (O. Bahrt).
2307.	*DBP*, IV (1927), 453-458 (Zöckler; Article only on "Hölderlin").
2308.	*DL*, XXVIII : 1 (Oct., 1925), 17-19 (Emil Lucka).
2309.	*DV*, 2.J. (1929), 270-274 (J. Klein).
2310.	*GOM*, 11.J.: 1 (1925), 511 (O. M. Fortana).
2311.	*Gr*, XIX (1924-1925), 493-494.
2312.	*KAZ*, No. 341 (Erich Jenisch) (Cf. *DL*, XXVII : 12 (Apr.-Sept., 1925)).
2313.	*LNN*, July 3, 1925 (K. Voss).
2314.	*LW*, Sept., 1925, p. 740 (R. H. Grützmacher).
2315.	*MMN*, XXVI (1927), 274 (Sudhoff).
2316.	*MNN*, Aug. 21, 1925 (Ernst Lissauer) (Cf. *DL*, XXVIII : 1 (1925-1926), 38).
2317.	*NFP*, May 20, 1925 (H. Bahr).
2318.	*NG*, 23.J.: 1 (1927), 168 (H. Stöcke).
2319.	*PNW*, 27.J. (1925), 531 (W. H. Becker).
2320.	*RG*, XVII : 9 (1926), 381-382 (L. Mis).
2321.	*TR*, Aug. 30, 1925 (Hanns Martin Elster) (Cf. *DL*, XXVIII : 2 (1925-1926), 99).
2322.	*ZB*, N.F. 19.J. (1927), 272 (H. Bethge).
2323.	*ZD*, 40.J. (1926), 618-619 (J. Stern).

Le Combat avec le Démon: Kleist-Hölderlin-Nietzsche. Tr. Alzir Hella. Paris: Stock, 1936.

2324.　*CdS*, 24.a. (1936-1937), 452-455.

Le Combat avec le Démon: Frédéric Nietzsche. Tr. Alzir Hella and Olivier Bournac. Paris: V. Attinger, 1930.

2325.　*NRe*, 4. sér, CXIII (1930), 240.
2326.　*NRF*, N.S. XXXVII (1933), 960 (J. Wahl).
2327.　*RHb*, 41.a.: 2 (1930), 350-355 (R. de Saint Jean).

Le Combat avec le Démon: Hölderlin. Tr. Alzir Hella and Olivier Bournac. Paris: V. Attinger, 1928.

2328.　*BU*, I (1929), 121 (M. Beaufils).
2329.　*NRF*, N.S. XXXIV (1930), 574-577 (J. Decour).
2330.　*RELV*, 45.a. (1928), 267-269 (H. Loiseau).
2331.　*RMd*, CLXXXIV (1930), 284-288 (N. Ségur).

ITALIAN

La Lotta col Demone: Hölderlin-Kleist-Nietzsche. Tr. A. Overdorfer. Milano: Sperling and Kupfer, 1930 (or later editions).

2332.　*IC*, 12.a. (1931), 285-289 (G. M. Tagliabue; Review only of "Nietzsche").
2333.　*ICS*, 17.a. (1934), 86 (L. Tonelli).
2334.　*RdP*, 30.a. (1936-1937), 279-281 (M. F. Canella; Review only of "Nietzsche").
2335.　*RN*, 3. sér., XX (1936-1937), 227.

GERMAN

Die Heilung durch den Geist. Franz Anton Mesmer-Mary Baker Eddy-Sigmund Freud. Leipzig: Insel, 1931.

2336.　*Äbl*, 1931, p. 101.
2337.　*BBZ*, Aug. 2, 1932 (F. Maraun).
2338.　*Bd*, Mar. 11, 1931 (M. Schnewlin).
2339.　*BM*, VIII (1931), 38, 75 (G. Feichtinger).
2340.　*Bng*, V (1931), 3 (F. Humbel) (Cf. *DL*, XXXIII : 12 (Apr.-Sept., 1931), 701).
2341.　*BT*, Jan. 30, 1931 (P. Flamm) (Cf. *DL*, XXXIII : 7 (Apr.-Sept., 1931), 399).
2342.　*ChW*, 46.J. (1932), 35 (Grabert).
2343.　*CVZ*, 10.J.: XI (1931), 237.
2344.　*DL*, 33.J.: 8 (May, 1931), 430-432 (Lutz Weltmann) (On page 430 is also a caricature-drawing of Stefan Zweig by B. F. Dolbin).
2345.　*DMW*, 57.J. (1931), 857-859 (K. Birnbaum).
2346.　*EAP*, II (1931-1932), 303 (A. Herzberg).
2347.　*Eck*, VII (1933), 409-413 (Theodor Spoerri).
2348.　*FdT*, 8.J. (1932), 220 (Haeberlin).
2349.　*Fu*, XVIII (1932), 213 (J. Schottky).
2350.　*Gdl*, 34.J. (1931), 207 (Kurzrock).

2351. *HFbl*, Feb. 28, 1931.
2352. *HK*, Mar. 7, 1931 (K. Voss).
2353. *KZ*, Mar. 15, 1931 (Emil Lucka).
2354. *MMN*, XXX (1930), 202 (Haberling).
2355. *MMW*, 78.J. (1931), 925 (E. Bleuler).
2356. *NB*, 7.J. (1930-1931), 185 (J. Peters).
2357. *NBL*, Kunst, No. 71 (Leonhard Adelt) (Cf. *DL*, XXXIII : 7 (Apr.-Sept., 1931), 399).
2358. *NFP*, Feb. 1, 1931 (Leonhard Adelt).
2359. *NlW*, 4.J.: 6 (1953), 10 (Karl August Horst: "Zum Wiederlasen empfohlen: Stefan Zweigs 'Heilung durch den Geist'").
2360. *PNW*, 33.J. (1931), 347 (Bresler).
2361. *SchR*, 31.J. (1931), 575.
2362. *SM*, IV (1931), 171 (Pryll).
2363. *Um*, 35.J. (1931), 686 (A. A. Friedländer).
2364. *Wt*, 13.J. (1931), 1019.

DANISH

Sjaelens Laegedom. Tr. Clara Hammerich. København: Hirschsprung, 1936.

2365. *UfL*, 95.a. (1937-1938), 1271.

DUTCH

Genezing door den Geest – Sigmund Freud. Tr. Reinier P. Sterkenburg. Arnhem: Van Loghum Slaterus, 1932.

2366. *Bks*, 26.J. (1932-1933), 252.
2367. *DNG*, 49.J. (Apr., 1934), 459-460 (F. S. Bosman).

ENGLISH

Mental Healers: Franz Anton Mesmer-Mary Baker Eddy-Sigmund Freud. Tr. Eden and Cedar Paul. New York: F. Ungar, 1932; London: Cassell, 1933.

2368. *AJPH*, XXII (June, 1932), 684 (Mazÿck P. Ravenel).
2369. *Bl*, XXVIII (Apr., 1932), 348.
2370. *Bm*, LXXXV (1933-1934), 458.
2371. *CC*, XLIX (Apr. 13, 1932), 483 (Paul Hutchinson: "Mesmer, Mrs. Eddy, Freud").
2372. *MH*, XVI (1932), 128-133 (Cl. M. Hincks).
2373. *N*, CXXXIV (Apr. 27, 1932), 494 (Benjamin Ginzberg).
2374. *NRep*, LXX (Apr. 13, 1932), 250.
2375. *NYEP*, Feb. 13, 1932, p. 7 (Joseph Jastrow).
2376. *NYHTB*, Feb. 21, 1932, p. 9 (Woodbridge Riley).
2377. *NYTBR*, Feb. 21, 1932, p. 9 (Herbert Gorman: "Seekers for the Power of Mind Over Matter").
2378. *NYTBR*, Feb. 13, 1932, p. 16.
2379. *PA*, V : 5 (1931), 242 (No. 2331) (A. B. Herrig: Review of "Sigmund Freud und die Situation der Jahrhundertwende," in *PB*, III (1931), 5-18).
2380. *PMB*, XXXVII (Oct., 1932), 61.
2381. *PQ*, VI (1932), 717 (Brown).

2382.   *SR*, Feb. 28, 1932, p. 7.
2383.   *SSR*, VII (1942), 332.
2384.   *Sy*, LXVIII (Oct. 1, 1932), 484 (George K. Pratt: "Healers Through the Mind").
2385.   *WLB*, XXVIII (May, 1932), 163.

FRENCH

La Guérison par l'Esprit. Tr. Alzir Hella and Juliette Parry. Paris: Stock, 1932 (or later editions).

2386.   *CdS*, 19.a. (1932), 221-222 (J. Audard; Review only of "Freud").
2387.   *CdS*, 20.a. (1933), 296-298 (R. Baumgarten: "La fantastique Existence de Mary Baker Eddy").
2388.   *E*, XXX (1932), 635-637 (P. Abraham; Review only of "Freud").
2389.   *JD*, XXXIX : 1 (Feb. 12, 1932), 234-236 (M. Muret).
2390.   *LLM*, 30.a. (1932), 565.
2391.   *MF*, CCXXXIX (1932), 179-181.
2392.   *MF*, 45.a., CCL (1934), 362-365 (P. Masson-Oursel; Review only of "Freud").
2393.   *P*, 3.sér., CXC (1935), 161-163 (J. Ferrand).
2394.   *RdF*, 12.a. (1932), 139-155 (L. Pierre-Quint; Review only of "Freud").
2395.   *RdF*, 12.a., IV (1932), 717-719 (P. Audiat: "Fantastique Existence de Mary Baker Eddy").
2396.   *RdV*, 7.a. (1939), 294 (P. Koruham-Europe).
2397.   *RdV*, 9.a. (1941), 435.
2398.   *RELV*, 49.a. (1932), 221 (H. Loiseau; Review only of "Freud").
2399.   *RELV*, 52.a. (1936-1937), 26-27 (H. Loiseau).
2400.   *RHb*, 41.a.: 2 (1926-1930), 350 ("Freud, ou la Guérison par l'Esprit").

ITALIAN

L'Anima che guarisce. Franz Anton Mesmer – Mary Baker Eddy – Sigmund Freud. Tr. Lavinia Mazzucchetti. Milano: Sperling and Kupfer, 1931.

2401.   *IC*, 13.a. (1932), 340-347.
2402.   *ICS*, XV (1932), 53 (E. Palmieri).
2403.   *L*, 2.a. (1931), 131-133 (Lavinia Mazzucchetti).
2404.   *L*, 3.a. (Mar., 1932), 119-122 (Astolfo).
2405.   *PeR*, 1934, pp. 261-276 ("L'Anima che guarisce").
2406.   *RN*, 54.a., 3. sér., XVI (1932), 310.

SPANISH

La Curación por el Espiritu. Tr. Francisco Payarols. Barcelona: Apolo, 1934.

2407.   *AUC*, 3. ser., I (1934), 132-133.

GERMAN

Sternstunden der Menschheit. Ed. Felix Wittmer and Theodore Geissendörfer. New York: Prentice Hall, 1931.

2408.   *MfDU*, XXIII (1931), 156 (Straube).

Noodlotsuren der Menschheid. Vijf historische Miniaturen. Tr. Reinier P. Sterkenburg. Zeist: J. Ploegsma, 1930; and, *Lotswendingen.* Tr. Reinier P. Sterkenburg. Amsterdam: Wereldbibliotheek, 1939.

2409.   *DNG*, 54.J. (1938-1939), 196.
2410.   *DWB*, 31.J. (1934), 153.

The Tide of Fortune. Twelve Historical Miniatures. Tr. Eden and Cedar Paul. New York: Viking, 1940.

2411.   *A,* LXIV (Nov. 30, 1940), 220.
2412.   *AM,* Jan., 1941.
2413.   *Bl,* XXXVII (Jan. 1, 1941), 172.
2414.   *CHF,* LII (Dec. 10, 1940), 3.
2415.   *Cwl,* XXXIII (Dec. 20, 1940), 235 (Euphemia van Rensselaer-Wyatt).
2416.   *LA,* CCCLIX (Dec., 1940), 391.
2417.   *LJ,* LXV (Nov. 15, 1940), 982 (J. B. Fogg).
2418.   *LT,* Dec. 14, 1940, p. 627.
2419.   *NSN,* XX (Dec. 28, 1940), 688 (Flora Grierson).
2420.   *NY,* XVI (Nov. 16, 1940), 100 (Clifton Fadiman).
2421.   *NYHTB,* Nov. 24, 1940, p. 9 (Albert Guerard: "Miniature Moments of Crisis in History").
2422.   *NYTBR,* Dec. 8, 1940, p. 7 (Herbert Gorman: "Stefan Zweig's Notes On History").
2423.   *Sp,* CLXVI : 1 (1941), 100.
2424.   *SR,* Jan. 5, 1941, p. 7 (F. G. Bratton).
2425.   *SRL,* XXIII (Nov. 23, 1940), 10 (Wm. H. Chamberlin: "There is a Tide").
2426.   *T,* XXXVI (Nov. 18, 1940), 90.

Les Heures Etoilées de l'Humanité. Tr. Alzir Hella. Paris: Grasset, 1928.

2427.   *RG,* 20.a. (1928-1929), 181-183.

Momenti Eccelsi. Cinque Miniature Storiche. Tr. Berta Burgio Ahrens; *La Resurrezione di Händel.* Tr. Marcella Gorra. Milano: Sperling and Kupfer, 1935.

2428.   *RN,* 3.sér., XXII (1936-1937), 435; XXIII (1936-1937), 78.

Brasilien, Land der Zukunft. Stockholm: Bermann-Fischer, 1942.

2429.   *CV,* 20.J. (1942), 73.

ENGLISH

Brazil, Land of the Future. Tr. Andrew St. James. New York: Viking, 1941.

2430.   *A*, LXVI (Oct. 25, 1941), 77.
2431.   *BA*, XVI : 4 (Autumn, 1942), 410-411 (Edward Murry Clark).
2432.   *Chm*, CLV (Nov. 1, 1941), 18 (A. L. Murray).
2433.   *Cwl*, XXXIV (Oct. 17, 1941), 617-618 (Philip Burnham).
2434.   *COS*, Oct., 1941, p. 17.
2435.   *HLAS*, 1941, p. 37 (James Granier).
2436.   *LJ*, LXVI (Sept. 1, 1941), 731 (F. A. Boyle).
2437.   *Ne*, XVIII (Sept. 29, 1941), pp. 50, 52.
2438.   *NRep*, CV (Oct. 20, 1941), 517.
2439.   *NY*, XVII (Oct. 4, 1941), 87.
2440.   *NYHTB*, Oct. 5, 1941, p. 650 (Nicholas Roosevelt).
2441.   *NYTBR*, Oct. 5, 1941, p. 9 (Ernesto Montenegro); Oct. 19, 1941, p. 32; Nov. 9, 1941, p. 36.
2442.   *SoS*, XXXIII (Jan., 1942), 38 (Elizabeth Wilder).
2443.   *SR*, Oct. 21, 1941, p. 8.

FRENCH

Le Brésil, Terre d'Avenir. New York: Edition de la Maison Française, 1942.

2444.   *VdF*, Mar. 15, 1942, p. 4 (Alceste (pseud.)).

GERMAN

Die Welt von gestern. Erinnerungen eines Europäers. Stockholm: Bermann-Fischer, 1944 (or later editions).

2445.   *Au*, IV (1948), 817-819 (H. Uhlig).
2446.   *BüK*, 11.J.: 2 (June 15, 1962), 28 (B.K.).
2447.   *DPbl*, LII (1952), 298-299 (Hans Jürgen Baden: "Stefan Zweig oder die Welt von gestern").
2448.   *Gwt*, III : 22 (1948), 19-20 (Sieburg).
2449.   *HAR*, I (1946-1947), 437-441 (E. Wolff).
2450.   *Uns*, IV : 10 (Oct., 1949), 1222 (Carl Augstein).

ENGLISH

The World of Yesterday. Tr. Eden and Cedar Paul. New York: Viking, 1943 (or later editions).

2451.   *A*, LXIX (June 26, 1943), 329.
2452.   *AM*, CLXXI (June, 1943), 129.
2453.   *Bl*, XXXIX (May 15, 1943), 367.
2454.   *CW*, CLVII (June, 1943), 332.
2455.   *CJR*, VII (Apr., 1944), 205.
2456.   *Cwl*, XXXVIII (June 4, 1943), 174 (Max Fischer).
2457.   *LJ*, LXVIII (Apr., 1943), 288 (F. E. Hirsch).
2458.   *LT*, Nov. 27, 1943, p. 574.
2459.   *MG*, Dec. 29, 1943, p. 3.

2460.	*MJ*, XXXI (Oct., 1943), 307-314 (Hannah Arendt: "Portrait of a Period; Based on Zweig's Autobiography 'World of Yesterday'").
2461.	*N*, CLVI (May 15, 1943), 711-712 (Hermann Kesten: "Citizen of the World").
2462.	*NRep*, CVIII (May 3, 1943), 600-602 (Irwin Edman: "World Not Without End").
2463.	*NY*, XIX (Apr. 24, 1943), 80.
2464.	*NYHTB*, Apr. 18, 1943, p. 4 (Virgilia Sapeiha).
2465.	*NYTBR*, Apr. 18, 1943, p. 2 (J. W. Krutch: "Stefan Zweig's Two Worlds").
2466.	*SR*, May 2, 1943, p. 7 (Helen Lowe).
2467.	*SRL*, XXVI (Apr. 24, 1943), 7 (Robert Pick: "The Storm Within a Storm").
2468.	*WLB*, XXXIX (June, 1943), 84.

POLISH

Swiat w Czorajsyy. Tr. Maria Wislowska. Warszawa: Panstwowy Instytut Wydawniczy, 1958.

2469.	*Ea*, 12 (1958), 10.

GERMAN

Stefan Zweig-Friderike Zweig: Briefwechsel 1912-1942. Bern: A. Scherz, 1951.

2470.	*Gwt*, VII (1952), 150 (B. Reifenberg).
2471.	*IP*, IX (1953), 232-233 (Lavinia Mazzucchetti).
2472.	*DFu*, I (1931), 1 (Cf. *DL*, XXXIV : 5 (Oct., 1931-Mar., 1932), 277).

ENGLISH

Stefan Zweig-Friderike Maria Zweig; Correspondence 1912-1942. Tr. and ed. Henry G. Alsberg, assisted by Erna MacArthur. New York: Hastings House Publishers, Inc., 1954.

2473.	*CR*, 1 (Spring, 1955), 127-129 (Sherman Lewis).
2474.	*NY*, XXX (Sept. 25, 1954), 142.
2475.	*NYHTB*, July 27, 1958, p. 2 ("Mail Pouch: Stefan Zweig and Friderike Maria Zweig").
2476.	*NYTBR*, Nov. 14, 1954, p. 4 (René Fülöp-Miller).
2477.	*SR*, Sept. 19, 1954, p. 9 (Richard McLaughlin).
2478.	*SRL*, XXIX (Oct. 19, 1946), 20 (F. C. Weiskopf).

GERMAN

Richard Strauss – Stefan Zweig: Briefwechsel. Ed. W. Schuh. Frankfurt am Main: S. Fischer, 1957.

2479.	*BA*, XXXII : 4 (Autumn, 1958), 425-426 (Robert Breuer).
2480.	*MA*, LXXVIII (Feb., 1958), 236-237 (Robert Breuer: "Strauss – Zweig Correspondence Reflects Nazi Persecution").
2481.	*Mkg*, 11.J. (1957-1958), 253-255 (E. H. M. von Asow).
2482.	*NYTBR*, June 22, 1958, p. 4.

2483. NZfM, CXIX (Mar., 1958), 131-136 (Heinz Joachim: "Europäisch und wahr-
       haft universal. Aus dem Briefwechsel von Richard Strauss und Stefan Zweig").
2484. ÖMz, XII (Dec., 1957), 502.
2485. SchMz, XCVII (Dec., 1957), 506-507.
2486. SoM, XXIII : 2 (1959), 192-194 (B. Cuckov: "R. Straus i St. Cveig v ich
       Perepiske").

XVII B. REVIEWS OF BOOKS WITH FOREWORDS BY ZWEIG

Anthologie jüngster Lyrik. Fr. Stefan Zweig. Ed. Klaus Mann und Willi Fehse, Hamburg:
       Gebrüder Enoch, 1927.

2487. *Gr*, 22.J. (1927), 189 (H. Bachmann).

Balzac. Sein Weltbild aus den Werken. Fr. Stefan Zweig. Ed. Lothar Brieger – Wasservogel.
       Stuttgart: R. Lutz, 1908.

2488. *DLE*, 11.J.: 14 (Apr. 15, 1909), 994-995 (Franz Servaes).
2489. *DLZg*, p. 1194.

Goethes Gedichte. Eine Auswahl. Fr. and ed. Stefan Zweig. Leipzig: Reclam, 1927.

2490. *DF*, XXVIII: 751/756 (Feb., 1927), 87-89 (Karl Kraus).

(E.M.) Lilien. Sein Werk. Fr. Stefan Zweig. Berlin-Leipzig: Schuster and Loeffler, 1903.

2491. *DLE*, 7.J.: 13 (Apr. 1, 1905), 992-995 (Max Osborn).

Rainer Maria Rilke: Aspects of His Mind and Poetry. Fr. Stefan Zweig. Ed. Wm. Rose and
       G. Craig Houston. London: Sidgwick and Jackson, 1938.

2492. *LM*, XXXVII (Apr., 1938), 649-650 (Edwin Muir).

Tolstoi. De Levende Gedachten van Tolstoi. (Verzameld door Stefan Zweig). Tr. Frank de
       Vries. Den Haag: Servire, 1939 (Levende Gedachten: Eerste Reeks, No. 3).

2493. *Bkg*, XVIII (1940), 87 (C. A. Bouman).

Tolstoy. Stefan Zweig Presents the Living Thoughts of Tolstoy. New York: Longmans and
       Green, 1939.

2494. *BA*, XIV (Winter, 1940), 92 (A.K.).

(Emile) Verhaerens Ausgewählte Gedichte. Tr. and ed. Stefan Zweig. Berlin: Schuster and
       Loeffler, 1904.

2495. *AZ*, No. 198, Beilage (K. H. Strobl).

(*Paul*) *Verlaine. Gesammelte Werke*. Ed. Stefan Zweig. Leipzig: Insel, 1922.

2496.   *BBC*, 411 (1923) (E. Werner: "Die deutschen Verlaine – Übersetzungen").

XVII C. REVIEWS OF WORKS ABOUT STEFAN ZWEIG

Arens, Hanns, ed. *Stefan Zweig. A Tribute to His Life and Work*. Tr. from German by
    Christobel Fowler. London: W. H. Allen, 1951.

2497.   *JLG*, III (Apr. 20, 1951), 1-2 ("The World of Yesterday").

Bauer, Arnold. *Stefan Zweig*. Berlin: Colloquium, 1961 (Köpfe des XX. Jahrhunderts,
    Band 21).

2498.   *GQ*, XXXVI : 1 (Jan., 1963), 75 (Randolph J. Klawiter).

Fitzbauer, Erich, ed. *Stefan Zweig Spiegelungen einer schöpferischen Persönlichkeit*. Wien: Berg-
    land, 1959.

2499.   *GQ*, XXXIII : 4 (Nov., 1960), 381-383 (George C. Schoolfield).
2500.   *MfDU*, LIII (1961), 223-224 (Robert Rie).
2501.   *MLJ*, Mar., 1961, p. 143 (Herbert Lederer).

Hünich, Fritz A. and Rieger, Erwin,eds. *Bibliographie der Werke von Stefan Zweig*. Leipzig:
    Insel, 1931.

2502.   *JBB*, 18.-19.J.: 104/107 (1931), 274.
2503.   *NaQ*, Jan. 16, 1932, p. 44 (Otto F. Babler).

Rieger, Erwin. *Stefan Zweig. Der Mann und das Werk*. Berlin: Spaeth, 1928.

2504.   *DFa*, XI (1928), 1 (Manfred Sturmann) (Cf. *DL*, XXXI : 6 (1928-1929),
    345).
2505.   *DL*, XXXI : 1 (1928-1929), 51 (Felix Braun).

Zech, Paul. *Stefan Zweig. Eine Gedenkschrift*. Buenos Aires: Quadriga, 1943.

2506.   *BA*, XVIII : 1 (1944), 42-43 (Harold von Hofe).

Zweig, Friderike Maria. *Stefan Zweig*. Tr. Erna MacArthur. New York: Thomas Y.
    Crowell Co., 1946.

2507.   *Bl*, XLIII (Oct. 15, 1946), 52.
2508.   *Bwk*, Sept. 29, 1946, p. 3 (Emily Schossberger).
2509.   *Cmy*, III (Jan., 1947), 95-96 (H. Politzer).
2510.   *Er*, III : 9/10 (June 10, 1950), 346-347) (Genevieve Bianquis).
2511.   *K*, XIV (July 15, 1946), 341.
2512.   *LJ*, LXXI (Sept. 15, 1946), 1206 (F. E. Hirsch).

2513. *NY*, XXII (Sept. 28, 1946), 102.
2514. *NYHTB*, Oct. 6, 1946, p. 26 (Virgilia Peterson).
2515. *NYTBR*, Sept. 29, 1946, p. 6 (Alfred Werner).
2516. *SFC*, Nov. 3, 1946, p. 12 (J. V.).
2517. *SRL*, XXIX (Oct. 19, 1946), 20 (F. C. Weiskopf).

Zweig, Friderike Maria. *Stefan Zweig, eine Bildbiographie.* München: Kindler, 1961.

2518. *BüK*, 11.J.: 2 (June 15, 1962), 22 (Georg Böse).
2519. *LT*, Oct. 27, 1961, p. 772.

XVIII. BOOKS AND ARTICLES ABOUT AND REFERENCES TO ZWEIG IN VARIOUS MONOGRAPHS

CZECHOSLOVAKIAN

2520. Hostovski, Egon. *Padesát let Egona Hostovského.* New York: Moravian Publishers House, 1958 (Liber amicorum to Hostovski in the Intro. to which Hostovski's blood relationship to Zweig is discussed).

DUTCH

2521. Kossmann, Alfred. "Het Noodlotsuur van Stefan Zweig," *DeG*, CXXI : 7 (July, 1958), 302-312.

ENGLISH

2522. Arendt, Hannah. *The Origins of Totalitarianism.* New York: Meridian Books, 1960, pp. 50, 52, 332 (Fourth printing; Original printing with Harcourt, Brace and Co., 1951).
2523. Arens, Hanns. "Stefan Zweig as a Collector of Manuscripts," *Ms*, 9 (1957), 43-45.
2524. Arens, Hanns, ed. *Stefan Zweig. A Tribute to His Life and Work.* Tr. from the German by Christobel Fowler. London: Allen, 1951.
2525. Auernheimer. Raoul. "Stefan Zweig," *Torch of Freedom.* Ed. Emil Ludwig and Henry B. Kranz. New York: Rinehart, 1943, pp. 409-426 (First printing New York-Toronto: Ferrare and Rinehart, 1939).
2526. Barricelli, J. P. and Harry Zohn. "Music in Stefan Zweig's Last Years," *JulR*, III (Spring, 1956), 3-11.
2527. Bartlett, Robert Merrill. "Conscience of Europe. An Interview with Stefan Zweig," *WU*, VII (Mar., 1931), 396-400.
2528. — "Spirit versus Force: Stefan Zweig," *They Dared to Live.* New York: Association Press, 1937, pp. 46-50.
2529. Baudouin, Charles. *Contemporary Studies.* Tr. from the French by Eden and Cedar Paul. London: Allen and Unwin, 1924, pp. 87, 117, 270, 283.
2530. Belmore, H. W. *Rilke's Craftsmanship. An Analysis of his Poetic Style.* Oxford, England: Basil Blackwell, 1954, p. 226 (Concerning the influence of Rilke's *Stundenbuch* on Zweig's "Taj Mahal" (Cf. *Fahrten*); Cf. "The Effect of Rilke's Style on Contemporary Language and Literature, pp. 221-232.
2531. Bergler, Edmund, M.D. *Homosexuality: Disease or Way of Life?* New York: Crowell-Collier, 1962, pp. 114, 122, 132, 133 (Discussion of and quotation from Zweig's biographical essay "Stendhal"; First printing with Hill and Wang, 1956).

2532. Bithell, Jethro. *Contemporary German Poetry*. Sel. and tr. from the German by Jethro Bithell. London-New York: Scott, 1909, pp. 190-191 (Contains two Zweig poems: "The Dark Butterfly" and "Bruges").

2533. Bratton, Fred Gladstone. *The Legacy of the Liberal Spirit. Men and Movements in the Making of Modern Thought*. Boston: Beacon Press, 1960, pp. 44, 47 (Quotations from Zweig's *Erasmus*; First printing New York: Charles Scribner's Sons, 1943).

2534. Brittin, Norman A. "Stefan Zweig: Biographer and Teacher," *SeR*, XLVIII (Apr., 1940), 245-254.

2535. Broadbent, Thomas L. *Stefan Zweig: An American Bibliography*. University of Utah, unpub., 1950.

2536. — "Stefan Zweig and his American Critics," *NBRMMLA*, IV : 11 (1951), 2-4.

2537. Brockway, Wallace and Herbert Weinstock. *Men of Music. Their Lives, Times and Achievements*. Revised and enlarged ed. New York: Simon and Schuster, 1950, p. 571 (Concerning the libretto to the Strauss opera "Die schweigsame Frau").

2538. Burckhardt, Oswald. "Introduction" to Zweig's *Novely*. Sjajvo, Ukraine: n.p., n.d.

2539. Cahnman, Werner J. "Stefan Zweig in Salzburg," *MJ*, XXX (July, 1942), 195-198.

2539a. "The Case of Stefan Zweig," *JSp*, VII : 6 (Apr., 1942), 5.

2540. Cousins, Norman. "Stefan Zweig," *SRL*, XXV (Mar. 14, 1942), 12.

2541. Curtiss, Thomas Q. "Stefan Zweig," *BA*, XIII : 4 (Autumn, 1939), 427-430.

2542. Da Cunha, Euclides. *Rebellion in the Backlands*. Tr. from the Portuguese by Livraria Francisco Alves. Chicago: University of Chicago Press, 1944, pp. iii-iv (Quotations from Zweig's *Brasilien*).

2543. Dali, Salvador. *The Secret Life of Salvador Dali*. Tr. from the Spanish by Haakon M. Chevalier. New York: Dial Press, 1942, pp. 23-25 (Dali, Zweig and Edward James visit Sigmund Freud in London).

2544. Dargan, E. Preston and Bernard Weinberg, eds. *The Evolution of Balzac's 'Comédie humaine'*. Chicago: University of Chicago Press, 1942, pp. 427-430 (Appendix: Wells Chamberlin, "The Zweig Manuscript Proof of 'Une ténébreuse Affaire'").

2545. Daviau, Donald G. "Stefan Zweig's Victors in Defeat," *MfDU*, LI : 1 (Jan., 1959), 1-12.

2546. Ende, Amelia von. "Literary Vienna," *Bm*, XXXVIII (Oct., 1913), 141-155 (p. 150, portrait of Zweig; p. 153, short discussion of Zweig).

2547. "European Writing Suffers – Summary of an Interview with Stefan Zweig," *PW*, CXXXV (Jan. 14, 1939), 110.

2548. Evensky, M. "Stefan Zweig," *YCD* (1951), 70-77.

2549. Ewen, David. "Stefan Zweig Calls Anti-Semitism a Moldering Evil," *AH*, CXXX: 22 (Apr. 15, 1932), 551.

2550. Feder, Ernst. "My Last Conversation with Stefan Zweig," *BA*, XVII (Jan., 1943), 2-9 (p. 1, sketch of Zweig by Stan Hess).

2551. Flower, Sir Walter Newman. "Stefan Zweig," *Just As It Happened*. London: Cassell, 1950; New York: Morrow, 1950, pp. 176-180 (Also contains a portrait of Zweig).

2552. Freud, Sigmund. "Four-and-Twenty Hours in a Woman's Life," *Collected Papers*. Vol. V. London: Hogarth, 1950, pp. 239-241 (Reprinted in "Dostoevsky and Parricide," *Art and Psychoanalysis*. Ed. William Phillips. New York: Criterion Books, 1957, 3-21 (Cf. esp. pp. 16-18)).

2552a. Gide, André. *Journal. 1939-1949*. Tr. from the French by Justin O'Brien. New York: Knopf, 1957, p. 318 (Ref. to Zweig's *Calvin*).

2553. — *Journals*. Vol. III. Tr. from the French by Justin O'Brien. New York: Knopf, 1949, p. 41.

2554. Gorki, Maxim. Preface to Zweig's Collected Works in Russian. Leningrad: Vremya, 1928-1930 (Cf. "Collected Works" of this bibliography).

2555. Griffin, Jonathan. Review of *Escape to Life* (Klaus and Erika Mann. Boston: Houghton, 1939), *SRL*, XIX : 26 (Apr. 22, 1939), 3-4 (Zweig portrait, p. 3.).

2556. Gunther John. *Inside Europe Today*. New York: Harper, 1961, p. 180.
2557. Heilblut, Ivan. "Graves by the Roadside. In Memory of Stefan Zweig," *MJ*, XXX (July-Sept., 1942), 199-200.
2558. "H. G. Wells Raises a Storm in the P.E.N. Congress," *LD*, CXVI (July 15, 1933), 17-18 (Discussion of a Nazi order banning certain German writers, Zweig among them. Portraits of Zweig, H. G. Wells, Thomas Mann, Erich Remarque, Leon Feuchtwanger, Ernst Toller and Harry S. Canby).
2559. "History of the Screen. Summary of an Interview with Stefan Zweig," *NYTBR*, Apr. 8, 1934, p. 4.
2560. "In Recollection of Stefan Zweig," *AIR*, XV : 167/168 (Feb.-Mar., 1947), 2 (Contains a letter from Zweig to the editor concerning Zweig's 1941 article in *Adam* on H. G. Wells).
2561. Jones, Ernest, M. D. *The Life and Work of Sigmund Freud. The Last Phase*, 1919-1939. Vol. III. New York: Basic Books, 1957, f.m.
2562. Kaufmann, Walter. *From Shakespeare to Existentialism*. Garden City (New York): Doubleday, 1960, pp. 283, 336, 371, 445 (Anchor Book, A 213).
2563. Koegler, H. "Stefan Zweig," *MC*, CLI (Feb., 1955), 101-102.
2564. Kracauer, Siegfried. *From Caligari to Hitler. A Psychological History of the German Film*. New York: Princeton University Press, 1947, p. 191.
2565. Kris, Ernst. *Psychoanalytic Explorations in Art*. New York: International Universities Press, 1952, p. 24.
2566. Krutch, Joseph Wood. "Woe to Israel!" *N*, CXLVIII (Feb. 18, 1939), 212.
2567. Leftwich, Joseph. "Stefan Zweig and the World of Yesterday," *Ybk*, III (1958), 81-100.
2568. Lengyel, Emil. "German Emigré Literature," *BA*, XII (1938), 5-8.
2569. Liptzin, Solomon, "Stefan Zweig," *Germany's Stepchildren*. Philadelphia: Jewish Publication Society of America, 1944, pp. 211-225.
2570. — "Young Vienna," *PoL*, XLVII : 4 (1941), 337-346.
2571. Lucas, Frank Laurence. *Tragedy: Serious Drama in Relation to Aristotle's 'Poetics'*. Rev. ed. New York: Collier Books, 1962, p. 39 (Ref. to *Beware of Pity (Ungeduld des Herzens)*; Originally appeared London: L. and Virginia Woolf, 1927 and New York: Harcourt, Brace, 1928).
2572. McClain, William H. "Romain Rolland and Russia," *RRev*, XXXIX : 2 (Apr., 1948), 122-129.
2573. — "Soviet Russia Through the Eyes of Stefan Zweig and Romain Rolland," *MLN*, LXIX : 1 (Jan., 1954), 11-18.
2574. McClain, William H. and Harry Zohn. "Zweig and Rolland – Literary and Personal Relationship," *GermR*, XXVIII : 4 (1953), 262-281.
2575. Mann, Klaus. "Stefan Zweig," *Treasury of the Free World*. Ed. B. Raeburn. New York: Arco, 1946, pp. 365-368.
2576. — "Victims of Fascism," *FW*, II (Apr., 1942), 274-276.
2577. Marshall, Margaret. "Stefan Zweig," *N*, CLIV (Mar. 14, 1942), 314.
2578. Mason, Eudoc. *Rilke, Europe and the English-speaking World*. Cambridge: Cambridge University Press, 1961, p. 200 (Quote from a conversation between Zweig, Emile Verhaeren, Romain Rolland and Rilke in 1913 on "the spiritual unity of Europe and the duty of the writer").
2579. Mathis, Alfred. "Stefan Zweig as Librettist and His Collaboration with Richard Strauss," *MaL* (1944), pp. 163-176, 226-245.
2580. Maurina, Zenta. *A Prophet of the Soul: Fyodor Dostoievsky*. Tr. from the Latvian by C. P. Finlayson. London: James Clarke, 1939, p. 25.
2581. Mileck, Joseph. *Hermann Hesse and His Critics*. Chapel Hill, N.C.: University of North Carolina Press, 1958, pp. 7, 49, 163, 291.
2582. Morgan, Bayard Quincy. "Literature in Exil," *BA*, XVIII : 3 (1944), 231-234.
2583. Neider, C., ed. "Beloved Returns," *Stature of Thomas Mann*. New York: New Directions, 1947, pp. 188-190.

2584. Niles, Blair Rice. "Stefan Zweig the Author," *Journeys in Time*. New York: Coward – McCann, 1946, pp. 50-53.
2585. — "Stefan Zweig the Man," *Journeys in Time*. New York: Coward – McCann, 1946, pp. 372-381.
2586. Norman, Charles. *Ezra Pound*. New York: Macmillan, 1960, p. 309 (Letter of Pound to Zukofsky of Nov. 22, 1931 referring to lectures to be given by him, Zweig, *et al.* in Florence).
2587. Norden, R. "Brazilian Diary," *LA*, CCCLI (Jan., 1937), 384-392.
2588. "On the War Effect on the Future of Writing. An Interview with Stefan Zweig," *NYT*, July 28, 1940, p. 2.
2589. Oechler, William F. "Reception of Emile Verhaeren in Germany. Some Unpublished Letters of Stefan Zweig," *MLN*, LXII (Apr., 1947), 226-234.
2590. Pick, Robert. "Stefan Zweig," *BMCN*, Nov., 1946, pp. 4-5.
2591. — "The Storm Within a Storm," *SRL*, XXVI (Apr. 24, 1945), 7.
2592. Puner, Helen Walker. *Freud, His Life and His Mind*. New York: Dell, 1959, p. 231 (Quote from Zweig's essay on Freud in *Heilung durch den Geist*).
2593. Putnam, Samuel. *Marvelous Journey. A Survey of Four Centuries of Brazilian Writing*. New York: Knopf, 1948, p. 203 (Quote from Zweig's *Brasilien*).
2594. Relgis, Eugen. "Stefan Zweig and Judaism," *JA*, XI : 10 (Oct., 1956), 4-9 (This article was translated into English by Dr. Harry Zohn from a chapter (slightly abridged) in Relgis' book *Profetas y Poetas*. Buenos Aires: Editorial Candelabro, 1955).
2595. Ring, O. T. "Life and Death of Stefan Zweig," *NM*, XLII : 10 (Mar. 10, 1942), 22-23.
2596. Romains, Jules. *Stefan Zweig, Great European*. Tr. from the French by James Whitall. New York: Viking, 1941 (A bibliography of the original works of Zweig, pp. 62-64).
2597. Rose, William. "German Literary Exiles in England," *GLL*, I (Apr., 1948), 3.
2598. Ross, Nan. "Books in Germany," *Sp* CLXXVIII (May 16, 1947), 554-555.
2599. Royce, William H. *A Balzac Bibliography*. Chicago: University of Chicago Press, 1929, pp. 231, 464.
2600. Schoenberner, Franz. "Stefan Zweig and Ourselves," *NRep*, CVI (Mar. 9, 1942), 333.
2601. Schreiber, Georges. "Stefan Zweig," *Portraits and Self-portraits*. New York-Boston: Houghton Mifflin, 1936, pp. 173-175.
2602. Selden-Goth, Gisella. "Stefan Zweig, Lover of Music," *BA*, XX : 2 (1946). 149-151.
2603. Sievers, W. David. *Freud On Broadway. A History of Psychoanalysis and the American Drama*. New York: Hermitage House, 1955, p. 256.
2604. Slochower, Harry. "In the Fascist Styx," *No Voice Is Wholly Lost*. New York: Creative Age Press, 1945, pp. 75-92.
2605. Slonim, Marc. *Three Loves of Dostoevsky*. New York: Rinehart, 1955; Toronto: Clarke, Irwin, 1955, p. 299 (Zweig's *Three Masters* listed in Slonim's bibliography as consulted but not specifically quoted).
2606. Slowacki, Juljusz. *Mary Stuart. A Romantic Drama*. Tr. from the Polish by Arthur Prudden Coleman and Marion Moore Coleman. Schenectady, N.Y.: Pub. by translators, 1937 (Foreword, pp. 3-4, by Arthur Prudden Coleman (May 1, 1937), discusses Zweig's influence on Slowacki's stage interpretation of the character of Mary Stuart).
2607. Sperry, W. L. "Foreshadows of the Present," *NRep*, LXXXIX (Jan. 20, 1937), 362.
2608. Starr, William Thomas. *A Critical Bibliography of the Published Writings of Romain Rolland*. Evanston, Ill.: Northwestern University Press, 1950, f.m.
2609. — *Romain Rolland and a World at War*. Evanston, Ill.: Northwestern University Press, 1956, f.m.
2610. Steinhauer, Harry. "Literary Survey of Republican Germany," *QR*, CI (Oct., 1934), 315-326.

2611. Taylor, Edmund. *The Fall of the Dynasties. The Collapse of the Old Order.* 1905-1922. New York: Doubleday, 1963, pp. 18, 30, 393, 395, 396.
2612. Teller, Gertrude E. "Virata or the Eyes of the Undying Brother and Stefan Zweig's Thought," *GermR*, XXVII : 1 (1952), 31-40.
2613. Teller, Judd L. "Expatriate from the 19th Century," *Cmy*, XVIII (Dec., 1954), 578-581.
2614. "The Tragic Case of Stefan Zweig," *JSp*, May, 1943, pp. 9-11.
2615. "Tribute to H. G. Wells at P.E.N. Club," *NYT*, Sept. 15, 1936, p. 27.
2616. Uhlman, Fred. *The Making of an Englishman.* London: Victor Gollancz, 1960, p. 217 (Ref. to Zweig's joining the "Free German League of Culture" in the spring of 1939).
2617. Van Gelder, R. "The Future of Writing in a World at War. Summary of an Interview with Stefan Zweig," *Writers and Writing.* New York: Scribner, 1946, pp. 86-89.
2618. W.E.G. "Has Intelligence Failed?" *CC*, LI (Dec. 19, 1934), 1626.
2619. "Werfel and Zweig," *IM*, LXXIII (Oct., 1945), 418-421.
2620. Werner, Alfred. "Pity for Stefan Zweig," *ConW*, IX : 14 (Apr. 10, 1942), 10-13.
2621. Wilson, Ronald A. *The Pre-War Biographies of Romain Rolland and Their Place in His Work and the Period.* London: Oxford University Press, 1939, f.m.
2622. Wilson, W. J. "Modern European History," *AHR*, XLVIII (Oct., 1942), 86.
2623. Wittlin, A. "Stefan Zweig," *ConR*, CLXXV (1949), 62.
2624. Wollf, Charles. *Journey into Chaos. Adventures and Experiences in Fifteen Countries of Europe.* 2. ed. London-New York-Melbourne: Hutchinson, n.d., p. 191 (Concerning Wollf's last conversation with Zweig (London, Mar., 1938)).
2625. Wunderlich, Eva C., ed. "The Author and His Work," Intro. to the school ed. of *Brennendes Geheimnis.* New York: Farrer and Rinehart, 1938.
2626. — "Stefan Zweig," *BET*, Dec. 10, 1932.
2627. Yust, Walter, ed. *Ten Eventful Years.* 1937-1946. 4. Vol. Chicago-London-Toronto: Encyclopedia Britannica, Inc., 1947, Vol. I, p. 485; Vol. II, p. 464; Vol. III, p. 394.
2628. Zarek, Otto. "Recalling a Tragedy: Stefan Zweig," *JeA*, CVIII : 5 (Mar. 1, 1951), 1.
2629. — "Stefan Zweig. A Jewish Tragedy," *Life-Work*, pp. 178-191.
2630. Zilboorg, Gregory. *Sigmund Freud.* New York: Charles Scribner's Sons, 1951, f.m.
2631. — *Sigmund Freud. His Exploration of the Mind of Man.* New York: Evergreen Books, 1960, f.m. (Evergreen NE-239).
2632. Zohn, Harry, ed. *Liber amicorum Friderike Maria Zweig. In Honor of Her Seventieth Birthday. Dec. 4, 1952.* Foreword Dr. George N. Schuster. Stamford, Conn.: Dahl, 1952 (Cf. esp. Zweig Bibliography, pp. 109-111).
2633. — "Stefan Zweig and Contemporary European Literature," *GLL*, V : 3 (1952), 202-212.
2634. — "Stefan Zweig and Verhaeren. In Memoriam Stefan Zweig," *MfDU*, XLIII (Apr.-May, 1951), 199-205.
2635. — "Stefan Zweig as a Collector of Manuscripts," *GQ*, XXV : 3 (May, 1952), 182-191.
2636. — "Stefan Zweig as Literary Mediator," *BA*, XXVI : 2 (1952), 137-140.
2637. — "Stefan Zweig's Last Years. Some Unpublished Letters," *MfDU*, XLVIII : 2 (Feb., 1956), 73-77.
2638. Zohn, Harry and J. P. Barricelli. "Music in Stefan Zweig's Last Years. Some Unpublished Letters to Alfred Einstein and Mme. Gisella Selden-Goth," *JulR*, III (Spring, 1956), 3-11.
2639. Zohn, Harry and William H. McClain. "Zweig and Rolland. Literary and Personal Relationship," *GermR*, XXVIII : 4 (1953), 262-281.
2640. Zweig, Friderike Maria. "Joseph Roth and the Zweigs," *BA*, XVIII (Jan., 1944), 4-8.
2641. — *Stefan Zweig.* Tr. from the German by Erna McArthur. New York: Thomas Y. Crowell, 1946 (Reprinted London: W. H. Allen, 1948).

2642. Angelloz, Jean François. *Rainer Maria Rilke. L'Evolution spirituelle du Poète.* Paris: Paul Hartmann, 1936, pp. 301, 376.

2643. Arcos, René. *Romain Rolland.* Paris: Mercure de France, 1950, p. 7 "A la mémoire de Stefan Zweig," thereafter f.m.

2644. Baudoin, Charles. *Hommage à Romain Rolland.* Intro. Charles Baudoin. Genève: Editions du Mont Blanc, 1945, m. (Article by Zweig, "Reconnaissance," Tr. from the German by Alzir Hella, pp. 86-91).

2645. Beaulieu, Paul. "Réflexions sur le Suicide de Stefan Zweig," *LNR*, X (Aug., 1942), 579-582.

2646. Béguin, Albert. *Essais et Témoignages: Etapes d'une Pensée. Rencontres avec Albert Béguin.* Neuchâtel: La Baconnière, 1957, p. 207 (Negative evaluation of Zweig's essays on Hölderlin and Kleist).

2647. Bon, Antoine. "Stefan Zweig et le Brésil," *MF*, CCCI : 1009 (Sept. 1, 1947), 73-78.

2648. Claudel, Paul and André Gide. *Correspondance.* 1899-1926. Intro. and Notes Robert Mallet. 5. ed. Paris: Gallimard, 1949, pp. 210, 357.

2649. Delarue, Henri. "Calvin, l'Histoire et Stefan Zweig," *MS*, Apr. 25, 1948 (Reprinted in *Schorer*, pp. 5-17).

2650. — "Histoire et Théologie font deux," *VP*, Feb. 18, 1948 (Reprinted in *Schorer*, pp. 19-24).

2651. Delarue, Henri and Paul F. Geisendorf. *Calvin, Stefan Zweig et M. Jean Schorer.* Genève: Georg and Cie, 1949.

2652. Décarreaux, Jean. "Le Message posthume de Stefan Zweig," *LMF*, XII (1948), 424-429.

2653. Demilly, Adolphe. "Sur une Mort," *VdF*, Mar. 15, 1942, p. 1.

2654. Geisendorf, Paul F. "Calvin Dictateur ou M. Schorer Historien," *LCP*, Apr.-May, 1948 (Reprinted in *Schorer*, pp. 33-64).

2655. Gide, André. *Journal 1939-1949.* Tr. from the French by Justin O'Brien. New York: Knopf, 1957, p. 318 (Ref. to Zweig's *Calvin*; Original version *Journal 1939-1949. Souvenirs.* Paris: Gallimard, 1954).

2656. Goffin, Robert. "Adieu à Stefan Zweig," *VdF*, Mar. 15, 1942, p. 4.

2657. Green, Julien. *Journal. Vol. I-IV.* Paris: Librairie Plon, 1938-1951, m.

2658. Hella, Alzir. "Avant-Propos," *Derniers Messages.* Tr. from the German by Alzir Hella. Paris: Attinger, 1949, pp. 9-10.

2659. — "Avant-Propos," *Vingt-quatre Heures de la Vie d'une Femme.* Tr. from the German by Alzir Hella. Paris-Neuchâtel: Attinger, 1929.

2660. Hellens, Frans. "Avant-Propos," *Souvenirs sur Emile Verhaeren.* Tr. from the German by Hendrik Coopman. Bruxelles: Kryn, 1931.

2661. Jouve, Pierre Jean. *Romain Rolland Vivant.* 1914-1919. Paris: Librairie Paul Ollendorff, 1920, m.

2662. Kadmi-Cohen. *Nomades. Essai sur l'Ame Juive.* Paris: Librairie Alcan, 1929 (Appraisals of Jewry by Jews and Gentiles).

2663. Kempf, Marcelle. *Romain Rolland et l'Allemagne.* Paris: Nouvelles Editions Debresse, 1962, f.m.

2664. Lang, C.-L. *Destin de l'Autriche.* Paris: Société d'Editions Françaises et Internationales, 1945, pp. 101, 103 (Zweig as a representative of the Freudian influence in literature).

2665. Lefevre, Frédéric. "Une Heure avec Stefan Zweig. Le Rôle de l'Intellectuel dans la Crise Actuelle," *LNL*, Jan. 23, 1932, p. 1.

2666. Levy, Arthur. *L'Idéalisme de Romain Rolland.* Paris: Nizet, 1946, m.

2667. Mazor, Michel. *Le Phénomène Nazi. Documents nazis commentés.* Intro. Rémy Rouvre. Paris: Editions du Centre, 1957, pp. 163-173.

2668. Muret, Maurice. *Le Désarroi de l'Esprit allemand.* Lyon: Edition la plus grande France, 1937, pp. 112-149.

2669. — "M. Stefan Zweig," *RP*, 42.a.: V (Oct. 15, 1935), 864-889 (Reprinted in *Le Désarroi de l'Esprit allemand*. Cf. above).
2670. Noth, Ernst Erich (pseud. for Paul Krantz). "Stefan Zweig et la France," *PlV*, Mar. 7, 1942, p. 6.
2671. Petijean, Armand. "Grands Hommes," *Ven*, IV : 121 (Feb. 25, 1938), 4-5.
2672. Rilke, Rainer Maria and André Gide. *Correspondance*. 1909-1926. Intro. and Commentaries Renée Lang. Paris: Corrêa, 1952, f.m.
2673. Rolland, Romain. *Cahiers Romain Rolland* (Vol. II. Louis Gillet-Romain Rolland). Paris: Albin Michel, 1950, p. 267; (Vol. III. Romain Rolland-Richard Strauss). Paris: Albin Michel, 1951, pp. 11, 172, 175; (Vol. XI. Lettres de Romain Rolland à Sofia Bertolini Guerrieri-Gonzaga). Paris: Albin Michel, 1960, pp. 167, 172, 230, 232, 340.
2674. — *Journal des Années de Guerre*. 1914-1919. Paris: Albin Michel, 1952 (Zweig is mentioned on some 100 pages, cf. esp. pp. 348-350, 1351-1362, 1473-1476).
2675. — "Préface," *Amok*. Tr. from the German by Alzir Hella and Olivier Bournac. Paris: Grasset, 1939.
2676. — "Vox Clamantis... 'Jeremias', Poème dramatique de Stefan Zweig," *Les Précurseurs*. Paris: Editions de l'Humanité, 1919, pp. 127-145 (This article originally appeared in *Coe*, Nov. 20, 1917).
2677. Romains, Jules. "Derniers Mois et dernières Lettres de Stefan Zweig," *RP*, 62.a.: 2 (Feb., 1955), 3-23.
2678. — "Souvenirs de mon Amitié avec Stefan Zweig," Lecture in the Französischer Institut (Wien), June 13, 1958 (Cf. *Blätter*, 3 (Oct., 1958), 5).
2679. *Stefan Zweig, Grand Européen*. New York: N.Y. Editions de la Maison française, 1941.
2680. — "Stefan Zweig, grand Européen," *Saints de notre Calendrier*. Paris: Flammarion, 1952, pp. 159-194.
2681. Schorer, Jean. "Calvin cet Inconnu," *EeL*, July, 1947.
2682. — *Jean Calvin et sa Dictature, d'après des Historiens anciens et modernes*. Genève: Grivet, 1948, f.m.
2683. Stern, Leopold. "Sur le Suicide de Stefan Zweig," *Car*, Aug. 19, 1947.
2684. Valentin, Antonina. "Stefan Zweig," *E*, 25.a.: 22 (Oct., 1947), 48-67.

GERMAN

2685. Adelt, Leonhard. "Werk und Leben Stefan Zweigs," *NFP*, Aug. 12, 1928, pp.27-28.
2686. Ahl, Herbert. "Stefan Zweig," *Literarische Portraits*. München-Wien: Langen-Müller, 1962, pp. 235-244 (Also scattered references).
2687. Arendt, Hannah. "Juden in der Welt von gestern. Anlässlich Stefan Zweigs 'The World of Yesterday. An Autobiography' (New York: Viking, 1943)," *Sechs Essays*. Heidelberg: Lambert Schneider, 1948, pp. 112-127.
2688. Arens, Hanns. "Dank an Stefan Zweig," *Un* (1931), 9 (Cf. *DL*, XXXIV : 5 (Oct., 1931-Mar., 1932), 277).
2689. — ed. *Der grosse Europäer Stefan Zweig*. München: Kindler, 1956. (Contents: Articles and Letters:
Hanns Arens, "Stefan Zweig," pp. 9-43
Richard Friedenthal, "Stefan Zweig und der humanitäre Gedanke," pp. 45-71
Stefan Zweig, "Besuch bei Emile Verhaeren," pp. 72-76
Rainer Maria Rilke, "Briefe an Stefan Zweig," pp. 78-82
Stefan Zweig, "Abschied von Rilke," pp. 83-86
Romain Rolland, "Briefe an Stefan Zweig," pp. 87-91
Stefan Zweig, "Dank an Romain Rolland," pp. 92-95
Oskar Maurus Fontana, "Stefan Zweig und die Jungen," pp. 96-101
Hans Carossa, "Uneigennützige Förderung," pp. 102-103
Hans Reisiger, "Freundliches Erinnern," pp. 104-106
Alexander Lernet-Holenia, "Ich wollte, er lebte noch!" pp. 108-109

Contents: Facsimiles
Contents: Pictures

Stefan Zweig, letzte Aufnahme, opp. p. 336
Stefan Zweig, letztes Gedicht, opp. p. 337
Stefan Zweigs Haus in Petropolis, opp. p. 352
Die Grabstätte in Petropolis, opp. p. 353).

2690. — "Ich besuche einen berühmten Dichter," *KNN*, Mar. 29, 1931 (Cf. *DL*, XXXIII : 9 (Apr.-Sept., 1931), 508).
2691. — "Die letzten Jahre Stefan Zweigs," *Wst*, XXV (1956), 15-19.
2692. — "Romain Rolland und Stefan Zweig," *DBei*, III : 5 (1949), 409-415 (Contains two letters of Rolland to Zweig).
2693. — "Der Sammler Stefan Zweig," *DNZg*, 121 (1949) (Reprinted in *Imp*, XI (1953), 199-205; *NDH*, 5 (1954), 394; *WidZ*, 10 (Oct., 1961), 36-40).
2694. — "Stefan Zweig," *Br*, XVII (1930), 447-449 (Cf. variations of this essay in *DeuR*, LXXVII : 8 (Aug., 1951), 712-717; *DL*, XXX : 9 (1927-1928), 528-529; *KHZ*, May 19, 1930; *Leben-Werk*, pp. 7-118; *SNT*, 177 (1928); *Wst*, July 21, 1952, pp. 49-52; *Europäer*, pp. 9-43).
2695. — *Stefan Zweig. Der Mensch im Werk.* Wien: Krystall, 1931.
2696. — ed. *Stefan Zweig. Sein Leben – sein Werk.* Esslingen: Bechtle, 1949 (Contents:
    Articles and Letters:
    Hanns Arens, "Stefan Zweig," pp. 7-119
    Stefan Zweig, "Stammbuchverse," p. 70
    Camoes-Zweig, "Gedicht," p. 89
    Carl Zuckmayer, "Did you know Stefan Zweig?" pp. 121-126
    Hans Reisiger, "Freundliches Erinnern an Stefan Zweig," pp. 128-129
    Walter Bauer, "Stefan Zweig der Europäer," pp. 130-145
    Rainer Maria Rilke, "Zwei Briefe an Stefan Zweig," pp. 146-148
    Alexander Lernet-Holenia, "Brief," p. 149
    Ernst Feder, "Stefan Zweigs letzte Tage," pp. 150-165
    René Fülöp-Miller, "Erinnerungsblatt für Stefan Zweig," pp. 167-168
    Romain Rolland, "Zwei Briefe an Stefan Zweig," pp. 169-172
    Richard Friedenthal, "Epistel an einen toten Freund," pp. 173-176
    Franz Werfel, "Stefan Zweigs Tod," pp. 177-187
    Benarsi Das Chaturvedi, "Bekenntnis zu Stefan Zweig," pp. 188-189
    Berthold Viertel, "Abschied von Stefan Zweig," pp. 191-199
    Richard Friedenthal, "Stefan Zweig und der humanitäre Gedanke," pp. 200-219
            Contents: Pictures and Facsimiles:
    Stefan Zweig, opp. p. 3
    Romain Rolland und Stefan Zweig, opp. p. 14
    Aufgang zum Hause Stefan Zweigs, opp. p. 15
    Korrekturblatt Stefan Zweigs, opp. p. 48
    Toscanini, Walter, Zweig, opp. p. 96
    Anton Kippenberg und Stefan Zweig, opp. p. 97
    Romain Rolland, opp. p. 113
    Manuskriptblatt von Stefan Zweig, opp. p. 144
    Manuskriptblatt aus Franz Werfels Rede, opp. p. 176
    Brief von Romain Rolland, opp. pp. 192-193
    Stefan Zweigs Haus in Petropolis, opp. p. 208
    Stefan Zweigs Grab in Petropolis, opp. p. 209
    Stefan Zweigs Brief-Signet, p. 26
    Brief Stefan Zweigs an Robert Faesi, p. 37
    Emile Verhaeren, Holzschnitt von Frans Masereel, p. 55
    Beethoven Noten, p. 66
    Richard Strauss, Widmungsblatt für Stefan Zweig, p. 80
    Karte von Frans Masereel, p. 112
    Stefan Zweigs Abschiedsbrief, p. 117
    Frans Masereel, Gedenkblatt für Stefan Zweig, p. 127
    Brief von Stefan Zweig an Ernst Feder, p. 157

Bruno Walter, Gedenkblatt für Stefan Zweig, p. 166
Franz Werfels Namenszug, p. 187).

2697. — "Stefan Zweig und die Musik," *NMz*, 4.J.: 9 (1950), 249-253 (Reprinted in *AMoz*, 5.J. (1958), 2-5; *DTp*, 23 (1952); *Mu*, 6.J.: 2 (1952), 59-62 ; *Vbü*, 3.J.: 5 (1952), 80-82; *Europäer*, pp. 139-149.

2698. Bab, Julius. *Die Chronik des deutschen Dramas*, Vol. I-IV. Berlin: Oesterheld, 1922, Vol. III, pp. 41-45 (Discussion of Zweig's *Haus am Meer*); Vol. IV, pp. 141-142 (Discussion of Zweig's *Jeremias*).

2699. — "Emile Verhaeren," *NR*, XXIII : 2 (July, 1912), 1020-1028.

2700. — *Richard Dehmel. Die Geschichte eines Lebenswerkes*. Leipzig: Haessel, 1926, p. 344.

2701. Belázs, Béla. *Der Geist des Films*. Halle, Saale: Wilhelm Knapp, 1930, pp. 67, 74 (Discussion of the film "Narkose" (1929), "based on a script by Balázs after a story by Stefan Zweig" (his "Brief einer Unbekannten"?)).

2702. Basil, Otto. "Stefan Zweig und Ben Jonson," *Blätter*, 4/5 (Apr., 1959), 8.

2703. Bauer, Arnold. *Stefan Zweig*. Berlin-Dahlem: Colloquium, 1961 (In the series "Köpfe des XX. Jahrhunderts," Vol. XXI).

2704. Bauer, Walter. "Die Beschwörung Europas. Ein Blatt des Gedenkens für Stefan Zweig," *Erz*, 1.J.: 8 (1947), 15 (Reprinted in *März*, 1.J.: 2 (1949), 49-51).

2705. — "Erinnerungen an einen Europäer," *KD*, 5.J. (1951), 1056-1060.

2706. "Der Europäer Stefan Zweig," *Leben-Werk*, pp.130-145.

2707. — "Stefan Zweig, Freund der Jugend," *Europäer*, pp. 110-127.

2708. Baum, Vicki. *Es war alles ganz anders*. Berlin-Frankfurt am Main-Wien: Ullstein, 1962, p. 246.

2709. Becker, Martha. "Emile Verhaeren. Nachträgliches zu seiner Würdigung," *GRM*, X : 5/6 (May-June, 1922), 172-180.

2710. Beierle, A. "Stefan Zweig, Dichter und Dulder," *DZe*, 2.J.: 22 (1947), 3.

2711. Benaroya, Mois. *Stefan Zweig*. Sofia: Hyperion, 1929.

2712. Berendsohn, Walter A. *Die humanistische Front. Einführung in die deutsche Emigranten-Literatur. Erster Teil von 1933 bis zum Kriegsausbruch 1939*. Zürich: Europa, 1946, f.m.

2713. — "Warum ging Stefan Zweig in den Tod?" *JüGbl*, 4.J.: 10 (1949), 6.

2714. Berger, Fritz. "Stefan Zweig als Deuter und Mahner," *IF*, IV : 5 (May, 1962), 16-17.

2715. Bertrand, P. "Das Problem der Toleranz. Castellio gegen Calvin oder Fanatismus," *DSa*, 2.J. (1947), 598-600.

2716. *Bibliographie der Werke von Stefan Zweig, dem Dichter zum 50sten Geburtstag dargebracht vom Insel-Verlag*. Ed. Fritz Adolf Hünich and Erwin Rieger. Leipzig: Insel, 1931 (Reprinted in *In*, XIII : 1 (Christmas, 1931), 17-25).

2717. Bieber, Hugo. "Deutscher und Jude," *DLE*, 24.J.: 6 (Dec. 15, 1921), 313-321.

2718. Bierotte, Wolf. "'Drei Dichter ihres Lebens'. Anmerkungen über die Sprache," *DSL*, XXIX : 11 (Nov., 1928), 520-523.

2719. Bin Gorion, Emanuel. "Die Augen des ewigen Bruders," *Ceterum*, pp. 51-63 (Criticism à la stultitia).

2720. — "Stefan Zweigs Novellen ('Brennendes Geheimnis,' 'Brief einer Unbekannten,' 'Verwirrung der Gefühle,' 'Untergang eines Herzens')," *Ceterum*, pp. 64-76 (Ludicrous criticism).

2721. — "Über Stefan Zweigs Legendenstil," *NZZ*, Lit. Beil., No. 1264 (Cf. also *DL*, XXXI : 12 (1928-1929), 714; Positively negative).

2722. Böttcher, Kurt. "Humanist auf verlorener Bastion," *NDL*, 4.J.: 11 (1956), 83-92.

2723. — "Der Lebensroman des unerschöpflichen Balzac," *NDL*, 7.J.: 11 (1959), 45-46.

2724. Braun, Felix. "Ein Besuch bei Stefan Zweig," *Spiegelungen*, pp. 42-44 (Cf. *Das Licht der Welt* below).

2725. — "Brief an Stefan Zweig," *Briefe in das Jenseits*. Salzburg: O. Müller, 1952 (Reprinted in *Blätter*, 8/10 (Oct., 1960), 12).

2726. — "Erinnerungen an Salzburg," *DeuR*, LXXXIV (Dec., 1958), 1156-1162.

2727. — "Das fremde Leben. Stefan Zweig" (poem), *Das neue Leben. Neue Gedichte*. Berlin: Reiss, 1912 (Reprinted in *Blätter*, 8/10 (Oct., 1960), 13).

2728. — *Das Licht der Welt. Geschichte eines Versuches, als Dichter zu leben.* Wien: Herder, 1949, f.m. (Cf. esp., pp. 457-461; Reprinted in *Spiegelungen*, pp. 42-44).

2729. — *Das musische Land. Versuche über Österreichs Landschaft und Dichtung.* Innsbruck: Österreichische Verlagsanstalt, 1952, pp. 191-206.

2730. — "Stefan Zweig," *Zeitgefährten.* München: Nymphenburger Verlagshandlung, 1963, pp. 59-77.

2731. — "Stefan Zweig," *Stefan Zweig. Sonderpublikation der Funktionärblätter* (London), Nov., 1943, pp. 2-6.

2732. — "Stefan Zweig und sein Dämon," *DPr*, 943 (1951).

2733. Braun, Robert. "Erinnerungen an Stefan Zweig," *WieZ*, 275 (1956) (Reprinted in *Spiegelungen*, pp. 78-85; *BuL*, 10 (Oct., 1962), 1-3).

2734. Brod, Max. "Stefan Zweig zum Gedenken," *Spiegelungen*, p. 41.

2735. — *Streitbares Leben. Autobiographie.* München: Kindler, 1960, f.m.

2736. Burchardt, Hansjürgen. "Die Autographen-Auktion bei Stargard vom 14ten November 1958", *BdBh*, 14.J.: 101 (1958), 1708-1711.

2737. Burschell, Friedrich. "Stefan Zweigs Novellen," *FZ*, Lit. Beil., No. 64 (Cf. also *DL*, XXXVII : 8 (Apr.-Sept., 1931), 449).

2738. Cahn, Alfredo. *Stefan Zweig. Ein Nachruf.* Buenos Aires: n.p., 1942.

2739. See Item 2539a.

2740. Chaturvedi, Benarsi Das. "Bekenntnis zu Stefan Zweig," *Leben-Werk*, pp. 188-189 (Reprinted in *Europäer*, pp. 150-152).

2741. Csokor, Franz Theodor. "Ihr Leben. Für Stefan Zweig" (poem), *Die Gewalten. Ein Band Balladen.* Berlin: Juncker, 1912 (Reprinted in Blätter, 8/10 (Oct. 1960), 11).

2742. — "Stefan Zweig, der Freund," *Spiegelungen*, pp. 109-110 (A photocopy of part of this essay is reprinted in *Blätter*, 8/10 (Oct., 1960), 10).

2743. Dehorn, W. "Psychoanalyse und neuere Dichtung," *GermR*, VII (1932), 245-262, 330-358 (Cf. esp. pp. 330-339).

2744. Deissinger, Hans. "Kleine Erinnerung an Stefan Zweig," *Blätter*, 13/14 (Apr., 1962), 2-4.

2745. Dolbin, Benedikt F. *Österreichische Profile.* Ed. Oskar Maurus Fontana. München: Albert Langen-Georg Müller, 1959, p. 22 (Caricature sketch of Zweig).

2746. Drews, Richard and Alfred Kantorowitz, eds. *Verboten und Verbannt. Deutsche Literatur – 12 Jahre unterdrückt.* Berlin-München: Ullstein-Kindler, 1947, pp. 5, 47, 182, 185.

2747. Ebermayer, Erich. "Letzte Stunden mit Stefan Zweig," *Pris*, 19/20 (1948), 40.

2748. "Echo der Zeitungen zum 50sten Geburtstag Stefan Zweigs," *DL*, XXXIV (1932), 267.

2749. Ecker, Karl. "Die Sammlung Stefan Zweigs in der Österreichischen National-bibliothek, Wien," *Festschrift zum 25 jährigen Dienstjubiläum des General Direktors Josef Bick.* Ed. Jasek Stummvoll. Wien: 1948, pp. 321-330.

2750. Eckhardt, Eduard. "Deutsche Bearbeitung älterer englischer Dramen," *ES*, LXVIII (1933), 195-208.

2751. Ehrentreich, Alfred. "Stefan Zweig und Henri Guilbeaux," *NphZ*, 4.J. (1952), 263-265.

2752. Eloesser, Arthur. "Verhaerens Drama 'Das Kloster'," *DLE*, XIII : 3 (Nov. 1, 1910), 208-209 (Discussion of the German premiere of Verhaeren's drama in Zweig's translation).

2753. Elster, Hanns Martin. *Deutsche Dichterhandschriften.* Vol. XIII. Intro. Hanns Martin Elster. Dresden: Lehmann, 1922 (Reproduction of the manuscript of Zweig's "Brief einer Unbekannten").

2754. — "Stefan Zweig," *BBB*, II : 138/139 (1923), 1-3; II : 140 (1923), 2-3; II : 141 (1923), 2 (Cf. also *DLE*, 25.J.: 9/10 (Feb. 1, 1923), 532).

2755. Erkelenz, K. H. "Stefan Zweig," *KZ*, 650 (1931) (Cf. also *DL*, XXXIV : 5 (Oct., 1931 - Mar., 1932), 267).

2756. Faesi, Robert. "Stefan Zweig zu seinem 50sten Geburtstag," *NZZ*, Nov. 29, 1931 (Cf. also *DL*, XXXIV : 5 (Oct., 1931 - Mar., 1932), 267).

2757. Faktor, Emil. "Stefan Zweig zum 50sten Geburtstag," *BBC*, 553 (1931) (Cf. also *DL*, XXXIV : 5 (Oct., 1931 - Mar., 1932), 267).

2758. Feder, Ernst. "Die letzten Tage Stefan Zweigs," *Begegnungen. Die Grossen der Welt im Zwiegespräch*. Esslingen: Bechtle, 1950, pp. 197-210 (Reprinted in *Leben-Werk*, pp. 150-165; *Europäer*, pp. 218-238).

2759. Fedin, Konstantin. "Die Tragödie Stefan Zweigs," *Au*, XII (1956), 959-961.

2760. Fehse, Willi. "Erinnerungen an Stefan Zweig," *Au*, II : 2 (1946), 1230-1233 (Reprinted in *LB*, II : 14 (Dec., 1947), 10-13).

2761. — "Das höchste Gut dieser Erde..." *Spiegelungen*, pp. 62-67.

2762. — "Stefan Zweig, Meister der Stimmungskunst," *DSta*, 2.J.: 25 (1947).

2763. Fitzbauer, Erich. "Einleitung," *Durch Zeiten und Welten*. Ed. Erich Fitzbauer. Graz-Wien: Stiasny, 1961, pp. 5-23 (Stiasny Bücherei, No. 79).

2764. — "Gedanken zu Klaus Manns 'Wendepunkt' mit dem Versuch einer Konfrontation des Verfassers mit Stefan Zweig. Im 10ten Todesjahr Klaus Manns," *Blätter*, 6/7 (Oct., 1959), 11-13.

2765. — "Die 'Schachnovelle' als Film," *Blätter*, 8/10 (Oct., 1960), 17-19.

2766. — "Stefan Zweig als Dramatiker," *DeuR*, 86.J. (1960), 434-437.

2767. — *Stefan Zweig (1881-1942). Ausstellung in der Residenz in Salzburg*. 15. *Juli* - 31. *Aug.*, 1961. Ed. of the Catalogue Erich Fitzbauer. Salzburg: Salzburger Residenzgalerie, Salzburger Kulturvereinigung, 1961.

2768. — "Stefan Zweig, dichterisch-menschlicher Einklang," *Spiegelungen*, pp. 5-18.

2769. — ed. *Stefan Zweig. Spiegelungen einer schöpferischen Persönlichkeit*. Wien: Bergland, 1959.

Contenst:

Erich Fitzbauer, "Stefan Zweig, dichterisch-menschlicher Einklang," pp. 5-18.
Stefan Zweig, "Ein Brief," pp. 19-21
Stefan Zweig, "Fünf Jugendgedichte," pp. 22-23
Harry Zohn, "Stefan Zweig und Emile Verhaeren," pp. 24-31
Stefan Zweig, "Fünf Nachdichtungen," pp. 32-35
Victor Fleischel, "Erinnerung an Stefan Zweig," pp. 36-40
Max Brod, "Stefan Zweig zum Gedenken," p. 41
Felix Braun, "Ein Besuch bei Stefan Zweig," pp. 42-43
Stefan Zweig, "Die Autographensammlung als Kunstwerk,", pp. 44-51
Joseph Gregor, "Stefan Zweig – Dank für zwei glückliche Jahrzehnte," pp. 52-55
Adelbert Muhr, "Bei Stefan Zweig auf dem Höhepunkt seines Lebens," pp. 56-61
Willi Fehse, "Das höchste Gut dieser Erde...'," pp. 62-67
Lee van Dovski, "Mit Stefan Zweig in Paris," pp. 68-73
Stefan Zweig, "Drei Briefe," pp. 74-77
Robert Braun, "Erinnerung an Stefan Zweig," pp. 78-85
Stefan Zweig, "Fünf Briefe," pp. 86-93
Siegfried Freiberg, "Stefan Zweig und Brasilien," pp. 94-100
Heinrich Eduard Jacob, "Aus den Polizeiakten von Petropolis," pp. 101-106
Ernst Waldinger, "Stefan Zweigs 'Feuilletonismus'," pp. 107-108
Franz Theodor Csokor, "Stefan Zweig – der Freund," pp. 109-110
Ludwig Ullmann, "Stefan Zweig, der grosse Europäer," pp. 111-116

Plates:

Stefan Zweig, Bronzebüste von Gustinus Ambrosi, opp. p. 3
Faksimile einer Karte Stefan Zweigs an Karl Klammer, p. 21
Einbandzeichnung zu Zweigs erstem Buch, von Hugo Steiner-Prag, opp. p. 48
Teilansicht von Stefan Zweigs Haus am Kapuzinerberg in Salzburg, opp. p. 64

2770. — "Stefan Zweig und Salzburg," *Blätter*, 2 (July, 1958), 4-5.

2771. Fleischel, Victor. "Erinnerung an Stefan Zweig," *Spiegelungen*, pp. 36-40.

2772. — "Stefan Zweig," *Stefan Zweig. Sonderpublikation der Funktionärblätter* (London), Nov., 1943.

2773. Foltin, Lore B. "Stefan Zweig," Intro. to "Die Legende der dritten Taube," *Aus Nah und Fern*. Boston: Houghton-Mifflin, 1950, pp. 152-154 (School ed.).
2774. Freiberg, Siegfried. "Stefan Zweig und Brasilien," *Spiegelungen*, pp. 94-100.
2775. Freud, Sigmund. *Briefe*. 1873-1939. Sel. and ed. Ernst L. Freud. Frankfurt am Main: Fischer, 1960, f.m.
2776. Friedenthal, Richard. "Epistel an einen toten Freund," *Leben-Werk*, pp. 173-176 (Reprinted in *Europäer*, pp. 239-241).
2777. — "Nachwort," *Angst. Novelle*. Stuttgart: Reclam, 1954, pp. 69-74.
2778. — "Nachwort des Herausgebers," *Balzac*. Stockholm: Bermann-Fischer, 1946, pp. 569-574.
2779. — "Nachwort des Herausgebers," *Zeit und Welt*. Stockholm: Bermann-Fischer, 1944, pp. 369-373.
2780. — *Stefan Zweig und der humanitäre Gedanke*. Esslingen: Bechtle, 1948 (Reprinted in *Leben-Werk*, pp. 200-219; *Europäer*, pp. 45-71).
2781. — "Stefan Zweigs literarischer Nachlass," *Stefan Zweig. Sonderpublikation der Funktionärblätter* (London), Nov., 1943, pp. 15-16.
2782. Friedrichs, Ernst. "Stefan Zweig zu seinem 45sten Geburtstag, "*GS*, No. 329 (Cf. also *DL*, XXIX : 5 (1926-1927), 279).
2783. Frischauer, Paul. "Stefan Zweig zum 50sten Geburtstag," *BT*, No. 559 (Cf. also *DL*, XXXIV : 5 (Oct., 1931 - Mar., 1932), 267).
2784. Fülöp-Miller, René. "Erinnerungsblatt für Stefan Zweig," *Leben-Werk*, pp. 167-168 (Reprinted in *Europäer*, pp. 203-205).
2785. "Gedenkabend zu Zweigs 80stem Geburtstag in Wien," *WieZ*, Nov. 30, 1961 (Reprinted in *Blätter*, 13/14 (Apr., 1962), 9).
2786. Götzfried, Hansleo. *Romain Rolland*. 2. ed. Stuttgart: Engelhorns Nachf., 1931, f.m.
2787. Green, Julien. *Tagebücher*. Vol. I (1928-1945), Vol. II (1946-1950). Tr. from the French by Hanns Winter. Wien: Herold, 1952, f.m.
2788. Gregor, Joseph. "An Stefan Zweig – Eine Aussprache über Wertungen und Ziele, zum 28sten November, 1931," *In*, XIII : 1 (Christmas, 1931), 1-10.
2789. — "Stefan Zweig – Dank für zwei glückliche Jahrzehnte," *Spiegelungen*, pp. 52-55.
2790. Grisson, Alexandra Carola."Stefan Zweig," Postscript to the Reclam ed. of "Angst". Stuttgart: Reclam, 1947, pp. 77-80.
2791. Grossberg, Mimi. "Gedenkabend für Stefan Zweig," Lecture given in the Austrian Forum (New York), Feb. 6, 1963 by Mme. Grossberg. Copyright by Mimi Grossberg. The following selections were read by Mr. Theodor Goetz:
    1. "Stefan Zweigs letzter Abend" (taken from Ernst Feder's "Stefan Zweigs letzte Tage", cf. above).
    2. One scene from *Jeremias* (highly abridged).
    3. Excerpts from Zweig's "Besuch bei Emile Verhaeren".
    4. Verhaeren's "Nun die Flimmer von Schnee auf unser Dach" in Zweig's translation.
    5. A passage from Camoens' *Lusiads* in Zweig's translation.
    6. The "Glockenmonolog" from *Die schweigsame Frau*.
    7. Zweig's "Ballade von einem Traum" (abridged).
2792. Günther, Herbert. "Stefan Zweig und Frankreich," *DGT*, 4.J.: 1 (1949), 83-88.
2793. Günther, Werner. *Weltinnenraum. Die Dichtung Rainer Maria Rilkes*. 2. ed. Berlin: Erich Schmidt, 1952, p. 331 (Reference to Zweig's "Abschied von Rilke").
2794. Hellwig, Hans. *Stefan Zweig. Ein Lebensbild*. Lübeck: Wildner, 1948.
2795. Herrmann, W. "Arnold und Stefan Zweig: der gestürzte Olymp," *BBZ*, June 25, 1933.
2796. Herrmann-Neisse, Leni. "Erinnerung an Stefan Zweig," *Blätter*, 11/12 (Oct., 1961), 15.
2797. Hinterberger, Heinrich, ed. *Repräsentative Original-Handschriften. Eine berühmte Autographen-Sammlung*. 1. *Teil*. Katalog IX. Wien: Heinrich Hinterberger, n.d. (Cf. also Katalog XX: *Interessante Autographen aus zwei bekannten Sammlungen*).

2798. Hirth, Friedrich. "Deutsche Literatur in Frankreich," *DL*, XXX : 7 (1927-1928), 385-387.
2799. Hofmann, Else. "Besuch bei Stefan Zweig," *FuT*, July, 1949, pp. 9-10.
2800. Holde, Artur. "Gedenkfeier des 'Aufbau' für Stefan Zweig," *Au (NY)*, VIII : 10 (Mar. 6, 1942), 19-20.
2801. Homeyer, Fritz. *Ein Leben für das Buch. Erinnerungen.* Aschaffenburg: Pottloch, 1961, f.m.
2802. Hünich, Fritz Adolf. "Stefan Zweig zum 50sten Geburtstag," *Bd*, No. 555 (Cf. also *DL*, XXXIV : 5 (Oct., 1931 - Mar., 1932), 267).
2803. Hünich, Fritz Adolf and Erwin Rieger, eds. *Bibliographie der Werke von Stefan Zweig.* Leipzig: Insel, 1931 (Reprinted in *In*, XIII (1931), 17-30).
2804. Huppert, Hugo. "Der das Glück als Schuld erachtete... Zum 75sten Wiederkehr von Stefan Zweigs Geburtstag," *Wbü*, XI (1956), 1534-1540.
2805. "In Memoriam Stefan Zweigs," *DWe*, 5.J.: 8 (1950), 4.
2806. Ippisch, Gottfried. "Nachwort," *Angst. Novelle*. Wien: Humboldt, 1947 (Kleine Humboldt Bibliothek, No. 104).
2807. Jacob, Heinrich Eduard. "Aus den Polizeiakten von Petropolis," *Spiegelungen*, pp. pp. 101-106.
2808. — "Stefan Zweig – Zehn Jahre nach seinem Tode," *NlW*, 3.J.: 5 (1952), 8.
2809. Jacob, P. Walter. "Stefan Zweig als Dramatiker," *Rampenlicht. Köpfe der Literatur und des Theaters.* Buenos Aires: Editorial Cosmopolita, 1945. pp. 75-82.
2810. Jacobi, Johannes and A. J. Seelmann-Eggebert. "Visionen der Entrechtung: Stefan Zweig und Georg Kaiser," *DZe*, 6.J.: 45 (1951), 3.
2811. "Jahre der Reife Stefan Zweigs," *AWJD*, 5.J.: 40 (1950), 6.
2812. J.D.L. "Stefan Zweig, ein gewissenhafter Dichter," *Bd*, No. 108 (Quote from same *DL*, XXXV : 8 (1932-1933), 463).
2813. Kayser, Rudolf. "Max Brod, 'Streitbares Leben. Autobiographie'," *Blätter*, 11/12 (Oct., 1961), 8.
2814. Kesten, Hermann. *Dichter im Café.* Wien-München-Basel: Kurt Desch, 1959, f.m.
2815. — *Der Geist der Unruhe. Literarische Streifzüge.* Köln-Berlin: Kiepenhauer-Witsch, 1959, f.m.
2816. — "Stefan Zweig," *Meine Freunde die Poeten.* Wien-München: Donau Verlag, 1953, pp. 114-126.
2817. — "Stefan Zweig," *WuW*, V : 13 (Mar., 1950), 97-99.
2818. — "Stefan Zweig – Erinnerungen an den Freund," *DMo*, 5.J.: 50 (1952), 225-228.
2819. Knevels, Wilhelm. "Stefan Zweig," *GdG*, LXVI : 4 (1930), 145-152.
2820. Kraus, Hans Johan. "Brasilien ehrt Stefan Zweig," *NVzt*, Mar. 14, 1942, p. 5.
2821. Kraus, Karl. "Pretiosen," *DF*, XXVIII : 726/729 (May, 1926), 55-56.
2822. — "Umsturz in der 'Neuen Freien Presse'," *DF*, XXVIII : 751/756 (Feb., 1927), 125-126.
2823. Kubin, Alfred. *Alfred Kubin – Leben-Werk-Wirkung.* Ed. Paul Raabe. Hamburg: Rowohlt, 1957, pp. 33, 53-54, 98 (Letters from Zweig to Kubin and reference to Kubin's illustrations for the 1931 edition of *Jeremias*, an edition that never appeared. These drawings are reprinted in *Blätter*, 8/10 (Oct., 1960), 26-27).
2824. Kuhn-Foelitz, August. "Begegnung in Salzburg. Gespräch mit Stefan Zweig," *MAZ*, 5 (1949).
2825. Kumming, Eugen. "Stefan Zweig – Weltbürger ohne Heimat," *AfdW*, 2.J. II: 10 (1950), 5-12.
2826. Landmann, Georg Peter. *Stefan George und sein Kreis. Eine Bibliographie.* Hamburg: Ernst Hauswedell, 1960, Nos. 178, 410a, 574.
2827. Lang, Wolf R. "Nachwort," *Menschen. Novellen.* Stuttgart-Zürich-Salzburg: Europäischer Buchklub, 1962, pp. 405-408.
2828. — "Stefan Zweig. Umrisse seines Lebens," *BuL*, 11 (Nov., 1962), 1-3.
2829. Lange, Herbert. "Ein Bildnis Stefan Zweigs," *OöN*, Oct. 27, 1947, p. 3.
2830. Lederer, Max. "Stefan Zweig," *Rad*, VI (1929), 2 (Cf. *DL*, XXXII : 3 (1929-1930), 158; *DL*, XXXII : 4 (1929-1930), 226).

2831. Lehrman, Charles. "Theodor Wolff und Stefan Zweig," *Au(NY)*, May 13, 1949, p. 32.
2832. Lenteritz, G. "Das unerloschene Leuchten, Stefan Zweig," *BdBh*, 114.J. (1947), 17-25.
2833. Lerch, Eugen. *Romain Rolland*. München: Max Hueber, 1926, f.m.
2834. Lernet-Holenia, Alexander. "Aus einem Brief von Alexander Lernet-Holenia," *Leben-Werk*, p. 149 (Reprinted as "Ich wollte, er lebte uns noch!" in *Europäer*, pp. 108-109).
2835. L. H. "Stefan Zweig zum 65sten Geburtstag," *ST*, Nov. 29, 1946, p. 8.
2836. Lie, Robert. "Amerika und die österreichische Literatur," *WidZ*, 4 (Apr., 1961), 42-45.
2837. Liess, Andreas. *Joseph Marx. Leben und Werk*. Graz: Sterische Verlagsanstalt, 1943 (Reference to Zweig's poem "Ein Drängen ist in meinem Herzen" (from *Silberne Saiten*) which Marx set to music in 1909).
2838. Lilge, Herbert. "Der Untergang eines Herzens. Nachruf auf Stefan Zweig," *Bng*, 6.J. (1951), 3-9.
2839. Lissauer, Ernst. "Zu Stefan Zweigs 50stem Geburtstag," *CVZ*, X : 47 (Nov. 20, 1931), 537-538.
2840. Lothar, Rudolf. "Aus dem Engeren. Literaturbilder aus deutschen Einzelgauen," *DLE*, IV : 8 (Jan., 1902), 509-524 (Cf. esp. p. 523).
2841. Lucka, Emil. "Stefan Zweig," *DLE*, XVII : 4 (Nov. 15, 1914), 193-199.
2842. — "Stefan Zweig, der Menschengestalter," *DLz*, XX : 6 (1933), 89-93.
2843. Ludwig, Emil. "Stefan Zweig zum 50sten Geburtstag," *DLW*, VII (1931), 47 (Cf. also *DL*, XXXIV : 5 (Oct., 1931- Mar., 1932), 277).
2844. Lukács, Georg. "Der Kampf zwischen Liberalismus und Demokratie im Spiegel des historischen Romans der deutschen Antifaschisten," *Essays über Realismus*. Berlin: Aufbau, 1948. pp. 88-128 (2. enl. ed. reprinted as *Probleme des Realismus*. Berlin: Aufbau, 1955. The article about the historical novel appears pp. 184-210).
2845. Maass, Joachim. "Neues von und über Stefan Zweig," *HFbl*, June 2, 1928 (Cf. also *DL*, XXX : 11 (1927-1928), 654).
2846. Maderno, Alfred. "Stefan Zweig," *RT*, I (n.d.), 44-45.
2847. Mann, Thomas. "Stefan Zweig zum 10ten Todestag," *Altes und Neues*. Frankfurt am Main: Fischer, 1953, pp. 263-265.
2848. Marti, Hugo. "Der Europäer Stefan Zweig," *Bd*, 113 (1933) (Cf. also *DL*, XXXV : 8 (1932-1933), 463).
2849. Maurer, Joseph, "Über Zweigs Aufsatz 'Herbstwinter in Meran'," *Blätter*, 6/7 (Oct., 1959), 18-19.
2850. Marina, Zenta. *Dostojewski. Menschengestalter und Gottsucher*. 2. ed. Memmingen: Maximilian Dietrich, 1960, pp. 12, 23, 138.
2951. Menter, L. "Stefan Zweig," *DWe*, 2.J.: 13 (1947), 9.
2852. Meyer-Benfey, Heinrich. "Stefan Zweig," *HK*, Lit. Beil. Oct. 28, 1923, pp. 505-506 (Cf. also *DL*, XXVI : 3 (Oct., 1923 - Mar., 1924), 157).
2853. Michaelis, Edgar. "Rückblick auf Freud," *Bng*, V : 2 (Mar.-Apr., 1950), 76-83.
2854. "Millionenblutopfer und Ideenforschung. Zu den Artikeln des A.H. Fried und Stefan Zweig," *NZZ*, Aug. 11, 1918.
2855. Mistral, Gabriela. "Un gran señor…" *Blätter*, 4/5 (Apr., 1959), 11.
2856. Molo, Walter von. "Erinnerungen an Stefan Zweig," *Blätter*, 3 (Oct., 1958), 4.
2857. Muhr, Adelbert. "Bei Stefan Zweig auf dem Höhepunkt seines Lebens," *Spiegelungen*, pp. 56-61.
2858. Mühsam, Paul. "Begegnung mit Stefan Zweig," *Blätter*, 15 (Jan., 1963), 10.
2859. Müller-Einigen, Hans. *Jugend in Wien. Erinnerungen an die schönste Stadt Europas*. Bern: Francke, 1945, f.m.
2860. Musil, Robert. *Tagebücher, Aphorismen, Essays und Reden*. Ed. Adolf Frisé. Hamburg: Rowohlt, 1955, f.m. (Vol. II of Musil collected works; in general Musil rejects Zweig as superficial and as an "opportunist").

2861. Neumann, Robert. "Abschied von Stefan Zweig," tr. from the English by Stefanie Neumann. *Blätter*, 11/12 (Oct., 1961), 1-4.
2862. Oetke, Herbert. "Stefan Zweig," *VuV*, 2. ser., 13 (1947), 22-31.
2863. Parandowski, Jan. "Erinnerungen an Stefan Zweig," *WidZ*, 11 (Nov., 1961), 40-44.
2864. Pisk, Egon. "Stefan Zweigs Tod," *WieZ*, 277 (1949).
2865. Poss, A. "Ein Gedankenaustausch mit Jugendlichen über Stefan Zweigs Legende 'Die Augen des ewigen Bruders'," *Mon*, Lit. Beil. 43.J. (1930), 1.
2866. Rainalter, Erwin H. "Nachwort," *Angst. Novelle*. Leipzig: Reclam, 1925, pp. 72-76.
2867. Rauscher, Bert. "Stefan Zweig: Ein Gewissen gegen die Gewalt. Zum 15ten Todestag von Stefan Zweig," *Brü*, 11.J.: 8 (1957), 1-3.
2868. Reim, Paul. *Probleme und Gestalten der österreichischen Literatur*. London: Verlag Jugend Voran (Junges Österreich), 1945, m.
2869. Reishofer, Karl. "Wie erklären sich grosse Bucherfolge? Eine Analyse der literarischen Wirkung," *BuI*, V : 203 (June 9, 1950), 2781-2782; V : 204 (June 16, 1950), 2797-2798.
2870. Reisiger, Hans. "Freundliches Erinnern an Stefan Zweig," *Leben-Werk*, pp. 128-129 (Reprinted in *Europäer*, pp. 104-107).
2871. Rieger, Erwin. "Stefan Zweig," *Rad*, VIII (1931), 8 (Cf. also *DL*, XXXIV : 5 (Oct., 1931 - Mar., 1932), 277).
2872. — "Stefan Zweig als Dramatiker," *HFbl*, 152 (June 2, 1928) (Cf. also *DL*, XXX : 11 (1927-1928), 654).
2873. — "Stefan Zweig als Essayist," *KZ*, Apr. 24, 1928 (Cf. *DL*, XXX : 9 (1927-1928), 528).
2874. — *Stefan Zweig, der Mann und das Werk*. Berlin: Spaeth, 1928 (Zweig bibliography, pp. 219-230).
2875. Rieger, Erwin and Fritz Adolf Hünich, eds. *Bibliographie der Werke von Stefan Zweig*. Leipzig: Insel, 1931 (Reprinted in *In*, XIII (1931), 17-30).
2876. Rieger, Harald. "Zwei Suchende: Siddhartha und Virata (Hermann Hesses 'Siddhartha' und Stefan Zweigs 'Die Augen des ewigen Bruders')," *Gespr*, 4 (Aug., 1959), 8f.
2877. Riemerschmid, Werner. "Salzburger Erinnerung. Aus einem Brief," *Blätter*, 6/7 (Oct., 1959), 2.
2878. Rilke, Rainer Maria. *Briefe* (Vol. I. 1897-1914). Wiesbaden: Insel, 1950, pp. 174-175.
2879. — *Briefe aus den Jahren* 1906 *bis* 1907. Leipzig: Insel, 1930, f.m.
2880. Rilke, Rainer Maria and André Gide. *Briefwechsel*. 1909-1926. Tr. from the French by Wolfgang A. Peters. Intro. and notes Renée Lang. Stuttgart: Deutsche Verlagsanstalt, 1957, f.m. (Also contains a letter from Zweig to Rolland (Dec. 30, 1915) and Rolland's response (Jan. 17, 1916)).
2881. Rilke, Rainer Maria and Katharina Kippenberg. *Briefwechsel*. Wiesbaden: Insel, 1954, f.m.
2882. Rilke, Rainer Maria and Maria von Thurn und Taxis. *Briefwechsel*. Vol. I/II. Zürich: Niehause, Rokitansky and Insel, 1951, Vol. I, p. 460.
2883. Ritzer, Walter. *Rainer Maria Rilke – Bibliography*. Wien: Kerry, 1951, f.m.
2884. Rolland, Romain. "Zwei Briefe an Stefan Zweig (Mar. 15, 1915, and May 4, 1915)," *Leben-Werk*, pp. 169-172 (Reprinted in *Europäer*, pp. 87-91).
2885. Rosenhaupt, Hans Wilhelm. *Der deutsche Dichter um die Jahrhundertwende und seine Abgelöstheit von der Gesellschaft*. Bern-Leipzig: Paul Haupt, 1939, f.m. (Cf. esp. pp. 145-147).
2886. Rosenthal, Friedrich. "Jungwiener Novellistik," *ÖR*, XXXVIII : 2 (Jan.-Mar., 1914), 90-103.
2887. Rosenzweig, Alfred. "Stefan Zweig als Operndichter," *Stefan Zweig. Sonderpublikation der Funktionärblätter* (London), Nov., 1943, pp. 10-14.
2888. Schäke, Gerd. "Stefan Zweig – Dichter, Essayist, Schriftsteller – sein tragisches Ende," *DWo*, 1.J.: 30 (1946), 5.
2889. Schaukal, Richard von. "Ein Abenteuer Henri Beyles und seine Verzweigung," *DeuV*, X : 9 (1928), 680-683.

L
2890. — "Deutsche Prosa auf Zeithöhe," *DeuV*, XII (1930), 551-552.
2891. — "Der Fall Stefan Zweigs. Beitrag zur Geschichte der Dummheit," *DeuE*, V : 7 (1931), 430-432 (Cf. also *DZ*, No. 170; *DL*, XXXIII : 12 (Apr.-Sept., 1931), 696).
2892. — "Krönung Stefans des Grossen," *DeuV*, XII (1930), 113-119.
2893. — "Stefan Zweig," *APzt*, Lit. Beil., 4 (1931).
2894. Scheller, Will. "Über Stefan Zweig als Lyriker und Erzähler," *KrZ* (Wissenschaft), 74 (1925) (Cf. *DL*, XXVII : 9 (Apr.-Sept., 1925), 537).
2895. Schlösser, Manfred, and Hans Rolf Ropertz, eds. *Kein ding sei wo das wort gebricht. Stefan George zum Gedenken.* Darmstadt: Agora, 1961 (2. enl. ed.; orig. 1958; Cf. *DLW*, IV : 29 (July 20, 1928), 24).
2896. Schlösser, Wilhelm. "Geleitwort," *Menschen. Novellen.* Stuttgart-Zürich-Salzburg: Europäischer Buchklub, 1962, pp. 7-8.
2897. Schneider, Wilhelm, ed. "Stefan Zweig über Sprach- und Stillehre," *Meister des Stils über Sprach-und Stillehre.* Leipzig: Teubner, 1926, p. 137.
2898. Schömann, Milian. "Stefan Zweig. Ein Humanist in unserer Zeit," *Philo*, III : 1/4 (1938), 347-358.
2899. Scholz, Wilhelm von. "Erinnerungen an Stefan Zweig," *Blätter*, 3 (Oct., 1958), 5.
2900. Seelig, Carl. "Stefan Zweig, ein europäisch gesinnter Schriftsteller," *WdA*, 1.J.: 31 (1950), 8.
2901. Selden-Goth, Gisella. "Stefan Zweig und die Musik," *Au(NY)*, I : 10 (Mar. 6, 1942).
2901a. Sieburg, Friedrich. "Stefan Zweigs Welt von gestern," *Nur für Leser. Jahre und Bücher.* Stuttgart: Deutsche Verlags-Anstalt, 1955, pp. 42-45.
2902. Simenauer, Erich. *Rainer Maria Rilke. Legende und Mythos.* Bern: Paul Haupt, 1953, f.m.
2903. "Die soziale Lage der deutschen Schriftsteller," *Bb*, 7/11 (Jan.-June, 1910).
2904. Spael, W. "Stefan Zweig," *Germ*, Jan. 20, 1923.
2905. Spanier, Max. "Stefan Zweig," *BrsZ*, No. 14 (Cf. *DL*, XXIX : 6 (1926-1927), 346).
2906. Specht, Richard. "Die Literatur der Gegenwart," *Ewiges Österreich.* Ed. Erwin Rieger. Wien: Manzscher Verlag, 1928, pp. 25-74.
2907. — *Stefan Zweig. Versuch eines Bildnisses.* Leipzig: Spamersche Buchdruckerei, 1927 (This essay was translated into Russian and forms the Intro. to Zweig's Collected Works in Russian, Leningrad: Vremya, 1928-1930).
2908. Stefan, Paul. "Zum Tode Stefan Zweigs," *NVzt*, Feb. 28, 1942, p. 3.
2909. "Stefan Zweig," *BZ*, Jan. 21, 1923.
2910. "Stefan Zweig," *Büg*, 6 (1951), 259.
2911. "Stefan Zweig," *NSchR*, N.F., 16.J. (1948-1949), 574-576.
2912. "Stefan Zweig," *DWo*, 3.J.: 18/19 (1948), 4.
2913. "Stefan Zweig, der Europäer," *Bd*, Mar. 8, 1933.
2914. "Stefan Zweig, Künder des Friedens und eines geeinten Europas," *Auf*, 4.J. (1952), 515-516.
2915. "Stefan Zweig spricht über den europäischen Gedanken," *BN*, Mar. 15, 1933.
2916. "Stefan Zweig wider Schieffenzahn," *Die Standarte.* Magdeburg: Frundsberg, 1930, p. 381.
2917. "Stefan Zweig zum 50sten Geburtstag," *DL*, XXXIV : 5 (1931), 267.
2918. "Stefan Zweig zum 50sten Geburtstag," *PL*, Nov. 27, 1931.
2919. "Stefan Zweig zum 50sten Geburtstag," *PP*, No. 322 (Cf. *DL*, XXXIV : 5 (1931), 267).
2920. "Stefan Zweig zum Gedächtnis," *Au(NY)*, VIII : 9 (Feb. 27, 1942), 15-16 (Brief contributions by Emil Ludwig, Paul Stefan, Bruno Frank, Hermann Kesten, Thomas Mann, Lion Feuchtwanger, Heinrich Mann, Walter Mehring, Alfred Polgar, Berthold Viertel, Lothar Wallerstein, Franz Werfel).
2921. Storz, Gerhard. "Über die Wirklichkeit von Dichtung," *WW* (Erstes Sonderheft), n.d. (ca. 1952), 94-103.

2922. Strich, Christian, ed. "Anekdote um Stefan Zweig," *Der Autorabend. Dichteranekdoten von Rabelais bis Thomas Mann.* Zürich: Diogenes, 1953.

2923. Sturmann, M. "Stefan Zweig, ein jüdischer Dichter," *BIG*, 1929, p. 104.

2924. — "Studie über Stefan Zweig," *JR*, 33.J. (1928).

2925. Thies, H. "Stefan Zweig," *HFbl*, Jan. 10, 1927.

2926. Thommen-Girard, G. H. "Stefan Zweig als Autographen-Sammler," *DAnq*, 10.J. (1954), 205-208.

2927. Tobias, J. "Stefan Zweig – zu seinem 50sten Geburtstag," *SLzt*, Nov. 28, 1931.

2928. Trebitsch, Siegfried. "Für Stefan Zweig (Gedicht zum 20sten Todestag Stefan Zweigs am. 22. Februar 1962)," *Blätter*, 13/14 (Apr., 1962), 1.

2929. Trenner, Franz. *Richard Strauss: Dokumente seines Lebens und Schaffens.* München: Beck, 1954, pp. 228 ff. (Concerning the stormy history of the opera "Die schweigsame Frau").

2930. — "Zur Entstehung der 'Schweigsamen Frau'," *BBSF* (1962).

2931. Trinius, B. "Stefan Zweig," *DAZ*, Nov. 25, 1931 (Cf. also *DL*, XXXIV : 5 (Oct., 1931 - Mar., 1932), 267).

2932. Truding, Lona. "Stefan Zweig und die Musik," *G*, XXXV (1956), 411-413.

2933. — "Stefan Zweig und die Musik," *NZfM*, CXIX (Mar., 1958), 136-139.

2934. "Über Sprach- und Stillehre," *Meister des Stils über Sprach- und Stillehre.* Ed. Wilhelm Schneider. Leipzig: Teubner, 1926, p. 137.

2935. "Über Stefan Zweig," *RoR*, 2 (1929), 120.

2936. Ullmann, Ludwig. "Stefan Zweig, der grosse Europäer," *Spiegelungen*, pp. 111-116.

2937. Ullrich, Hermann, ed. *Salzburg. Bildnis einer Stadt. Essays, Briefe und Dokumente.* Wien: Sexl, 1948 (Cf. *Blätter*, 8/10 (Oct., 1960), 7).

2938. — "Zum Geleit," *Stefan Zweig. Sonderpublikation der Funktionärblätter* (London), Nov., 1943, pp. 1-2.

2939. Van Dovski, Lee. "Mit Stefan Zweig in Paris," *Spiegelungen*, pp. 68-73.

2940. Van Gelder, Robert. "Stefan Zweig: Wie sich die Schriftstellerei in einer kriegerischen Welt entwickeln wird," *Prominente plaudern.* Tr. from the English by Gottfried Ippisch. Wien: Humboldt, 1947, pp. 72-75.

2941. "Verwirrung der Gefühle – Todestag des Dichters Stefan Zweigs," *BdBh*, 118.J. (1951), 113.

2942. Viertel, Berthold. "Abschied von Stefan Zweig," *Leben-Werk*, pp. 191-199 (Reprinted in *Europäer*, pp. 250-260).

2943. — "Das gestohlene Jahr," *Blätter*, 8/10 (Oct., 1960), 14-17 (Concerning the Zweig/Viertel collaboration on the film by the same name).

2944. Vogelsang, Hans. "Stefan Zweig, ein Enthusiast des Dramas," *WidZ*, 12 (Dec., 1961), 53-59.

2945. Waibler, Helmut. *Hermann Hesse. Eine Bibliographie.* Bern-München: Francke, 1962, Nos. P 1558-1561, L 120, 907, 1926.

2946. Waldinger, Ernst. "Stefan Zweigs 'Feuilletonismus'," *Spiegelungen*, pp. 107-108.

2947. Walter, Bruno. *Thema und Variationen. Erinnerungen und Gedanken.* Stockholm: Bermann-Fischer, 1947 (Tr. into English by James A. Galstone. New York: Knopf, pp. 262, 307, 311).

2948. Weiss, Hansgerhard. *Romain Rolland.* Berlin-Leipzig: Volk und Wissen, 1948, f.m.

2949. Wendel, Hermann. "Ein Vorläufer von Karl Marx. Auseinandersetzungen mit Stefan Zweig," *V*, No. 246 (Cf. *DL*, XXXII : 4 (1929-1930), 222).

2950. Werfel, Franz. "Stefan Zweigs Tod," *Leben-Werk*, pp. 177-187 (Reprinted in *Europäer*, pp. 269-282; *Unsterblicher Genius. Deutsche Dichter in Gedenken ihrer Freunde.* Ed. Paul Schneider. Ebenhausen bei München: Hartfrid Voss, 1959, pp. 317-323).

2951. Werremeier. "Der Arzt in der Dichtung Stefan Zweigs und Hans Carossas," *DNSch*, 14.J. (1953), 175-176.

2952. Wilhelm, Paul. "Stefan Zweig," *NWJ*, 6829 (1912) (Cf. *DLE*, 15.J.: 5 (Dec. 11, 1912), 328).

2953. Winternitz, Friderike Maria von. "Die Übersetzer und der Krieg," *DLE*, XVIII : 8 (Jan. 15, 1916), 483-485.

2954. Wittek, Suzan von. "Erinnerung an Stefan Zweig," *OöN*, Oct. 27, 1947, p. 3.
2955. Wittner, V. "Altösterreichische Abschiede." *DLW*, I (1946-1947), 300-304.
2956. Wolbe, Eugen. "Stefan Zweig als Autographensammler," *DKw*, XIII (Nov., 1931), 72-73.
2957. Wolf, H. "Stefan Zweig," *Zweigs Ausgewählte Prosa*. Ed. W. Kuiper. Amsterdam: Meulenhoff, 1931.
2958. Wolff, Theodor. "Die Wohltat des Exils," *Au(NY)*, XV : 18 (May 6, 1949), 3.
2959. Zarek, Otto. "Stefan Zweig. Zu seinem 50sten Geburtstage," *NR*, 42.J.: II (1931), 861-862.
2960. Zech, Paul. "Erinnerungen an Stefan Zweig," *Greifenalmanach auf das Jahr* 1956, pp. 170-189.
2961. — "Stefan Zweig," *BT*, Oct. 5, 1914.
2962. — *Stefan Zweig. Eine Gedenkschrift*. Buenos Aires: Quadriga, 1943.
2963. Zohn, Harry. "Schulausgaben von Werken Stefan Zweigs," *Blätter*, 6/7 (Oct., 1959), 20.
2964. — "Stefan Zweig," *Wiener Juden in der deutschen Literatur*. Tel Aviv: Olamenu, 1963, pp. 19-30 (Contains a Zweig portrait; p. 6, excerpts from Zweig's autobiography, cf. *WvG*, pp. 23, 31, 32, 33).
2965. — "Stefan Zweig," *Wie sie es sehen*. New York: Holt, 1951, p. 130 (School edition; "Die Augen des ewigen Bruders," pp. 131-171).
2966. — "Stefan Zweigs Lebensabend," *DeuR*, 82.J. (1956), 1195-1197.
2967. — "Stefan Zweig und Emile Verhaeren," *Spiegelungen*, pp. 24-32.
2968. — "Worte zum Gedächtnis Stefan Zweigs," *Blätter*, 11/12 (Oct., 1961), 10-12.
2969. Zimmermann, Walter. "Stefan Zweigs 'Die Augen des ewigen Bruders'," *Deutsche Prosadichtungen der Gegenwart. Interpretationen für Lehrende und Lernende*. Düsseldorf: Pädagogischer Verlag Schwann, 1954-1956, pp. 81-98.
2970. Zuckmayer, Carl. "Did you know Stefan Zweig?" *Leben-Werk*, pp. 121-126 (Reprinted in *Europäer*, pp. 242-249; *NASG*, 1 (1950), 25-28).
2971. — "Tage und Nächte," *Mer*, XVII : 1 ("Salzburg") (Jan., 1964), 66-74 (Zuckmayer's remembrances of Salzburg and the people he knew there; picture of Zweig's house on the Kapuzinerberg, p. 74).
2972. "Zwei Dichter: Thomas Mann und Stefan Zweig," *Colq*, 1.J.: 7 (1947), 23-24.
2973. Zweig, Arnold. "Biblische Stücke, Judenstücke," *Juden auf der deutschen Bühne*. Berlin: Welt-Verlag , 1928, pp. 257-267.
2974. Zweig, Friderike Maria. *Stefan Zweig. Eine Bildbiographie*. München: Kindler, 1961 (Cf. Rev. of same by Georg Böse, *BüK*, 11.J.: 2 (June 15, 1962), 22).
2974a. — *Spiegelungen*. Wien: Hans Deutsch Verlag, 1964 (Memoirs of Mrs. Zweig or, as she referred to them, "Fragmente meines Lebens").
2975. — *Stefan Zweig wie ich ihn erlebte*. Stockholm-New York: Neuer Verlag, 1947 (Reprinted Frankfurt am Main: Frankfurter Verlagsanstalt, 1947 and Berlin-Grunewald: Herbig, 1948).

HEBREW

2976. Kastein, Josef (pseud. Julius Katzenstein). "Stefan Zweig," *Midot Va'arakhim*. Intro. Azrael Karlebach. Tel Aviv: Olympia, 1947.

HINDI

2977. Chaturvedi, Benarsi Das. "Stefan Zweig," *The Navyug* (India), XVIII (Feb. 26, 1950), 9.
2978. Jain, Yashpal. "Author Who Ended His Life. Life and Work of Stefan Zweig," (In Hindi), *Leader* (Allahabad), Oct. 1, 1944.
2979. — "Stefan Zweig," *Social Welfare*, 1944.

ITALIAN

2980. Burich, Enrico. "I due Zweig: Stefan e Arnold," *NA*, N.S., 4.a.: 2 (Mar.-Apr., 1956), 122-127.
2981. De Lorenzo, Giuseppe. "Stefan Zweig ed il Buddhismo," *AAP*, N.S., II (1948-1949), 51-56.
2982. Mazzucchetti, Lavinia. "Introduzione," *Incontri e Amicizie*. Tr. from the German by Anita Limentani. Milano-Verona: Mondadori, 1950, pp. 7-13.
2983. — "Richard Strauss e Stefan Zweig," *LAM*, 2.a.: 5 (Jan.-Mar., 1959), 19-52.
2984. — "Ricordando Stefan Zweig," *Novecento in Germania*. Milano: Mondadori, 1959, pp. 266-272 (Cf. also pp. 55, 160, 220, 249-250; Reprinted in *IP* (1959)).
2985. Robertazzi, M. "Tre Maestri: Balzac-Dickens-Dostoievski," *Poesia e Realta*. Modena: Guandi, 1934, pp. 293-304.
2986. Settanni, E. "Freud visto da Zweig," *Romanzi e Romanzieri d'oggi*. Napoli: Guida, 1933, pp. 11-17.
2987. Tilgher, Adriano. "Stefano Zweig," *La Scena e la Vita. Nuovi Studi sul Teatro Contemporaneo*. Roma: Libreria di Scienze e Lettere, 1925, pp. 206-216.
2988. Zampa, Gregor. "Una Gloria che non ha resistada," *CorS*, May 19, 1961, p. 3.
2989. Zweig, Friderike Maria. *Stefan Zweig. Compagno della mia Vita*. Tr. from the German by Ervino Pocar. Milano: Rizzoli, 1947.

JAPANESE

2990. Iizuka, Nobuo. "Goethe und Stefan Zweig," *GoeJb*, II (1960), 98-114.
2991. — "Stefan Zweig und der europäische Geist," *DoiB*, XVIII (1957), 121-129.

NORWEGIAN

2992. Berendsohn, Walter A. "Hvorfor søkte Stefan Zweig døden?" *Vin*, VII (Sept., 1950), 533-537.
2993. Bredsdorff, Viggo. "Stefan Zweig som Dramatiker," *Ed*, LIII (1953), 257-274.

POLISH

2994. Nowaczynski, Adolf. "Clio again in Fashion," *WiaL*, Apr. 12, 1936.
2995. "Nowelistyka Stefana Zweiga," *Two*, 7 (1936), 128-133.
2996. Wislowska, Maria. "Krótko o Stefanie Zweigu," *NLW*, 14 (1957), 4.

PORTUGUESE

2997. Azevedo, Raul de. *Vida e Morte de Stefan Zweig*. Rio de Janeiro: Brasil ("Aspectos"), 1942.
2998. Fedèr, Ernesto. "Stefan Zweig," *IBra*, Mar., 1942, pp. 16-17.
2999. — "Os últimos Dias de Stefan Zweig," *Diálogos dos Grandes do Mundo*. Rio de Janeiro: Dois Mundos Editora, 1944, pp. 185-200.
3000. Garcia, Antonio Augusto Apio. *Algunos Aspectos da Vida e Obra de Stefan Zweig*. Porto: n.p., 1942.
3001. Lima, Claudio de Araujo. *Ascençao e Queda de Stefan Zweig*. Rio de Janeiro: Olympio, 1943.
3002. Navarro, Eugenio. "Stefan Zweig," *Oc*, II : 6 (Oct., 1938), 403-414.
3003. Souza, Claudio de. *Os últimos Dias de Stefan Zweig*. Rio de Janeiro: Valverde, 1942.
3004. Stern, Leopold. *A Morte de Stefan Zweig*. Rio de Janeiro: Civilização Brasiliera, 1942 (Pub. by the same company in French as *La Mort de Stefan Zweig*).

RUSSIAN

3005. Rapoport, O. "Tvorcheskij Put' Stefana Zweigs," *Yevreiskie Pisateli*. Shanghai: n.p., 1942, pp. 217-225.

SPANISH

3006. Arias, Alejandro C. *Ensayos*: *Goethe, José Asunción Silva, Stefan Zweig*. Salto (Uruguay) Editado por Tipografía Mazzara, 1936.
3007. Arrieta, Rafael Alberto. "Stefan Zweig y las Letras francesas," *Dickens y Sarmiento. Otros Estudios*. Buenos Aires: El Ateneo, 1928, pp. 111-120.
3008. Cahn, Alfredo. *Literaturas Germánicas*. Buenos Aires: Talleres Gráficos de la Compañía General Fabril Financeira, 1961, m.
3009. Feder, Ernest. "Stefan Zweig," *ID*, XXVIII (Feb., 1952), 55-57.
3010. — "Las últimas Conversaciones con Stefan Zweig," *RdA*, June, 1945, pp. 20-25.
3011. — "Los últimos Dias de Stefan Zweig," *Encuentros*. Rosario: Editorial Rosario, 1945, pp. 175-186.
3012. Franulic, Lenka, ed. "Stefan Zweig," *Cien Autores Contemporaneos*. Vol. II. Santiago de Chile: Ediciones Ercilla, 1941, pp. 511-523.
3013. Fuente Gonzáles, Efrain de la. *Stefan Zweig. Juan Tenorio. Ensayos*. Santiago de Chile: Carabineros de Chile, 1946.
3014. Gandia, Enrique de. "Stefan Zweig y el Nombre de América," *Ver*, Mar. 31, 1947, pp. 263-271 (Contains Zweig portrait).
3015. Goldbaum, Wenzel. *Stefan Zweig, su Vida, Obra y Muerte*. Quito: Imprenta de la Universidad central, 1942.
3016. Jarnés, Benjamín Millán. *Stefan Zweig, Cumbre Apagada. Retrato*. México, D.F.: Proa, 1942.
3017. Jarpa, Hugo Lazo. "Stefan Zweig y Benjamín Jarnés," *Ate*, LXXIII : 12 (Sept., 1943), 283-289.
3018. Moreno, Artemio. *De Stefan Zweig a Jacques Maritain. Muerte y Resurrección del Espiritu*. Buenos Aires: Claridad, 1943.
3019. Ortiz Oderigo, Alicia. *Stefan Zweig. Un Hombre de Ayer*. Buenos Aires: Nova, 1945.
3020. Osorio Lizarazo, J. "La Tragedia de Petrópolis," *RdII*, Jan., 1944, pp. 436-462.
3021. Relgis, Eugen. *El Espíritu Activo*. Buenos Aires: Humanidad, 1959, f.m. (Rev. ed.).
3022. — *El Hombre Libre frente a la Barbarie Totalitaria. Un Caso de Conciencia*: *Romain Rolland*. Montevideo: Anales de la Universidad, 1954. f.m.
3023. — *Homenaje a Eugen Relgis en su 60. Aniversario*. Montevideo: Comité Nacional de Adhesión a la Candidatura de Eugen Relgis al Premio Nobel de la Paz, 1955. m.
3024. — *La Paz del Hombre*. Montevideo: Humanidad, 1961, f.m.
3025. — *Profetas y Poetas*. Buenos Aires: Candelabro, 1955, f.m.
3026. — *Stefan Zweig, Cazador de Almas. Entrevista y Paseo en Salzburgo. Post-mortem. Sus Huellas en Montevideo. Algunas Cartas*. Montevideo: Humanidad, 1952.
3027. Romera, Antonio R. "Esquema de Stefan Zweig," *Ate*, XIX : 200 (Feb., 1942), 220-238.
3028. Sanchez Tricado, José Luis. "Una Novela de Stefan Zweig," *Stendhal y Otras Figuras*. Buenos Aires: Republica Argentina (Imprenta López), 1943, pp. 85-92.
3029. Souza, Claudio de. *Los últimos Dias de Stefan Zweig*. Pref. André Maurois, pp. 10-16. Mexico, D.F.: Quetzal, 1944.
3030. Tiempo, César (pseud.). "Stefan Zweig, el Poeta de su Vida," *Bre*, 4/5 (Jan., 1960), 16-20.
3031. Wills Ricaurte, Gustavo. "Porque murio Stefan Zweig?" *RdA*, Oct., 1946, pp. 41-48.
3032. Zweig, Friderike Maria. *Stefan Zweig*. Tr. from the German by Alfredo Cahn. Barcelona: Hispano Americana de Ediciones, 1947.

130

3033. Zagul, Dmitro. "Stefan Zweig," *Zbirnyk Tvoriv*. Kiev: n.p., 1929 (Ukranian translation of some of Zweig's works).

3034. Goldkorn, Yitzchak. "Stefan Zweig," *Fun Welt-Kwal*. Tel Aviv: Hamenorah, 1963, pp. 219-224.
3035. Hameiri, Avigodor. *Yirmiyahn*. Jerusalem: n.p., 1949 (Translation of Zweig's *Jeremias* with a critical essay about Zweig and his drama).
3036. Kreitner, R. L. "A Shu mit Stefan Zweig," *DoA*, II : 9 (May, 1950), 21-22.

XIX. LITERARY AND BIOGRAPHICAL PERSONALIA

3037. *AHR*, XLVII (Apr., 1942), 724-725 (Zweig portrait and obituary).
3038. *Ate*, XIX : 200 (Feb., 1942), 220-238 (Antonio R. Romera, "Esquema de Stefan Zweig").
3039. *Au*, XII (1956), 959-961 (Konstantin Fedin, "Die Tragödie Stefan Zweigs").
3040. *Au(NY)*, VIII : 9 (Feb. 27, 1942), 15-16 ("Stefan Zweig zum Gedächtnis").
3041. *Au(NY)*, VIII : 10 (Mar. 6, 1942), 19-20 (Artur Holde, "Gedenkfeier des 'Aufbau' für Stefan Zweig").
3042. *AWJD*, 5.J.: 40 (1950), 6 ("Jahre der Reife Stefan Zweigs").
3043. *BA*, XIII : 4 (Autumn, 1939), 427-430 (Thomas Q. Curtiss, "Stefan Zweig").
3044. *BBB*, II : 138/139 (1923), 1-3 (Hanns Martin Elster, "Stefan Zweig").
3045. *BBC*, 553 (1931) (Emil Faktor, "Stefan Zweig zum 50sten Geburtstag").
3046. *Bd*, 555 (1931) (Fritz Adolf Hünich, "Stefan Zweig zum 50sten Geburtstag").
3047. *Bd*, Mar. 8, 1933 ("Stefan Zweig, der Europäer").
3048. *BdBh*, 114.J. (1947), 17-25 (G. Lenteritz, "Das unerloschene Leuchten, Stefan Zweig").
3049. *BdBh*, 118.J. (1951), 113 ("Verwirrung der Gefühle – Todestag des Dichters Stefan Zweig").
3050. *Bm*, XXXVIII (Oct., 1931), 150 (Zweig portrait and note).
3051. *BMCN*, Nov., 1946, pp. 4-5 (Robert Pick, "Stefan Zweig").
3052. *Bng*, 6.J. (1951), 3-9 (Herbert Lilge, "Der Untergang eines Herzens. Nachruf auf Stefan Zweig").
3053. *Br*, XVII (1930), 447-449 (Hanns Arens, "Stefan Zweig").
3054. *Bre*, 4/5 (Jan., 1960), 16-20 (César Tiempo, "Stefan Zweig, el Poeta de su Vida").
3055. *BT*, Oct. 5, 1914 (Paul Zech, "Stefan Zweig").
3056. *BT*, 559 (1931) (Paul Frischauer, "Stefan Zweig zum 50sten Geburtstag").
3057. *BTr*, Dec. 10, 1932, p. 1 ("Stefan Zweig").
3058. *Büg*, 6 (1951), 259 ("Stefan Zweig").
3059. *BuL*, 11 (Nov., 1962), 1-3 (Wolf R. Lang, "Stefan Zweig, Umrisse seines Lebens").
3060. *BZ*, Jan. 21, 1923 ("Stefan Zweig").
3061. *Car*, Aug. 19, 1947 (Leopold Stern, "Sur le Suicide de Stefan Zweig").
3062. *ConR*, CLXXV (1949), 62 (A. Wittlin, "Stefan Zweig").
3063. *ConW*, IX : 4 (Apr. 10, 1942), 10-13 (Alfred Werner, "Pity for Stefan Zweig").
3064. *CorS*, May 19, 1961, p. 3 (Gregor Zampa "Una Gloria che non ha resistada").
3065. *CurBio*, 1942, pp. 902-903 ("Stefan Zweig").
3066. *CVZ*, X : 47 (Nov. 20, 1931), 537-538 (Ernst Lissauer, "Zu Stefan Zweigs 50sten Geburtstag").
3067. *DAZ*, Nov. 25, 1931 (B. Trinius, "Stefan Zweig zu seinem 50sten Geburtstag").

3068. *DeG*, CXXI : 7 (July, 1955), 302-312 (Alfred Kossmann, "Het Noodlotsuur van Stefan Zweig").
3069. *DGT*, 4.J.: 1 (1949), 83-88 (Herbert Günther, "Stefan Zweig und Frankreich").
3070. *DL*, XXVII : 12 (Apr.-Sept., 1925), 746 (A. Busse, "Amerikanischer Brief," ref. to *Passion and Pain*).
3071. *DL*, XXVIII : 4 (1925-1926), 250 (Ref. to French translations of Zweig's works; Cf. also *VZ*, No. 522).
3072. *DL*, XXVIII : 10 (1925-1926), 624 (Ref. to Japanese translations of Zweig's works *Romain Rolland*, "Die Augen des ewigen Bruders" and "Amok").
3073. *DL*, XXXI : 3 (1928-1929), 174 (Ref. to the warm reception given to Zweig at the Tolstoy Jubilee and that a second collected works of Zweig was about to appear in Russian translation).
3074. *DL*, XXXI : 10 (1928-1929), 602 (Hermann Sternbach, "Polnischer Brief," ref. to Polish translation of "Verwirrung der Gefühle").
3075. *DL*, XXXI : 10 (1928-1929), 617 (Ref. to Italian translation of *Baumeister*).
3076. *DL*, XXXIII : 1 (Oct., 1930 - Mar., 1931), 58 (Ref. to English translation of *Drei Meister*).
3077. *DL*, XXXIII : 10 (Apr.-Sept., 1931), 584 (Ref. to Swedish translation of *Fouché*).
3078. *DL*, XXXIV : 5 (1931), 267 ("Stefan Zweig zum 50sten Geburtstag").
3079. *DLE*, 9.J.: 5 (Dec. 1, 1906), 363 (Ref. to translation of Zweig into Norwegian).
3080. *DLE*, 9.J.: 11 (Mar. 1, 1907), 849-855 (S. Meisels, "Jüngjüdische Lyrik").
3081. *DLE*, XVII : 4 (1914), 193-199 (Emil Lucka, "Stefan Zweig").
3082. *DLE*, 17.J.: 24 (Sept., 1915), 1519 (Ref. to English translation of Zweig's *Emile Verhaeren*).
3083. *DoA*, II : 9 (May, 1950), 21-22 (R. L. Kreitner, "A Shu mit Stefan Zweig").
3084. *DWe*, 2.J.: 13 (1947), 9 (L. Menter, "Stefan Zweig").
3085. *DWo*, 1.J.: 30 (1946), 5 (Gerd Schäke, "Stefan Zweig – Dichter, Essayist, Schriftsteller – sein tragisches Ende").
3086. *DWo*, 3.J.: 18/19 (1948), 4 ("Stefan Zweig").
3087. *DZe*, 2.J.: 22 (1947), 3 (A. Beierle, "Stefan Zweig, Dichter und Dulder").
3088. *E*, 25.a.: 22 (Oct., 1947), 48-67 (Antonina Valentin, "Stefan Zweig").
3089. *Europäer*, pp. 218-238 (Ernst Feder, "Die letzten Tage Stefan Zweigs").
3090. *Frw*, Feb., 1942(?) (Salman Shneour, "Stefan Zweig").
3091. *GB*, XV (Feb., 1932), 190 ("Stefan Zweig").
3092. *GdG*, LXVI : 4 (1930), 145-152 (Wilhelm Knevels, "Stefan Zweig").
3093. *GS*, 329 (1926) (Ernst Friedrichs, "Stefan Zweig zu seinem 45sten Geburtstag").
3094. *IBra*, Mar., 1942, pp. 16-17 (Ernesto Feder, "Stefan Zweig").
3095. *IN*, July, 1960 ("Stefan Zweig Correspondence").
3096. *JR*, 33.J. (1928) (M. Sturmann, "Studie über Stefan Zweig").
3097. *JSp*, VII : 6 (Apr., 1942), 5 ("The Case of Stefan Zweig").
3098. *JSp*, May, 1943, pp. 9-11 ("The Tragic Case of Stefan Zweig").
3099. *KZ*, 444 (1921) (Claims by Zweig that a Novelle entitled "Untreue" submitted to the *KZ* in 1914 by Gräfin D. Stourza von Katschuro was in reality a slightly changed version of his "Angst": "Es liegt also literarischer Diebstahl unverschämtester Art vor"; Cf. also *DLE*, 23.J.: 21 (Aug., 1921), 1342).
3100. *KZ*, 650 (1931) (K. H. Erkelenz, "Stefan Zweig").
3101. *LD*, CXVI (July 15, 1933), 17-18 ("H. G. Wells Raises a Storm in the P.E.N. Congress"; Contains a Zweig portrait).
3102. *LD*, CXX (Sept. 21, 1935), 24 (Rev. of *Queen of Scots*; Contains a Zweig portrait).
3103. *Leader* (Allahabad, India), Oct. 1, 1914 (Yashpal Jain, "Author Who Ended His Life. Life and Work of Stefan Zweig").
3104. *LMF*, XII (1948), 424-429 (Jean Décarreaux, "Le Message posthume de Stefan Zweig").
3105. *LNR*, X (Aug., 1942), 579-582 (Paul Beaulieu, "Réflexions sur le Suicide de Stefan Zweig").
3106. *LT*, Feb. 24, 1942, p. 3 and Feb. 25, 1942, p. 7 ("Stefan Zweig's Death").

3107. *MA*, LXXIV (Oct., 1954), 15 (Portrait: "A Threesome at the Salzburg Festival of 1934: Arturo Toscanini, Bruno Walter and Stefan Zweig").

3108. *MC*, CLI (Feb., 1955), 101-102 (H. Koegler, "Stefan Zweig").

3109. *N*, CLIV (Mar. 14, 1942), 314 (Margaret Marshall, "Stefan Zweig").

3110. *Navyug* (India), XVIII (Feb. 26, 1950), 9 (Benarsi das Chaturvedi, "Stefan Zweig").

3111. *Ne*, I (Apr. 8, 1933), 28.

3112. *Ne*, XI (Feb. 7, 1938), 29 (Portrait).

3113. *Ne*, XIII (Mar. 20, 1939), 43 (Portrait).

3114. *Ne*, XVII (Sept. 29, 1941), 52 (Portrait).

3115. *Ne*, XIX (1942), 37 ("Stefan Zweig Epilogue").

3116. *NFP*, Aug. 12, 1928, pp. 27-28 (Leonhard Adelt, "Werk und Leben Stefan Zweigs").

3117. *NM*, XLII : 10 (Mar., 1942), 22-23 (O. T. Ring, "Life and Death of Stefan Zweig").

3118. *NR*, 42.J. II (1931), 861-862 (Otto Zarek, "Stefan Zweig zu seinem 50sten Geburtstag").

3119. *NSchR*, N.F., 16.J. (1948-1949), 574-576 ("Stefan Zweig").

3120. *NVzt*, Feb. 28, 1942, p. 3 (Paul Stefan, "Zum Tode Stefan Zweigs").

3121. *NVzt*, Mar. 14, 1942, p. 5 (Hans Johan Kraus, "Brasilien ehrt Stefan Zweig").

3122. *NYT*, Apr. 23, 1933, p. 22 ("German Students Purge Libraries").

3123. *NYT*, May 11, 1933, p. 12 ("Berlin Lukewarm to Book-Burning").

3124. *NYT*, Nov. 1, 1933, p. 14 ("Nazis Raise Swastika on Vienna City Hall").

3125. *NYT*, Nov. 2, 1933, p. 19 ("Zweig in London").

3126. *NYT*, Jan. 18, 1935, p. 7 ("Stefan Zweig Arrives in the United States – An Interview about His Plans").

3127. *NYT*, Jan. 2, 1939, p. 27 ("Zweig Says Unrest Hampers Writers").

3128. *NYT*, Feb. 21, 1939, p. 4 ("Institute Honors Stefan Zweig").

3129. *NYT*, Apr. 10, 1940, p. 2 ("Stefan Zweig Becomes a Briton").

3130. *NYT*, July 8, 1940, p. 4 ("Stefan Zweig Arrives to Study the Americas"; Portrait of Stefan and Lotte Zweig).

3131. *NYT*, Feb. 24, 1942, pp. 1, 23 ("Stefan Zweig and Wife End Lives in Brazil").

3132. *NYT*, Feb. 25, 1942, p. 3 ("Brazil Pays Honor to Zweigs in Death").

3133. *NYT*, Feb. 25, 1942, p. 18 ("One of the Dispossessed – A Tribute to Stefan Zweig").

3134. *NYT*, Feb. 27, 1942, p. 5 ("Stefan Zweig's Will").

3135. *NYT*, Mar. 1, 1942, p. 28 ("Memorial Meeting in Honor of Stefan Zweig").

3136. *NYT*, Feb. 23, 1943, p. 11 ("Stefan Zweig Monument Unveiled by Jewish Colony in Petropolis").

3137. *NYTBR*, June 14, 1931, p. 7 (Rev. of American ed. of *Amok* with Zweig portrait).

3138. *NYTBR*, Apr. 8, 1934, p. 4 (Article by Zweig: "History and the Schreen. On the Filming of Events of Bygone Times"; Ed. comment: MGM preparing to make film based on Zweig's *Marie Antoinette*).

3139. *NYTBR*, Aug. 25, 1940, p. 2 ("Letter in Honor of Stefan Zweig").

3140. *NYTBR*, Oct. 19, 1941, p. 32 ("About Brazil" – concerning the Ernesto Montenegro rev. of Zweig's *Brasilien*).

3141. *NYTBR*, Nov. 9, 1941, p. 36 ("The Word 'Decent'").

3142. *NYTBR*, Mar. 1, 1942, p. 6 (Austin Stevens, "Tribute to Stefan Zweig").

3143. *NYTBR*, Mar. 8, 1942, p. 2 ("Speaking of Books").

3144. *NZZ*, Nov. 29, 1931 (Robert Faesi, "Stefan Zweig zu seinem 50sten Geburtstag").

3145. *OöN*, Oct. 27, 1947, p. 3 (Herbert Lange, "Ein Bildnis Stefan Zweigs").

3146. *Philo*, III : 1/4 (1938), 347-358 (Milian Schömann, "Ein Humanist in unserer Zeit").

3147. *PL*, Nov. 27, 1931 ("Stefan Zweig zum 50sten Geburtstag").

3148. *PP*, No. 322 ("Stefan Zweig zum 50sten Geburtstag").

3149. *Pris*, 19/20 (1948), 40 (Erich Ebermayer, "Letzte Stunden mit Stefan Zweig").

3150. *PW*, CXLI (Feb. 28, 1942), 950 ("Stefan Zweig").

3151. *Rad*, VI (1929), 2 (Max Lederer, "Stefan Zweig").

3152. *Rad*, VIII (1931), 8 (Erwin Rieger, "Stefan Zweig").

3153. *RD*, XXXIX (1941), 39-43 ("Stefan Zweig").
3154. *RdlI*, Jan. 1944, pp. 436-462 (Osorio Lizarazo, "La Tragedia de Petrópolis").
3155. *RP*, 42.a.: 5 (Oct. 15, 1935), 864-889 (Maurice Muret, "Stefan Zweig").
3156. *RP*, 62.a.: 12 (Feb., 1955), 3-23 (Jules Romains, "Derniers Mois et dernières Lettres de Stefan Zweig").
3157. *RR*, LI : 5 (May, 1915), 620-621 ("Stefan Zweig: Austrian Poet, Critic and Dramatist").
3158. *SLzt*, Nov. 28, 1931 (J. Tobias, "Stefan Zweig zu seinem 50sten Geburtstag").
3159. *Spiegelungen*, pp. 68-73 (Lee Van Dovski, "Mit Stefan Zweig in Paris").
3160. *SRL*, VIII (June 18, 1932), 791 (Rev. of "Letter from an Unknown Woman"; Portrait of Zweig).
3161. *SRL*, XVI (Oct. 16, 1937), 22, 26 (Stephen Vincent Benet, Rev. of "Buried Candelabrum").
3162. *SRL*, XVII (Feb. 5, 1938), 1, 5 (Oliver La Farge, Rev. of *Magellan*; Portrait of Zweig).
3163. *SRL*, XIX (Apr. 22, 1939), 3 (Jonathan Griffin, Rev. of *Escape to Life* by Klaus and Erika Mann; Zweig portrait).
3164. *SRL*, XXI (Nov. 25, 1939), 11 (Paul Rosenfeld, Rev. of *Master Builders*; Portrait of Zweig from a drawing by George Schreiber).
3165. *SRL*, XXIII (Nov. 23, 1940), 10 (William H. Chamberlin, Rev. of *Tide of Fortune*; Zweig portrait).
3166. *SRL*, XXV (Mar. 14, 1942), 12 (Thomas Q. Cousins, "Stefan Zweig").
3167. *SRL*, XXVII (Feb. 26, 1944), 5 (Christopher La Farge, "Say It With Fiction"; Zweig portrait).
3168. *SRL*, XLI (Feb. 8, 1958), 24.
3169. *T*, XXXII (July 25, 1938), 30 ("Bad Boy" concerning the Richard Strauss-Stefan Zweig collaboration; Zweig portrait).
3170. *T*, XXXIX (Mar. 2, 1942), 53 (Zweig obituary).
3171. *VdF*, Mar. 15, 1942, p. 1 (Adolphe Demilly, "Sur une Mort").
3172. *VdF*, Mar. 15, 1942, p. 4 (Robert Goffin, "Adieu à Stefan Zweig").
3173. *Vin*, VII (Sept., 1950), 533-537 (Walter A. Berendsohn, "Hvorfor søkte Stefan Zweig Døden?").
3174. *VuV*, 2. ser., 13 (1947), 22-31 (Herbert Oetke, "Stefan Zweig").
3175. *WieZ*, 277 (1949) (Egon Pisk, "Stefan Zweigs Tod").
3176. *WLB*, V (Sept., 1930), 8 (Rev. of *Fouché*; Biographical sketch and portrait of Zweig).
3177. *WLB*, XVI (Apr., 1942), 598 (Biographical sketch of Zweig).
3178. *Wst*, XXV (1950), 15-17 (Hanns Arens, "Die letzten Jahre Stefan Zweigs").
3179. *YCD*, 1951, pp. 70-77 (M. Evensky, "Stefan Zweig").

XX. UNPUBLISHED MASTERS' THESES AND DOCTORAL DISSERTATIONS

3180. Bak, Olga. *Stefan Zweig, sa Vie et son Oeuvre*. Diss., Quebec (Laval University), 1950.
3181. Berry, Robert M. *The French Symbolist Poets in Germany: Criticism and Translations*. 1870-1914. Diss., Harvard University, 1944.
3182. Böttcher, Kurt. *Stefan Zweig und die Welt von gestern*. Diss., Jena (Friedrich Schiller University), 1951.
3183. Diamond, Helena. *Protest gegen den Krieg als Hauptmotiv in den Dramen von 1917 bis 1931*. Thesis, Hunter College, 1933 (Zweig's *Jeremias*).
3184. Eichbaum, Gerda. *Die Krise der modernen Jugend im Spiegel der Dichtung*. Diss., Giessen, 1929.
3185. Firon, Erich. *Stefan Zweig als Dramatiker*, Diss., Wien, 1949.
3186. Frese, Hans. *Das Deutsche Buch in Amerika: Übersetzungen der Jahre 1918-1935*. Diss., Marburg, 1937.

3187. Frets, Huberta. *L'Elément germanique dans l'Oeuvre d'Emile Verhaeren.* Diss., Paris, 1935.
3188. Götzfried, Johannes L. *Der heroische Idealismus bei Romain Rolland.* Diss., Bonn-Freudenstadt, 1929.
3189. Grebert, Ludwig. *Paul Verlaine und seine deutschen Übersetzer.* Diss., Giessen, 1923.
3190. Gschiel, Martha. *Das dichterische Werk Stefan Zweigs.* Diss., Wien, 1953.
3191. Kaemmer, Kurt. *Die Versdichtungen Baudelaires und Verlaines in deutscher Sprache.* Diss., Köln, 1922.
3192. Kaempffer, Annemarie. *Romain Rollands Frauengestalten.* Diss., Jena, 1931.
3193. Klawiter, Randolph J. *Stefan Zweig's Novellen – An Analysis.* Diss., University of Michigan, 1960.
3194. Lent, Ingrid. *Das Novellenwerk Stefan Zweigs. Eine Stil- und Typenuntersuchung.* Diss., München, 1956.
3195. Mertens, Gerhard M. *Stefan Zweig's Biographical Writings as Studies of Human Types.* Diss., University of Michigan, 1950.
3196. Rosenberg, Justus. *The German Translations of Paul Verlaine's Poetry.* Diss., University of Cincinnati, 1950.
3197. Rosnovsky, Karl. *Erinnerungsbücher an das alte Österreich. Raoul Auernheimer und Stefan Zweig.* Diss., Wien, 1951.
3198. Starr, William T. *Romain Rolland's Internationalism.* Diss., University of Oregon, 1938.
3199. Thornton, Luanne. *The Critical Reception in the United States of the Novellen of Stefan Zweig.* Thesis, Emory University (Georgia), 1963.
3200. Vanicek, Hilde. *Der Einfluss der französischen Lyrik auf Anton Wildgans, Stefan Zweig und Felix Dörmann.* Diss., Wien, 1952.
3201. Wahrheit, Israel Albert. *Jung-Wien as a Literary School. Schnitzler – Beer Hofmann – Hofmannsthal.* 1890-1914. Diss., University of Michigan, 1940.
3202. Welter, M. L. *Typus und Eros. Eine Untersuchung des Menschenbildes in den Novellen Stefan Zweigs.* Diss., Freiburg i. Br., 1957.
3203. Werner, Bruno. *Die deutschen Übersetzungen der Gedichte Paul Verlaines.* Diss., München, 1922.
3204. Wolff, Gerhart. *Die Geschichte und ihre Künstler. Bewältigungen im Werk von Stefan Zweig. Ein Beitrag zum Problem geschichtlicher Wortkunst.* Diss., Bonn, 1958.
3205. Zohn, Harry. *Stefan Zweig as Literary Mediator.* Diss., Harvard University, 1951.

XXI. GENERAL REFERENCE WORKS

3206. *Autorenlexikon des XX. Jahrhunderts* (Ed. Karl August Kutzbach). Bonn: Bouvier, 1952, pp. 179-180.
3207. *The Best Short Stories of* 1926 (Ed. Edward J. O'Brien). New York: Dodd, Mead and Co., 1926, pp. 378, 464.
3208. *Bibliographia Philosophica.* 1934-1945. (Ed. G. A. De Brie). Vol. I/II. Bruxelles: Editiones Spectrum, 1950, f.m.
3209. *Bibliographie der deutschen Literaturwissenschaft* (Ed. Hanns W. Eppelsheimer). Vol. I/IV. Frankfurt am Main: Vittorio Klostermann, 1957-1961, Vol. I (1957), pp. 417-418; Vol. II (1958), pp. 8, 273, 293, 296; Vol. III (1960), p. 192; Vol. IV (1961), p. 236.
3210. *Bibliographie deutscher Übersetzungen aus dem Französischen.* 1700-1948 (Ed. Hans Fromm). Vol. I/VI. Baden-Baden: Verlag für Kunst und Wissenschaft, 1950-1953, f.m.
3211. *Bibliographisches Handbuch des deutschen Schrifttums* (Ed. Josef Körner). Bern: Francke, 1949, p. 505 (3. ed.).
3212. *Bibliography Index. A Cumulative Bibliography of Bibliographies for* 1943 (Ed. Joseph Bea). New York: H. W. Wilson, 1944, p. 243.

3213. *Bibliography of Critical and Biographical References for the Study of Contemporary French Literature* (Ed. Douglas Alden, Gertrude Jasper, Robert Waterman). Vol. I/III. New York: Stechert-Hafner, 1949-1954, Vol. I (1949), No. 4955; Vol. II (1951), No. 5108; Vol. III (1954), No. 12191.

3214. *The Bookman's Manual. A Guide to Literature* (Ed. Bessie Graham). New York: R. R. Bowker, 1941 (4. ed.; List of Zweig's books in English, by whom translated and when and where published).

3215. *Cassell's Encyclopaedia of Literature* (Ed. S. H. Steinberg). London: Cassell, 1953, Vol. II, p. 2086.

3216. *Chamber's Biographical Dictionary* (Ed. J. O. Thorne). New York: St. Martin's Press, 1962, p. 1396.

3217. *Collier's Encyclopedia* (Charles P. Barry, Editor-in-Chief). Vol. I/XX with Index and Bibliography. New York: Collier and Son, 1951 ed., f.m.

3218. *Columbia Dictionary of Modern European Literature* (Ed. Horatio Smith). New York: Columbia University Press, 1947, pp. 898-899 (Article on Zweig by William K. Pfeiler, University of Nebraska).

3219. *The Columbia Encyclopedia in One Volume* (Ed. William Bridgewater, Elizabeth Sherwood). New York: Columbia University Press, 1950, p. 2202 (2. ed.).

3220. *Compton's Pictured Encyclopedia and Fact-Index*. Vol. I/XV. Chicago: F. E. Compton, 1961, Vol. XV, p. 433.

3221. *Current Biography. Who's News and Why*. 1942. (Ed. Maxime Block). New York: H. W. Wilson, 1942, pp. 902-903 (Zweig obituary and short bibliography).

3222. *Deutsche Dichterhandschriften von 1400 bis 1900*. Ed. Wilhelm Frels). Leipzig: Hiersemann, 1934, p. 375 (Concerning Zweig's manuscript collection).

3223. *Deutsche Geschichte* (Hubertus Prinz zu Löwenstein). Berlin: Haude und Spenersche Verlagshandlung, 1962, p. 423.

3224. *Deutsches Literaturlexikon* (Ed. Wilhelm Kosch). Vol. I/II. Halle (Saale): Max Niemeyer, 1930, p. 3223.

3225. *Deutsches Literatur-Lexikon. Biographisches und bibliographisches Handbuch* (Ed. Wilhelm Kosch). Vol. I/IV. Bern: Francke, 1958, Vol. IV, pp. 3559-3560 (2. ed.).

3226. *Diccionario de la Literatura* (Ed. F. C. Sainz de Robles). Madrid: Aguilar, 1950, p. 1652.

3227. *Dictionnaire des Auteurs*. Vol. I/II. Paris: Laffont/Bompiani, 1956, Vol. II, p. 729 (Article by Michel Mourre).

3228. *Dictionnaire des Biographes* (Ed. Pierre Crimal et al.). Vol. I/II. Paris: Presses Universitaires de France, 1958, Vol. II, pp. 1562-1563.

3229. *Dictionnaire des Lettres* (Ed. Pierre Clarac). Paris: Société d'Edition de Dictionnaires et Encyclopédies et Bompiani, 1961, p. 937.

3230. *Dictionnaire des Oeuvres de tous les Temps et de tous les Pays*. Vol. I/IV and Index. Paris: Laffont/Bompiani, 1955, Vol. I, p. 83 ("Amok"), p. 509 ("La Confusion des Sentiments"); Vol. III, p. 288 ("La Lutte avec le Démon"); Vol. IV, p. 15 ("La Pitié dangereuse"), p. 705 ("Vingt-quatre Heures de la Vie d'une Femme").

3231. *Dizionario Enciclopedico Italiano*. Vol. I/XII. Roma: Instituto della Enciclopedia Italiana, 1961, Vol. XII, p. 1025.

3232. *Dizionario Letterario Bompiani degli Autori di tutti Tempi e di tutte le Letterature*. Vol. I/III. Milano: Bompiani, Vol. III, pp. 954-955.

3233. *Dizionario Universale della Letteratura Contemporanea* (Ed. Orlando Bernardi). Vol. I/IV. Milano: Mondadori, 1959, Vol. IV, pp. 1259-1261.

3234. *Enciclopedia Cattolica*. Vol. I/XII. Città del Vaticano: Ente per l'Enciclopedia Cattolica e per il Libro Cattolico, 1954, Vol. XII, pp. 1834-1835 (Article by Sergio Lupi).

3235. *Encilopedia de la Literatura* (Ed. Benjamín Jarnés). Vol. I/VI. Mexico City: Editora Central, n.d., Vol. VI, pp. 428-430.

3236. *Enciclopedia Italiana di Scienze, Lettere ed Arti*. Vol. I/XXXVI and Index. Roma: Instituto della Enciclopedia Italiana, 1939, f.m. (Cf. also Appendice. Vol. I/II (1938-1948), Vol. I, pp. 729, 1046; Vol. II, p. 1144).

136

3237. *Enciclopedia Universal Illustrada – Europeo-Americana.* Vol. I/X and Appendix. Bilbao-Madrid-Barcelona: Espasa-Calpe, 1933. Vol. X, p. 1326 (1930 ed., Vol. I/LXX. Vol. LXX, p. 1573 (Cf. also Supplemento 1942-1944, p. 309).

3238. *Enciclopedia Vergara – Universal Didáctica Illustrada* (Ed. Jaime Berenguer Amenós). Barcelona: Editorial Vergara, 1961, p. 1546 (3 ed.).

3239. *Encyclopedia Americana.* Vol. I/XXX. New York-Chicago-Washington, D.C.: Americana Corp., 1956, Vol. II, p. 639; Vol. XII, p. 589.

3240. *Encyclopedia of Jewish Knowledge* (Ed. Jacob De Haas). New York: Behrman's Jewish Book House, 1934, p. 661.

3241. *Encyclopédie des Citations* (Ed. P. Dupré). Paris: Éditions de Trévise, 1959, Nos. 6174-6177 (Quotations from "Angst" and "Verwirrung der Gefühle" in French translation).

3242. *Everyman's Encyclopedia.* Vol. I/XII. New York: Macmillan, 1951, Vol. XII, p. 853 (3. ed.).

3243. *Der grosse Brockhaus. Handbuch des Wissens.* Vol. I/XX. Leipzig: Brockhaus, 1935, Vol. XX, p. 741 (15. ed.; 16. ed., 1957, Vol. XII, p. 757).

3244. *Der grosse Herder. Nachschlagewerk für Wissen und Leben.* Vol. I/IX. Freiburg: Herder, 1956, Vol. IX, p. 1527.

3245. *Grove's Dictionary of Music and Musicians* (Ed. Eric Blom). London: Macmillan, 1954; New York: St. Martin's Press, 1954, Vol. IX, Photogramme," 2. "Demuth – three songs with orchestra," 3. "Radó – songs with orchestra, translated from Verhaeren," 4. "Reger – two songs," 5. "Schibler – 'Augen des ewigen Bruders,' radio opera; 'Polyhem,' choral work," 6. "'Schweigsame Frau,' R. Strauss libretto," 7. "Seiber – 'Volpone,' translated from Ben Jonson," 8. "Szelényi – 'Virata,' oratorio," 9. "Toch – 'Heilige aus USA',").

3246. *The Guide to Catholic Literature.* 1888-1940 (Ed. Walter Romig). Part V. Detroit: Walter Romig, 1940, pp. 1229-1230.

3247. *Harvard Guide to American History* (Ed. Oscar Handlin *et al.*). Cambridge, Mass.: Harvard University Press, 1954, p. 205.

3248. *Das kleine Lexikon der Weltliteratur* (Ed. Hermann Pongs). Stuttgart: Union Verlag, 1961, p. 1757 (4. ed.).

3249. *Kleines literarisches Lexikon* (Ed. Wolfgang Kayser). Bern: Francke, 1953, p. 580 (2. ed. rev.; Sammlung Dalp, Nos. 15-17).

3250. *Kleines literarisches Lexikon. Vol. II. Autorenlexikon des 20. Jahrhunderts* (Ed. Horst Rüdiger). Bern-München: Francke, 1961, pp. 453-454 (3. ed.).

3251. *Kleines österreichisches Literatur-Lexikon* (Ed. H. Giebisch *et al.*). Wien: Hollinek, 1948, pp. 536-537.

3252. *Knaurs Buch vom Film* (Ed. Rune Walderkranz, Arpe Verner). München: Droemersche Verlagsanstalt, 1956, p. 468.

3253. *Larousse du XXe Siècle* (Ed. Paul Augé). Vol. I/VI. Paris: Libraire Larousse, 1933, Vol. VI, p. 1145.

3254. *Lexikon der Weltliteratur* (Ed. Heinz Kindermann, Margarete Dietrich). Wien-Stuttgart: Humboldt, 1951, pp. 901-902 (3. ed.).

3255. *Lexikon der Weltliteratur* (Ed. Gero von Wilpert). Stuttgart: Kröner, 1963, p. 1471.

3256. *Lexikon der Weltliteratur im 20sten Jahrhundert.* Vol. I/II. Freiburg-Basel-Wien: Herder, 1961, f.m.

3257. *The Lincoln Library of Essential Information.* Buffalo, New York: The Frontier Press, 1959, p. 2010.

3258. *Living Authors. A Book of Biographies* (Ed. Tante Dilly). New York: H. W. Wilson, 1931, pp. 461-462 (Contains Zweig portrait).

3259. *Meyers Opernbuch.* Leipzig: Bibliographisches Institut, 1935, pp. 438-439 (Otto Schumann, "Die schweigsame Frau").

3260. *Das musikalische Theater. Ein Führer durch das Repertoire der Oper und Operette der Welt bis in die neueste Zeit* (Ed. Francisco Curt Lange). Linz a. D.: Österreichischer Verlag für Belletristik und Wissenschaft, 1948.

3261. *Philosophen-Lexikon. Handwörterbuch der Philosophie nach Personen* (Ed. Werner

Ziegenfuss, Gertrud Jung). Vol. I/II. Berlin: de Gruyter, 1950, Vol. II, p. 957.

3262. *Reallexikon der deutschen Literaturgeschichte* (Ed. Paul Merker, Wolfgang Stammler). Vol. I/III. Berlin: de Gruyter, 1928-1929, Vol. III, pp. 394-402 (R. Leppla, "Übersetzungsliteratur").

3263. — Vol. I/IV. Berlin: de Gruyter, 1931, f.m.

3264. *Riemann Musik Lexikon* (Ed. Willibald Gurlitt). Vol. I/III. Mainz: B. Schott's Söhne, 1961, Vol. II, pp. 742-745 (Cf. also the article "Richard Strauss").

3265. *Der Romanführer. Teil III* (Ed. Johannes Beer, Wilhelm Olbrich, Karl Weitzel). Vol. I/V. Stuttgart: Hiersemann, 1954, pp. 984-987 (Plot summaries of *Ungeduld des Herzens, Erstes Erlebnis*, "Amokläufer," "Verwirrung der Gefühle," *Sternstunden der Menschheit, Schachnovelle*).

3266. *Salmonsens Konversations Leksikon* (Ed. Johannes Brøndum-Nielsen, Palle Raunkjaer). Vol. I/XXV. København: Schultz, 1928, Vol. XXV, pp. 659-660.

3267. *Der Schauspielführer* (Ed. Joseph Gregor). Stuttgart: Hiersemann, 1954, Vol. II, pp. 25-26 ("Volpone"), p. 26-28 ("Die Flucht zu Gott").

3268. *Schweizer Lexikon.* Vol. I/VII. Zürich: Encyclios Verlag, 1948, VII, p. 1671.

3269. *60 Years of Best Sellers. 1895-1955* (Ed. Alice Payne Hackett). New York: R. R. Bowker, 1956, pp. 155, 159-160.

3270. *Standard Catalog for Public Libraries. Literature and Philology Section* (Ed. Minnie Earl Sears). New York: W. W. Wilson, 1931, p. 99.

3271. *A Treasury of Jewish Quotations* (Ed. Joseph L. Baron). New York: Crown, 1956, f.m.

3272. *Twentieth Century Authors* (Ed. Stanley Kunitz, Howard Haycraft). New York: H. W. Wilson, 1942, pp. 1576-1577 (Contains a copy of Zweig's "Abschiedsbrief"; Cf. also Supplement I, 1955, p. 1123).

3273. *The Universal Jewish Encyclopedia* (Ed. Isaac Landman). Vol. I/X. New York: Universal Jewish Encyclopedia Co., 1943, Vol. X, p. 680 (Article by Emil Langyel; Also contains a Zweig bibliography).

3274. *Who Was Who. 1941-1950.* London: Adam and Charles Black, 1952, Vol. IV. p. 1277.

3275. *Winkler Prins Encyclopaedia* (Ed. E. De Bruyne, G. B. J. Hiltermann, H. R. Hoetink). Vol. I/XVIII. Amsterdam-Brussel: Elsevier, 1954, Vol. XVIII, p. 871.

3276. *A World Bibliography of Bibliographies and of Bibliographical Catalogues, Calendars, Abstracts, Digests, Indexes and the like* (Ed. Theodore Besterman). Vol. I/III. Genève: Societas Bibliographica, 1955, Vol. III, col. 4408.

3277. *The World Book Encyclopedia.* Vol. I/XVIII. Chicago: Quarrie, 1947, Vol. XVIII, p. 9012.

3278. *Writings on American History. 1902-1940.* Washington, D.C.: American Historical Association, 1937, col. 894.

XXII. HISTORIES OF LITERATURE

3279. Alker, Ernst. *Geschichte der deutschen Literatur von Goethes Tod bis zur Gegenwart.* Stuttgart: Cotta, 1950, Vol. II, pp. 381-382.

3280. Bennett, E. K. and H. M. Waidson. *A History of the German Novelle.* Cambridge: University Press, 1961, pp. 272-273, 276 (2. ed.).

3281. Bertaux, Félix. *A Panorama of German Literature from 1871 to 1931.* New York: McGraw Hill, 1935, pp. 176, 197-198, 277, 325.

3282. Bithell, Jethro, ed. *Germany. A Companion to German Studies.* London: Methuen, 1959, p. 366 (5. ed.).

3283. — *Modern German Literature. 1880-1950.* London: Methuen, 1959, f.m. (Cf. esp. pp. 384-385; 3. ed. rev.).

3284. Boesch, B. *Deutsche Literaturgeschichte in Grundzügen.* Bern: Francke, 1946, pp. 330-331 (2. ed. Bern-München: Francke, 1946, pp. 386, 403).

3285. Brand, Guido K. *Werden und Wandlung.* Berlin: K. Wolff, 1933, pp. 45, 60, 117.
3286. Castle, Eduard *et al. Deutsch-österreichische Literaturgeschichte.* Vol. I/IV. Wien: Frommer, 1937, Vol. IV, pp. 1884-1889 (Article "Stefan Zweig" by Erwin Rieger).
3287. Clark, Barrett H. and George Freedley, eds. *A History of Modern Drama.* New York: Appleton-Century-Crofts, 1947, pp. 144-145.
3288. Diebold, Bernhard. *Anarchie im Drama.* Frankfurt am Main: Frankfurter Verlagsanstalt, 1921, pp. 431-433 (Discussion of *Jeremias* as a drama of pacifism).
3289. Duwe, Wilhelm. *Deutsche Dichtung des 20sten Jahrhunderts.* Vol. I/II. Zürich: Drell Füssli, 1962, f.m.
3290. Edschmid, Kasimir. *Lebendiger Expressionismus. Auseinandersetzungen, Gestalten, Erinnerungen.* Wien-München-Basel: Kurt Desch, 1961, pp. 22, 47, 199.
3291. Eloesser, Arthur. *Die deutsche Literatur von der Romantik bis zur Gegenwart.* Berlin: Bruno Cassirer, 1931 (Tr. into English by C. A. Phillips as *Modern German Literature.* New York: Knopf, 1933, p. 393 (2. ed.)).
3292. Franwallner, E., H. Giebisch and E. Heinzel. *Die Welt-Literatur.* Vol. I/II. Wien: Hollinek, 1953, f.m.
3293. Frenzel, Herbert A., ed. *Daten deutscher Dichtung.* Köln-Berlin: Kiepenheuer and Witsch, 1953, pp. 360, 368, 411, 415; Biography p. 344).
3294. Fricke, Gerhard *et al. Geschichte der deutschen Dichtung.* Lübeck-Hamburg: Matthiesen, 1962, pp. 355-356 (9. ed.).
3295. Friedmann, Hermann and Otto Mann, eds. *Deutsche Literatur im 20sten Jahrhundert.* Heidelberg: Wolfgang Rothe, 1956, pp. 48, 131, 311, 324 (2. ed. rev.).
3296. Friedrich, Werner P. *An Outline History of German Literature.* New York: Barnes and Noble, 1948, pp. 226-227, 250 (College Outline Series; 5. printing, 1960).
3297. Fuchs, Albert. "Stefan Zweig," *Moderne österreichische Dichter.* Wien: Globus-Verlag, 1946, pp. 55-59.
3298. Garten, H. F. *Modern German Drama.* Fair Lawn, New Jersey: Essential Books, 1959, pp. 123, 125-126, 241.
3299. Hieble, Jacob. *An Outlihe of German Literature with Reading References to Cheap German Editions and English Translations.* Ithaca: The Thrift Press, 1935, pp. 30-31.
3300. Highet, Gilbert. *A Clerk of Oxenford. Essays on Literature and Life.* New York: Oxford University Press, 1954, p. 239.
3301. Horst, Karl August. *Die deutsche Literatur der Gegenwart.* München: Nymphenburger, 1957, pp. 64-65, 99, 209 (Zweig portrait p. 96).
3302. — *Kritischer Führer durch die deutsche Literatur der Gegenwart.* München: Nymphenburger, 1962, f.m.
3303. Kindermann, Heinz. *Wegweiser durch die moderne Literatur in Österreich.* Innsbruck: Österreichische Verlagsanstalt, 1954, p. 12.
3304. Klein, Johannes. *Geschichte der deutschen Novelle von Goethe bis zur Gegenwart.* Wiesbaden: Franz Steiner, 1956, pp. 502-512 (3. ed.).
3305. Körner, Josef. *Bibliographisches Handbuch des deutschen Schrifttums.* Bern: Francke, 1949, p. 505 (3. ed.).
3306. Krell, Leo and Leonhard Fiedler. *Deutsche Literaturgeschichte.* Bamberg: Buchners, 1962, pp. 372, 400 (9. ed.).
3307. Kummer, Friedrich. *Deutsche Literaturgeschichte des 19ten und 20sten Jahrhunderts.* Vol. I/II. Dresden: Carl Reissner, 1924, Vol. II, p. 451.
3308. Kutscher, Artur. *Stilkunde der deutschen Dichtung.* Vol. I/II. Bremen-Horn: Dorn, 1952, Vol. I, p. 33; Vol. II, p. 244.
3309. Laaths, Erwin. *Geschichte der Weltliteratur. Eine Gesamtdarstellung.* München: Knauer, 1953, p. 727 (3. ed.).
3310. Langer, Norbert. "Stefan Zweig," *Dichter aus Österreich.* Wien: Österreichischer Bundesverlag, 1957, pp. 122-127.
3311. Lennartz, Franz. *Die Dichter unserer Zeit.* Stuttgart: Kröner, 1952, pp. 571-573 (5. ed.).

3312. Lockemann, Fritz. *Gestalt und Wandlungen der deutschen Novelle. Geschichte einer literarischen Gattung im 19ten und 20sten Jahrhundert*. München: Max Hueber, 1957, pp. 364-366.
3313. Lueth, Paul E. H. *Literatur als Geschichte. Deutsche Dichtung von 1885 bis 1947*. Vol. I/II. Wiesbaden: Limes, 1947, Vol. I, p. 111.
3314. Maderno, Alfred. *Die deutsch-österreichische Dichtung der Gegenwart*. Leipzig: Gerstenberg, 1920, pp. 39, 175, 260.
3315. Martini, Fritz. *Deutsche Literaturgeschichte*. Stuttgart: Kröner, 1960, pp. 457, 485-486.
3316. Meyer, Richard M. *Die deutsche Literatur des 19ten und 20sten Jahrhunderts*. Berlin: Bondi, 1921, p. 638 (Volksausgabe).
3317. Mittner, Ladislao. *La Letteratura tedesca del Novecento*. n.l.: Ein-audi Editore, 1960, p. 183.
3318. Mumbauer, Johannes. *Die deutsche Dichtung der neuesten Zeit*. Vol. I/II. Freiburg i.B.: Herder, 1931, Vol. I, pp. 528-532.
3319. Nadler, Josef. *Literaturgeschichte Österreichs*. Salzburg: Otto Müller, 1951, pp. 431-433, 437 (2. ed.).
3320. Naumann, Hans. *Die deutsche Dichtung der Gegenwart*. Stuttgart: Metzler, 1924, p. 77.
3321. Pellegrini, Carlo. *Storia della Letteratura e d'America*. Vol. I/VI. Milano: Vallardi, 1958-1960 Vol. IV, pp. 371-373, 411, 470.
3322. Pongs, Hermann. *Das Bild in der Dichtung*. Vol. I/II. Marburg: Elwert, 1927, f.m.
3323. — *Im Umbruch der Zeit. Das Romanschaffen der Gegenwart*. Göttingen: Göttinger Verlagsanstalt, 1956, pp. 149-150, 154.
3324. Prampolini, Giacomo. *Storia universale della Letteratura*. Vol. I/VII. Torinese: Unione Tipografico Editrice, n.d.; Cf. esp. Vol. VI, pp. 496-498.
3325. Priestley, J. B. *Literature and Western Man*. New York: Harper, 1960, pp. 333, 336.
3326. Robertson, J. G. *A History of German Literature*. Edinburgh-London: William Blackwood, 1959, p. 563 (3. ed.; 4. ed. rev. Edna Purdie *et al.*, New York: British Book, Centre, 1962, p. 563).
3327. Rocca, Enrico. *Storia della Letteratura tedesca dal 1870 al 1933*. Firenze: Samsoni, 1950, f.m. (Cf. esp. pp. 285-304).
3328. Rose, Ernst. *A History of German Literature*. New York: New York University Press, 1960, p. 291.
3329. Salzer, Anselm. *Illustrierte Geschichte der deutschen Literatur von den ältesten Zeiten bis zur Gegenwart*. Vol. I/V. Regensburg: Josef Habbel, 1931, Vol. IV, pp. 1666-1667, 1739; Vol. V, p. 2288.
3330. Samuel, Richard and Thomas R. Hinton. *Expressionism in German Life and Literature and the Theater*. 1910-1924. Cambridge: W. Heffer, 1939, f.m.
3331. Scherer, Wilhelm and Theodor Schultz. *Geschichte der deutschen Literatur*. Wien: Concordia, 1948, p. 695.
3332. Schmidt, Adalbert. *Deutsche Dichtung in Österreich*. Wien-Leipzig: Adolf Luser, 1935, pp. 24, 31, 123, 201.
3333. Schmitt, Fritz and Gerhard Fricke. *Deutsche Literaturgeschichte in Tabellen*. Vol. I/III. Bonn: Athenäum, 1952, Vol. III, pp. 238, 283.
3334. Soergel, Alabert and Curt Hohoff. *Dichtung und Dichter der Zeit*. Vol. I/II. Düsseldorf: August Bagel, 1961, Vol. I, p. 421; Vol. II, pp. 448-450 (Reprinted 1963).
3335. Walzel, Oskar. *Die deutsche Dichtung seit Goethes Tod*. Berlin: Akademischer Verlag, 1920, pp. 297, 431-432, 489, 491 (5. ed. 1929, pp. 151 ff.).
3336. Weiskopf, Franz Karl. *Unter fremden Himmeln. Ein Abriss der deutschen Literatur im Exil*. 1933-1947. Berlin: Dietz, 1948, f.m.
3337. Wiegand, Julius. *Geschichte der deutschen Dichtung*. Köln: Schaaffstein, 1922, pp. 365-391 (Excellent discussion of New Romanticism).
3338. Wiegler, Paul. *Geschichte der deutschen Literatur*. Vol. I/II. Berlin: Ullstein, 1930, Vol. II, pp. 821, 858.
3339. Wilpert, Gero von. *Deutsche Literatur in Bildern*. Stuttgart: Kröner, 1957, pp. 786, 812.

XXIII. MISCELLANY

Films Made from Zweig's Works (Cf. *Knaurs Buch vom Film*. Ed. Rune Walderkranz and Werner Arpe. München: Droemersche Verlagsanstalt, 1956, p. 468; *Blätter*, 1 (Apr., 1958), 8).

3340. "Amok," 1927 (Russia; Directed by Konstantin Mardschanow).
3341. — 1934 (France; Directed by Fedor Ozep).
3342. "Angst," 1928 (Germany; Directed by Hans Steinhoff).
3343. — 1934 (France; Directed by Viktor Tourjansky).
3344. — 1954 (Germany; Directed by Roberto Rosellini, starring Ingrid Bergmann).
3345. "Brennendes Geheimnis," 1933 (Germany; Directed by Robert Siodmak; Cf. also *NYT*, Nov. 6, 1946, p. 30 ("M.G.M. Buys Film Rights to Story 'Burning Secret'")).
3346. "Brief einer Unbekannten" ("Narkose"), 1929 (Germany; Directed by Alfred Abel).
3347. — 1943 (Finnland; Directed by Hannu Leminen, starring Helena Kara).
3348. — 1948 (USA; Directed by Max Ophüls, starring Joan Fontaine).
3349. "Das gestohlene Jahr" (Unpublished scenario with the collaboration of Berthold Viertel), 1951 (Austria; Directed by Wilfred Frass, starring Ewald Baeler).
3350. *Das Haus am Meer* (Drama), 1924 (Germany; Directed by Fritz Kaufmann, starring Asta Nielsen and Albert Steinrück).
3351. *Marie Antoinette* (Biography), 1938 (USA; Directed by W. S. van Dyke, starring Norma Shearer, Tyrone Power and John Barrymore).
3352. "Schachnovelle" (Film version written by Herbert Reinecker, Harold Medford and Gerd Oswald), 1960 (Austria; Starring Curd Jürgens; German premiere in Austria Sept. 2, 1960 (Wien); English premiere Sept. 1, 1960; Cf. rev. in *Die neue Film-Post*, 7.J.: 4 (1960)).
3353. "Das Schicksal einer Nacht" (*Sternstunden der Menschheit*), 1927 (Germany; Directed by Erich Schönfelder, starring Erna Morena and Harry Liedtke).
3354. *Ungeduld des Herzens* (Novel), 1946 (England; English title *Beware of Pity*; Directed by Maurice Elvey, starring Lilli Palmer and Albert Lieven).
3355. "Vierundzwanzig Stunden aus dem Leben einer Frau," 1944 (Argentina; Directed by Carlos Borcosqu, starring Amelia Bence).
3356. — 1952 (England; English title *Twenty-four Hours in the Life of a Woman*; Produced by Associated British Picture Corp.; Released in USA in 1953 as *Affair in Monte Carlo* by the Allied Artists Production; TV version written by John Mortimer in 1960, starring Ingrid Bergmann and Maximilian Schell).

Zweig's Works set to Music:

3357. Demuth, Norman. Three poems (1944).
3357a. Ebenhöh, Horst. "Virata oder die Augen des ewigen Bruders" (Used as text basis for an oratorio in six scenes; Cf. *Blätter*, 8/10 (Oct., 1960), ?1).
3357b. Radó, Aladar. Four poems by Emile Verhaeren in Zweig's translation (1913).
3357c. Reger, Max. Two poems ("Ein Drängen ist in meinem Herzen" and "Neue Fülle").
3358. Röntgen, Johannes. "Two poems from 'Musik der Jugend' (For soprano with instrumental accompaniment; Amsterdam: Alsbach, 1936).
3359. Schibler, Arnim. "Polyphem" (Cantata for Chorus, solo-tenor and two pianos; Opus 34; Zürich: Selbstverlag, 1952). Radio opera based on "Die Augen des ewigen Bruders."
3359a. Seiber, Matyas. Incidental music to *Volpone*.
3359b. Strausz, Richard. Music to the text *Die schweigsame Frau*.
3359c. Szelényi, Istvan. Oratorio based on "Varata oder die Augen des ewigen Bruders".
3359d. Toch, Ernst. Music to the text of "Die Heilige aus U.S.A." (1932).

Recordings of Zweig's Works:

3360. "Brief einer Unbekannten," Read by Ruth Leuwerik. Deutsche Grammophon Gesellschaft, No. 44011.
3361. "Novemberwind," (Original text by Emile Verhaeren in French, translated into German by Stefan Zweig). Shortened version read by Alexander Moissi. Monarch Record Gramophone, No. 041-023 (Cf. *Blätter*, 1 (Apr., 1958), 7).
3362. "Schachnovelle," Read by Curd Jürgens. Amadeo, No. AM-AVRS 1015.
3363. "Vierundzwanzig Stunden aus dem Leben einer Frau," Read by Lil Dagover. Deutsche Grammophon Gesellschaft, No. 44009.
3364. German tape entitled "Stefan Zweig" available at the German Consulate, Detroit, Michigan. Tape No. 358 (27 min. 30 sec.).
3365. "Zweig im 'Osterreichischen Rundfunk'," *Blätter*, 8/10 (Oct., 1960), 22.

Further Reference Works to be Consulted:

3366. Bürgin, Hans. *Das Werk Thomas Manns. Eine Bibliographie* (unter Mitarbeit von Walter A. Reichert und Erich Neumann). Frankfurt am Main: Fischer, 1959, Nos. I, 10a; III, 4; V, 447.
3367. Garraty, John A. *The Nature of Biography*. New York: Knopf, 1957, pp. 126, 131.
3368. Jonas, Klaus W. *Fifty Years of Thomas Mann Studies. A Bibliography of Criticism*. Minneapolis: University of Minnesota Press, 1955, Nos. 760, 764, 1749, 2635.
3369. Reference to Zweig's Tolstoi essay in *BA*, III : 3 (July, 1929), 296-297 in H. G. Wendt's review of Philipp Witkop's *Leo Tolstoi*. Wittenberg: Ziemsen, 1928.
3370. The Dutch fragment from *Jeremias* (Cf. item 100) was originally chosen as the lustrum-play (70th anniversary) of the Christian Philanthropic Institute at Doetinchem, Holland. The whole *Jeremias* was performed in 1938 as the lustrum-play (2nd anniversary) of the Vrijzinnig Christelijke Jeugd Centrale (in Dutch translation) at Ermelo, Holland. Translation and adaptation by Halbs C. Kool; Leader of the performance was the late Abraham van der Vies.

I have seen references to the following but have not been able to trace them down:

3371. Articles about Zweig in the following:
    Aufbau, 12 (1946).
    Der Bogen, 2.J.: 13 (1946).
    Das goldene Tor, 6 (1947).
    Neue Auslese, 2.J.: 2 (1947).
    Wiener Revue. Ein Jahr Wiener Theater, Folge 7/8 (1946).

XXIV. GERMAN MANUSCRIPTS IN ZWEIG'S MANUSCRIPT COLLECTION

3372. Frels, Wilhelm. *Deutsche Dichterhandschriften von 1400 bis 1900* (Gesamtkatalog der eigenhändigen Handschriften deutscher Dichter in den Bibliotheken und Archiven Deutschlands, Österreichs, der Schweiz und der CSR). Leipzig: Verlag von Karl W. Hiersemann, 1934, p. 375.
Salzburg. *Sammlung Stefan Zweig*, Besitzer: Dr. Stefan Zweig, Kapuzinerberg 5. Nur Handschriften, keine Briefe. Aufnahme nach dem Bestand 1928 bis 1929.
    1. Arndt, Ernst Moritz (1769-1860): 2 Gedichte (p. 10).
    2. Arnim, Achim von (Ludwig Acbimo) (1781-1831): Gedicht "Der Leuchtturm," (p. 11).

3. Arnim, Bettina v., geb. Brentano (1785-1859): 1 Gedicht "Petöfy dem Sonnengott," (p. 13).
4. Bäuerle, Adolf Johann (1786-1859): Ms. e. Kritik (5 1/2 S.) (p. 16).
5. Bauernfeld, Eduard von (1802-1890): 1 Einakter "Der Zweifler" (1827) (p. 18).
6. Bierbaum, Otto Julius (1865-1910): 2 Gedichte (p. 25).
7. Blumauer, Joh. Alsys (1755-1798): Ein Bruchstück der *Aeneide* (Buch 7, 55-88) (p. 27).
8. Bodenstedt, Friedrich von (1819-1892): 2 Gedichte (p. 29).
9. Börne, Ludwig (1786-1837): "Briefe aus Paris," Anfang (1/2 S.) u. 1 Sinnspruch (p. 30).
10. Brentano, Clemens (1778-1842): 5 Gedichte (p. 37).
11. Chamisso, Adalbert von (1781-1838): einige Gedichte (p. 46).
12. Claudius, Matthias (1740-1815): 1 Gedicht "Ihr Leute gross u. klein," (p. 48).
13. Cornelius, Peter (1824-1874): 1 Gedicht an Liszt (p. 50).
14. Dehmel, Richard (1863-1920): 2 Gedichte (p. 55).
15. Droste-Hülshoff, Annette Elizabeth Freiin von (1797-1848): 4 Gedichte (2 S. 8°) (p. 58).
16. Eckermann, Johann Peter (1792-1854): 3 Gedichte (p. 62).
17. Eichendorff, Joseph Freiherr v. (1788-1857): mehrere Mss. (p. 63).
18. Fontane, Theodor (1819-1898): Entwurf u. Inhaltsskizze von "Cécile" mit 3 Briefen, das Gedicht "Der alte Derffling" mit Begleitbrief (p. 71).
19. Fouqué, Friedrich Heinrich Karl Baron de la Motte (1777-1843): einige Gedichte (p. 73).
20. Freiligrath, Ferdinand (1810-1876): 2 Gedichte (p. 76).
21. Geibel, Emanuel (1815-1884): 2 Gedichte (p. 81).
22. Gellert, Christian Fürchtegott (1715-1769): Ode auf den Tod Bernhard Christian Willes (p. 83).
23. Gleim, Johann Wilhelm Ludwig (1719-1803): 1 Gedicht an Jean Paul (1798) (p. 89).
24. Goethe, Johann Wolfgang von (1749-1832):
    a. 52 Verse aus Faust II, Akt I (Plutusszene),
    b. Brautlied aus d. Maskenzuge 1810,
    c. 2 S. aus Vorarbeiten zu d. "Principes de philosophie zoologique" Tl. 2,
    d. Gedichte: Eigenthum
       Im May ("Zwischen Weizen u. Korn")
       An Amalie Wolf 1812
    e. 1 Seite Sprüche aus d. Westöstl. Divan,
    f. "Will einer sich gewöhnen" aus d. Zahmen Xenien V,
    g. Die 2 letzten Strophen aus "An die verehrten 18 Frankfurter Festfreunde,"
    h. Hochzeitsgedicht für Willemers "Reicher Blumen goldene Ranken" (1815),
    i. 2 S. aus d. Jugend arbeiten 1759 (p. 96).
25. Gotthelf, Jeremias (wirklicher Name: Albert Bitzius) (1797-1854). Vorwort zu "Zeitgeist u. Bernergeist" (4 S.) (p. 98).
26. Gottsched, Johann Christoph (1700-1766): 1 Gedicht "Du bist des Phöbus Sohn" (1731) (p. 99).
27. Grabbe, Christian Dietrich (1801-1836): ein Fragment aus "Don Juan u. Faust" (2. S) u. eines aus d. "Hermannsschlacht," erster Entwurf (8 S.) (p. 100).
28. Grillparzer, Franz (1791-1872): 3 Gedichte: "Napoleon 1821," "Vision," "Entsagung," (p. 104).
29. Groth, Klaus (1819-1899): Ms. "Vor de Gorn" (106 S.) mit vielen unveröffentlichten Gedichten (p. 106).

30. Grün, Anastasius (wirklicher Name: Anton Alexander Graf von Auersperg) (1806-1876): 1 Gedicht u.a. (p. 107).
31. Gryphius, Andreas (1616-1664): 1 Sonett "Was sindt wir Menschen doch" (1640) (p. 107).
32. Hagedorn, Friedrich von (1708-1754): 1 Promemoria über Voltaires Rechtgläubigkeit (p. 111).
33. Haller, Albrecht von (1708-1777): 1 Gedicht an Gessner (p. 113).
34. Halm, Friedrich (wirklicher Name: Franz Joseph Eligius Reichsfreiherr von Münchhausen-Belling) (1806-1871): 1 Gedicht "Beim Tode Lenaus," (p. 113).
35. Hamann, Johann Georg (1730-1788): 1 Ms. von 8 S. (vgl. Klüber im Jahrbuch d. Goethe-Ges. 15. S. 89f.) (p. 114).
36. Hamerling, Robert (1830-1889): 1 Gedicht (p. 115).
37. Hammer-Purgstall, Joseph von (1774-1856): 3 Gedichte (p. 115).
38. Hardenberg, Friedrich von (Deckname: Novalis) (1772-1801):
    a. Das Gedicht "Der Fremdling" (Anfang)
    b. 1 Sonett an d. Bruder Karl (auf demselben Blatt noch ein Verzeichnis d. Werke J. Böhmes)
    c. Trinklied u. Liebesgedicht (2. S).
    d. Eingangsgedicht zum 2. Tl. des Ofterdingen (4 S.)
    e. Fragment aus d. 2. Tl (1/2 S.)
    f. 1 Gedichtfragment "Die Vermählung der Jahreszeiten" (2 S.) (p. 116)
39. Hartleben, Otto Erich (1864-1905): 1 Gedicht "Franzensfeste," (p. 118).
40. Hauff, Wilhelm (1802-1827):
    1 Gedicht "Serenade"
    2 S. Notizen zu d. Skizzen aus Schwahen u. zum Fischerstechen (p. 119).
41. Haug, Johann Christoph Friedrich (1761-1829): 1 Gedicht an Hebel (p. 120).
42. Hebbel, Friedrich (1813-1863): Novelle "Schnock" u. Schluss des Vorspiels der Niebelungen (p. 122).
43. Hebel, Johann Peter (1760-1826): 2 S. in 4° mit Erzählungen (p. 122).
44. Heine, Heinrich (1797-1856): "Die Weber" in der ersten Fassung, 1 Gedicht aus d. Wintermärchen, erste Fassung, 1/2 S. mit 3 Gedichten (p. 124).
45. Heinse, Wilhelm (1746-1803): 1 Gedichtfragment "In einem Tal am Fusse des Vesuv..." (p. 125).
46. Herder, Johann Gottfried (1744-1803): 2 Gedichte (p. 128).
47. Herwegh, Georg (1817-1875): 1 Gedicht "Den Reichstäglern," (p. 130).
48. Heyse, Paul (1830-1914): Die Novelle "Einer von Hunderten" (45 S.) u. 1 Gedicht an Georg Scherer 1898 (p. 132).
49. Helle, Peter (1854-1904): 10 Gedichte (p. 132).
50. Hölderlin, Friedrich (1770-1843):
    a. 16 Gedichte
    b. Die Fragmente des Pindar 3-9 (früher in der Slg. der Frhrn v. Bernus)
    c. Fragment aus d. Hyperion (6 vom gedruckten Text abweichende Briefe)
    d. Die Abschrift Sinclairs von "Patmos," (p. 135).
51. Hölty, Ludwig Christoph Heinrich (1748-1776): 1 Gedicht "Aufmunterung zur Freude" u. "Maylied," (p. 135).
52. Hoffmann, Ernst Theodor Amadeus (1776-1833): "Kreislers musikalische Leiden," u. 2 S. aus d. Erzählung "Neueste Schicksale des Hundes Berganza."
53. Hoffmann von Fallersleben, August Heinrich (1798-1874): 3 Gedichte.
54. Jean Paul (d.i. Johann Paul Friedrich Richter) (1763-1825): 4 S. "Vom Verfasser der Auswahl aus des Teufels Papieren" u. Ms. der 1. Fassung der "Rede des toten Christus vom Weltgebäude herab."
55. Immermann, Karl Lebrecht (1796-1840): 2 Sonette.

56. Karschin, Anna Luisa (1722-1791): 2 Gedichte.
57. Keller, Gottfried (1819-1890): "Feueridylle" (erste Fassung – 13 S. in gr. – 4°).
58. Kerner, Justinus (richtig Justinus Andreas Christian) (1786-1862): Gedicht "Der Wanderer in der Sägemühle" u. 1 Klexographie mit Gedicht 1854.
59. Kinkel, Johann Gottfried (1815-1882): 1 Gedicht 1862 "Die Veteranen des Exils."
60. Kleist, Ewald Christian von (1715-1759): 4 S. in 8° mit 1 Gedicht "Einladung aufs Land" u. einigen Epigrammen.
61. Kleist, Heinrich von (1777-1811): Fabel "Die Bedingung des Gärtners" u. 6 Gedichte: Sonett an d. Königin Louise (3. Fassung), An Friedrich Wilhelm III., Germania an ihre Kinder, an Kaiser Franz I., Kriegslied der Deutschen, An Wilhelmine von Zenge: "Nicht aus des Herzens Blossem Wunsche."
62. Klopstock, Friedrich Gottlieb (1724-1803): Ode "An die rheinischen Republikaner."
63. Körner, Karl Theodor (1791-1813): Der Einakter "Die Blumen" (1 S. in gr. 2°).
64. Kotzebue, August Friedrich Ferdinand von (1761-1819): Ms. des Lustspiels "Der Hagestolz u. die Körbe."
65. Laube, Heinrich (1806-1884): 1 S. mit d. Abschiedsworten am Grabe Grillparzers.
66. Lenau, Nikolaus (wirklicher Name: Nikolaus Franz Niembsch Edler von Strehlenau) (1802-1850): Das Widmungsgedicht zu den Albigensern, die Gedichte: Crucifix, Der Maskenball, Die Waldkapelle, sämtliche Schilflieder u. 1 Gedichtentwurf von 6 Versen.
67. Lenz, Jakob Michael Reinhold (1751-1792): Gedicht "Ach, wo brennt sie himmlisch schön...".
68. Lessing, Gotthold Ephraim (1729-1781): 1 lat. Stammbuchblatt f. Seydel.
69. Leuthold, Heinrich (1827-1879): 1 Gedichtentwurf.
70. Lichtenberg, Georg Christoph (1742-1799): 2 S. Aphorismen u. Sentenzen.
71. Liliencron, Detlev Freiherr von (1844-1909): Ms. der Novelle "Die Mergelgrube" (39 S.), Prosagedicht "Schmetterlinge" (1 1/2 S.), Korrekturbogen des Gedichts "Das verschüttete Dorf" mit Anmerkungen L's.
72. Lingg, Hermann von (1820-1905): 2 Gedichte.
73. Ludwig, Otto (1813-1865): Fragment e. Dramas.
74. Meyer, Conrad Ferdinand (1825-1898): 1 Gedicht "Lenz, wer kann Dir widerstehen!"
75. Mörike, Eduard (1804-1875): Gedicht, "Jedem das Seine".
76. Müller, Wilhelm (1794-1827): 1 Br. an Ludw. Tieck 14.10.1826.
77. Nietzsche, Friedrich (1844-1900): Gedichtzyklus "Heimkehr" 1863 u. Novellenanfang "Euphorion," "Die Geburt des tragischen Gedankens" (Vorarbeit zur Geburt d. Tragödie), letzter Brief an Avenarius.
78. Opitz, Martin (1597-1639): 1 lat. Gedicht.
79. Pestalozzi, Johann Heinrich (1746-1827): 1 Fragment aus e. Roman (2. S.).
80. Pfeffel, Gottlieb Konrad (1736-1809): 1 Gedicht "Der schwarze Schwan."
81. Platen-Hallermünde, August Graf v. (1796-1835): Gedicht "Gnome."
82. Raimund (eigentlich Raimann), Ferdinand (1790-1836) 1 1/2 Bl. zu "Der Bauer als Millionär," 1 Gedicht "An Gutenstein."
83. Ramler, Karl Wilhelm (1725-1798): 2 Gedichte "Amyntas" u. "Der zerbrochene Krug."
84. Reuter, Fritz (1810-1874): Gedicht "Hei is dod."
85. Rilke, Rainer Maria (1875-1926): Die 1. Fassung d. "Weise von Liebe u. Tod des Cornets Chr. Rilke." 5 Gedichte: "Vor Ostern," "Die Greisin," "Das Bett," "Papageienpark," "Archäischer Torso Apollos."

86. Rodenberg, Julius (1831-1914): 1 Gedicht.
87. Rosegger, Peter (1843-1918): Ms. der Novelle "Der Lachenmacher."
88. Rückert, Friedrich (1788-1866): Gedicht "Jusuff u. Suleika."
89. Saar, Ferdinand von (1833-1906): 2 Gedichte.
90. Scheffel, Joseph Viktor (seit 1876: von) (1826-1886): Gedicht "Waidmann u. Minne."
92. Schiller, Friedrich von (1759-1805):
    2 Fragmente aus Phädra,
    1 aus Don Carlos,
    7 Xenien,
    2 S. mit Gedichtentwürfen.
92. Schlegel, August Wilhelm (1767-1845): 2 Gedichte "Auf die Taufe eines Negers" u. "Die veredelte Hexenzunft."
93. Schlegel, Friedrich (1772-1829): Aufsatz "Über die Aussichten der Kunst im österr. Kaiserstaat" (1812) (16 S.).
94. Seidel, Heinrich (1842-1906): Ms. der Novelle "Eva."
95. Seume, Johann Gottfried (1763-1810): Elegie "An das deutsche Volk" (1810) u. das Ms. von "Mein Leben."
96. Stelzhamer, Franz (1802-1874): 1 Gedicht "Radikale Lieder. 1."
97. Stolberg, Friedrich Leopold Graf zu (1750-1819): Gedicht "An Agnes" usw.
98. Storm, Theodor (1817-1888): Ergänzung d. Novelle "Im Sonnenschein" (12 S.) u. der Gedichtzyklus "Die rote Rose" (4 S.).
99. Strachwitz, Graf Moritz von (1822-1847): 1 Liebesgedicht an Harrie.
100. Tieck, Ludwig (1773-1853): 1 S. zum Versdrama "Isodir u. Olga" u. 1 Buchbesprechung (1 S.).
101. Uz, Johann Peter (1720-1796): 1 Gedicht "Hagedorn" (1744).
102. Varnhagen von Ense, Karl August (1785-1858): 4 Gedichte.
103. Varnhagen von Ense, Rahel, geb. Levin (1771-1833): Eine philosophische Abhandlung 13.9.1820.
104. Vogl, Johann Nepomuk (1802-1866): 3 Gedichte.
105. Voss, Johann Heinrich (1751-1826): "Idylle," "Die Bleicherin."
106. Vulpius, Christian August (1762-1827): Aufsatz von 1 1/2 S.
107. Wackenroder, Wilhelm Heinrich (1773-1798): 2 Entwürfe "Sprachbemerkungen über die Minnesinger" u. "Wörter u. Redensarten aus Hans Sachs."
108. Wagner, Richard (1813-1883): 8 S. aus "Siegfried," Akt 1, Szene 1, u. Festrede f. Friedrich Schneider, Dresden 1846 (3 S.).
109. Waiblinger, Friedrich Wilhelm (1804-1830): 2 Gedichte "Der Griechin Klage" u. "Die Griechin v. Korinth."
110. Werner, Zacharias (1768-1823): Der 165. Gesang über Michelangelos jüngstes Gericht 1810 (1 1/2 S.).
111. Wieland, Christoph Martin (1733-1813): 1 S. zur Horazübersetzung.
112. Zschokke, Johann Heinrich Daniel (1771-1848): Aufsatz "Die Republik Krakau u. die Neutralität" (3 S.).

XXV. ARTICLES BY ZWEIG CONCERNING HIS MANUSCRIPT COLLECTION AND ARTICLES ABOUT ZWEIG AS A MANUSCRIPT COLLECTOR

3373. "Das Autographensammeln," *VZ*, Sept. 14, 1913.
3374. "Die Autographensammlung als Kunstwerk," *DBK*, II (1914), 44-50 (Reprinted in *Spiegelungen*, pp. 44-51).
3375. "Die drei Meyer-Sammlungen," *BT*, June 17, 1924 (Arthur Meyer, Cornelius Meyer, R. M. Meyer).

3376. "Echte und falsche Autographen," *ARsch*, VII (1926), 115.
3377. "Meine Autographensammlung," *Ph*, III : 7 (1930), 279-289.
3378. Mozart, Wolfgang Amadeus. *Ein Brief von Wolfgang Amadeus Mozart an sein Augsburger Bäsle*. Wien-Leipzig-Zürich: Reichner, 1931 (Intro. by Zweig with a four page facsimile of Mozart's letter and a transcription of it).
3379. "Neue Napoleon Manuskripte," *Ph*, II (1929), 246.
3380. "Die Sammlung Morrison," *VZ*, Sept. 6, 1917 (Cf. *DBK*, VI (1918), 73).
3381. "Sinn und Schönheit der Autographen," *DNSch*, 19.J. (1958), 118 (Cf. also *Begegnungen* (1937 ed.), pp. 469-476; *Begegnungen* (1955 ed.), pp. 441-448; Excerpts of this essay are used as the Intro. to *Lyrische Handschrift unserer Zeit*. Ed. Hartfrid Voss. Ebenhausen bei München: Hartfrid Voss, 1958, p. 5).
3382. "Die Welt der Autographen," *DBK*, 12./13.J. (1927), 70-77.
3383. Arens, Hanns. "Der Sammler Stefan Zweig," *DNZg*, 121 (1949) (Reprinted in *Imp*, XI (1953), 199-205; *NDH*, 5 (1954), 394; *WidZ*, 10 (Oct., 1961), 36-40).
3384. — "Stefan Zweig as a Collector of Manuscripts," *Ms*, 9 (1957), 43-45.
3385. *Blätter*, 6/7 (Oct., 1959), 9 ("Zweigs Sammlung von Autographenkatalogen noch geschlossen vorhanden im Privatbesitz von Herrn Heinrich Eisemann").
3386. Burchardt, Hansjürgen. "Die Autographen-Auktion bei Stargard vom 14. November 1958," *BdBh*, 14.J.: 10 (1958), 1708-1711.
3387. Claudel, Paul and André Gide. *Correspondance*. 1899-1926. Pref. and Notes Robert Mallet. 5. ed. Paris: Gallimard, 1949, pp. 210, 357 (Ref. to Zweig's attempt to purchase Claudel's *L'Annonce faite à Marie*).
3388. Dargan, E. Preston and Bernard Weinberg, eds. *The Evolution of Balzac's 'Comedie humaine'*. Chicago: University of Chicago Press, 1942, pp. 427-430 (Appendix: Wells Chamberlin, "The Zweig Manuscript Proof of 'Une ténébreuse Affaire'").
3389. Ecker, Karl. "Die Sammlung Stefan Zweigs in der Österreichischen Nationalbibliothek – Wien," *Festschrift zum 25 jährigen Dienstjubiläum des General Direktors Josef Bick*. Ed. Jasek Stummvoll. Wien, 1948, pp. 321-330 ("Stefan Zweig Autographen:
a. In der Handschriftensammlung: 17 Autographen verschiedener Art (Briefe, Postkarten, Widmungen, teilweise nur Unterschriften)
b. In der Theatersammlung: *Die schweigsame Frau*, Oper für Richard Strauss").
3390. Hintenberger, Heinrich, ed. *Repräsentative Original-Handschriften. Eine berühmte Autographen-Sammlung*. 1. Teil. Katalog IX. Wien: Heinrich Hintenberger, n.d. (Cf. also Katalog XX: *Interessante Autographen aus zwei bekannten Sammlungen*).
3391. Thommem-Girard, G. H. "Stefan Zweig als Autographen-Sammler," *DAnq*, 10.J. (1954), 205-208.
3392. Wolbe, Eugen. "Stefan Zweig als Autographensammler," *DKw*, XIII (Nov., 1931), 72-73.
3393. Zohn, Harry. "Stefan Zweig as a Collector of Manuscripts," *CQ*, XXV : 3 (May, 1952), 182-191.

ADDENDA

3394. Arens, Hanns. "Erinnerungen an Stefan Zweig. Aufgezeichnet aus Anlass seines 80. Geburtstags," *Welt und Wort*, XVI (1961), 334-336, 340.
3395. Barthel, L. F., ed. *Das war Binding. Ein Buch der Erinnerung*. Wien-Berlin-Stuttgart, 1955 (Contributions by Thomas Seidenfaden, Karl Rauch, O. Jancke, Tilla Fleischel, Stefan Zweig, Richard Scheibe, Willi Fehse, *et al.*).
3396. Berenson, Bernard. *Sunset and Twilight. From the Diaries of 1947-1958*. Intro. by Iris Origo. Epilogue by Nicky Mariano. New York: Harcourt, Brace and World, 1963, p. 9 (Reference to Zweig's *Balzac*).
3397. Butler, E. M. *The Tyranny of Greece over Germany*. Boston: Beacon Press, 1958, pp. 214n, 333 (Reference to Zweig's *Der Kampf mit dem Dämon*).

3398. Courts, Gerd. *Das Problem des unterliegenden Helden in den Dramen Stefan Zweigs*. Köln, 1962 (Unpub. Doctoral Dissertation).
3399. Faesi, Robert. "Erinnerung an Stefan Zweig. Zu seinem 20. Todestag," *Schweizer Monatshefte* (Zürich), XLI (1961-1962), 1301-1310.
3400. Grossberg, Mimi. "Joseph Roth, sein Schicksal und sein Werk," *Bulletin des Leo Baeck Instituts* (Tel-Aviv), VII (1964), 76-94.
3401. Huder, Walther. "Stefan Zweig," *Sinn und Form. Beiträge zur Literatur* (Berlin), XIV (1962), 135-140.
3402. Kesten, Hermann. *Hermann Kesten. Ein Buch der Freunde. Zum 60. Geburtstag*. München: Desch; Köln: Kiepenheuer and Witsch. Frankfurt am Main: Büchergilde Gutenberg, 1960 (Contributions by Heinrich Mann, Joseph Roth, Stefan Zweig, Alfred Döblin, Thomas Mann *et al.*).
3403. — "Stefan Zweig," *Meine Freunde, die Poeten*. München: Kindler, 1959, pp. 141-154 (Cf. No. 2816).
3404. Kohn, Hans. *Karl Kraus – Arthur Schnitzler – Otto Weininger. Aus dem Jüdischen Wien der Jahrhundertwende*. Tübingen: Mohr, 1962, pp. 14, 30-31, 68-69.
3405. Langer, N. "Stefan Zweig," *Dichter aus Österreich* (Wien), 2.F. (1957), 122-127.
3406. Prater, Donald A. "Stefan Zweig and England," *German Life and Letters*, XVI (1962), 1-13.
3407. Schramm, Werner. *Stefan Zweig. Essay*. Itzehoe: Selbstverlag, 1961.
3408. Zweig, Stefan. "Abschiedsrede (In memoriam Joseph Roth)," *Österreichische Post* (Paris), July 1, 1939 (Reprinted in *Sie trugen Österreich mit sich in die Welt*. Ed. Arthur Breycha-Vauthier. Wien: Weltbund der Österreicher im Ausland, 1962, pp. 126-130).
3409. — "An Arthur Schnitzler: Kundgebungen österreichischer Zeitgenossen," *Moderne Welt*, III: 12 (?), 10-15 (Contributions by Felix Salten, Anton Wildgans, Stefan Zweig *et al.*).
3410. — "Das Geheimnis des künstlerischen Schaffens," *Wort und Tat* (Mainz-Weisenan), 9 (1948), 7-21 (Cf. No. 1224).
3411. — "Die Geschichte als Dichterin," *Erbe und Zukunft*, 1 (1946), 54-64 (Cf. No. 1226).
3412. — "Persönliche Erinnerungen an Arthur Schnitzler," *Literarische Welt*, VII (?), 45 (Contributions by Hermann Bahr, Felix Salten, Stefan Zweig).
3413. — *Der Turm zu Babel*. Wien: Im Verlag der Internationalen Stefan-Zweig-Gesellschaft, 1964 (4. Sonderpublikation der Stefan Zweig Gesellschaft; Cf. No. 1361).
3414. — *Die Welt von gestern. Erinnerungen eines Europäers*. Frankfurt am Main-Berlin: G. B. Fischer, 1962.

NOTES

[1] These words, attributed to Marguerite of Austria, are used as the motto to the last chapter of Zweig's *Calvin* (1954 ed.), p. 262.

[2] Kurt Böttcher, "Humanist auf verlorener Bastion, *NDL*, XI (Nov., 1956), p. 83.

[3] Stefan Zweig, *WvG*, pp. 17-23. Zweig's autbiography first appeared in English as: *The World of Yesterday*. New York City: Viking, 1943; the following year it appeared in German with the Berman-Fischer Verlag.

[4] Friderike M. Zweig, *SZ*, pp. 9-12.

[5] *Ibid.*, pp. 18-22.

[6] S. Zweig, *WvG*, pp. 23-69.

[7] For Zweig's evaluation and appreciation of Rimbaud, Verlaine, Rilke and Hofmannsthal compare the following:
   a. Stefan Zweig, "Arthur Rimbaud" (1907), *Begegnungen*, pp. 432-441.
   b. S. Zweig, *Verlaine*.
   c. S. Zweig, "Abschied von Rilke" (1927), *Begegnungen*, pp. 59-74.
   d. S. Zweig, "Hugo von Hofmannsthal. Gedächtnisrede zur Trauerfeier im Wiener Burgtheater," *Zeit und Welt*, pp. 33-49.

[8] S. Zweig, "Erinnerung an Theodor Herzl" (1929), *Begegnungen*, pp. 88-96.

[9] S. Zweig, *WvG*, pp. 100-121.

[10] For succinct, penetrating appraisals of this characteristic of Zweig see:
   a. Willi Fehse, "Das höchste Gut dieser Erde...," *Spiegelungen*, pp. 64-65.
   b. Romain Rolland, Preface to the French edition of Zweig's *Amok* (Paris: Ferenczi and Fils, 1939), pp. 11-12. The Preface first appeared in Nov., 1926 in the first edition of the text cited above.

[11] K. Böttcher, *op.cit.*, pp. 84-85.

[12] S. Zweig, *WvG*, p. 120; compare the same sentiment expressed in a letter Zweig had received 32 years previously from Richard Dehmel, which in its latter part anticipates some of Zweig's own editorial problems:

Blankensee, 1.11.9.

Lieber Herr Zweig!

Es ist in jeder Hinsicht bewundernswert, wie Sie für Verhaeren eintreten; und Sie werden sehen, dass Sie dadurch unmerklich auch für Ihren eignen Weg schrittfester geworden sind. Es ist ja vollkommen einerlei, an was für Aufgaben man seine Kräfte setzt, wenn's nur zu höchsten Aufgaben sind und nach besten Kräften geschieht. Auch ich werde noch einige Zeit für den höchsten Wert eines andern arbeiten müssen: die Säuberung des Liliencronschen Gedächtnisbildes von dem wohlgemeinten, aber übelbeschaffenen Firnis der vulgären Reklame wird mich noch mindestens ein halbes Jahr lang beschäftigen (Sichtung des Briefnachlasses u. dergl.). Ich halte die Zeit nicht für verloren an mir selber; denn man wird sich bei solcher Arbeit klarer über seelische Allgemeinwerte, als wenn man sich immer bloss mit seinen eignen Spielen und Zielen befasst. Übrigens war es vielleicht eine Dummheit von mir, die Poesie meiner letzten Jahre unter die Titel meiner früheren Bücher miteinzuschachteln; infolgedessen merken die meisten Leute garnicht, was mir wesentlich Neues zugewachsen ist. Aber das sagt mir wohl bloss das Bewusstsein meiner persönlichen Entwickelung, also die liebe Eitelkeit; schliesslich kommt es doch nur darauf an, was als sachliches Werk von uns übrig bleibt.

Mit allen guten Wünchen
Ihr Dehmel.

Richard Dehmel, *Ausgewählte Briefe*. 1902-1920. Berlin: Fischer, 1923, No. 573, p. 189.

[13] S. Zweig, "Erinnerungen an Emile Verhaeren" (1916), *Begegnungen*, pp. 9-59; cf. *WvG*, pp. 116-121.

[14] For a vibrant, loving description of Paris compare S. Zweig, *WvG*, pp. 126-128.

[15] For Zweig's work on Desbordes-Valmore cf:
a. *Marceline Desbordes-Valmore*.
b. "Marceline Desbordes-Valmore," *Begegnungen*, pp. 318-373.

[16] S. Zweig, "Auguste Rodin" (1913), *Begegnungen*, pp. 74-78.

[17] S. Zweig, *WvG*, pp. 122-148.

[18] *Ibid.*, pp. 148-151.

[19] Zweig's essay "Die Autographensammlung als Kunstwerk" (of which the original manuscript is at present in the Manuscript Collection of the Wiener Stadtbibliothek) was first published in the *DBK*, II (1914), 44-50; reprinted in *Spiegelungen*, pp. 44-52; "Sinn und Schönheit der Autographen," *Begegnungen*, pp. 441-449.

[20] S. Zweig, "Benares: die Stadt der tausend Tempel," *Begegnungen*, pp. 254-262; reprinted from *Fahrten*.

[21] S. Zweig, *WvG*, pp. 171-173.

[22] S. Zweig, "Der Rythmus von New York" (1912), *Begegnungen*, pp. 264-271; reprinted from *Fahrten*.

[23] S. Zweig, *WvG*, pp. 299-308.

[24] S. Zweig, "Die Stunde zwischen zwei Ozeanen" (1912), *Begegnungen*, pp. 239-248; reprinted from *Fahrten*.

[25] S. Zweig, *WvG*, p. 198.

[26] S. Zweig, "Das schönste Grab der Welt" (1928), *Begegnungen*, pp. 262-264; "Tolstoi als religiöser und sozialer Denker," *Zeit und Welt*, pp. 65-89; "Reise nach Russland," *Zeit und Welt*, pp. 203-249.

[27] S. Zweig, *WvG*, pp. 299-308.

[28] Cf. footnote 13.

[29] For a far too effervescent, though undoubtedly sincere appraisal of Rolland see: *Rolland*.

[30] S. Zweig, *WvG*, pp. 222-224.

[31] *Ibid.*, p. 220.

[32] *Ibid.*, pp. 224-225.

[33] Donald G. Daviau, "Stefan Zweig's Victors in Defeat," *MfDU*, LI : 1 (Jan., 1959), pp. 1-12.

[34] S. Zweig, *Begegnungen*, pp. 207-219; cf. *WvG*, pp. 277-278.

[35] S. Zweig, *WvG*, pp. 227-234.

[36] *Ibid.*, pp. 255-256.

[37] *Ibid.*, pp. 246-253.

[38] S. Zweig, "Der Turm zu Babel," *VZ*, May 8, 1916; reprinted as "La tour de Babel," *LC*, April-May, 1916.

[39] A small number of Zweig's articles written during the First World War have recently been reprinted and are collected in his *Begegnungen*. See:
a. "Die schlaflose Welt" (1914), pp. 175-181.
b. "Bei den Sorglosen" (1916), pp. 181-187.
c. "Bertha von Suttner" (1917), pp. 187-194.
d. "Das Herz Europas" (1917), pp. 194-207.
e. "Das Feuer" (1918), pp. 207-219.

[40] In his article "Humanist auf verlorener Bastion" (see footnote 2), Kurt Böttcher makes several interesting observations, which, though easily enough misinterpreted, even

detrimentally so, do have more than a mere grain of truth in them. His argument runs somewhat as follows: After the war Zweig sought to promote international understanding, justice and the abolition of force through a spiritual reformation, a transformation of human consciousness, completely misunderstanding, no, ignoring the proletarian movement which was steadily forcing itself to the fore. Although his ideas found almost no sympathy in an era of revolutionary ideals and revenge, he remained true to these ideals of serving the realm of the spirit and "... hierin liegt das grosse (politische!) Verdienst seines Schaffens" (p. 87). Around 1918 Zweig sought to actively mould public opinion, and when this attempt failed (a fact which he doesn't mention in his autobiography) he was faced with an important decision: should he aid the propagation of the new social ideas which advocated removal of economic inequality of states, imperialism, misery of the lower classes and oppression of minorities, ideas which he decidedly championed? When Barbusse, after his tour of Russia openly advocated Communism, believing democracies incapable of accomplishing international brotherhood, attempted to turn their international peace group "Clarté" into a class-machine for the spread of Communism, Zweig withdrew his support. "Wieder hatten wir im Kampf um die geistige Freiheit versagt aus zu grosser Liebe zur eigenen Freiheit und Unabhängigkeit" (S. Zweig, *WvG*, p. 278). Böttcher interprets this sentence as a self-remonstrance on Zweig's part for not having openly advocated Communism and for not having given up his personal wealth. Thus to avoid an unequivocal decision Zweig fled again into the realm of spirit ("... die blosse Auseinandersetzung mit dem Menschen als Individuum." Böttcher, p. 88), reasserting his former inclination that society can only be understood if we first have grasped the mental and the emotional essence of the individual. Böttcher sees this individualism in combination with philosophic relativism as the basis upon which Zweig based his defense of the worth of the individual, or should we say "individuals", individuals who need one another, that is society, ergo Communism.

Böttcher's article is based on extracts from his Doctoral Dissertation, "Stefan Zweig und 'die Welt von Gestern'," which was written in 1951 at the Friedrich-Schiller-Universität, Jena.

[41] Mrs. Zweig's book, *SZ*, is a pertinent accout of Zweig's life as an individual, his life with her, and an exceptionally penetrating discussion of his works. Upon reading the work, however, one is left with a strange feeling that she showed somewhat too much heroism with respect to Stefan's escapade in his 50s and was far too tolerant with respect to his moodiness. G. Bianquis in her review of this work (*Er*, III (June 10, 1959), 347) brings this fact out rather too bluntly, reducing Zweig's actions to mere selfishness.

[42] F. M. Zweig, *SZ*, pp. 125-128.

[43] S. Zweig, *WvG*, pp. 264-265.

[44] S. Zweig, "Salzburg: die Stadt als Rahmen," *Begegnungen*, pp. 271-274; reprinted in *Blätter*, 2 (July, 1958), 1-4.

[45] S. Zweig, "Arturo Toscanini" (1935), *Begegnungen*, pp. 78-88.

[46] S. Zweig, "Bruno Walter: Kunst der Hingabe" (1936), *Begegnungen*, pp. 127-130.

[47] S. Zweig, "Geburtstagsbrief an Hermann Bahr" (1923), *Begegnungen*, pp. 106-111.

[48] S. Zweig, "Unvergessliches Erlebnis. Ein Tag bei Albert Schweitzer" (1932), *Begegnungen*, pp. 113-123.

[49] S. Zweig, "Der Dirigent (Gustav Mahler)," *Begegnungen*, pp. 123-127.

[50] S. Zweig, "Frans Masereel" (1923), *Begegnungen*, pp. 130-140.

[51] S. Zweig, *WvG*, pp. 315-317.

[52] S. Zweig, "Die moralische Entgiftung Europas" (1932), *Begegnungen*, pp. 223-239; "Der europäische Gedanke in seiner historischen Entwicklung," *Zeit und Welt*, pp. 299-327.

[53] Olga Bak, "Stefan Zweig, sa vie et son oeuvre," (Unpub. diss., Laval Université,. Quebec, 1950), pp. 67-68.

[54] For a summary bibliography of Zweig's major works consult *Blätter*, 1 (April, 1958), 5-7 and "Bibliographie der Werke von Stefan Zweig," *In*, XIII (1931), 17-30.

[55] Otto Zarek, "Stefan Zweig zum 50sten Geburtstag," *NR*, XLII : 2 (Dec., 1931), 861-863.

[56] S. Zweig, *WvG*, pp. 334-343.

151

57 Walter A. Berendsohn, *Die humanistische Front; Einführung in die deutsche Emigranten-Literatur. Erster Teil von 1933 bis zum Kriegsausbruch 1939*. Zürich: Europa, 1946.
58 S. Zweig, *WvG*, p. 345.
59 Mary Lamberton Becker, "The Most Readable and the Most Reliable," *NYHTB*, Aug. 25, 1935, p. 3.
60 Werner J. Cahnmann, "Stefan Zweig at Salzburg," *MJ*, XXX (July, 1942), 195-198.
61 F. M. Zweig, *SZ*, pp. 364-388.
62 S. Zweig, *WvG*, pp. 359-362.
63 S. Zweig, "Dank an Brasilien," *Zeit und Welt*, pp. 151-159; "Kleine Reise nach Brasilien" (1936), *Begegnungen*, pp. 274-309; *Brasilien*.
64 S. Zweig, "Geschichtsschreibung von Morgen," *Zeit und Welt*, pp. 275-299.
65 To demonstrate that Zweig realized these ideals in his own life was the purpose of an article by Normal A. Brittin entitled "Stefan Zweig: Biographer and Teacher," *SeR*, XLVIII (April, 1949), 245-254; that Zweig himself was not always the "eternal idealist" is obvious from much of his correspondence. To this effect compare the letters written by Zweig to Alfred Wolfenstein and Felix Braun reprinted in *Spiegelungen*, pp. 86-88.
66 S. Zweig, *Heilung durch den Geist*; "Worte am Sarge Sigmund Freuds," *Zeit und Welt*, pp. 49-55.
67 F. M. Zweig, *SZ*, pp. 402-433.
68 S. Zweig, *Balzac*. This work was completed and published posthumously by Dr. Richard Friedenthal, the executor of Zweig's literary estate; cf. "Die unterirdischen Bücher Balzacs" (1920), *Begegnungen*, pp. 427-432; *Drei Meister*.
69 For a photographic reprint of Zweig's last declaration see Hanns Arens, "Stefan Zweig," *Europäer*, p. 44; the printed text of the letter is found on the preceding page.
70 F. M. Zweig, *SZ*, pp. 416-424.
71 S. Zweig, *WvG*, pp. 7-10.
72 F. M. Zweig, *SZ*, pp. 356-363.
73 Raoul Auernheimer, "Stefan Zweig," *The Torch of Freedom*. Ed. Emil Ludwig and Henry B. Kranz. New York City: Farrar and Rinehart, 1943, pp. 409-426.
74 Paul Beaulieu, "Reflexions sur la suicide de Stefan Zweig," *LNR* (Montreal, Canada), X (Aug., 1942), 579-582; Thomas Mann, "Stefan Zweig zum 10. Todestag," *Altes und Neues*. Frankfurt am Main: S. Fischer, 1943, 263-265; Franz Schoenberner, "Stefan Zweig and Ourselves," *NRep*, CVI (March, 1942), 333.
75 In his article "Erinnerungen an Stefan Zweig" (*Spiegelungen*, pp. 78-85) Robert Braun maintains that he believes Zweig was more than passively interested in conversion to Christianity, indeed to Roman Catholicism, following the example of some of the leading German literary Jews, among them Franz Werfel. Had he (Braun) only dared be more forceful Zweig would possibly have chosen the only possible line of salvation left open to men of humanistic idealism - religion.

> Vielleicht wäre Stefan Zweig damals geneigter gewesen denn je, meinen Schritt zum religiösen Bekenntnis, der dieser Einsicht gefolgt war, nicht allein zu tolerieren, sondern auch als eine Möglichkeit zu begreifen, die nicht allein für den fremden Anderen annehmbar blieb. Unsere Feinden konnten uns ja alles absprechen, Heimat, Besitz, Freiheit, ja das Recht zu leben, nur das Bekenntnis zum Kreuz nicht. Noch nie war es verbunden mit jahrtausende altem Schicksal so an uns herangetreten wie unter dem Schatten Hitlers. Hätte ich damals gewagt, Stefan Zweig dies in Zusammenhang mit der politischen Situation zu bekennen, hätte er vielleicht aufgehorcht. Es hätte freilich auch sein können, dass er, ähnlich wie Franz Werfel, gerade unter dem Druck der Verfolgung sich weiter denn je von einer Anerkennung dessen entfernt hätte, was mir die einzige Rettung schien. Ich erwähnte jedoch kein Wort davon. Es war nich seine Schuld, sondern allein die menige, dass ich es nicht wagte, die Rede auf das mir Wichtigste zu bringen, und es so – durch Zuhören geheimhielt. p.78.

This of course may be true but judging strictly from Zweig's own writings there seems nothing to substantiate such a view.
76 K. Böttcher, *op. cit.*, p. 92.
77 Antoine Bon, "Stefan Zweig et le Brésil," *MdF*, CCCI (Sept. 1, 1947), 78.

152

INDEX

Note: Roman numerals refer to pages in the Introduction, Arabic numbers in parentheses refer to the foot-notes in the Introduction, Arabic numbers without parentheses refer to the entries in the body of the text.

WORKS BY STEFAN ZWEIG: BIOGRAPHICAL STUDIES

155

POETRY

PROSE FICTION

MONOGRAPHS ABOUT STEFAN ZWEIG

Stefan Zweig. Ein Lebensbild (H. Hellwig), 2794
Stefan Zweig. Ein Nachruf (A. Cahn), 2738
Stefan Zweig. Eine Bildbiographie (F. M. Zweig), 2518-2519, 2974
Stefan Zweig. Eine Gedenkschrift (P. Zech), 2506, 2962
Stefan Zweig, grand Européen (Romains), 2679-2680
Stefan Zweig, Great European (Romains), 2596
Stefan Zweig. Juan Tenario. Ensayos (Fuente Gonzáles), 3013
Stefan Zweig. Der Mensch im Werk (H. Arens), 2695
Stefan Zweig. Sonderpublikation der Funk- *tionärblätter*, 2731, 2772, 2781, 2887, 2938
Stefan Zweig, su Vida, Obra y Muerte (Goldbaum), 3015
Stefan Zweig und der humanitäre Gedanke (R. Friedenthal), 2780
Stefan Zweig. Un Hombre de Ayer (Ortiz Oderigo), 3019
Stefan Zweig. Versuch eines Bildnisses (R. Specht), 2907
SZ, (4-5), (41-42), (61), (67), (70), (72), 2975, 2989, 3032
Os últimos Dias de Stefan Zweig (Souza), 3003, 3029
Vida e Morte de Stefan Zweig (Azevedo), 2997

MONOGRAPHS IN GENERAL

(Excluding works by or about Stefan Zweig, general reference works (Cf. 3206-3278) and histories of literature (Cf. 3279-3339)):

Abendgluten, 1598
De Achterhoede, 1506
Adventures in Modern Literature, 301
ALA, 25, 31, 85
Albert Schweitzer. Leven en Werk, 1513
Alfred Kubin. Leben - Werk - Wirkung, 976, 2823
Altes und Neues, (74), 2847
Das Amselnest, 1563
L'Annonce faite à Marie, 2648, 3387
Eine Antologie der besten Übersetzungen (Verlaine), 1474, 1538
Anthologie jüngster Lyrik, 1514, 2487
Antlitz, 1460
Der arme Lukas, 1576
Art and Psychoanalysis, 2552
Arthur Rimbaud. Leben und Dichtung, 1149
Art of Modern Fiction, 277
Arturo Toscanini, 1530-1531
Assessor Karlchen, 1619
L'Aube, XXXI
Au-dessus de la mêlée, XXXI
Auf höherer Warte, 209
Ausgewählte Briefe (R. Dehmel), (12), 979
Ausgewählte Gedichte (E. Verhaeren), 1442-1443, 2495
Ausgewählte Romane und Novellen (C. Dickens), 1491, 1182
Aus Nah und Fern, 171, 2773
Aus Tag und Traum, 1618
Aus toten Fragen, 1591
Aus unserer Zeit, 158
Der Autorabend. Dichteranekdoten von

Rabelais bis Thomas Mann, 2922
Aux peuples assassinés, 1435
A Balzac-Bibliography, 2599
Balzac. Historia dos treze, 1272
Balzac. Sein Weltbild aus den Werken, 1484, 2488-2489
Bass-Bassina-Bulu, 1501
Begegnungen. Die Grossen der Welt im Zwiegespräch, 2759
Bekenntnisse eines Egoisten, 1615
Das bekränzte Jahr, 1589
La Belgique sanglante, XXXI
Best of Modern European Literature, 278
Ein Blatt aus der Chronik unserer Stadt, 1597
Blick ins Chaos, 1571
Die Blumen des Bösen, 1402
Book of Contemporary Short Stories, 267
Briefe aus den Jahren 1906 bis 1907 (Rilke), 2879
Briefe aus Einsamkeiten, 1263, 1503
Briefe: 1873-1939 (S. Freud), 981, 2775
Briefe: 1897-1914 (Rilke), 2878
Briefe in das Jenseits, 2725
Ein Brief von Mozart an sein Ausburger Bäsele, 1517, 3378
Briefwechsel (Rilke-Gide), 977-978, 2880
Briefwechsel (Rilke-Kippenberg), 2881
Briefwechsel (Rilke-Marie von Thurn und Taxis), 2882
Brigitte und Regine und andere Dichtungen, 1495
Brod, 1281

159

PERIODICALS AND NEWSPAPERS

163

Ré, 1924
REH, 2042
REI, 1052
RELM, 2122
RELV, 1850, 1980, 2043, 2165, 2261,
2295, 2330, 2398-2399
RG, 2123, 2296, 2299, 2320, 2427
RH, 1040, 1981, 2166
RHb, 2327, 2400
RHEF, 1982
RHG, 1024, 1053, 1074, 1106
RHPR, 1983
RM, 2077
RMd, 2254, 2331
RN, 1854, 2169, 2304, 2335, 2406, 2428
RoR, 2935
RP, 997, 1010, 1122-1123, 2044, 2669,
2677, 3155-3156
RQH, 2124
RR, 2034, 2110, 2154, 2201, 3157
RRev, 2572
RRh, 1454, 1459, 1470, 1473, 2207a
RT, 1659, 2846
RvB, 1377
RX, 2290
S, 1712
SAQ, 1966
SC, 1925
SchM, 1032
SchMz, 2485
SchR, 2017, 2361
SE, 2068
SeR, (65), 1967, 2534
Sewanee Review, cf. SeR
SFC, 1897, 2516
SG, 2111
SGM, 2069
Si, 1898
SLR, 2035, 2246, 2291
SLzt, 2927, 3158
SM, 1055, 2362
SNT, 1172
Social Welfare (India), 2979
SoM, 2486
SoS, 2442
Soz, 1660
SP, 1323
Sp, 1731-1732, 1793, 1828, 1917, 1968,
2112, 2155, 2423, 2598
SR, 1776, 1794, 1805, 1826, 1833, 1848,
1918, 1969, 2070, 2113, 2156, 2382,
2424, 2443, 2466, 2477
SRL, 1355, 1733, 1777, 1806, 1827, 1834,
1849, 1899, 1919, 1970, 2036, 2071,
2292, 2425, 2467, 2478, 2517, 2540,
2555, 2591, 3160-3168

SS, 1752
SSA, 1056
SSR, 2383
ST, 2835
Sy, 2384
T, 1672, 1796, 1807, 1900, 2072, 2426,
3169-3170
Tab, 1920
TAM, 1673, 1734-1735
Tb, 1622
Th, 1971, 2115, 2158
TL, 1859
TR, 1713, 2321
Tr, 1184
TrG, 1926
Tribune de Genève, 1902
Ts, 2045
Two, 2995
U, 2048
Ud, 1327, 2204
UfL, 2365
Um, 2363
Un, 1173, 1216, 2688
Uns, 2450
V, 1033, 1363, 2949
Vbü, 2697
VdF, 2444, 2653, 2656, 3171-3172
Ven, 2671
Ver, 3014
VFZM, 1138, 1170, 1185, 1208, 1277,
1302, 1356
Vin, 2992, 3173
VK, 1748
VP, 1927-1928, 2650
VQR, 1284
VuV, 2862, 3174
VV, 1937, 2274
VZ, (38), 1061, 1072, 1155, 1273, 1335,
1361, 1661, 2018, 2087, 2275, 3373,
3380
W, 1884
WaM, 1250
WAZ, 2185
Wbü, 2804
WdA, 2900
WE, 1230, 1267
Wi, 1280
WiaL, 2994
WidZ, 2693, 2836, 2863, 2944, 3383
Wiener Revue, 3371
WieZ, 2733, 2785, 2864, 3175
WL, 1871, 1938, 2187
WLB, 1736, 1797, 1882, 1972, 2073, 2116,
2159, 2385, 2468, 3176-3177
WM, 1684, 1939
WR, 2208

Wst, 2691, 2694, 3178
Wt, 2364
WU, 2527
WuW, 1041, 2817
WW, 2921
WZ, 1181, 1331
WZV, 2276
Ybk, 2567
YCD, 2548, 3179
YR, 2160, 2216, 2248

Z, 38, 65, 83, 1149, 1182, 1244, 1340,
    1629-1630
ZB, 1758, 1868, 1940, 2277, 2322
ZD, 2323
Ze, 1203, 1278, 1430, 1638
ZfB, 1685
ZFEU, 2188-2189
ZfG, 1258
ZP, 2019

TRANSLATORS AND EDITORS

Abels, Lucy (Tr.), 1607
Adler, Paul (Tr.), 1268, 1509, 1555
Ahrens, Berta Burgio (Tr.), 403, 405-406,
    837, 916, 1856, 1858, 2300-2304,
    2428
Akiyama, Hideo (Tr.), 658, 725, 862
Aladár, Sajó (Tr.), 815
Alden, Douglas (Ed.), 3213
Aleksov, Lazo (Tr.), 687
Almagro Rodiera, G. (Tr.), 785
Alsberg, Henry G. (Tr.), 972, 2473-2478
Alves, Livraria Francisco (Tr.), 2542
Amann, Paul (Tr.), 1487
Ammer, K. L. (Cf. K. Klammer, Tr.),
    988, 1521-1522, 2769
Ammer, R. (Tr.), 1586
Andresen, N. (Tr.), 257
Androulidakis, I. (Tr.), 723
Angelloz, J. (Tr.), 809, 1536
Aoyagi, Mizuho (Tr.), 817
Araryo, Milton (Tr.), 1272
Arens, Hanns (Ed.), (69), 2497, 2524
Arpad, Burhan (Tr.), 929
Arpe, Werner (Ed.), 3252, 3340-3356
Ascutan, Mavelikkara (Tr.), 395
Asteriadis, Ioannes (Tr.), 721, 754
Augé, Paul (Ed.), 3253
Babler, Otto F. (Tr.), 226, 229
Baedeker, Peer (Ed.), 980
Ballester Escalas, Rafael (Tr.), 479-480
Bamberger, Max (Tr.), 1614
Bandy-Opadhyay, Shantiranjan (Tr.), 383,
    386-387
Banerji, Shantiranjan (Tr.), 380-382, 384-
    385
Baron, Joseph L. (Ed.), 3271
Barry, Charles P. (Ed.), 3217
Baseggio, Cristina (Tr.), 406
B'ase'wis, I. (Tr.), 786
Bea, Joseph (Ed.), 3212
Bedford, Herbert (Tr.), 119
Beer, Johannes (Ed.), 3265

Bekata, Kemal (Tr.), 507-508
Belmont, L. (Tr.), 887
Beneš-Šumavsky, Vaclav (Tr.), 638
Beratis, Ioannes (Tr.), 587, 835
Bernardi, Orlando (Ed.), 3233
Berenguer Amenós, Jaime (Ed.), 3238
Bernstein, P. (Tr.), 4, 459-460, 462-463,
    466, 663, 820, 841
Besterman, Theodore (Ed.), 3276
Bhattacharya, Vidhayek (Tr.), 379
Birsel, Salah (Tr.), 505
Bithell, Jethro (Tr.), 788-789, 2209-2216,
    2532, 3282-3283
Blaustein, Phyllis M. and Albert P. (Eds.
    and Trs.), 261
Blewitt, Phyllis and Trevor (Trs.), 264,
    1778-1797
Bloch, Henri (Tr.), 832-833, 2297-2299
Block, Maxime (Ed.), 3221
Blom, Eric (Ed.), 3245
Bobetsky, Victor (Ed.), 164a
Bobynskyj, Vasil (Tr.), 511-512, 514
Boon, Josef (Tr.), 101
Botez, Joachim (Tr.), 450
Boudouin, Louis Charles (Tr.), 105
Bournac, Olivier (Tr.), 306, 308, 311,
    315, 317, 325-326, 612, 648-651,
    807-808, 831, 852-853, 1504, 1850-
    1852, 2037-2045, 2253-2261, 2293-
    2296, 2325-2331, 2675
Br'aq'azs, Hayim (Cf. Ch. Brakarz, Tr.),
    111, 515-518, 970
Brewster, Dorothy (Ed.), 267
Bridgewater, William (Ed.), 3219
Brieger-Wasservogel, Lothar (Ed.), 1484,
    2488-2489
Brøndum-Nielsen, Johannes (Ed.), 3266
Brosniowskaja, O. (Tr.), 461
Buacidze, S. (Tr.), 693
Budtz-Jørgensen, Jørgen (Tr.), 232, 244,
    1769
Bukovinszky, Peter (Tr.), 376

Burke, Kenneth (Tr.), 1182, 2192
Cahn, Alfredo (Tr.), 11, 109-110, 114,
    481-483, 555, 569, 697, 784, 891,
    926, 939, 966, 2204, 3032
Calendo, Albina (Tr.), 605
Carlsen, G. H. (Tr.), 422
Carvalho, Cándido de (Tr.), 108
Cassvan-Pas, Sarina (Tr.), 451
Castanakis, L. (Tr.), 342
Castle, Eduard (Ed.), 3286
Castro Henriques Oswald, Maria de (Tr.),
    554, 690
Catalano, S. (Tr.), 1492
Cauris, E. (Tr.), 547
Centnerszwerowa, R. (Tr.), 613, 661, 819
Cerf, Bennett (Ed.), 262
Cerny, Rudolf (Tr.), 226
Changi, Bag (Tr.), 417
Charodschinskaja, I. E. (Tr.), 459, 464
Chaudhuri, Dipak (Tr.), 388
Chauhan, Shivadanasimha and Vijaya
    (Trs.), 390, 392
Chayadevi, Abburi (Tr.), 396
Chernet, Henri (Tr.), 790, 2217
Chevalier, Haakon (Tr.), 2543
Clarac, Pierre (Ed.), 3229
Clark, Barrett H. (Ed.), 3287
Codjioulas, G. (Tr.), 755
Coenen, F. E. (Ed.), 209
Cohn, A. (Tr.), 363
Coleman, Arthur and Marion (Trs.), 2606
Constantinidis, N. (Tr.), 349
Cooper, Page (Ed.), 286
Coopman, Hendrik (Tr.), 546
Cornelius, P. (Tr.), 1510, 1647
Cory, Donald W. (Ed.), 275
Cournos, John (Ed.), 295
Cranaki, M. (Tr.), 339
Cunningham, William (Ed.), 301
Czermakowa, Izabella (Tr.), 427
Dániel, Anna (Tr.), 370
Dargan, E. Preston (Ed.), 2544, 3388
De Brie, G. A. (Ed.), 3208
De Bruyne, R. (Ed.), 3275
De Haas, Jacob (Ed.), 3240
Delmas, Fernand (Tr. and Ed.), 586, 912
Des Gouttes, Jacqueline (Tr.), 318
Dezsö, Kiss (Tr.), 369, 373
Dietrich, Margarete (Ed.), 3254
Dilly, Tante (Ed.), 3258
Dimitriou, D. (Tr.), 356
Dolezil, Zdenek (Tr.), 1303
Dominques, Mário José (Tr.), 592
Drews, Richard (Ed.), 2746
Dreyfus, Marcella (Tr.), 398, 1853-1854
Dupré, P. (Ed.), 3241

Dzapharidzis, Leli (Tr.), 331-332
Eckstein, Friedrich (Ed.), 1549
Elster, Hanns Martin (Ed.), 155
Engberg, Harold (Tr.), 243
Enking, Ottomar (Tr.), 1505
Eppelsheimer, Hanns (Ed.), 3209
Esen, Muzaffer (Tr.), 1020
Eskeland, Severin (Tr.), 423
Etzel-Kühn, Gisela (Tr.), 610-611
Farhad (Tr.), 757
Farrán y Mayoral, J. (Tr.), 480, 495
Fehse, Willi (Ed.), 1514, 2487
Feijii, Toshiak (Tr.), 686
Feuerstein, Emil (Tr.), 366
Fico, Enver (Tr.), 221
Finlayson, C. P. (Tr.), 2580
Fitzbauer, Erich (Ed.), (10), 163, 528,
    1759-1760, 2499-2501, 2763, 2767-
    2769
Fitz Gibbon, Constantine (Tr.), 302
Flerè, Pavle (Tr.), 696
Fodor, Pal (Tr.), 370
Foltin, Lore B. (Ed.), 171
Fónagy, Iván (Tr.), 378
Fontana, Oskar M. (Ed.), 2745
Fowler, Christobel (Tr.), 2497, 2524
Franulic, Lenka (Ed.), 3012
Franwaller, E. (Ed.), 3292
Franzos, Birta (Tr.), 1500
Freedley, George (Ed.), 3287
Freeman-Ishill, Rose (Tr.), 1519
Frels, Wilhelm (Ed.), 3222, 3372
Frenzel, Herbert (Ed.), 3293
Friedenthal, Richard (Ed.), (68), 533,
    560, 574-579, 1864
Friedmann, Hermann (Ed.), 3295
Friedrich, Paul (Tr.), 1516
Frisé, Adolf (Ed.), 2860
Fromm, Hans (Ed.), 3210
Fülöp-Miller, René (Ed.), 1549
Gallard, Alfredo (Tr.), 822
Gallotti, Odilon (Tr.), 434, 606, 937-938,
    963
Gal'perinoj, R. (Tr.), 762-763
Galstone, James (Tr.), 2947
Ganboa, Arístides (Tr.), 11, 493, 594
Gebsattel, Emil von (Tr.), 1570
Geissendörfer, Theodore (Ed.), 901, 2408
Gelovani, A.P. (Tr.), 693
Gentilli, G. (Tr.), 1079
Ghion, A. (Tr.), 360
Giebisch, H. (Ed.), 3251, 3292
Gilli, Clementina (Tr.), 446
Gorfinkel, D. M. (Tr.), 454, 561-562
Gorra, Marcella (Tr.), 917, 2428
Góth, Ferenc (Tr.), 372

PROPER NAMES

179

Cabelentz, Hanns Conon von der, 768
Gabrielli, G., 2046
Gandia, Enrique de, 3014
Gannett, Lewis, 1962
Garraty, John A., 3367
Garten, H. F., 3298
Gausebeck-Dörper, L., 1935
Geibel, Emanual, 3372
Geisendorf, Paul F., 2651, 2654
Geismar, Maxwell, 1785
Geissendörfer, Theodore, 901, 2408
Gelber, A., 1562
Gellert, Christian F., 3372
George, Stefan, 1276, 1347, 1452, 1455, 1469, 2826, 2895
Gerhardt-Amytor, Dagobert von, 1563
Gershoy, Leo, 2101
Gibson, Wilfred, 1784
Gide, André, 977-978, 1347, 2552a-2553, 2648, 2655, 2672, 2880, 3387
Giese, R., 1966
Gilder, Rosamund, 1734
Gillet, Louis, 2673
Ginskey, Franz Karl, 1216, 1495-1496
Ginzberg, Benjamin, 2373
Girosi, Raolo, 2075
Gleim, Johann W. L., 3372
Godfrey, Eleanor, 2054
Goethe, Johann Wolfgang von, 165, 526-527, 545, 900-903, 909, 911, 1114, 1136, 1191, 1238, 1307, 1497, 2490, 2990, 3006, 3372
Goffin, Robert, 2656, 3172
Goldbaum, Wenzel, 3015
Goldkorn, Yitzchak, 3034
Goll, Claire, 1498
Gordon, Franklin, 2232
Gorki, Maxim, XXXIII, 8, 526, 545, 1284, 1499, 2554
Gorman, Herbert, 2106, 2377, 2422
Gotthelf, Jeremias, 1253, 3372
Gottsched, Johann Cgr., 3372
Götzfried, Hansleo, 2786, 3188
Grabbe, Christian D., 3372
Grabert, ?, 2342
Grandmaison, Geoffroy de, 2040
Granier, James, 2435
Grebert, Ludwig, 3189
Green, Julien, 2657, 2787
Greene, Graham, 1828
Gregor, Joseph, 2129, 2769, 2788-2789, 3267
Greiner, Leo, 1564, 1628
Grenville, Vernon, 1665
Grierson, Flora, 2419
Griffin, Francis Vielé, 1347

Griffin, Jonathan, 2555, 3163
Grillparzer, Franz, 3372
Grisson, Alexandra Carola, 140, 2790
Grossberg, Mimi, 2791, 3400
Groth, Klaus, 3372
Grün, Anastasius, 3372
Grützmacher, R. H., 2314
Gryphius, Andreas, 3372
Gschiel, Martha, 3190
Guerard, Albert, 2105, 2226, 2421
Guerrieri-Gonzaga, Sofia B., 2673
Guilbeaux, Henri, 2751
Guillemin, B., 1710
Gundolf, Friedrich, 1565
Günther, Christian, 1566
Günther, Herbert, 2792, 3069
Günther, John, 2556
Günther, Werner, 2793
Guth, Alfred, 1567
Haas, Willy, 1994
Haberling, ?, 2354
Hachtman, O., 1934
Hackett, A., 1792
Haeberlin, ?, 2348
Hagedorn, Friedrich von, 3372
Hall, C. R., 2024
Hallener, ?, 1676
Haller, Albrecht von, 3372
Halm, Friedrich, 3372
Hamann, Johann Georg, 3372
Hamecher, Peter, 1987
Hameiri, Avigodor, 3035
Hamerling, Robert, 3372
Hammer-Purgstall, Joseph von, 3372
Hampe, Theodor, 1645
Händel, Georg Friedrich, 165, 896, 902-904, 909, 911, 917, 926-927, 1109, 1120, 1122, 1275, 2428
Hardt, Ernst, 1478
Hartleben, Otto E., 3372
Hartmann, F., 1700
Hartrott, 1235
Hartung, P. T., 1781
Hasenclever, Walter, XXVI
Hauff, Wilhelm, 3372
Haug, Johann Christian, 3372
Hauptmann, Gerhardt, XXVII, 1168
Hauser, H., 1981
Hauser, Otto, 1478
Haushofer, Karl, 1258
Haynes, Renée, 2151
Hayward, J., 2100
Hearn, Lafcadio, 533, 1500
Hebbel, Friedrich, 3372
Hebel, Johann Peter, 3372
Heijermans, Hermann, 1568

Heilblut, Ivan, 2557
Heine, Heinrich, 1569, 3372
Heinse, Wilhelm, 3372
Hella, Alzir (Cf. Hella as translator), 2658-2659
Helle, Peter, 3372
Hellens, Franz, Cf. F. van Ermengem
Hellpach, Willy, 1347
Hellwig, Hans, 2794
Hemmingway, Ernest, 266
Henriquez-Urena, P., 1207
Herder, Johann G., 3372
de Herédia, José Maria, 1570
Hermann-Neisse, Max. 1283, 1367, 1502
Herrig, A. B., 2108, 2379
Hermann-Neisse, Leni, 2796
Herrsmann, W., 2795
Herwegh, Georg, 3372
Herzberg, A., 2346
Herzl, Theodor, XXVII, (8), 526-527, 1262
Hess, Stan, 2550
Hesse, Hermann, 1192, 1217, 1367, 1381, 1480, 1571-1573, 1761, 1937, 2186, 2274, 2581, 2876, 2945
Heuschele, Otto, 1263, 1503
Heynen, H., 1683
Heynen, W., 1936, 2016
Heyse, Paul, 3372
Hieble, Jacob, 3299
Hift, I., 2175
Highet, Gilbert, 3300
Hille, Peter, XXVIII
Hincks, Cl. M., 2372
Hinterberger, Heinrich, 2797, 3390
Hinton, Thomas R., 3330
Hirn, H., 2161
Hirsch, F. E., 1890, 2457, 2512
Hirth, Friedrich, 1658, 2798
Hitler, Adolf, XXXV, 1235, 2564
Hochstetter, Sophie, 1574
Hofe, Harold von, 2506
Hoffmann, Camill, 1403, 1762
Hoffmann, E. T. A., 533, 1504, 3372
Hoffmann von Fallersleben, August Heinrich, 3372
Hofmann, Else, 2799
Hofmannsthal, Hugo von, XXVII, XXXIV, (7), 541, 544, 558, 1127-1128, 1245, 1575, 3201
Hohlfeld, J., 2085
Hohoff, Curt, 3334
Holburn, T., 1726
Holde, Artur, 2800, 3041
Hölderlin, Friedrich, XXXIII, 9, 851-852, 854-856, 861-865, 870-871,

1073, 1075-1081, 1590, 2218-2228, 2305-2324, 2328-2335, 3372
Holitscher, Arthur, 767
Hölty, Ludwig Chr., 3372
Holz, Herbert Johann, 1867
Holzamer, Wilhelm, 1385, 1576
Homann, Hans Joachim, 1744, 2263
Homeyer, Fritz, 2801
Hönigsberg, Margret, 1577
Hoppe-Meyer, H., 2178
Hornfeld, A. G., 116
Horst, Karl August, 2359, 3301-3302
Horvaths, Ödön von, 1388
Hostovski, Egon, 2520
Hugo, Victor, 1370, 1428
Humbel, F., 2340
Hünich, Fritz Adolf, (54), 170, 2716, 2802-2803, 2875, 3046
Huppert, Hugo, 2804
Hutchinson, Paul, 2371
Hutchinson, Percy, 1964
Ibarguren, C., 1207
Iizuka, Nobuo, 552-553, 2990-2991
Immermann, Karl L., 3372
Ippisch, Gottfried, 141, 2806, 2940
Jack, Peter Monro, 2153
Jackson, George, 1911
Jacob, Henrich Eduard, 1988, 2769, 2807-2808
Jacob, P. Walter, 2809
Jacobi, Johannes, 2810
Jacobsens, Jens Peter, 533, 1505
Jacquot, Michel, 309
Jain, Yashpal, 2978-2979, 3103
Jaloux, Edmond, 533, 1198
James, Edward, 2543
Jacke, Otto, 1860
Janitschek, Maria, 1578
Jarnés, Benjamin Millán, 3016-3017, 3235
Jarpa, Hugo Lazo, 3017
Jastrow, Joseph, 2375
Jaurès, Jean Leon, 533, 1363
Jean Paul (Johann P. Richter), 1253, 3372
Jefsen, Jes. 946
Jenisch, Erich, 2312
Joachim, Heinz, 2483
John, K., 1961
Jonas, Klaus W., 3368
Jones, Ernest, 2561
Jones, H. M., 2219
Jonsen, O., 2172
Jonson, Ben, 118-120, 125-135, 1162-1163, 1708-1743, 2702, 3245
Josephson, Matthew, 1895
Jourda, P., 1982

182

Matkowsky, Adalbert, 60a
Mattingly, Garret, 1919
Matzdorff, W. S., 1642
Maurer, Joseph, 1240, 2849
Marina, Zenta, 2580, 2850
Maurois, André, 3029
Maury, J. W., 2092, 2234
Mayer, Paul, 1515
Mazor, Michel, 2667
Mazzucchetti, Lavinia (Cf. L. Mazzuc-
   chetti as translator), 2251, 2403,
   2471, 2982-2984
Means, Philip A., 1881
Medford, Harold, 3352
Mehring, Wlater, 2920
Meier-Cräfe, Julius, 1588
Meisels, S., 3080
Mell, Max, 1589
Mensch, L., 2253
Menter, L., 2851, 3084
Mércereau, Alexander, 1516
Mertens, Gerhard M., 3195
Mesmer, Franz Anton, XXXIV, (66),
   9, 11, 872-875, 877-879, 882-888,
   892, 894-895, 1054-1072, 2336-2365,
   2368-2407
Meunier, Constant, 1185
Meyer, Arthur, 3375
Meyer, Conrad F., 3372
Meyer, Cornelius, 3375
Meyer, Richard, 3316, 3375
Meyer-Benfey, Heinrich, 2852
Michael, F., 1929
Michaelis, Edgar, 2853
Michel, Wilhelm, 1590
Mileck, Joseph, 2581
Minnigerode, Meade, 2114
Miran, L., 2042
Mis, L., 2320
Mistral, Gabriela, 2855
Mittner, Ladislo, 3317
Moehlman, C. H., 1907
Moissi, Alexander, 533, 1287, 3361
Molo, Walter von, 1357a, 1635, 2856
Montaigne, Michel, XXXVI, XXXVIII,
   533, 1289, 2689
Montenegro, Ernesto, 2441
Moore, George, 1591
Moore, Harry, T. 1802
Morena, Erna, 3353
Moreno, Artemio, 3018
Morgan, Bayard Q., 2582
Mörike, Eduard, 3372
Morley, Christopher, 263
Morris, Lawrence S., 2233
Morrison, Samuel E., 1878

Mortimer, John, 3356
Mortimer, Raymond, 1892
Mottram, R. H., 1207
Moulin, René, 2041
Mourre, Michel, 3227
Mozart, Wolfgang Amadeus, XXXIII,
   1517, 3378
Muckermann, Friedrich, 1347
Mueller, G., 2020
Muhr, Adelbert, 2769, 2857
Mühsam, Paul, 2858
Muir, Edwin, 2492
Müller, Wilhelm, 1675, 3372
Müller-Einigen, Hans, 2859
Mumbauer, Johannes, 3318
Munn, L. S., 1848
Münz, J. B., 1639
Muret, Maurice, 2039, 2119, 2389, 2668-
   2669, 3155
Murray, A. L., 1906, 2432
Musil, Robert, 2860
Musset, Alfred de, 1292
Nadler, Josef, 3319
Naldoni-Centenari, N., 2074, 2077
Napoleon Bonaparte, 165, 523, 525, 899-
   903, 909, 911, 1051-1053, 1113,
   1115-1116, 1119, 1121, 1178, 1296,
   2032, 2044, 3379
Narciss, G. A., 1989
Naumann, Hans, 3320
Navarro, Eugenio, 3002
Nazaroff, Alexander, 2032
Neale, J. E., 2157
Necker, Moritz, 1707
Netto, Hadrian Maria, 1592
Neuburger, P., 1229
Neumann, Erich, 3366
Neumann, Robert, 2861
Niebuhr, Reinhold, 1914
Nielsen, Asta, 3350
Nietzsche, Friedrich, XXVII, XXXIII,
   528, 541, 544, 588, 829, 851, 853-
   856, 859-861, 863, 868-871, 1073,
   1088-1092, 1279, 2218-2228, 2305-
   2327, 2332-2335, 3372
Niles, Blair Rice, 2584-2585
Nobel, Alfred, XXXII
Norden, R., 2587
Norman, Charles, 2586
Noth, Ernst E. (Cf. Paul Krantz), 2670
Novalis (Friedrich von Hardenberg),
   3372
Nowaczynski, Adolf, 2994
Noyes, R. G., 1725
O'Brien, Kate, 1793
Oechler, William F., 996, 2589

Oetke, Herbert, 2862, 3174
Ophüls, Max, 3348
Opitz, Martin, 3372
Orrick, James, 2224
Oritz Oderigo, Alicia, 3019
Orzeszko, Helene, 1593
Osborn, Max, 2491
Osorio Lizarazo, J., 3020, 3154
Oswald, Gerd, 3352
Overbeck, Franz, 541, 544, 558, 1279
Ozep, Fedor, 3341
Palmer, Lilli, 3354
Palmieri, E., 2047, 2125, 2402
Pankow, H., 1643
Pannwi z, Rudolf, 1313
Paquet, Alfons, 1357a
Parandowski, Jan, 2863
Parsons, Alice Beal, 1912
Partridge, David, 291
Peixoto, Afrancio, 1207
Pellegrini, Carlo, 3321
P.E.N. Club, XXXV, 1226, 2558, 2615
Perfall, Anton von, 1594-1596
Pestalozzi, Johann H., 3372
Peters, J., 2356
Peterson, Virgilia, 2514
Petijean, Armand, 2671
Petit, G., 2118
Petry, L., 2205
Peyre, Henri, 1896
Pfeffel, Gottlieb K., 3372
Pfeiler, William K., 3218
Pick, Robert, 899, 1899, 2467, 2590-2591, 3051
Piérard, Louis, 1207
Pierre-Quint, L., 2394
Pierson, Edgar, 1696
Pirandello, Luigi, 1433
Pirker, M., 2273
Pisani, P., 2298
Piscatur, 1033
Pisk, Egon, 2864, 3175
Pitollet, C., 2043
Pitrou, R., 1624, 2296
Platen-Hallermünde, August Graf von, 3372
Poerio, Alessandro, 1136
Poggioli, R., 2249
Pohl, G., 1367
Polgar, Alfred, 2920
Politzer, H., 2509
Pommeranz-Liedtke, Gerhard, 768
Pompeati, A., 2127, 2303
Pongs, Hermann, 3322-3323
Ponten, Josef, 1347
Porena, E., 1984

Porterfield, Allen W., 2033
Poss, A., 2865
Pound, Ezra, 2586
Powell, F-M., 1916
Power, Tyrone, 3351
Prager, Hans, 1518
Prampolini, Giacomo, 3324
Pratt, George K., 2384
Priestley, J. B., 3325
Proust, Marcel, 541, 558, 1278, 1312
Pruschanski, N., 1597
Pryll, ?, 2362
Puner, Helen Walker, 2592
Purdie, Edna, 3326
Pury, Roland de, 1924
Putnam, Samuel, 2593
Puttkammer, Alberta von, 1135, 1629-1630, 1702
Radebeul, ?, 2006
Radó, Aladar, 3245, 3357b
Rafael, L. (Cf. Hedwig Kiesekamp), 1598
Raff, Helene, 1599
Raimund, F., 3372
Rainalter, Erwin H., 139, 2866
Ramler, Karl W., 3372
Ramuz, Charles Ferdinand, 533, 1308
Randall, A. W. G., 2036
Ranicki, Marceli, 1859
Ranschoff, Georg, 1930
Rapoport, O., 3005
Rasputin, 1031, 1033
Rathenau, Walter, XXXIII, 533, 1319, 1375
Rauscher, Bert, 2867
Ravel, Maurice, XXXIII
Ravenel, Mazyck P., 2368
Read, C., 2160
Reger, Max, 3245, 3357c
Reichert, Walter, A., 3366
Reichmann-Jungmann, Eva, 1641
Reicke, Ilse, 1640
Reifenberg, B., 2470
Reik, Theodor, 1753
Reim, Paul, 2868
Reinecker, Herbert, 3352
Reinfels, Hans von, 1600
Reinhardt, Max, XXXIII
Reischl, Friedrich, 1601
Reishofer, Karl, 2869
Reisiger, Hans, 1686, 2689, 2696, 2870
Relgis, Eugen, 1519, 2594, 3021-3026
Remarque, Erich Maria, XXXIV, 1367, 2558
Rembrandt, van Rijn, 1448
Renan, Ernest, 526-527, 545, 1206, 1520
Renier, M., 322

Renoir, Auguste, XXIX
Rensselaer-Wyatt, Euphemia van, 2221,
 2415
Reuter, Fritz, 3372
Rexroth, Franz von, 1480
Rey Alvarez, R., 2257
Reyes, Alfonso, 1207
Reyles, Carlos, 1207
Reynolds, F. H., 2158
Rice, Muriel, 1602
Richter, Helene, 1709
Richter, Johann Paul F. (Jean Paul), 1253,
 3372
Rie, Robert, 2500
Rieger, Erwin, (54), 1440, 1745, 2502-
 2505, 2716, 2803, 2871-2875, 2906,
 3152, 3286
Rieger, Harald, 2876
Riemerschmid, Werner, 2877
Ries, Theresa Feodor, 1356
Riley, Woodbridge, 2376
Rilke, Rainer Maria, XXVII, (7), 519-
 521, 526, 533, 545, 659, 792, 977-
 978, 1002-1005, 1314, 1316-1318,
 1452, 1455, 1469, 1478, 1480, 1525,
 1603, 2492, 2530, 2578, 2642, 2672,
 2689, 2696, 2793, 2878-2883, 2902,
 3372
Rimbaud, Arthur, XXVII, (7), 526-527,
 545, 1149, 1521-1522, 1622
Ring, O. T., 2595, 3117
Ritzer, Walter, 2883
Robakidse, Grigol, 1523
Robertazzi, M., 2300, 2985
Robertson, J. G., 3326
Robespierre, Maximilien François, 1050
Rocca, Enrico, 1688, 3327
Roces Suárèz, Wenceslas, 849
Rodenberg, Julius, 3372
Rodin, Auguste, XXIX, (16), 23, 526-
 527, 1230, 1267, 1625
Rolland, Romain, XXX, XXXI, XXXII
 XXXIII, (10), (29), 9, 306, 308, 311,
 533, 769-786, 977-978, 982-983,
 994-995, 1153, 1168, 1188, 1243,
 1252, 1320, 1324-1329, 1434-1436,
 1524, 1528, 2171-2204, 2572-2574,
 2578, 2608-2609, 2621, 2639, 2643-
 2644, 2661, 2663, 2666, 2673-2676,
 2689, 2692, 2696, 2786, 2833, 2880,
 2884, 3022, 3072, 3188, 3192, 3198
Romain, Jules, 132, 989, 997, 1207, 1737-
 1743, 2596, 2677-2680, 2689, 3156
Romera, Antonio R., 3027, 3038
Romero, Francisco, 1207
Ronayne, Charles, F., 1948

Röntgen, Johannes, 3358
Roosevelt, Nicholas, 2440
Rops, Daniel, 1852
Rose, Ernst, 3328
Rose, William, 584, 1525, 1885-1900,
 2492, 2597
Rosegger, Peter, 533, 1306, 3372
Rosellini, Roberto, 3344
Rosenberg, Justus, 3196
Rosenfeld, Paul, 2228, 3164
Rosenhaupt, Hans Wilhelm, 2885
Rosenkranz, ?, 1943, 2007
Rosenthal, Friedrich, 2886
Rosenzweig, Alfred, 2887
Rosenzweig, Franz, 1347
Rosnovsky, Karl, 3197
Ross, Nan, 2598
Rössler, Arthur, 1604
Roth, Joseph, 533, 1255, 2640, 3400,
 3402, 3408
Rouget de Lisle, Claude Joseph, 902-903,
 905, 909, 911, 923-926
Rousseau, Jean Jacques, 1331, 1526
Rouvre, Rèmy, 2667
Rowse, A. L., 1917, 1968, 2155
Royce, William H., 2599
Rubens, Peter Paul, 1449
Rückert, Friedrich, 3372
Rudens, S. P., 2290
Russell, Archibald B. H., 1437
Rychner, Max, 1347
Saar, Ferdinand von, 3372
Sachaczewer, H., 2262
Sachs, Erich, 1605
Sainte-Beuve, Charles Augustin, 526-527,
 545, 1333, 1527
Saint Jean, R. de, 2327
Saint Paul, Albert, 1347
Salpeter, Harry, 1814-1815, 2245
Salten, Felix, 1637, 3409, 3412
Salus, Hugo, 1606
Salzburg (City of), XXXIII, XXXIV,
 XXXVI, (44), (60), 526-528, 1129,
 1334, 1601, 1612, 2539, 2726, 2770,
 2824, 2877, 2937, 2971
Salzer, Anselm, 3329
Samain, Albert, 1607
Samuel, Richard, 3330
Sanchez Tricado, José Luis, 3028
Sanderson, Elizabeth, 1839
Sanin Cano, B., 1207
Sapieha, Virhilia, 2464
Sarnetzki, D. H., 2084
Schaeffer, Albrecht, 2689
Schäfer, Wilhelm, 1347, 1357a, 1608
Schäke, Gerd, 2888, 3085

Schatz, Otto R., 181
Schaukal, Richard von, 1478, 1480, 2889-2893
Schaumann, Ruth, 1347
Scheffel, Joseph, 3372
Schell, Maximilian, 3356
Scheller, Will, 2009, 2894
Scherer, Wilhelm, 3331
Schibler, Armin, 3245, 3359
Schieffenzah, ?, 2916
Schiff, Martha, 2182
Schiller, Friedrich von, 3372
Schinz, A., 2213
Schlaf, Johannes, 1254, 1609
Schlegel, August W., 3372
Schlegel, Friedrich, 3372
Schlegelmilch, W., 1768a
Schlösser, Wilhelm, 178
Schmidt, Adalbert, 3332
Schmidt, P. Expeditus, 1347
Schmidtbonn, Wilhelm, 1148, 1866
Schmitt, Fritz, 3333
Schmitz, Oskar A. H., 1301, 1347, 1610
Schnewlin, M., 2338
Schnitzler, Arthur, XXVII, XXXIV, 533, 1150-1151, 1337, 3201, 3404, 3412
Schoenberner, Franz (74), 2600
Schoen-Rene, O. E., 1779
Scholz, Wilhelm von, 1357a, 1367, 1566, 2899
Schömann, Milian, 2898, 3146
Schönfelder, Erich, 3353
Schoolfield, George C., 2499
Schorer, Jean, 978, 2649-2651, 2654, 2681-2682
Schossberger, Emily, 2508
Schottky, J., 2349
Schreiber, George, 2601, 3164
Schtschegolew, ?, 1033
Schullern, Heinrich von, 1611
Schultz, Theodor, 3331
Schumann, Otto, 3259
Schuster, George N., 2632
Schwarz, Heinrich, 1612
Schweitzer, Albert, XXXIII, (48), 526-527, 1158, 1365, 1482, 1513, 2689
Scott-James, R. A., 2240
Scott, Robert Falcon, 165, 523, 525, 898-903, 909, 911, 921, 1107, 1112, 1117-1118
Seelig, Carl, 1938, 2187, 2900
Seelmann, Eggebert, U., 2810
Ségur, N., 2331
Seiber, Matyas, 3245, 3359a
Seidel, Heinrich, 3372
Seidel, Ina, 1347

Selden-Goth, Gisela, 975, 1000-1001, 2602, 2638, 2901
Seldes, Gilbert, 1835
Semmig, Jeanne Bertha, 1613
Servaes, Franz, 1661, 2207, 2488
Settanni, E., 2986
Seume, Johann, 3372
Shakespeare, William, 1311, 1341
Shearer, Norma, 3351
Shneour, Salman, 3090
Shukry, Muhammed 'Ayyad, 1535
Sieburg, Friedrich, 2448, 2901a
Sievers, W. David, 2603
Silbergeist, ?, 2128
Silva, José Asunción, 3006
Silvestre, Armand, 1438-1439
Simenauer, Erich, 2902
Simon, E., 1651
Siodmak, Robert, 3345
Slochower, Harry, 2604
Slonim, Marc, 2605
Slowacki, Juljusz, 2606
Smertenko, ?, 1837
Smith, Preserved, 1963
Snell, George, 1897
Sochaczewer, H., 1367
Soederberg, Eduard, 1614
Soergel, Albert, 3334
Soldevilla, Carlos, 10
Soskin, William, 2104
Soulie, Gaston, 1528
Souza, Claudio de, 3003, 3029
Soyka, ?, 1346
Speal, W., 2904
Spanier, Max, 2905
Specht, Richard, 8, 1529, 2906-2907
Spender, S., 2145
Spenlée, J. E., 1977, 2259
Sperry, W. L., 1913, 2607
Spörri, Theodor, 2080, 2347
Squire, John, 1889, 2059
Starr, William Thomas, 983, 2608-2609, 3198
Steersma, J. G., 146
Stefan, Paul, 1655, 2908, 2920, 3120
Stefan-Gruenfeldt, Paul, 522, 1171, 1530-1531
Steinbrinck, O., 1986
Steiner, Rudolf, XXVIII
Steiner-Prag, Hugo, 2769
Steinhauer, Harry, 2610
Steinhoff, Hans, 3342
Steinrück, Albert, 3350
Stelzhauer, Franz, 3372
Stendhal (Pseud. for Henri Beyle), 9-10, 801-806, 810-811, 813, 816-817,

ADDENDA

UNIVERSITY OF NORTH CAROLINA
STUDIES IN THE GERMANIC LANGUAGES
AND LITERATURES

1. Herbert W. Reichert. THE BASIC CONCEPTS IN THE PHILOSOPHY OF GOTTFRIED KELLER 1949. Pp. 164. Paper $ 3.00.
2. Olga Marx and Ernst Morwitz. THE WORKS OF STEFAN GEORGE. Rendered into English. 1949. Out of print.
3. Paul H. Curts. HEROD AND MARIAMNE, A Tragedy in Five Acts by Friedrich Hebbel, Translated into English Verse. 1950. Pp. 96. Cloth $ 3.00.
4. Frederic E. Coenen. FRANZ GRILLPARZER'S PORTRAITURE OF MEN. 1951. Pp. xii, 135. Cloth $ 3.50.
5. Edwin H. Zeydel and B. Q. Morgan. THE PARZIVAL OF WOLFRAM VON ESCHENBACH. Translated into English Verse, with Introductions, Notes, and Connecting Summaries. 1951, 1956, 1960. Pp. xii, 370. Paper $ 4.50.
6. James C. O'Flaherty. UNITY AND LANGUAGE: A STUDY IN THE PHILOSOPHY OF JOHANN GEORG HAMANN. 1952. Out of print.
7. Sten G. Flygt. FRIEDRICH HEBBEL'S CONCEPTION OF MOVEMENT IN THE ABSOLUTE AND IN HISTORY. 1952. Out of print.
8. Richard Kuehnemund. ARMINIUS OR THE RISE OF A NATIONAL SYMBOL. (From Hutten to Grabbe.) 1953. Pp. xxx, 122. Cloth $ 3.50.
9. Lawrence S. Thompson. WILHELM WAIBLINGER IN ITALY. 1953. Pp. ix, 105. Paper $ 3.00.
10. Frederick Hiebel. NOVALIS. GERMAN POET - EUROPEAN THINKER - CHRISTIAN MYSTIC. 1953. Pp. xii, 126. 2nd rev. ed. 1959. Paper $ 3.50.
11. Walter Silz. Realism and Reality: Studies in the German Novelle of Poetic Realism. 1954. Third printing, 1962. Pp. xiv, 168. Paper $ 4.00.
12. Percy Matenko. LUDWIG TIECK AND AMERICA. 1954. Out of print.
13. Wilhelm Dilthey. THE ESSENCE OF PHILOSOPHY. Rendered into English by Stephen A. Emery and William T. Emery. 1954, 1961. Pp. xii, 78. Paper $ 1.50.
14. Edwin H. Zeydel and B. Q. Morgan. GREGORIUS. A Medieval Oedipus Legend by Hartmann von Aue. Translated in Rhyming Couplets with Introduction and Notes. 1955. Out of print.
15. Alfred G. Steer, Jr. GOETHE'S SOCIAL PHILOSOPHY AS REVEALED IN CAMPAGNE IN FRANKREICH AND BELAGERUNG VON MAINZ, With three full-page illustrations. 1955. Pp. xiv, 178. Paper $ 4.00.
16. Edwin H. Zeydel. GOETHE THE LYRIST. 100 Poems in New Translations facing the Original Texts. With a Biographical Introduction and an Appendix on Musical Settings. 1955. Pp. xviii, 182. 2nd ed. 1958. Paper $ 1.75.
17. Hermann J. Weigand. THREE CHAPTERS ON COURTLY LOVE IN ARTHURIAN FRANCE AND GERMANY. Out of print.
18. George Fenwick Jones. WITTENWILER'S ,,RING" AND THE ANONYMOUS SCOTS POEM ,,COLKELBIE SOW". Two Comic-Didactic Works from the Fifteenth Century. Translated into English. With five illustrations. 1956. Pp. xiv, 246. Paper $ 4.50.
19. George C. Schoolfield. THE FIGURE OF THE MUSICIAN IN GERMAN LITERATURE. 1956. Out of print.
20. Edwin H. Zeydel. POEMS OF GOETHE. A Sequel to GOETHE THE LYRIST. New Translations facing the Originals. With an Introduction and a List of Musical Settings. 1957. Pp. xii, 126. Paper $ 3.25. Out of print.
21. Joseph Mileck. HERMANN HESSE AND HIS CRITICS. The Criticism and Bibliography of Half a Century. 1958. Out of print.
22. Ernest N. Kirrmann. DEATH AND THE PLOWMAN or THE BOHEMIAN PLOWMAN. A Disputatious and Consolatory Dialogue about Death from the Year 1400. Translated from the Modern German Version of Alois Bernt. 1958. Pp. xviii, 40. Paper $ 1.85.
23. Edwin H. Zeydel. RUODLIEB, THE EARLIEST COURTLY NOVEL (after 1050). Introduction, Text, Translation, Commentary, and Textual Notes. With seven illustrations. 1959, Second printing, 1963. Pp. xii, 165. Paper $ 4.50.
24. John T. Krumpelmann. THE MAIDEN OF ORLEANS. A Romantic Tragedy in Five Acts by Friedrich Schiller. Translated into English in the Verse Forms of the Original German. 1959. Out print.
25. George Fenwick Jones. HONOR IN GERMAN LITERATURE. 1959. Pp. xii, 208. Paper $ 4.50.
26. MIDDLE AGES—REFORMATION—VOLKSKUNDE. FESTSCHRIFT for John G. Kunstmann Twenty Essays. 1959. Out of print.
27. Martin Dyck. NOVALIS AND MATHEMATICS. 1960. Pp. xii, 109. Paper $ 3.50.
28. Claude Hill and Ralph Ley. THE DRAMA OF GERMAN EXPRESSIONISM. A German-English Bibliography. 1960. Pp. xii, 211. Out of print.
29. George C. Schoolfield. THE GERMAN LYRIC OF THE BAROQUE IN ENGLISH TRANSLATION. 1961. Pp. x, 380. Paper $ 7.00.
30. John Fitzell. THE HERMIT IN GERMAN LITERATURE. (From Lessing to Eichendorff.) 1961. Pp. xiv, 130. Paper $ 4.50.
31. Heinrich von Kleist. THE BROKEN PITCHER. A Comedy. Translated into English Verse by B. Q. Morgan. 1961. Pp. x, 74. Paper $ 2.00.